Sources for the
History of Cyprus

Volume V

English Texts:
Frankish and Turkish Periods

Sources for the History of Cyprus

Edited by
Paul W. Wallace and Andreas G. Orphanides

Volume V

English Texts:
Frankish and Turkish Periods

Selected and Edited, with Introduction and Notes by
DAVID W. MARTIN
(University at Albany, State University of New York)

Greece and Cyprus Research Center
1998

ISBN: 0-9651704-5-4

ISBN set: 0-9651704-0-3

TABLE OF CONTENTS

INTRODUCTION

Volume V of *Sources for the History of Cyprus* attempts to collect the English texts written by visitors to Cyprus from the early 15th century to 1878, during the times that the Franks and the Turks ruled the island. To the texts of authors who actually visited the island have been added two passages from Chaucer, as well as the colorful description by Sir John Mandeville, who, if he existed, probably never visited Cyprus.

The visitors to the island during this period were pilgrims, diplomats, scholars, antiquarians, soldiers, bankers, and others, as well as those who traveled just for the sake of travel. Their accounts of the island therefore vary greatly, and the historical value of some of the texts is much greater than that of others. Since one of the main purposes of the series, however, is to make historical documents readily available, it seemed best at this point not to exercise too vigorous a judgment of inclusion or exclusion; we have accordingly included nearly everything we could discover written about the island in English during this period. The amount written about Cyprus by any one author is usually not very large, since the visit to the island was often incidental to the main purpose of the trip. Only toward the end of this period do book-length texts begin to appear, when Cyprus is itself the main object of study. In those cases it was necessary to excerpt the book and to present in this volume, it is hoped, only the more important observations or descriptions.

Some of the texts in this volume were published by Claude Delaval Cobham in *Excerpta Cypria*. That excellent volume, intended to include within the covers of one book historical documents from all languages and all periods, necessarily omits many texts which we have thought worthy of inclusion. We believe that all the texts in the present volume have some historical relevance; they were chosen because of their first-hand observation of places, conditions, and customs, and sometimes simply because of their general interest. On the other hand, some English texts, usually archaeological, have been omitted either because they are easily found in libraries or have been re-printed (e.g. Cesnola).

As mentioned above, although the occupations and areas of interest of the travelers to Cyprus during this period vary considerably, the reader will probably note a similarity in their outlook and biases. They are all men, all of the higher ranks of society, all classically educated, and all from Great Britain, with the exception of a few Americans, mostly missionaries, from near the end of the period. Their sympathy for things Greek is readily perceived and derives to a great extent from their education. The advance of the Turk into Europe in recent history also undoubtedly contributed to the anti-Turkish feeling which is generally evident in the texts. The American texts, perhaps because they were written only toward the end of the period, and by missionaries, seem to have a different flavor. It should be noted that the diary of one of those American missionaries, Lorenzo Pease, is being prepared for this series separately.

Scholarly attitudes about the presentation of the texts themselves have changed since the time of Cobham, when it was thought appropriate to correct the text according to modern usage. That practice resulted in an inaccurate representation of the text, based on the assumptions of the editor. Current practice seems to favor an exact presentation of the text, allowing corrections to be made by future commentators. We have accordingly retained eccentricities of spelling and punctuation, except for obvious mistakes, as they appear in the earliest editions that we have been able to obtain. We edited by the principle that readers of the present volume should make their own corrections and draw their own conclusions. Historical and topographical mistakes abound, but corrections in these areas alone would require another volume. Therefore, the selections reproduced here attempt to preserve the spelling, diacritical marks, italics, paragraphing, punctuation, and hyphenation of the original texts, which practice not only presents the texts more accurately, but also illustrates the usage and understanding of those eras. This practice applies especially to place-names and Turkish terminology, since earlier editors have sometimes changed them to conform to the usage in vogue in their own times. One exception to this practice is our occasional deletion of words, or place-names, written in Greek. The entries are often so filled with errors that it seemed pointless to reproduce them, but in such cases we have warned the reader of their omission.

The orthography of letters has not been a great problem, for most of the earliest texts that we have been able to obtain have already been updated. The one change made in our oldest obtainable texts is the standardization of the letter "s". We have done this despite Benjamin Franklin's complaint to Noah Webster in 1789: "And lately another fancy has induced some Printers to use the short round S instead of the long one, which formerly served so well to distinguish a word readily by its varied appearance. Certainly the omitting this prominent letter makes the line appear more even; but renders it less immediately legible; as the paring all Men's Noses might smooth and level their Faces, but would render their Physiognomies less distinguishable." Place-names, terminology, and orthography become less of a problem as we move to texts closer to the present era.

The discovery of all the texts included in the present volume owes much to modern technology. Recent Cypriot scholarship has given little attention to English speaking visitors to the island, and few bibliographies exist to suggest who they were. The bibliography in Cobham's *Excerpta Cypria*, and Cobham's *Attempt at a Bibliography of Cyprus*, edited by G. Jeffery, provided some sources. Many more were found by using the computerized data bases of RLIN and OCLC (World Catalog). Judith Place and other reference librarians at the University at Albany, State University of New York, provided invaluable assistance.

The staff of the Interlibrary Loan Department of the University Libraries of the University at Albany worked unstintingly to obtain these texts from university and public libraries across the United States. Libraries of the Metropolitan Museum of Art, Harvard University, and the University of Pennsylvania provided access to their data bases and to non-circulating materials in their rare book collections. Other non-circulating materials were made accessible by the Free Library of Philadelphia, the College of Physicians and Surgeons in Philadelphia, and the University of Virginia.

In addition to those already mentioned, it is a pleasure to thank Fran Martin for her support and great patience throughout the process, Laina Swiny for her help, and Paul W. Wallace for his extraordinary effort in producing this volume.

ENGLISH TEXTS: FRANKISH AND TURKISH PERIODS

Mandeville 1322–1356

The record of a possible early visit of an English-speaking traveler to Cyprus between 1322 and 1356 is surrounded by controversy that has continued over six hundred years. *Mandeville's Travels* was well and widely received as a vivid record of travel to the Holy Land and far beyond to lands rarely visited. It now appears that the *Travels* was written in French, somewhere around 1356. By the end of that century it had been translated into English and every major European language. Over three hundred manuscripts still exist. Over the centuries its popularity has fallen and risen again, and its reputation has changed from a respected record of the travels of Sir John Mandeville, Knight, of St. Albans, England, to a fanciful elaboration of others' travels. It is recognized, however, that the text has importance for the history of geographic discovery, (and, therefore, to later world travelers), for the history of text-making, and for the history of imaginative world literature.

Some scholars have felt that despite the dependence on other sources, there was so much travel to the Holy Land in Mandeville's time that there is a slight possibility of his travel there if not farther east. In *The Rediscovery of Sir John Mandeville*, New York: Modern Language Association, 1954, Josephine Bennett chose Mandeville's description of details about Cyprus that "intensive source-hunting has found no authority earlier than the *Travels*" to propose that he could well have traveled to Cyprus and the Holy Land. Bennett claims Mandeville was the first to reveal that the True Cross in the monastery at Stavrovouni was really that of the good thief. On the contrary, it is called the cross of the good thief by many early travelers including Von Oldenburg (1211), Von Boldensele (1333), Jacobus de Verona (1335), and Ozier d'Anglure (1395). Bennett continues the argument with Mandeville's description of a good wine of Cyprus called "de Marrea" not reported again until 1395 by d'Anglure except by J. de Verona in 1335 whose report Mandeville could not have seen. Mandeville's story about the "papyons" or leopards used in hunting in Cyprus has been traced to other travelers. Bennett felt that his depiction of Cypriots sitting on the ground to eat and dangling their feet into pits dug for cooling comfort seemed to have no prior written record, but may be Mandeville's poor observation of pits for cooling wine. Bennett's evidence that he visited Cyprus is not convincing.

In the recent study *Writing East: The "Travels" of Sir John Mandeville* (Philadelphia: University of Pennsylvania Press, 1997), Iain Macleod Higgins, through close textual analysis of several Mandeville manuscripts, concurs with other scholars that the author was probably a well-educated noble or a cleric who not merely spliced together the "principal underlying intertexts" of William of Boldensele and Odoric of Pordenone, but "overwrote and augmented" with words from still other texts. Unconvinced of the existence of Sir John, he prefers "the Mandeville-author." Because we never see Sir John on the road and the work is a compilation of texts rather than a travel document, Higgins prefers the medieval title, "The Book of John Mandeville."

Although the "Mandeville-author" probably never visited Cyprus, the *Travels* is an important medieval work that deserves quotation here as one of the earliest descriptions of Cyprus in English. These selections are taken from *The Voiage and Travaile of Sir John Maundevile, Kt. which Treateth of the Way to Hierusalem; and of Marvayles of Inde, with Other Ilands and Countryes,* London: F. S. Ellis, 1866. This is a reprint of an 1839 edition for which J. O. Halliwell had added an introduction, notes and glossary to the 1725 Cotton manuscript.

Cap. II.

Of the Crosse and the Croune of oure Lord Jesu Crist.

At Costantynoble is the Cros of our Lord Jesu Crist, and his Cote withouten Semes, that is clept *Tunica inconsutilis,* and the Spounge, and the Reed, of the whiche the Jewes zaven oure Lord Eyselle and Galle, in the Cros. And there is on of the Nayles, that Crist was naylled with on the Cros. And some Men trowen, that half the Cros, that Crist was don on, be in Cipres, in an Abbey of Monkes, that Men callen the Hille of the Holy Cros; but it is not so: For that Cros, that is in Cypre, is the Cros, in the whiche Dysmas the gode Theef was honged onne. But alle Men knowen not that; and that is evylle y don. For profyte of the Offrynge, thei seye, that it is the Cros of oure Lord Jesu Crist. Aud zee schulle undrestonde, that the Cros of oure Lord was made of 4 manere of Trees, as it is conteyned in this Vers,

In Cruce fit Palma, Cedrus, Cypressus, Oliva.

Cap. IV.

Of the Weye fro Costantynoble to Jerusalem . . .

. . . And from this Ile of Rodes, Men gon to Cipre, where bethe many Vynes, that first ben rede, and aftre o Zeer, thei becomen white: and theise Wynes that ben most white, ben most clere and best of smelle . . .

Fro Rodes to Cypre ben 500 Myle and more. But Men may gon to Cypre, and come not at Rodes. Cypre is righte a gode Ile and a fayr and a gret, and it hathe 4 princy-palle Cytees within him. And there is an Erchebyssshoppe at Nichosie, and 4 othere Bysschoppes in that Lond. And at Famagost is on of the princypalle Havenes of the See, that is in the World: and there arryven Cristene Men and Sarazynes and Men of alle Na-ciouns. In Cipre is the Hille of the Holy Cros; and there is an Abbeye of Monkis blake; and there is the Cros of Dismas the gode Theef, as I have seyd before. And summe Men trowen, that there is half the Crosse of oure Lord: but it is not so: and thei don evylle, that make Men to beleeve so. In Cipre lythe Seynt Zenomyne: of whom Men of that Contree maken gret Solempnytee. And in the Castelle of Amours lythe the Body of Seynt Hyl-larie; and Men kepen it righte worschipfully. And besyde Famagost was Seynt Barnabee the Apostle born. In Cipre Men hunten with Papyonns, that ben lyche Lepardes: and thei taken wylde Bestes righte welle, and thei ben somdelle more than Lyouns; and thei taken more scharpely the Bestes and more delyverly than don Houndes. In Cipre is the manere of Lordis and alle othere Men, alle to eten on the Erthe. For thei make Dyches in the Er-the alle aboute in the Halle, depe to the Knee, and thei do pave hem: and whan thei wil ete, thei gon there in and sytten there. And the Skylle is, for thei may ben the more fressche: For that Lond is meche more hottere than it is here. And at grete Festes and for Straungeres, thei setten Formes and Tables, as Men don in this Contree: but thei had lever sytten in the Erthe.

From Cypre, Men gon to the Lond of Jerusalem be the See: and in a Day and in a Nyghte, he that hathe gode Wynd may come to the Havene of Thire, that now is clept Surrye . . . Men myghte go more right to that Havene, and come not in Cypre: but thei gon gladly to Cypre, to reste hem on the Lond, or elles to bye thingis, that thei have nede to here lyvynge . . .

And whoso wil go longe tyme on the See, and come nerrer to Jerusalem, he schal go fro Cipre, be See, to the Port Jaff. For that is the nexte Havene to Jerusalem.

Cap. XI.
Of the Cytee of Damasce. Of 3 Weyes to Jerusalem . . .

. . . And so gon men by a Cytee, that men clepen Beruche. And thare men gon un to the See, that schal goon un to Cypre. And thay aryve at Porte de Sure or of Tyrye; and thanne un to Cypre. Or elles men mowen gon from the Porte of Tyrye ryzt welle, and com not yn to Cypre; and aryve at som Haven of Grece: and thanne comen men un to theis Countrees, by weyes, that I have spoken of by fore . . .

And thare fore I telle yow schorttely, how a man may goon with lytel costage and schortte tyme. A man that cometh form the Londes of the Weste, he gothe thorewe Fraunce, Borgoyne and Lumbardye, and to Venys and to Geen, or to som other Havene of the Marches, and taketh a Schyppe thare, and gon by See to the Isle of Gryffle; and so aryveth hem yn Grece or in Port Myroche or Valon or Duras, or at som other Havene, and gon to Londe, for to reste hem; and gon ayen to the See, and aryves in Cypre; and cometh nouzt yn the Ile of Roodes; and aryves at Famegoste, that ys the chefe Havene of Cypre, or elles at Lamatoun.

Cap. XIV.
. . . Of the knouleche and vertues of the verray Dyamant.

. . . And other Dyamandes also men fynden in the Ile of Cipre, that ben zit more tendre; and hem men may wel pollische.

Chaucer 1340?–1400

Although Chaucer never traveled to Cyprus, these excerpts are included here as some of the earliest references to Cyprus by an author in the English language. It has been suggested that the first excerpt (*General Prologue* I, 43-78), partly because of some of the places mentioned, may have been inspired by the presence of Peter I of Cyprus, who visited England in 1362-63. The second selection, lamenting the death of Peter (who was murdered in 1369 in Rome), is from *The Monk's Tale,* VII, 2390–2398.

A KNYGHT ther was, and that a worthy man,
That fro the tyme that he first bigan
To riden out, he loved chivalrie,
Trouthe and honour, fredom and curteisie.
Ful worthy was he in his lordes werre,
And therto hadde he riden, no man ferre,
As wel in cristendom as in hethenesse,
And evere honoured for his worthynesse.

At Alisaundre he was whan it was wonne.
Ful ofte tyme he hadde the bord bigonne
Aboven alle nacions in Pruce;
In Lettow hadde he reysed and in Ruce,
No Cristen man so ofte of his degree.
In Gernade at the seege eek hadde he be
Of Algezir, and riden in Belmarye.
At Lyeys was he and at Satalye,
Whan they were wonne; and in the Grete See
At many a noble armee hadde he be.
At mortal batailles hadde he been fiftene,
And foughten for oure feith at Tramyssene
In lystes thries, and ay slayn his foo.
This ilke worthy knyght hadde been also
Somtyme with the lord of Palatye
Agayn another hethen in Turkye.
And everemoore he hadde a sovereyn prys:
And though that he were worthy, he was wys,
And of his port as meeke as is a mayde.
He nevere yet no vileynye ne sayde
In al his lyf unto no maner wight.
He was a verray, parfit gentil knyght.
But, for to tellen yow of his array,
His hors were goode, but he was nat gay.
Of fustian he wered a gypon
Al bismotered with his habergeon,
For he was late ycome from his viage,
And wente for to doon his pilgrymage.

De Petro Rege de Cipro

O worthy Petro, kyng of Cipre, also,
That Alisandre wan by heigh maistrie,
Ful many an hethen wroghtestow ful wo,
Of which thyne owene liges hadde envie,
And for no thyng but for thy chivalrie
They in thy bed han slayn thee by the morwe,
Thus kan Fortune hir wheel governe and gye,
And out of joye brynge men to sorwe.

Wey 1458

William Wey, the first known traveler to Cyprus to write at least partially in English, visited the island for the first time in 1458. His journeys are recorded in *The Itineraries of William Wey, Fellow of* ·

Eton College, to Jerusalem, A.D. 1458 and A.D. 1462; and to Saint James of Compostella, A.D. 1456 from the original manuscript in the Bodleian Library printed for the Roxburghe Club, London: J. B. Nichols and Sons, 1857.

The first two entries here were written by Wey in Middle English on pages 3 and 4 of *The Itineraries*. He wrote the remaining entries in Latin. They were translated for this volume by Louis W. Roberts and Paul W. Wallace.

Records show that Wey was a fellow of Eton College, which had been founded by Henry VI and incorporated in 1442. Although not one of the original fellows, he appears to have transferred from Exeter College, Oxford, to Eton within ten years of its founding. The college normally allowed leaves of absence for only six weeks annually, but Wey petitioned King Henry directly and received leave and license "to passe over the See on perigrinage, as to Rome, to Jerusalem, and to other Holy Places." As a secular priest he was concerned with a number of issues regarding the Holy Land and evidently felt satisfied when he returned thirty-seven weeks and three days later. Apparently some time after his second voyage to Jerusalem Wey joined the brotherhood of the Edyngdon Monastery, in Wiltshire, which automatically voided his fellowship at Eton. He presented the monastery with considerable church furniture, relics, and curiosities from Palestine. A dedicated pilgrim, he had set out at age 70 on his last voyage.

Chavnges of money from Englond to Rome and Venyse.
* * * * *

In Cipresse ye schal haue grotis of sylver and half grotis, and other denars of black money, and besavntis; and halfe a besavnte ys worth xlvij. denars, and vij. besauntys and half to a doket of Venyse. A grot of Cypres ys worth xxxviij. denars . . .

From Rodys to Baffe in Cipres iiij c. myle; from Baffe to Port Jaffe iij. c. myle, withowȝte more. But make covenaunte that ye com nat at Famagust in Cipres for no thyng, for meny Englysch men and other have dyde, for that eyre ys so corupte ther abowte, and in the water also.

[p. 52]
First, twenty miles from the port of Salinis is the cross of the holy robber which, as is said, hangs in a chapel without any support of any kind.

[p. 57]
And on the 15th of the same month (June) I came to the port of Baffe in the region of Cyprus. In that city Paul was imprisoned beneath the church. Pilgrims buy vessels there for carrying wine to the Holy Land.

[p. 78]
. . . and so we were in the Holy Land for thirteen days. On the 5th of July we began to sail and arrived at the port of Salynis in Cyprus on July 8th. And in that same place on a high mountain is a cross of the holy robber hanging in the air, and it cannot be removed from that place. Sometimes it appears to be white and sometimes red. Also there is a stream of white salt. And the King of Cyprus gives to the Sultan of Babylon as tribute ten thousand ducats a year in a cloth called Chamelet. In the same region near Famacost Saint Catherine was born who was converted to the faith by a holy hermit.

And on the 13th of July we sailed from Salynys and came to Rhodes.

[p. 90]

. . . to Paphos on Cyprus three hundred miles . . . Make also an agreement that the patron not lead you to Famacosta in Cyprus, because the air in that place is very harmful to Englishmen; also that the patron give you twice a day warm food and that the wine be good and the water fresh.

[p. 95]

From Rhodes we came to Paphus on the 9th of July. Here Saint Paul was imprisoned in a place belonging to the Friars Minor, and here is a fountain of Saint Paul. Also two miles from Famacosto, in a city called Constantia, Saint Catherine was born. Also in Famacosta is a chapel in the church of the Friars Minor behind the large altar, and the place where Saint Catherine learned her letters. Also in the city of Nicocee, which is one of the main cities of Cyprus, there lies the undecomposed body of a lord Mountford, once an English Knight, in the abbey of the Order of Saint Benedict, and here he is revered as a saint, and it has been two hundred years and a little more since he was buried there. Also outside Nicocea is the body of Saint Mamma, whose body exudes oil: also the body of the Abbot Illarion. Further, we did not journey through Seleeucia, because there were there eleven thousand Mamalukes, Moors, and Saracens; and at Nicosetum with the bastard king were one thousand of the aforementioned pagans. There is also twenty miles from Seleeucia a cross of the sacred robber, which hangs in a chapel on the mountain without any visible support. And on July 12th we came to Haifa, port of the Holy Land.

[p. 99]

Having completed out business in the Holy Land, we resumed our journey by sea and arrived at the port of Pafus on August 9th in the kingdom of Cyprus. The bastard had entered this kingdom with the aid of the Sultan of Babylon and caused both the true king and queen to flee. Thence we came to Rhodes on August 19th.

Locke 1553

Little is known about M. John Locke (Lok) who made a voyage to Jerusalem, embarking on March 26, 1553. After changing ships over several months, he finally joined a group of other pilgrims, and they sighted Cyprus on August 11. He visited until they set sail on August 14 only to return along the coast on September 25, visiting the island and leaving again on October 15. His account "The Voyage of Mr. John Locke to Jerusalem" is contained in Volume 3 of the 8-volume set *The Principal Navigations, Voyages, Traffiques & Discoveries of the English Nation Made by Sea or Overland to the Remote and Farthest Distant Quarters of the Earth at Any Time Within the Compass of These 1600 Years* edited by Richard Hakluyt, published in London and Toronto by J. M. Dent and Sons Limited and in New York by E. P. Dutton & Co. in 1927. It was first published in 1589 and the first complete edition was published in 1599.

. . . The 11 in the morning, we had sight of the Iland of Cyprus, and towards noone we were thwart the cape called Ponta Malota, and about foure of the clocke we were as farre as Baffo, and about sunne set we passed Cavo Bianco, and towards nine of the clocke at night we doubled Cavo de le gatte, and ankered afore Limisso, but the wind blew so hard, that we could not come neere the towne, neither durst any man goe on land. The towne is from Cavo de le gatte twelve miles distant.

The 12. of August in the morning wee went on land to Limisso: this towne is ruinated and nothing in it worth writing, save onely in the mids of the towne there hath bene a fortresse, which is now decayed, and the wals part overthrowen, which a Turkish Rover with certaine gallies did destroy about 10. or 12. yeeres past. This day walking to see the towne, we chanced to see in the market place, a great quantitie of a certaine vermine called in the Italian tongue Cavalette. It is as I can learne, both in shape and bignesse like a grassehopper, for I judge but little difference. Of these many yeeres they have had such quantitie that they destroy all their corne. They are so plagued with them, that almost every yeere they doe well nie loose halfe their corne, whether it be the nature of the countrey, or the plague of God, that let them judge that best can define. But that there may no default be laied to their negligence for the destruction of them, they have throughout the whole land a constituted order, that every Farmor or husbandman (which are even as slaves bought and sold to their lord) shall every yeere pay according to his territorie, a measure full of the seede or egges of these forenamed Cavalette, the which they are bound to bring to the market, and present to the officer appointed for the same, the which officer taketh of them very straight measure, and writeth the names of the presenters, and putteth the sayd egges or seed, into a house appointed for the same, and having the house full, they beate them to pouder, and cast them into the sea, and by this policie they doe as much as in them lieth for the destruction of them. This vermine breedeth or ingendereth at the time of corne being ripe, and the corne beyng had away, in the clods of the same ground do the husbandmen find ye nestes, or, as I may rather terme them, cases of the egges of the same vermine. Their nests are much like to the keies of a hasel-nut tree, when they be dried, and of the same length, but somewhat bigger, which case being broken you shall see the egges lie much like unto antes egges, but somewhat lesser. Thus much I have written at this time, because I had no more time of knowledge, but I trust at my returne to note more of this island, with the commodities of the same at large.

The 13. day we went in the morning to the Greekes church, to see the order of their ceremonies, & of their communion, of the which to declare the whole order with the number of their ceremonious crossings, it were to long. Wherefore least I should offend any man, I leave it unwritten: but onely that I noted well, that in all their Communion or service, not one did ever kneele, nor yet in any of their Churches could I ever see any graven images, but painted or portrayed. Also they have store of lampes alight, almost for every image one. Their women are alwayes separated from the men, and generally they are in the lower ende of the Church. This night we went aboord the ship, although the wind were contrary, we did it because the patrone should not find any lacke of us, as sometimes he did: when as tarying upon his owne businesse, he would colour it with the delay of the pilgrimes.

The 14. day in the morning we set saile, and lost sight of the Island of Cyprus.

* * * * *

The 23. 24. and 25. we sailed our direct course with a small gale of winde, and this day we had sight of the Island of Cyprus. The first land that we discovered was a headland called Cavo de la Griega, and about midnight we ankered by North of the Cape.

This cape is a high hil, long and square, and on the East corner it hath a high cop, that appeareth unto those at the sea, like a white cloud, for toward the sea it is white, and it lieth into the sea Southwest. This coast of Cyprus is high declining toward the sea, but it hath no cliffes.

The 26. we set saile againe, and toward noone we came into the port of Salini, where we went on land and lodged that night at a towne one mile from thence called Arnacho di Salini, this is but a village called in Italian, Casalia. This is distant from Jaffa 250. Italian miles.

The 27. we rested, and the 28. we hired horses to ride from Arnacho to Salina, which is good mile. The salt pit is very neere two miles in compasse, very plaine and levell, into the which they let runne at the time of raine a quantitie of water comming from the mountaines, which water is let in until the pit be full to a certaine marke, which when it is full, the rest is conveyed by a trench into the sea. This water is let runne in about October, or sooner or later, as the time of the yeere doth afforde. There they let it remaine untill the ende of July or the middest of August, out of which pits at that time, in stead of water that they let in they gather very faire white salt, without any further art or labour, for it is only done by the great heate of the sunne. This the Venetians have, and doe maintaine to the use of S. Marke, and the Venetian ships that come to this Iland are bound to cast out their ballast, and to lade with salt for Venice. Also there may none in all the Iland buy salt but of these men, who maintaine these pits for S. Marke. This place is watched by night with 6. horsemen to the end it be not stolne by night. Also under the Venetians dominions no towne may spende any salt, but they must buy it of Saint Marke, neither may any man buy any salt at one towne to carie to another, but every one must buy his salt in the towne where he dwelleth. Neither may any man in Venice buy more salt then he spendeth in the city, for if he be knowen to carie but one ounce out of the citie and be accused, hee looseth an eare. The most part of all the salt they have in Venice commeth from these Salines, and they have it so plentifull, that they are not able, never a yeere to gather the one halfe, for they onely gather in July, August, and September, and not fully these three monethes. Yet notwithstanding the abundance that the shippes carie away yeerely, there remaine heapes like hilles, some heapes able to lade nine or tenne shippes, and there are heapes of two yeeres gathering, some of three and some of nine or tenne yeeres making, to the value of a great summe of golde, and when the ships do lade, they never take it by measure, but when they come at Venice they measure it. This salt as it lyeth in the pit is like so much ice, and it is six inches thicke: they digge it with axes, and cause their slaves to cary it to the heapes. This night at midnight we rode to Famagusta, which is eight leagues from Salina, which is 24 English miles.

The 29 about two houres before day, we alighted at Famagusta, and after we were refreshed we went to see the towne. This is a very faire strong holde, and the strongest and greatest in the Iland. The walles are faire and new, and strongly rampired with foure principall bulwarkes, and betweene them turrions, responding one to another, these walles did the Venetians make. They have also on the haven side of it a Castle, and the haven is chained, the citie hath onely two gates, to say, one for the lande and another for the sea, they have in the towne continually, be it peace or warres, 800 souldiers, and fortie and six gunners, besides Captaines, petie Captaines, Governour and Generall. The lande gate hath alwayes fiftie souldiers, pikes and gunners with their harnes, watching thereat night and day. At the sea gate five and twentie, upon the walles every night doe watch fifteene men in watch houses, for every watch house five men, and in the market place 30 sould-iers continually. There may no soldier serve there above 5. yeres, neither will they with-out friendship suffer them to depart afore 5. yeres be expired, and there may serve of all nations except Greekes. They have every pay, which is 45. dayes, 15 Mozenigos, which is 15 shillings sterling. Their horsemen have onely six soldes Venetian a day, and prov-ender for their horses, but they have also certaine lande therewith to plow and sowe for the maintenance of their horses, but truely I marvell how they live being so hardly fed, for all the sommer they feede onely upon chopt strawe and barley, for hey they have none, and yet they be faire, fat and serviceable. The Venetians send every two yeeres new rul-ers, which they call Castellani. The towne hath allowed it also two gallies continually armed and furnished.

The 30 in the morning we ridde to a chappell, where they say Saint Katherin was borne. This Chappell is in olde Famagusta, the which was destroyed by Englishmen, and is cleane overthrowne to the ground, to this day desolate and not inhabited by any person, it was of a great circuit, and there be to this day mountaines of faire, great, and strong buildings, and not onely there, but also in many places of the Iland. Moreover when they digge, plowe, or trench they finde sometimes olde antient coines, some of golde, some of silver, and some of copper, yea and many tombes and vautes with sepulchers in them. This olde Famagusta is from the other, foure miles, and standeth on a hill, but the new towne on a plaine. Thence we returned to new Famagusta againe to dinner, and toward evening we went about the towne, and in the great Church we sawe the tombe of king Jaques, which was the last king of Cyprus, and was buried in the yere of Christ one thou-sand foure hundred seventie & three, and had to wife one of the daughters of Venice, of the house of Cornari, the which family at this day hath great revenues in this Island, and by means of that mariage the Venetians chalenge the kingdom of Cyprus.

The first of October in the morning, we went to see the reliefe of the watches. That done, we went to one of the Greekes Churches to see a pot or Jarre of stone, which is sayd to bee one of the seven Jarres of water, the which the Lord God at the mariage con-verted into wine. It is a pot of earth very faire, white enamelled, and fairely wrought upon with drawen worke, and hath on either side of it, instead of handles, eares made in fourme as the Painters make angels wings, it was about an elle high, and small at the bottome, with a long necke and correspondent in circuit to the bottome, the belly very great and round, it holdeth full twelve gallons, and hath a tap-hole to drawe wine out thereat, the Jarre is very auncient, but whether it be one of them or no, I know not. The aire of Fama-gusta is very unwholesome, as they say, by reason of certain marish ground adjoyning unto it. They have also a certaine yeerely sicknesse raigning in the same towne, above all the rest of the Island: yet neverthelesse, they have it in other townes, but not so much. It is a certain rednesse and paine of the eyes, the which if it bee not quickly holpen, it taketh away their sight, so that yeerely almost in that towne, they have about twentie that lose their sight, either of one eye or both, and it commeth for the most part in this moneth of October, and the last moneth: for I have met divers times three and foure at once in com-panies, both men and women. Their living is better cheape in Famagusta then in any other place of the Island, because there may no kinde of provision within their libertie be solde out of the Citie.

The second of October we returned to Arnacho, where wee rested untill the sixt day. This towne is a pretie Village, there are thereby toward the Sea side divers monuments, that there hath bene great overthrow of buildings, for to this day there is no yere when they finde not, digging under ground, either coines, caves, and sepulchres of antiquities, as we walking, did see many, so that in effect, all alongst the Sea coast, throughout the whole Island, there is much ruine and overthrow of buildings: for as they say, it was disinhabited sixe and thirtie yeres before Saint Helens time for lacke of water. And since that time it hath bene ruinated and overthrowen by Richard the first of that name, king of England, which he did in revenge of his sisters ravishment comming to Jerusalem, the which inforcement was done to her by the king of Famagusta.

The sixt day we rid to Nicosia, which is from Arnacho seven Cyprus miles, which are one and twentie Italian miles. This is the ancientest citie of the Island, and is walled about, but it is not strong neither of walles nor situation: It is by report three Cyprus miles about, it is not throughly inhabited, but hath many great gardens in it, and also very many Date trees, and plentie of Pomegranates and other fruites. There dwell all the Gentilitie of the Island, and there hath every Cavallier or Conte of the Island an habitation. There is in this citie one fountaine rented by saint Marke, which is bound every eight dayes once, to water all the gardens in the towne, and the keeper of this fountaine hath for every tree a Bizantin, which is twelve soldes Venice, and six pence sterling. He that hath that to farme, with a faire and profitable garden thereto belonging, paieth every yeere to saint Marke, fifteene hundred crownes. The streetes of the citie are not paved, which maketh it with the quantitie of the gardens, to seeme but a rurall habitation. But there be many faire buildings in the Citie, there be also Monasteries both of Franks & Greekes. The Cathedrall church is called Santa Sophia, in the which there is an old tombe of Jaspis stone, all of one piece, made in forme of a cariage coffer, twelve spannes long, sixe spannes broad, and seven spannes high, which they say was found under ground It is as faire a stone as ever I have seene.

The seventh day we rid to a Greeke Frierie halfe a mile without the towne. It is a very pleasaunt place, and the Friers feasted us according to their abilitie. These Friers are such as have bene Priests, and their wives dying they must become Friers of this place, and never after eate flesh, for if they do, they are deprived from saying masse: neither, after they have taken upon them this order, may they marry againe, but they may keepe a single woman. These Greekish Friers are very continent and chast, and surely I have seldome seen (which I have well noted) any of them fat.

The 8. day we returned to Arnacho, and rested there. The 9. after midnight my company rid to the hill called Monte de la Croce (but I not disposed would not go) which hill is from Arnacho 15. Italian miles. Upon the sayd hill is a certaine crosse, which is, they say, a holy Crosse. This Crosse in times past did by their report of the Island, hang in the ayre, but by a certaine earthquake, the crosse and the chappell it hung in, were overthrowen, so that never since it would hang againe in the aire. But it is now covered with silver, and hath 3. drops of our lordes blood on it (as they say) and there is in the midst of the great crosse, a little crosse made of the crosse of Christ, but it is closed in the silver, you must (if you will) beleeve it is so, for see it you cannot. This crosse hangeth nowe by both endes in the wall, that you may swing it up and downe, in token that it did once hang in the aire. This was told mee by my fellow pilgrims, for I sawe it not.

The 10. at night we went aboord by warning of the patron: and the 11. in the morning we set saile, and crept along the shore, but at night we ankered by reason of contrary windes.

The 12. we set saile toward Limisso, which is from Salinis 50. miles, and there we went on land that night.

The 13. and 14. we remained still on land, and the 15. the patrone sent for us; but by reason that one of our company was not well, we went not presently, but we were forced afterward to hire a boate, and to overtake the ship tenne miles into the sea. At this Limisso all the Venetian ships lade wine for their provision, and some for to sell, and also vineger. They lade also great store of Carrobi: for all the countrey thereabout adjoining, and all the mountaines are full of Carrobi trees, they lade also cotton wooll there. In the sayd towne we did see a certaine foule of the land (whereof there are many in this Island) named in the Italian tongue Vulture. It is a fowle that is as big as a Swanne, and it liveth upon carion. The skinne is full of soft doune, like to a fine furre, which they use to occupie when they have evill stomacks, and it maketh good digestion. This bird (as they say) will eate as much at one meale as shall serve him fortie dayes after, and within the compasse of that time careth for no more meate. The countrey people, when they have any dead beast, they cary it into the mountaines, or where they suppose the sayd Vultures to haunt, they seeing the carion doe immediately greedily seaze upon it, and doe so ingraft their talents, that they cannot speedily rise agayne, by reason whereof the people come and kill them: sometimes they kill them with dogs, and sometimes with such weapons as they have. This foule is very great and hardy, much like an Eagle in the feathers of her wings and backe, but under her great feathers she is onely doune, her necke also long and full of doune. She hath on the necke bone, between the necke and the shoulders, a heape of fethers like a Tassell, her thighs unto her knees are covered with doune, her legs strong and great, and dareth with her talents assault a man. They have also in the Island a certaine small bird, much like unto a Wagtaile in fethers and making, these are so extreme fat that you can perceive nothing els in all their bodies: these birds are now in season. They take great quantitie of them, and they use to pickle them with vineger and salt, and to put them in pots and send them to Venice and other places of Italy for presents of great estimation. They say they send almost 1200. Jarres or pots to Venice, besides those which are consumed in the Island, which are a great number. These are so plentifull that when there is no shipping, you may buy them for 10. Carchies, which coine are 4. to a Venetian Soldo, which is peny farthing the dozen, and when there is store of shipping, 2. pence the dozen, after that rate of their money. They of the limites of Famagusta do keep the statutes of the Frenchmen which sometimes did rule there. And the people of Nicosia observe the order of the Genoueses, who sometimes also did rule them. All this day we lay in the sea with little wind ...

Toward night we ankered under Cavo Bianco, but because the winde grew faire, we set saile againe presently.

Aldersey 1581, 1586

Master Laurence Aldersey, Marchant of London, published his first voyage in a book titled "to the Cities of Jerusalem, Tripolis, &c. In the yeere 1581. Penned and set downe by himselfe." It included a brief stop in Cyprus on August 2. In 1586 his second voyage took him to the "Cities of Alexandria, and Cayro in Ægypt," and he arrived in Cyprus on the 24th of June. His second trip illustrates the extortion at sea by stronger fleets.

This account is set forth in Volume 3 of *The Principal Navigations, Voyages, Traffiques & Discoveries of the English Nation Made by Sea or Overland to the Remote and Farthest Distant Quarters of the Earth at any time within the compass of these 1600 Years,* published by Richard Hakluyt in the late 1500s. This selection comes from the edition published in London and Ontario by J. M. Dent & Sons, Ltd. and in New York by E. P. Dutton & Co. in 1907 and reprinted in 1926.

[First voyage—1581]

[p. 77]

The second day of August we arrived in Cyprus, at a towne called Missagh: the people there be very rude, and like beasts, and no better, they eat their meat sitting upon the ground, with their legges a crosse like tailors, their beds for the most part be hard stones, but yet some of them have faire mattraces to lie upon.

[Second voyage—1586]

[p. 355]

The 15. of May, wee came to Sio, where I stayed thirtie and three dayes. In it is a very proper Towne, after the building of that Countrey, and the people are civil: and while we were here, there came in six Gallies, which had bene at Alexandria, and one of them which was the Admiral, had a Prince of the Moores prisoner, whom they tooke about Alexandria, and they meant to present him to the Turke . . .

The 24. of June wee came to Cyprus, and had sight in the way of the aforesaide six Gallies, that came from Alexandria, one whereof came unto us, and required a present for himselfe, and for two of the other Gallies, which we for quietnesse sake gave them.

Wrag 1595

Richard Wrag undertook a "Voiage" from England to Constantinople and Syria aboard the ship *Ascension* on the 21st of March 1593 and returned overland arriving the 9th of August 1595. In March 1597 he completed his written account of his journey and sent it to his uncle noting that he had accompanied Edward Barton, the British ambassador as the latter presented to "Sultan Murad Can, Emperour of Turkie" a present from the Queen that had been transported on the *Ascension*. Wrag appears to have landed in Cyprus on March 14, 1595. This selection appears in Volume 4 of Richard Hakluyt's *The Principal Navigations of the English Nation.*

[p. 14]

The 27 of February I departed from Aleppo, and the fifth of March imbarked my selfe at Alexandretta in a great ship of Venice called the Nana Ferra, to come for England. The 14 we put into Salino in Cyprus, where the ship staying many dayes to lade cotton wooll, and other commodities, in the meane time accompanied with M. William Barret my countrey man, the master of the ship a Greeke, and others we tooke occasion to see Nicosia, the chiefe city of this Iland, which was some twenty miles from this place, which is situated at the foot of an hill: to the East is a great plaine, extending it selfe in a great length from the North to the South: it is walled about, but of no such strength as Famagusta (another city in this Iland neere the Sea side) whose walles are cut out of the maine rocke. In this city be many sumptuous and goodly buildings of stone, but uninhabited; the cause whereof doth give me just occasion to shew you of a rare judgement of God upon the owners sometime of these houses, as I was credibly informed by a Cipriot a marchant of good wealth in this city. Before it came in subjection to the Turks, while it was under the Venetians, there were many barons and noble men of the Cipriots, who partly by usurping more superiority over the common people then they ought, and partly through their great revenues which yeerely came in by their cotton wooll and wines, grew so insolent and proud, and withall so impiously wicked, as that they would at their pleasure command both the wives and children of their poore tenants to serve their uncleane lusts, & holding them in such slavery as though they had beene no better then dogges, would wage them against a grayhound or spaniell, and he who woon the wager should ever after holde them as his proper goods and chattels, to do with them as he listed, being Christians as well as themselves, if they may deserve so good a name. As they behaved themselves most unchristianly toward their brethren, so and much more ungodly (which I should have put in the first place) did they towards God: for as though they were too great, standing on foot or kneeling to serve God, they would come riding on horsebacke into the church to heare their masse: which church now is made a publike basistane or market place for the Turkes to sell commodities in: but beholde the judgement of the righteous God, who payeth the sinner measure for measure. The Turkes the yeere before the overthrowe given them at Lepanto by Don John tooke Cyprus. These mighty Nimrods fled some into holes & some into mountaines to hide themselves; whereupon the Turkes made generall proclamation, that if they would all come in and yeeld themselves, they would restore them to their former revenues and dignities: who not mistrusting the mischievous pretense of the Turkes, assembled together to make themselves knowen; whom after the Turkes had in possession, they (as the Lords executioners) put them with their wives and children all to the sword, pretending thereby to cut of all future rebellion, so that at this day is not one of the noble race knowen alive in the Iland, onely two or three remaine in Venice but of litle wealth, which in the time of the warres escaped. After we had stayed in this Iland some thirty dayes, we set saile in the foresayd shippe being about the burthen of 900 tunnes, having in her passengers of divers nations, as Tartars, Persians, Jewes, and sundry Christians.

Moryson 1596

Born in 1566 Fynes Moryson, also recorded as Fines or Fiennes, completed studies at Cambridge, London and Oxford before beginning his journeys to Europe and the Mediterranean on May 1, 1591. He wandered through Europe for four years. He returned to London to find his brother Henry preparing for a journey to Jerusalem and Turkey and joined him, leaving London on November 29, 1595. Henry died of dysentery near Antioch, and Fynes was critically ill, but recovered to complete his travels, arriving in London July 10, 1597. His visit to Cyprus occurred in 1596.

During the period from 1609 to 1617 he wrote an account of his journeys in Latin and then translated it himself into English. The Latin version was never published, but his English version was published with the title *An Itinerary: Containing His Ten Yeeres Travell through the Twelve Dominions of Germany, Bohmerland, Sweitzerland, Netherland, Denmarke, Poland, Italy, Turky, France, England, Scotland & Ireland,* by John Beale, Aldersgate street, London, 1617. Our selections were taken from an edition reprinted in Glasgow: James MacLehose and Sons, 1907.

The first selection, from Volume I, contains Moryson's visit to Cyprus. Some short selections about money, islands, weather, and generalizations about the region of the Mediterranean, from Volumes II and IV, follow this longer selection.

[Vol. I, p. 458]

On Sunday the nineteenth of May, we came to the first Promontory of the Iland Cyprus, towards the West, and after eight houres sayling, we came to the old City Paphos (or Paphia), now called Baffo, and the wind failing us, and gently breathing upon this Castle of Venus, we hovered here all the next night, gaining little or nothing on our way. This place is most pleasant, with fruitfull hils, and was of old consecrated to the Goddesse Venus, Queene of this Iland; and they say that Adamants are found here, which skilfull Jewelers repute almost as precious as the Orientall. A mile from this place is the Cave, wherein they faigne the seven sleepers to have slept, I know not how many hundred yeeres. The twenty one of May towards the evening, we entred the Port of Cyprus, called Le Saline, & the two & twentieth day obtaining licence of the Turkish Cady to goe on land, we lodged in the Village Larnica, within a Monastery of European Friars. Here some of us being to saile to Joppa, and thence to goe by land to Jerusalem, did leave the Venetian ship, which sailed forward to Scanderona. The Turkes did conquer the Iland Ciprus from the Venetians, in the yeere 1570, and to this day possesse it, the chiefe Cities whereof are Nicosia, (seated in the middest of the Iland) and Famagosta (seated in the furthest part of the Iland towards the East). The Turkish Basha or Governour, useth to chuse Famogosta for his seate, (though Nicosia be the fairer City), because it hath a good Haven, and a most strong fort, which the Venetians built. The Iland lieth two hundred & forty miles in length from the west to the East, and hath some eighty miles in bredth, & six hundred miles in compasse . . .

This Iland yeeldeth to no place in fruitfulnesse or pleasure, being inriched with Corne, Oile, Cheese, most sweet Porkes, Sheepe, (having tailes that weigh more than twenty pound) Capers (growing upon pricking bushes) Pomegranats, Oranges, and like fruites; Canes or Reedes of sugar, (which they beat in mils, drawing out a water which they seeth to make sugar), with rich wines, (but gnawing or burning the stomacke) odoriferous Cipres trees, (whereof they make fiers,) store of Cotton, and many other blessings of nature. Neere the Promontory Del' Gatto, so called of Cats that use to kill Serpents, they take Falcons, which Hawkes the Governours are commanded to send to Constantinople. They sowe corne in the month of October, and reape it in Aprill. I know not how it comes to passe that in this Iland of Venus, all fruites taste of salt, which Venus loved well. And I thought that it was onely proper to the place at which we landed, where they make salt, till many Ilanders affirmed to me, that the very earth, the sweet hearbs, the beasts feeding there, and the fountaines of waters had a naturall saltnes. The houses are built after the manner of Asia, of a little stone, one roofe high, and plaine in the top, which is plastered, and there they eate and sleepe in the open aire . . .

I formerly said, that we lodged at Cyprus in a Monastery, whence being now to depart, the Friers of our company, and also the Lay-men, gave each of us eight lires of Venice to the Guardian of the Monastery, and one lire to the Frier that attended us, in the name of gift or almes, but indeede for three dayes lodging and dyet.

Upon Friday the twentie foure of May, we seven Consorts (namely, two Franciscan Friers, one Erimitane Frier, and two Lay men, all Frenchmen, and my selfe and my brother) hired a boat in the Haven for foure lires of Venice, to carrie us to the Cyprian Barke we had hired, and we carried with us our food, a cheese costing foure Aspers, a Jarre of Oyle costing sixe Aspers, and a vessell of Wine (called Cuso, somewhat bigger then an English barrell, and full of rich Wine, but such as fretted our very intrals) costing one Zechine, and foure soldi of Venice, and two Turkish aspers; and egges costing twenty three aspers, beside Bisket which we brought out of the Greeke ship. In twilight (for the nights use not here to be darke) we set saile, and were forced to goe backe towards the West, along the shoare of Cyprus, to the Promontory called Capo di Gatti, that is, the Cape of Cats, that we might from thence (according to the Marriners experience) fetch a faire winde. So we sailed that evening thirtie miles (of Italy I meane) and the next day twentie miles to a Village of Cyprus called Lemisso (where Christians ships use to put in.) Here we cast anchor, & all the six & twentie day of May expected a winde, which we got at midnight following.

[Vol. II, p. 159]

The Greeke Iland Cyprus, subject to the Turkes, spends the Venetian gold and silver lires, but receives not the peeces of eight soldi, nor the lesser moneys of Venice, neither are the Venetian lires currant any further then this Iland, though perhaps they may be spent with some losse upon the Coast adjoyning. At Cyprus the gold zechine was given for eleven lires of Venice, and for 120 aspers of Turkey; and the silver crown called piastro, or a piece of eight Reali Spanish, was given for seventy Aspers, and the gold Sultanon of Turkey, was of the same value with the zechine of Venice: yet the very Subjects more willingly received the zechines. The Turkish Asper is a little peece of silver, which at Haleppo in Syria was worth some three farthings English: and eight aspers at Cyprus made one scahy (a Turkish money which the Italians call Seya) being esteemed at little more then sixe pence English, and fifteene scahy made a zechine, twelve scahy made a French or Spanish Crowne, ten scahy made a piastro or Spanish peece of eight Reali. And sixteene brasse Mangouri made one silver Asper, neither can any money of Cyprus be spent in Palestine without losse.

[Vol. IV, p. 114]

Cyprus is an Iland in the same Sea, and it is most fertile, yeelding Canes of Hony, whence Suger is made, and rich Wines, and abounding with many things required for life and for pleasure, and this Iland the Turks in the last Age took from the Venetians by force of Armes, the chiefe Cities whereof are Famagosta and Nicosia.

* * * * *

Lastly in Palestine, Cyprus and those parts, partly I understood by others, partly I found by experience, that it seldome raines, and that about September and October onely, and not often at that time, but so violently for the time, as if it would beate downe the very houses, falling (as it were) by palefulls at once, and that the fields are watred with night dewes, at the fall whereof no man stirres out of dores, but with his head well covered, for danger of sicknesse, all men using to keepe in the house till the dew be dried, while in the meane time by day the heate is so excessive, as a man can hardly indure his apparrell, though it be of linnen or silke, if it hang not loose but be close about him.

Dallam 1599

Thomas Dallam was a master organ builder in England during the reign of Queen Elizabeth I. She chose him to build an organ as a gift to Sultan Mahomed III and to take it to Constantinople in 1599. The Queen was hoping to enlist the Sultan in her battle against Spain, which he promised but never performed. The secondary intention of the gift was to smooth the way for the newly organized Levant Company of Turkish Merchants. The Levant Company was to exist for 244 years and become second only to the East India Company in its mercantile success.

Dallam's brief visit to "Siprus" is contained in *Early Voyages and Travels in the Levant*, which consists of "The Diary of Master Thomas Dallam, 1599–1600" and "Extracts from the Diaries of Dr. John Covel, 1670–1679." Edited by J. Theodore Bent, the book was originally published by the Hakluyt Society and reprinted by Burt Franklin, New York, undated.

Dr. Covel went to Constantinople in 1670 as chaplain to the embassy. He mentions Cyprus only as an area of some possible danger during his trip because of the presence of "twelve Algerine men of war."

The 8 and 9 we weare in a maner be calmede. The tenthe, and eleventhe, and 12th we sayled by the Coste of Siprus, havinge it upon our lefte hande. Neare unto the weste ende we saw a towne caled Baffa. Eyghte leagues further, at Cape Gata, we sett a man a shore, who was a Greke, and borne in Siprus, and thare dwelled, but havinge a brother dwellinge in Candie, whom he had not in a longe time seene, he gott passage in a shipe to goo to Candie; but the wynde would not suffer the ship to tuche thare, but carried that man to Zante, and in 3 monthes space he could not meete wythe any ship to carrye him backe, againe to Candie. When our shipe came, he hearinge that we weare to sayle by Candie, he fell at our Maysteres feet, and craved passage in our shipe thether. So he was taken in. Yeat when we sayled cloce by the shore of Candie, our Mr. would not land him thare, but carried him to Siprus, and sett him on shore thare; the which I thought was the man's hard fortun, and so he thoughte himselfe, for he wepte bitterly, because he had spente so muche time, and could not se his brother, whom he so dearly lovede.

Aboute ten leagus from the easte end of this Iland, in Siprus, near unto Cape Grego, thare is a greate and large towne caled Famagusta. It is a harber, or good porte. Thare dothe lye the moste of there gallis and other shipinge.

The 13th daye we sayled Juste to the easte ende of Siprus, for the wynde was verrie smale.

This Iland is the moste pleasante of any that hetherto I did ever see. The shores be lowe, and playne feeldes risinge into the lande still hier and hier, that a man maye se neare twentie myles into the Contrie, wheare we sett the man a shore. We saw great store of wylde swine; but, out of all question, it is a verrie fruitful contrie.

When we weare about the mydle of Siprus, we sawe the Mounte Lebynus, which is in Assirria, and but tow smale dayes Journaye from Jerusalem. The 14th, havinge a freshe gale of wynde, we recovered the Cape Cansele, the which is neare unto Scandaroune.

Sandys 1610

A Relation of a journey begun An. Dom. 1610 was first published in 1615 in London by George Sandys, who Cobham tells us was the son of Edwin, Archbishop of York and lived from 1577 to 1644. This folio edition from which Cobham transcribed consisted of four books, one each on Turkey, Egypt, and Palestine. The fourth book covered Sandys' observations about Italy and the islands of Cyprus, Crete, Malta and Sicily.

This selection is from the sixth edition titled *Sandys Travailes* printed in London in 1658 by R. and W. Leybourn. In contrast to Sandys' description of other lands, there is no first person narrative about Cyprus that indicates his actual travel on the island. Nonetheless, there are indications that he did indeed visit the island, and his account is included here because of its broad and interesting survey of what was known of Cyprus at that time.

Sandys gives his poetic selections both in English and in the Latin original, with Greek translated into Latin. We have given only Sandys' translations here, along with citations according to current usage.

THE FOVRTH BOOK.

. . . Our sails now swelling with the first breath of May, on the right hand we left *Cyprus,* sacred of old unto *Venus,* who (as they fain) was here first exhibited to mortalls.

> *I sing of Venus crown'd with gold, renown'd*
> *For fair: that Cyprus guards, by Neptune bound.*
> *Her in soft fome mild-breathing Zephyre bore*
> *On murmuring waves unto that fruitfull shore.*
>
> (*Hymn. Hom. Ven.* 1-5)

Thither said to be driven in regard of the fertility of the soil, or beastly lusts of the people, who to purchase portions for their daughters, accustomed to prostitute them on the shore unto strangers: an offering besides held acceptable to their goddesse of Viciousnesse. Some write that *Cyprus* was so named of the Cypresse trees that grew therein. Others, of *Cyrus,* who built in it the ancient City of *Aphrodisia,* but grosly: for *Cyrus* lived six hundred years after *Homer,* who hath used that name: but more probably of *Cryptus,* the more ancient name; in that often concealed by the surges. It stretcheth from East unto West in form of a fleece, and thrusteth forth a number of promontories: whereupon it was called *Cerastis,* which signifieth horned; so terming Promontories: as in *Phillis* to *Demophoon,*

A Bay there is like to a bow when bend,
Steep horns advancing on the shores extend.

(Ov. *Her.* 2.131)

the occasion of that fable of *Venus* her metamorphosing the cruell sacrificers of that Island into oxen, or else called so of the tumors that grew in many of their foreheads: It is in circuit according unto *Strabo,* 427 miles, 60 miles distant from the rocky shore of *Cilicia;* and from the main of *Syria* an hundred: from whence it is said to have been divided by an earthquake. Divided it was into four Provinces; *Salamina, Amathusia, Lapethia,* and *Paphia,* so named of their principall Cities. *Salamina* was built by *Teucer* in memoriall of that from whence he was banished by his father *Telamon,* for not revenging the death of his brother.

When Teucer fled from sire, and Salamine,
Crown'd with a wreath of poplar dipt in wine,
He thus his sad friends cheers: Go we lov'd mates
Which way soever fortune leads; the Fates
Are kinder than my father: nor despaire
When Teucer guides you. He whose answers are
Most sure, Apollo, in another land
Did say another Salamine should stand.

(Hor. *Carm.* 1.7.21)

The Island being assigned to him by *Belus,* if *Didoes* relation may be beleeved.

Teucer, exiled Greece, to Sidon came:
Who a new kingdome sought by Belus aid.
My father Belus then did Cyprus tame:
And that rich countrey tributory made.

(Verg. *Aen.* 1.619-622)

This city was afterwards called *Constantia;* but destroyed by the *Jews* in the dayes of the Emperour *Trajan,* and finally by the *Saracens* in the reign of *Heraclius;* upon the ruines thereof, the famous *Famagosta* was erected by King *Costa,* as they say, the father of S. *Katherine.* Eternized in fame by the unfortunate valour of the *Venetians,* and their anxiliary forces under the command of *Signior Bragadino;* who with incredible fortitude withstood the furious assaults, made by the populous army of *Selymus* the second, conducted by *Mustapha:* and after surrendered it upon honourable conditions, infringed by the perjured and execrable *Bassa.* Who entertaining at his tent with counterfeit kindnesse the principall of them, suddenly picking a quarrel, caused them all to be murdered, the Governour excepted, whom he reserved for more exquisite torments. For having cut off his ears, and exhibited him by carrying of earth on his back to the derision of the Infidels, hee finally fleyed him alive; and stuffing his skin with chaffe, commanded it to bee hung at the main yard of his Galley. *Famagosta* is seated in a Plain, between two promontories: in form welnigh quadrangular, whereof two parts are washt with the Sea, indifferent strong, and containing two miles in circumference. It standeth almost opposite unto *Tripoly,* having a haven which openeth South-east; the mouth thereof being straightened with two rocks which defend it from the weather. There was Saint *Barnaby* borne, there suffered Martyrdome under *Nero,* and there buryed: to whom the Cathedrall Church was dedicated. This greatly ruined City is yet strongest in the Island, the seat of the *Zanziack*: who was late put into such an affright upon the approach of the *Florentine* ships, that he fully purposed, as is credibly reported, to have surrendered it upon their landing. But they (perhaps possest with a mutuall terror) forbear to attempt it. The aforesaid region of *Salamina* (which lyeth on the East of the Island) contained also the celebrated Cities of *Aphrodisium, Tamassus* abounding with Vitrioll, and Verdigrease; *Arsinoe, Idalium,* and the neighbouring groves so chanted of; the Olympian Promontory (where *Venus* had her Temple, into which was lawfull for no woman to enter) with the hill on the opposite *Pedasium,* square on the top like a table, and sacred unto her, as all the aforenamed. In the territory of *Lapathia* comprehending the North part, where once stood *Tremitus,* in the heart almost of the Island, and midst of a goodly Plain stands the late regall City of *Nicosia*: circular in form, and five miles in circumference; not yeelding in beauty (before defaced by the *Turk*) unto the principall Cities of *Italy:* taken by the aforesaid *Mustapha* on the ninth of September, in the year 1570 with an uncredible slaughter, and death of *Dandalus* the unwarlike Governour. The chief of the prisoners, and richest spoiles, he caused to be imbarqued in two tall ships, and a great Gallion, for a present to send unto *Selymus:* when a noble and beautifull Lady, preferring an honorable death, before a life which would prove so repleat with slavery, and hated prostitutions: set fire on certain barrells of powder, which not only tore in pieces the vessels that carryed her, but burnt the other so low, that the sea devoured their reliques. The *Franks* have their factors resident in *Nicosia;* partly inhabited by the ancient *Greek Cypriots,* and partly by *Turks* and *Moores.* The buildings are low, flat rooft, the entrances little, for the most part ascended by stairs for the more difficult entry. North of this, and upon the sea, stood *Cerévina,* erected by *Cyprus,* (now of great strength, and called *Cerines*: yet surrendered to the *Turk* before it was besieged) and at the West and of that Province, the city of the Sunne, with the Temples of *Venus,* and *Isis,* built by *Phalerus* and *Achamus* the *Athenians.* The mountain of *Olympus* lies on the South of *Lapathia,* high, and taking up fifty miles with his basis; now called, The mountain of the holy Crosse: clothed with trees of all sorts, and stored with fountaines; whereon are a number of Monasteries possest by the *Greek Coloieros* of the order of Saint *Basil.* South of the which even to the sea, extendeth *Amathusia,*

> ——*heavy with mines of brasse:*

(Ov. *Met.* 10.220)

so called of the City *Amathus,* now scarcely shewing her foundation, sacred unto *Venus,* and wherein the rites of her *Adonis* were annually celebrated. Built perhaps by *Amasis* (for I do but so conjecture by the name, & in that it lieth opposite unto *Egypt*) who was the first that conquered *Cyprus.* East thereof are the *Saline,* so named of the abundance of salt that is made there; where the *Turk* did first land his Army: the shore thereabout being fit for that purpose. On the West side of *Amathus* there is a promontory, in form of a peninsula, called formerly *Curias* (of the not far distant City built by the *Argives,* at this day named *Episcopia,* where *Apollo* had a grove hard by a promontory, from whence they were thrown that but presumed to touch his Altar) now called the *Cape* of *Cats:* whereon are the ruines of a Monastery of *Greek Coloieros,* fair when it flourished, with a sumptuous Temple, dedicated to St. *Nicholas.* The Monks, as they say, being obliged to foster a number of Cats for the destruction of the abundance of Serpents that infested those quarters; accustoming to return to the Convent at the sound of a Bell when they had sufficiently hunted. *Paphia* comprehendeth the West of *Cyprus:* so called of the maritime City, built by the son of *Pigmalion* by his Ivory statue: such said to be in regard of her beauty; of whom having long lived a single life (in detestation of those lustfull women) he became inamoured.

> *She Paphus bare, whose name that Iland bears.*
>
> (Ov. *Met.* 10.297)

But *Paphus,* according to others, was built by *Cyneras* (both father and grandfather to *Adonis)* who called it so in remembrance of *Paphus* his father. This *Cyneras* having sworn to assist *Menelaus* with fifty ships, sent him onely one, with the modells of the other in clay to colour his perjury. No place there was through the whole earth where *Venus* was more honoured.

> *An hundred fires Sabean gums consume*
> *There in her fane, which fragrant wreaths perfume.*
>
> (Verg. *Aen.* 1.416-417)

Five miles from thence stands the City of *Baffo* called New *Paphos* heretofore, and built by *Agapenor,* frequented from all parts both by men and women; who went from thence in a solemn procession unto the Old, to pay their vows and celebrate her solemnities. But her Temples both in the one, and in the other (as thorowout the whole Island) were razed to the ground by the procurement of St. *Barnaby.* West of this stood *Cythera,* a little village, at this day called *Conucha;* sacred also unto *Venus,* and which once did give a name unto *Cyprus.* That, and not the Island that lies before *Peloponnesus,* being meant by this:

> *Mine Amathus, high Paphos, Cythera,*
> *Idalia groves——*
>
> (Verg. *Aen.* 10.51-52)

The uttermost promontory that stretcheth to the West, with the supereminent mountain, now called *Capho,* Saint *Pifano;* bore formerly the name of the *Athenian Acamus:* East of which stood the City of *Arsinoe* (at this day *Lescare*) renowned for the groves of *Jupiter.* This Island boasts of the births of *Æsclapiades, Solon, Zeno,* the Stoick, and author of that Sect, *Apollonius,* and *Xenophon.* At the first it was so overgrown with wood, that besides the infinite wast made thereof in the melting of metalls, it was decreed that every man should inherit as much as hee could make champian. A countrey abounding with all things necessary for life; and therefore called *Macaria.* Whose wealth allured the *Romanes* to make a conquest thereof: a prey that more plentifully furnished their coffers, then the rest of their triumphs. It affordeth matter to build a ship from the bottome of the keele to the top of her top-gallant, and to furnish her with tackle and munition. It produceth oyle and grain of severall sorts; wine that lasteth until the eight year; grapes whereof they make Raisins of the Sunne; Citrons, Oranges, Pomegranates, Almonds, Figs, Saffron, Coriander, Sugar-canes: sundry herbs as well Physicall as for food, turpentine, rubarbe, colloquintida, scammony, &c. But the staple commodities, are, Cotton wools (the best of the Orient) chamolets, salt, and sope-ashes. They have plentifull Mines of brasse, some small store of gold and silver; green soder, vitrioll, allome, orpiment, white and red lead, iron, and divers kinds of precious stones of inferiour value, amongst which the emerald and the turkie. But it is in the Summer exceeding hot, and unhealthy, and annoyed with serpents. The brooks (for rivers it hath none) rather merit the name of Torrents, being often exhausted by the Sunne: insomuch as in the time of *Constantine* the Great the Iland was for six and thirty yeers together almost utterly abandoned; rain never falling during that season. It was first possesed by the sons of *Iaphet:* payed tribute first to the *Egyptian Amasis:* then conquered by *Belus*, & governed by the posterity of *Teucer*, untill *Cyrus* expulsed the nine kings that there ruled. But after the *Grecians* repossest the soveraignty, and kept it untill the death of *Nicocles:* and then it continued under the government of the *Ptolemees*, till the *Romans* tooke it from the last of that name: restored it was againe to *Cleopatra,* and her sister *Arsinoe*, by *Antonius*. But he over-throwne, it was made a province of *Rome*, and with the transmigration of the Empire, submitted to the *Bizantine* Emperours: being ruled by a succession of Dukes for the space of eight hundred yeares. When conquered by our *Richard* the first, and given in exchange for the titular Kingdome of *Ierusalem* unto *Guy* of *Lusignan*, it continued in his family untill in the yeare 1473 it was by *Catharina Cornelia* a *Venetian* Lady, the widow to King *James* the bastard, who had taken the same by strong hand from his sister *Carlotte*, resigned to the *Venetians*, who ninety seven years after did lose it to the infidels: under whose yoke it now groneth. But is for the most part inhabited by *Grecians*, who have not long since attempted an unfortunate insurrection. Their Ecclesiasticall estate is governed by one Archbishop and three Bishops: the Metropolitan of *Nicosia*, the Bishop of *Famagosta, Paphus,* and *Amathus*, who live upon stipends.

Lithgow 1611

William Lithgow was born about 1582 in Lanark, Scotland. He evidently began his travels while still in adolescence visiting the Orkney and Shetland Islands and continued in Europe in his twenties. He admitted to the wandering spirit common to his country-men and referred to an "undeserved Dalida wrong" that spurred his travels. The "wrong" is unknown but there is a story that four brothers of a young lady finding their sister with Lithgow cut off his ears, earning him the nicknames of "Cutlugged" or "Lugless" Will. He was also luckless as he was captured and tortured severely in Spain, jailed in England for assaulting the Spanish ambassador, committed again after publication of his book which attacked the Spanish, and even during his journey in Cyprus he was pulled by his heels from his mule, beaten and left for dead.

Lithgow's visit to Cyprus in 1611 occurred during one of the three trips described in *The Totall Discourse of the Rare Adventures & Painfull Peregrinations of Long Nineteene Yeares Travayles from Scotland to the most famous Kingdomes in Europe, Asia and Affrica,* published originally in 1632 by Nicholas Okes in London. This selection is from a reproduction of that first full edition, with conversions of the letters i, j, u, and v to modern usage, published in 1906 in Glasgow by James MacLehose and Sons. Lithgow went on to publish accounts of several shorter journeys until 1645 when all account of him was lost.

THE FIFTH PART

> Close bounded Hellespont, Earths Mother sport
> I leave: longst the Æolid lists, I Smirna court:
> Thence Samothrace, and Rhodos, I accoast,
> Which Lilidamus Viliers, manly lost:
> The Lycian bounds, and steepe Pamphilian shoares
> I strictly view: The sea Carpathian roares,
> I land at Cyprus: Seline is the place,
> Whence I that Kingdome, to Nicosia trace:
> From Famagust, fair Asia, then I courted
> And Libanon . . .

. . . Twelve dayes I was betweene Rhodes and Limisse in Cyprus; where arrived, I received more gracious demonstrations from the Ilanders, then I could hope for, or wish, being farre beyond my merit or expectation; only contenting my curiosity with a quiet mind, I redounded thankes for my imbraced courtesies.

The people are generally strong and nimble, of great civility, hospitality to their neighbours, and exceedingly affectionated to strangers. The second day after my arrival, I tooke with me an Interpreter, and went to see Nicosia, which is placed in the midst of the Kingdome. But in my journey thither, extreame was the heate and thirst I endured; both in respect of the season, and also want of water: And although I had with me sufficiency of Wine, yet durst I drinke none thereof, being so strong, and withall had a tast of pitch; and that is, because they have no barrels, but great Jarres made of earth, wherein their Wine is put. And these Jarres are all inclosed within the ground save onely their mouthes, which stand alwayes open like to a Source or Cisterne; whose insides are all interlarded with pitch to preserve the earthen vessells unbroke a sunder, in regard of the forcible Wine; yet making the taste thereof unpleasant to liquorous lips; and turneth the Wine, too headdy for the braine in digestion, which for health groweth difficult for strangers; and to themselves a swallowing up of diseases.

> To cherish life and blood, the health of Man,
> Give me a Tost, plung'd in a double Cann,
> And spic'd with Ginger: for the wrestling Grape,
> Makes Man, become from Man, a sottish Ape.

Nicosia is the principall Citie of Cyprus, and is invironed with mountaines, like unto Florence in Ætruria; wherein the Beglerbeg remaineth; The second is Famegusta, the chiefe strength and Sea-port in it: Selina, Lemisso, Paphos, and Fontana Morosa, are the other foure speciall Townes in the Iland.

This Ile of Cyprus was of old called Achametide, Amatusa, and by some Marchara, that is happy: It is of length extending from East to West, 210. large 60. and of circuit 600. miles. It yeeldeth infinite canes of Sugar, Cotten-wooll, Oyle, Honney, Cornes, Turpentine, Allum, Verdegreece, Grogranes, store of Mettals and Salt; besides all other sorts of fruit and commodities in abundance. It was also named Cerastis, because it butted toward the East with one horne: and lastly Cyprus, from the abundance of Cypresse trees there growing. This Iland was consecrated to Venus, where in Paphos she was greatly honoured, termed hence, Dea Cypri,

Festa Dies Veneris tota celeberrima Cypro,
Venerat, ipsa suis aderat Venus aurea festis.

Venus feast day, through Cyprus hallowed came,
Whose feasts, her presence, dignified the same.

Cyprus lyeth in the gulfe betweene Cilicia and Syria, having Ægypt to the West: Syria to the South: Cilicia to the East: and the Pamphilian Sea to the North: It hath foure chiefe Capes or headlands: first, Westward the Promontore of Acanias, modernely Capo di Santo Epifanio: to the South the Promontore Phæuria, now Capo Bianco: to the East Pedasia, modernely Capo di Greco: to the North, the high foreland Cramineon, now Capo di Cormathita: these foure are the chiefest Promontores of the Iland, and Cape di S. Andrea in the furthest poynt Eastward toward Cilicia: Diodore and Pliny say that anciently it contained nine Kingdomes, and fifteene good Townes: Cerania, now Selina, was built by Cyrus, who subdued the nine petty Kings of this Ile: Nicosia is situate in the bottome or plaine of Massara, and thirty foure miles from Famagusta; and the Towne of Famagusta was formerly named Salamus: I was informed by some of sound experience here, that this Kingdome containeth about eight hundreth and forty Villages, besides the sixe capitall Townes, two whereof are nothing inferiour for greatnesse and populosity to the Townes in Candy, Sicily, or Greece.

The chiefest and highest mountaine in this Ile, is by the Cypriots called Trohodos, it is of height eight, and of compasse forty eight miles, whereon there are a number of Religious Monasteries, the people whereof are called Colieros, and live under the order of Saint Basile. There is abundance here of Coriander seede, with medicinable Reubarbe, and Turpentine. Here are also mines of gold in it, of Chrysocole, of Calthante, of Allome, Iron, and exceeding good Copper. And besides these mines, there are diverse precious stones found in this Ile, as Emeraulds, Diamonds, Chrystall, Corall, red and white, and the admirable stone Amiante, whereof they make Linnen cloth, that will not burne being cast into the fire, but serveth to make it neate and white.

The greatest imperfection of this Ile, is scarcity of water, and too much plenty of scorching heate, and sabulous grounds. The Inhabitants are very civill, courteous, and affable; and notwithstanding of their delicious and delicate fare, they are much subject to Melancholy, of a Robust nature, and good Warriours, if they might carry Armes: It is recorded, that in the time of Constantine the Great, this Ile was all uterly abandoned of the Inhabitants, and that because it did not raine for the space of sixe and thirty yeares. After which time, and to replant this Region againe, the chiefest Colonies came from Ægypt, Judea, Syria, Cilicia, Pamphilia, Thracia, and certaine Territories of Greece: And it is thought, in the yeares 1163. after that Guy of Lusingham, the last Christian King of Jerusalem had lost the Holy Land, a number of French men, stayed and inhabited here; of whom sprung the greatest race of the Cyprian Gentility; and so from them are discended the greatest Families of the Phenician Sydonians, modernely Drusians: though ill divided, and worse declined; yet they are sprung both from one Originall: the distraction arising from Conscience of Religion, the one a Christian, the other a Turke.

The three Iles of Cyprus, Candy, and Sicily, are the onely Monarchicke Queenes of the Mediterranean Seas: and semblable to other in fertility, length, breadth, and circuit: save onely that Candy is somewhat more narrow than the other two, and also more Hilly and sassinous: yet for Oyles and Wines, she is the Mother of both the other: Sicily being for Graine and Silkes the Empresse of all: and Cyprus for Sugar and Cotton-wooll, a darling sister to both; onely Sicily being the most civill Ile, and nobly gentilitat, the Cypriots indifferently good, and the Candiots the most ruvid of all.

The chiefe Rivers are Teno, and Pedesco: Cyprus was first by Teucer made a Kingdome, who after the Trojane Warre came and dwelt here: and afterwards being divided betweene nine petty Princes, it was subdued by Cyrus, the first Monarch of the Meedes and Persians. After the subversion of which Empire, this Ile was given to the Potolemies of Ægypt: from whom Cato conquered it to the benefit of the Romans. The Dukes of Savoy were once Kings of Cyprus; but the Inhabitants usurping their authority, elected Kings to themselves, of their owne generation: and so it continued, till the last king of Cyprus, James the Bastard (marrying with the daughter of a noble Venetian, Catherina Cornaro) died without children, leaving her his absolute heire. And she perceiving the factious Nobility, too headstrong to be bridled by a female authority, like a good child, resigned her Crowne and Scepter to the Venetian Senate, Anno 1473. Whereupon the Venetians embracing the opportunitie of time, brought her home, and sent Governours thither to beare sway in their behalfe; paying onely as tribute to the Ægyptian Sultans 40000. Crownes, which had been due ever since Melecksala, had made John of Cyprus his tributary.

It was under their Jurisdiction 120. years and more; till that the Turkes, who ever oppose themselves against Christians (finding a fit occasion in time of peace, and without suspition in the Venetians) tooke it in with a great Armado. Anno 1570. and so till this day by them is detayned. Oh great pitty! that the usurpers of Gods word, and the worlds great enemy, should maintaine (without feare) that famous Kingdome, being but one thousand & fifty Turkes in all, who are the keepers of it: unspeakable is the calamitie of that poore afflicted Christian people under the terrour of these Infidels; who would, if they had Armes, or asistance of any Christian Potentate, easily subvert and abolish the Turkes, without any disturbance; yea, and would render the whole Signiory thereof to such a noble Actor. I doe not see in that small judgement, which by experience I have got, but the redemption of that Countrey were most facile; if that the generous heart of any Christian Prince, would be moved with condigne compassion to relieve the miserable afflicted Inhabitants. In which worke, he should reape (questionlesse) not onely an infinite treasure of Worldly commodities, that followeth upon so great a conquest, but also a heavenly and eternall reward of immortall glory. The which deliverance Ferdinando Duke of Florence, thought to have accomplished (having purchased the good will of the Ilanders) with five Gallounes, and 5000. Souldiers: Who being mindfull to take first in the Fortresse of Famogusta, directed so their course, that in the night, they should have entred the Haven, disbarke their men, and scale the walles.

But in this plot they were farre disappointed by an unhappy Pilot of the Vice-admirall, who mistaking the Port, went into a wrong bay: which the Florentines considering, resolved to returne, and keepe the sea, till the second night; but by a dead calme, they were frustrated of their aymes, and on the morrow discovered by the Castle: Whereupon the Turkes went presently to armes, & charged the Inhabitants to come to defend that place: But about foure hundred Greekes in the West part, at Paphos, rebelled; thinking that time had altered their hard fortunes, by a new change: but alas, they were prevented, & every one cut off by the bloody hands of the Turkes. This massacre was committed in the yeare 1607. Such alwaies are the torturing flames of Fortunes smiles, that he who most affecteth her, she most, and altogether deceiveth: But they who trust in the Lord, shall be as stable as Mount Syon, which cannot be removed; and questionlesse, one day God, in his all-eternall mercie, will relieve their miseries, and in his just judgements, recompence these bloody oppressors with the heavy vengeance of his all-seeing Justice.

In my returne from Nicosia, to Famogusta, with my Trench-man, we encountered by the way with foure Turkes, who needs would have my Mule to ride upon; which my Interpreter refused: But they in a revenge, pulled me by thee heels from the Mules backe, beating me most pittifully, and left me almost for dead. In this meanewhile my companion fled, and escaped the sceleratnesse of their hands; and if it had not beene for some compassionable Greekes, who by accident came by, and relieved me, I had doubtless immediately perished . . .

From the Fort and City Famogusta, I embarked in a Germo, and arrived at Tripoly being 88. miles distant . . .

Ricaut 1678

Paul Ricaut (Rycaut), a former consul at Smyrna and Fellow of the Royal Society was charged by King Charles II to provide an account of Greek and Armenian churches. The result was a book titled *The Present State of the Greek and Armenian Churches, Anno Christi 1678.* His 452-page book published in London by John Starkey in 1679 devoted 380 pages to the Greek Church, including this short selection of the church in Cyprus and a paragraph on the long life claimed by a monk at Kykko Monastery.

The Island of *Cyprus* was in its Ecclesiastical Government subjected once to the Patriarch of *Antioch;* but afterwards by the Council of *Ephesus* as Canon the Eighth, and the same again confirmed by the Grace and Favour of Justinian the Emperour, (whose Mother was a *Cypriot* by birth;) this Church was made absolute and independent of any other, and a priviledge given to *Anthemius*, the Arch-Bishop in that age, to subscribe his Name to all Publick Acts in red Letters, which was an honour above that of any Patriarch, who writes his Name or Firm in black Characters, the which was afterwards confirmed by the Authority of *Zeno* the Emperour: This Favour and Indulgence was granted in honour to the apostle *Barnaby*, who primarily governed this Diocess, where now his Sepulcher remains. The Arch-Bishoprick, during the time that it was under the Duke of *Savoy* and the Republick of Venice, was the Mother of 32 Bishopricks, but now by the oppression and violence of the *Turks* hath been reduced to one Arch-Bishoprick and three Bishopricks. The first hath its Cathedral Church at *Nicosia*, and receives its Revenue from *Famagosta*, *Carpasi* and *Tamasea*, which are immediately subject thereunto. The Bishopricks are,

First, that of *Pafo*, and *Arsenoia,* or *Arsinoe*.

The Second, that of *Cyti*, and *Amathunta,* anciently *Cetium* or *Citium* and *Amathusia*.

The third, that of *Cerinia* and *Solea*, anciently called *Salines,* or *Salamine* from *Salamis*, and was the most renowned City of all the others.

This island before it was taken by the *Turks,* contained 14 thousand Villages: but after a Rebellion they made against the *Turk, Anno* 1580. and 1593. the greatest part of the Inhabitants were either killed or exterminated: to which the grievous Pestilence which succeeded in the Year 1624. added so irreparable a desolation that of the 14 thousand Villages there remain not 700 at this present time.

The Archbishop of this Island in this year 1678. is named *Hilarion*, and sirnamed *Cicala*, created and promoted to this Dignity in the year 1674. a learned man, and well skilled in the *Greek* and *Latine* Tongues. His Revenue or maintenance arises from the Churches of *Famagosta*, *Carpasi,* and *Tamasea*, according to the Ecclesiastical Endowments: but from the Villages he receives nothing, unless at the Visits which he makes twice a year, some Collection is made of Corn, Oyl, Wine, and other Fruits, in like nature of Tythes, but rather by way of Presents and Free-will Offerings, than of Duties. From the Monasteries he receives a certain annual Income or Rent, according to the Abilities and Possessions thereof, and from every *Papa* or Priest, a Dollar yearly *per* Head: All which will scarce maintain a Patriarch, or yield him other than a poor livelihood. For when a Patriarch is first constituted, a Purse of Money or 500 Dollars is exacted, and paid to the *Pasha*, and as much more to the *Janisaries;* besides the ordinary growing charges, which are yearly about 2500 dollars. For to the *Pasha* every three Months are paid 166 dollars; and to the *Janisary*, which is set for a guard to the Patriarch, 20 or 25 dollars, as he thinks fit to agree: also upon the coming of a new *Kadi* there is always a new Expence, who commands what he pleases in Money or Presents; so that with these Taxes and Exactions the Church is always harassed and made poor.

The Bishop of *Pafo*, named at present *Leontius*, who hath the city of *Arsinoia* under his Jurisdiction, gathers his maintenance after the manner of the Archbishop. *Pafo* was anciently a Port of good fame and renown, and is so at present; from whence is yearly shipped off a considerable quantity of Cottons, Silk, and other Merchandise: but by the oppression and hard usage of the *Turks*, and the covetousness of the Officers, is reduced to poverty and want of people. The second Diocess govern'd by its Bishop, is that of *Cetium*, or after the Vulgar *Cyti*, hath under its Government the City of *Limeson*, *Cilan*, *Amathunte,* and another City anciently a Diocess, adjoined to it, called *Cyrion*: of which place one *Cosma* was Bishop some few years past, a person of good Ingenuity and Learning, born at *Tunis* in *Africa*, his Father of *Thessalonica*, and his Mother of *Cyprus*, with whom having some acquaintance, I had the opportunity to make these Collections relating to the state and condition of that place.

The third Diocess is of *Cerinia*, the Bishops name at present *Leontius*, having three Cities under it, *viz. Solea*, *Pentasia,* and *Marathusa*, the which is governed and maintained in the same manner as the other Diocesses.

* * * * *

Many of this sort of people (*Kaloires*) are long-lived in regard they are temperate in eating and drinking, and ever unacquainted with Women. I once knew one of them who was an Ἀπανδόχους of a monastery in Cyprus called Παναγία τοῦ κύκκου Μαραθάσα τῆς Λεύκας, whereunto belonged 200 *Kaloirs*, he told me that he was 119 years of age; and the better to assure me he was not mistaken in his Calculate, he confidently affirmed, that he remembered the taking of *Cyprus* by the *Turk*, when the Channels of his Town ran with blood, which according to History may be about the space of 107 years past, and at that time he conceived that he might have been about 12 years of age, when he remembers, that the cruel Souldiers bloodily massacring all persons which met them in their fury, his Mother defended him from violence; for having the fortune to meet with a Souldier more flexible then the rest, she fell on the body of this her Son, and by her Prayers and Tears prevailed to rescue him from death: in commemoration of which deliverance, she afterwards dedicated him to the service of God, speedily entering him into the Order of *Kaloires*; he never remembers to have eaten flesh; his Father lived but to 80 years of age, but his Grandfather to 158.

Thompson 1734

Charles Thompson undertook a trip best described by the title of his book, *Travels through Turkey in Asia, the Holy Land, Arabia, Egypt, and other parts of the World: Giving a Particular and Faithful Account of What is most Remarkable in the Manners, Religion, Polity, Antiquities, and Natural History of those Countries: With a Curious Description of Jerusalem, as it now Appears, and other Places Mentioned in the Holy Scriptures,* Carlisle: Archibald Loudon, 1813. Thompson sailed from Constantinople in 1733 and visited Cyprus in 1734. Of the ten pages he devoted to Cyprus only the few paragaphs below contain any personal observations. The remainder surveys the history of the island as determined by writers preceding him.

TRAVELS
THROUGH
TURKEY IN ASIA

. . . Our vessel sailed from Rhodes on the 6th of February in the morning, with a fresh gale at West, whereby we ran about ten miles an hour for the greatest part of the day; but the wind slackened in the evening, and before midnight we were quite becalmed. We had a continual rain till morning, and some thunder; but about nine in the forenoon a gentle gale sprung up again, and we had pleasant sailing all that and the following day. On the 9th it blew very hard, but more rain falling towards the evening, the wind abated. We did not make much way that night, but the next day we ran at least twenty-five leagues, and made the island of Cyprus a little before sun-set. The 11th in the morning we found ourselves off Cape de Gate, the most Southern point of the island; which having doubled, and passed by the point of Lymisso, and afterwards Cape Grega, we arrived the same evening in the harbour of Famagusta . . .

The town of Famagusta, supposed to be the ancient Salamis, which was said to be built by Teucer when banished by his father, stands on the Eastern part of the island, almost over against Tripoli in Syria. It is a place of considerable strength, and has a pretty good harbour, but the entrance is somewhat dangerous for vessels of large burthen. It is inhabited by Turks, Greeks, Jews, Armenians, and some few Latins; but the Greeks are most numerous, as they are all over the island. While Cyprus was under the dominion of the Christians, it was well peopled, having no less than eight hundred or a thousand villages in it, besides several handsome cities; but since it has unhappily fallen under the Turkish yoke, they have spread ruin and desolation over the country, and it is now so thinly inhabited, that half the lands lie uncultivated; and the noble buildings, which the Venetians erected when they were masters of it, are most of them demolished. Many of the finest churches were taken from the Christians when the Turks conquered the island, and turned into mosques; particularly the cathedral church of St. Sophia in the city of Nicosia. In a word, as far as I can learn, the people are loaded with taxes, and in other respects are rigorously treated by their Mahometan masters, which occasions many of them to apostatize, and embrace the Turkish faith, at least in appearance; especially the wicked and profligate, who are generally observed to shake off the profession of Christianity, when it is attended with reproach and oppression . . .

Montague 1738

John Montague, fourth Earl of Sandwich, of some culinary fame, sailed around the Mediterranean and published his reflections under the title *A Voyage Performed by the Late Earl of Sandwich Round the Mediterranean in the Years 1738 and 1739.* It was printed in London for T. Cadell Jun. and W. Davies in 1799.

There is in Montague's account more recapitulation of the history of Cyprus than of his own personal observations. This selection comprises the last thirteen pages (pp. 379–391) of his thirty-five pages on Cyprus, omitting the earlier history, which contains no first person narrative.

[p. 379]

The figure under which the goddess was symbolized in the temple of Paphos, was of a pyramidical form, as we find it expressed in several medals; particularly in one, which I saw when I was at Cyprus: on one side of which was the head of Venus, and on the other a temple, in the middle of which stood a pyramid with the inscription, ΠΑΦΙΩΝ. It was esteemed by the Cyprians so great an honour to officiate as high priest in the Paphian temple, that it was usually annexed to the royal dignity; and hence we find the ancient king Cinyras at the same time invested with the character of chief priest of Venus and monarch of Cyprus. Paphos was several times destroyed by earthquakes, and as often rebuilt by the joint benefactions of the nine sovereigns, who looked upon it as an holy city. During the Roman civil wars it was by a violent earthquake wholly levelled with the ground; but was afterwards raised from its ruins by the emperor Augustus, who changed its name to Augusta; ordering that the proconsul should make it the place of his residence; which is confirmed by a passage in the Acts of the Apostles, in which we are told that Barnabas and Paul, in the city of Paphos, met with a certain false prophet named Barjesus, who was in the presence of Sergius Paulus, at that time proconsul of the island.

> And when they had gone through the isle unto Paphos, they found a cer-
> tain sorcerer, a false prophet, a Jew, whose name was Barjesus: Which was
> with the deputy of the country, Sergius Paulus, a prudent man, who called
> for Barnabas and Saul, and desired to hear the word of God.
>
> Acts, C. xiii. v: 6, 7.

These two apostles were the first, who preached the gospel in the island of Cyprus, the inhabitants of which pretend that they left behind them Epaphras, who was the first bishop of Paphos. There was another Paphos, distant from this about sixty stadiums, which for the sake of distinction was called Palaepaphos, being founded by Agapenor, on his return from the siege of Troy. Of these two cities there are now little or no remains, both of them having long since been destroyed by earthquakes, which are very frequent in these parts. There is, however, upon the site of Palaepaphos a village, called by the inhabitants Baffo, (which is undoubtedly a corruption of the old name,) and near it some fragments of marble, but no inscription, or other curiosity worthy a traveller's attention. The country round Baffo is extremely fertile, being watered by a small rivulet, which renders it abundant in corn and fruits of all sorts. The city of Salamis, which was next in renown to that of Paphos, stood upon the opposite part of the island; its origin is too well known to be mentioned in this place, though it may not, perhaps, be improper to take notice, that after its foundation, the other Salamis in Attica was called by the Greeks the true Salamis, to distinguish it from this in Cyprus;

> Exhausit totas quamvis delectus Athenas,
> Exiguae Phoebea tenet navalia puppes,
> Tresque petunt veram credi Salamina carinae.
>
> Lucan. L. iii. l. 181.

> Though Athens now had drain'd her naval store,
> And the Phoebean arsenal was poor;
> Three ships of Salamis to Pompey came;
> To vindicate it's true and antient name.
>
> Rowe

Diodorus Siculus represents Salamis as one of the largest and most powerful cities in all Cyprus; and we are informed by other authors, that it was as remarkable for its beauty and regularity, as for its strength and extent. Among many stately temples the principal were that of Jupiter Salaminius, founded by Teucer; those of Venus Prospiciens, of Diomede, Minerva, and Aglaura, at whose altar the Cypriots annually, in the month called by them Aphrodisium, observed a cruel ceremony of sacrificing an human creature; till Diphilus, king of Salamis, abolished the barbarous custom, and changed the victim to an ox. Salamis was so totally destroyed by Richard the First, king of England, that it is now only an heap of ruins, which account, from the people of the country, together with the inconvenience of its being situated in the most remote part of the island, prevented my visiting the remains of that renowned city. Lapethus, another of the royal cities, founded by Belus, is now reduced to a small village, known under the name of Lapitho, the territories of which are productive of fruits of all sorts, and in the greatest abundance. Curias, built by Cureas, son of Cinyras, was situated at a small distance from a promontory of the same name, now called Capo di Gatto. It is owen to the authority of Herodotus, that I venture to place this among the number of the royal cities, since that author, in the hundred and thirteenth chapter of Terpsichore, mentions Stesenor as king of Curias, or Curium, as he calls it, differing in that point from Pliny and other authors, who give the same name to the town and promontory. Near this city was a temple in the middle of a wood, dedicated to Apollo Hylates, which was held in great veneration by all the inhabitants of the island. Both the city and temple are now entirely buried under their ruins, insomuch that their situation is at present by no means determined. Cytium is supposed by some authors to have owed its foundation to Belus, though others give it a much higher date of antiquity, pretending that its name is only a corruption of Chetim, grandson to Noah, from whom they trace the original of this city. In effect, we read in the seventh book of Josephus, that it was called Cytium by those, who were willing to adapt the name of Chetim to the Greek pronunciation. In the time of Alexander the Great, when the nine sovereigns of Cyprus made a voluntary offer of their dominions to that conqueror, the king of Cytium distinguished himself beyond the others, by a present which he made to him of a fine sword, the make and form of which was so much approved of by Alexander, that he for the future never made use of any other weapon. Zeno, the first institutor of the sect of stoic philosophers, was a native of this city, which has many ages since dwindled into a small village, situated in a fertile country, upon a cape, not far from the town of Arnicho, and known by the inhabitants of the island under the name of Chiti; which, although it be a manifest corruption of Cytium, and by that means points out the exact situation of that city; yet I could not, after the strictest search, find out the least remains of antiquity any where in that part of the island. Amathus, the most ancient city in the whole island, being said to have been founded by Amatheus, son of Hercules, was under the peculiar protection of Venus; whose statue, though it was dressed in a woman's habit, had the face of a man with a long beard; whence Catullus calls the goddess duplex Amathusia;

Nam mihi quam dederit duplex Amathusia curam
Scitis, et in quo me torruerit genere.

CAT. El. lx. L.v. l. 51.

Oft has this bosom, ye chaste muses, know,
Sharp pangs from double Amathusia tried,
Burnt, like fierce Ætna, or the baths which flow
From Malia's fount near Ætna's scorching side.

OZELL

I mention this passage, because a late commentator has taken a great deal of pains to give a quite different explanation to it, which trouble he might have spared himself, had he not been unacquainted with the above-mentioned particularity. Near the temple of Venus was an altar dedicated to Jupiter Ξένιος, where the Cypriots inhumanly sacrificed all strangers that were by stress of weather driven upon their island, and even such as they had at first relieved with tokens of hospitality. We are beholden to Ovid for an account of this horrid barbarity:

> Ante fores horum stabat Jovis Hospitis ara,
> Lugubris sceleris; quam si quis sanguine tinctam
> Advena vidisset, mactatos crederet illic
> Lactentes vitulos, Amathusiacasve bidentes:
> Hospes erat caesus.
>
> OVID. Met. L. x. l. 224

> Before whose gates a rev'rend altar stood,
> To Jove inscrib'd, the hospitable god:
> This had some stranger seen, with gore besmear'd,
> The blood of lambs and bulls it had appear'd:
> Their slaughter'd guests it was.
>
> OZELL

There were also temples erected to Ariadne, Hercules, and Onesilus; who, as I before mentioned, induced the Cypriots to revolt from the Persian government. The remains of this city are so inconsiderable, that its situation is uncertain, though it is most commonly imagined to have stood at about five miles distance from Limisso; which opinion is in some measure favoured by a few fragments of marble, which are to be found in that place. The city of Soli, which, according to Strabo, was situated near that of Arsinoe, had for its founders two Athenians, named Apamus and Phalerus; though Plutarch gives it a very different origin. We are informed by that learned historian, that during the reign of Philocyprus, king of this province, Solon happening to come to Cyprus, was entertained in that prince's court with very great hospitality, and had by his merit insinuated himself so much into his favour, that he was treated by him, and always behaved to him with the utmost familiarity. Solon, in recompence of his friendship, observing that the capital of his dominions stood in a barren and mountainous country, advised him to build a new city in the plains beneath, which by their beauty and fertility seemed to invite him to the enjoyment of the benefits of so advantageous a situation. Solon at the same time promised to superintend the work, and the prince, who in every thing put an entire confidence in that great man, readily agreed to his proposal, and in compliment to his friend named the city Soli. Plutarch has preserved to us some verses of Solon himself upon this occasion, in which he addresses himself to Philocyprus:

> Νῦν δὲ σὺ μὲν Σολίοισι πολὺν χρόνον ἐνθάδ' ἀνάσσων,
> Τήν τε πόλιν ναίοις, καὶ γένος ὑμέτερον·
> Αὐτὰρ ἐμὲ ξὺν νηὶ θοῇ κλεινῆς ἀπὸ Νήσου

'Ασκηθῆ πέμποι Κύπρις ἰοστέφανος.

PLUT. In Vit. Sol.

Long time mayest thou, O king! in Soli reign:
Thou, and thy progeny, a lengthening train.
But me from this famed isle, with guardian care,
May Venus, crown'd with violets, quickly bear.

This city was placed under the protection of the goddesses Venus and Isis, both of whom were honoured with temples, frequent sacrifices, and festivals. There are at present no remains existing to point out the true situation of this city, unless it be the small village of Solea, situated upon the western coast of the island, which has nothing but its name to countenance such a supposition. The city of Chytros, so called from Chytrus, grandson of Acamas, who built and peopled it, was once the capital of a kingdom contiguous to that of Salamis, but is now reduced to an inconsiderable village; which retains no other mark of antiquity than the name of Chitri. Malum, the ninth royal city, is recorded in history only upon account of its having been besieged and taken by Cimon the Athenian, and afterwards destroyed by Ptolomy the First, king of Ægypt; who took prisoner the monarch who resided in it, and transported all the inhabitants to Paphos. The situation of it is absolutely unknown, nor is it so much as determined upon what part of the island it was placed. Beside these royal cities there were several private ones, which might very well dispute with the capitals in grandeur and magnificence. Such were these mentioned by Pliny, namely, Cythera, Corineum, Tamassus, Epidarum, Arsinoe, Carpasium, Golgos, Marium, and Idalium, which two latter he informs us were utterly destroyed before his time. Cythera, famous for the worship there paid to the goddess Venus, stood almost in the centre of the island, and is now sunk into a small village, which has preserved its ancient name. Tamassus, which in all probability is the modern Famagusta, was situated about ten leagues distant from the easternmost point of the island. This was the most fertile part of all Cyprus, and particularly sacred to Venus, who had here a very ancient temple with a temenos, wherein grew the tree which produced the three golden apples, by her presented to Hippomenes. This we may collect from Ovid:

Est ager, indigenae Tamasenum nomine dicunt,
Telluris Cypriae pars optima; quem mihi prisci
Sacravere senes, templisque accedere dotem
Hanc jussere meis; medio nitet arbor in arvo,
Fulva comam, fulvo ramis crepitantibus auro.

Ov. Met. L. x. l. 644.

The Cyprian lands, though rich, in richness yield
To that surnam'd the Tamasenian field.
That field of old was added to my shrine,
And its choice products consecrated mine.
A tree there stands, full glorious to behold,

Gold are the leaves, the crackling branches gold.

EUSDEN.

Claudian seems to allude to Tamassus, in his beautiful description of the court of Venus, as one may conclude from several particulars, but especially from his placing it on the eastern part of the island. The ancients had a notion, that in the neighbourhood of this city were two fountains, the waters of which were of so very different a nature, that as a draught of one incited to love, the other on the contrary utterly extinguished that passion. It seems to me, as if Claudian hinted at this in the following lines:

Labuntur gemini fontes, hic dulcis, amarus
Alter, et infusis corrumpit mella venenis;
Unde Cupidineas armavit fama sagittas.

CLAUD. de Nupt. Hon. & Mar.

Hence flow two fountains, sweet of taste the one,
The other bitter, and of poisonous taint,
Whence Cupid ting'd, as fame reports, his darts.

Golgos and Idalium were also favourite cities of Venus, upon which account Theocritus has joined them together.

Δέσποιν ἁ Γολγόντε, καὶ ᾽Ιδαλίον ἐφίλασας.

THEOC. Idyl. xv. 1. 100.

O, chief of Golgos, and the Idalian grove,
And breezy Eryx, beauteous queen of love!

FAWKES.

In the forests near Idalium, Adonis received his death, as we read in the poet:

Testis qui niveum quondam percussit Adonin
Venantem Idalio vertice durus Aper.

PROP. L. ii. El. xiii. 1. 53.

Venus was so afflicted at the loss of her beloved youth, that she ordered the inhabitants of Idalium every year, upon the anniversary of his death, to express their sorrow with cries and lamentations, in imitation of those she herself uttered.

Desiluit, pariterque sinus, pariterque capillos
Rupit, et indignis percussit pectora palmis.
Questaque cum fatis, at non tamen omnia vestri
Juris erunt, inquit, luctus monumenta manebunt
Semper, Adoni, mei, repetitaque mortis imago

Annua plangoris repetet simulamina nostri.

Ov. Met. L. x. 1. 722.

Down with swift flight she plung'd, nor rage forbore,
At once her garment and her hair she tore.
With cruel blows she beat her guiltless breast,
The fates upbraided and her love confest.
Nor shall they yet (she cry'd) the whole devour
With uncontroll'd, inexorable power:
For thee, lost youth, my tears and restless pain,
Shall in immortal monuments remain.
With solemn pomp in annual rites return'd,
Be thou for ever, my Adonis, mourn'd.

EUSDEN.

This was the origin of the festivals termed Αδωνεια, which were afterwards celebrated with many ridiculous ceremonies in Greece, Ægypt, and particularly upon the banks of the river Adonis in Syria. Golgos fell to decay soon after the building of Paphos; Idalium is at present a small town called Dali, about twelve miles from the city of Nicosia, without the least remains of antiquity any where in its neighbourhood. The chief cities of Cyprus at present are Famagusta, Nicosia, Arnicho, and Limisso. Famagusta was founded in the year one thousand two hundred and ninety by Henry king of Cyprus, after the destruction of Ptolemais in Syria. Its situation is advantageous, being upon the sea-shore, at the extremity of a spacious gulph, towards the most eastern part of the island. It is some miles in circumference, is tolerably well built, and has a very good harbour for small vessels. Some authors there are, who pretend to give it a much higher date of antiquity, by affirming that the emperor Augustus, after the battle of Actium, willing to perpetuate his name in all parts of the world, erected this city, which he called Fama Augusta, in memory of the fame he had acquired in that signal victory. This city was rendered a strong place by the Venetians, whose works are still remaining, though by the neglect of the present possessors they are in a very ruinous condition. Nicosia, which is now the capital of the island, and residence of the Mouhassil, or exactor of the tribute, (who is invested with his authority by the grand visier, to whom belongs the whole revenue of Cyprus,) is situated near the centre of the island, and is said to owe its foundation to one of the kings of the Lusignan family, who constituted it the metropolis of his dominions. It was originally near nine miles in circumference, till the Venetians, to render it more capable of defence, reduced it to three, surrounding it with a fortification, which in those days was esteemed considerable. Arnicho, where all the European factories reside, stands about a mile from the sea-shore, at the extremity of a deep bay, which is the place of resort of a great number of English, French, Dutch, and Venetian ships, which carry on a great trade. The town is of a pretty large extent, without any sort of defense; the houses are low, and but of ordinary structure. Close to the sea-shore is a small village called Saline, from the neighbouring salt-works, with a castle garrisoned by Turks, who in this place collect their duties. These salt-works, in the time of the Venetians, afforded an immense revenue to the republic; but, since they have been in the hands of the Turks, they have been so much neglected, that the product of them is very inconsiderable, in comparison of what it has been formerly. The salt is owen to a great number of springs, which rise in a large valley near the sea, impregnated to a vast degree with particles of salt, which the nature of the earth undoubtedly administers. These springs being augmented by the torrents, which fall from the mountains in the winter seasons, form themselves into a lake of five or fix feet in depth, and almost a mile in circumference, the waters of which being dried up by the excessive heats of the summer leave the surface of the earth entirely covered with the finest salt, which in the month of August is thrown up into one large heap, where it remains ready either for exportation, or to be disposed of among the inhabitants of the island. Limisso stands upon the sea-coast, about thirty-three miles to the westward of Saline. It is defended by a castle, which seems by its structure to have been built by the Turks, who maintain a sufficient garrison in it to prevent the Maltese from making their descents upon that part of the island. The town itself consists in about three hundred houses, which are low and ill built, as are indeed the generality of them throughout all Cyprus. These are the only towns of note; there are several others indeed, but all of too little consequence to deserve mention. The island is three hundred and thirty miles in circuit, and extends itself forty-five leagues in length, from east to west; it lies between the thirty-fifth and thirty-sixth degrees of latitude, about fifteen leagues distant from the coast of Syria. None of the islands in the Mediterranean can dispute with it in fertility, since it produces a prodigious quantity of silk, cotton, flax, honey, oil, wax, fruits of all sorts, corn in abundance, and the best wine of the universe. Its inhabitants are most of them Greeks, and are computed at one hundred thousand, including about three thousand Turks, who live in the towns of Nicosia, Famagusta, and Limisso. None of the Grand Signor's subjects are more oppressed, or live in greater poverty, than the inhabitants of this island; since they are taxed entirely according to the will of the mouhassil, who, buying his employment at a very high price, is obliged to reimburse himself at the expense of his miserable subjects. Cyprus, in the winter, is one of the most agreeable habitations in the world, the climate is mild and temperate, the air wholesome, and the face of the country covered with a most delightful verdure; in the summer it bears a quite different appearance, being burnt up by the scorching rays of the sun, and frequently overwhelmed by incredible numbers of locusts, which, after having devoured all the products of the earth, die in the months of July and August, and by the infected vapours which arise from the putrefaction of their carcasses, either produce the plague or malignant fevers, no less fatal to the inhabitants of this island. I was surprised during my stay at Cyprus to find so few remains of antiquity, notwithstanding I was very exact in my search after curiosities of that nature; but when I confider the many revolutions, to which it has been subject, and the frequent ravages it has suffered from the Arabs, and other barbarous nations, its sterility in that respect is very easy to be accounted for.

Pococke 1738

Richard Pococke published two volumes of his *Description of the East, and Some other Countries* in London, 1745, printed by W. Bowyer. In Volume II, Part I, *Observations on Palæstine or the Holy*

Land, Syria, Mesopotamia, Cyprus, and Candia, Pococke described his travels of about two months in Cyprus, from his arrival off "Limesol" on October 28, 1738, until his departure from that port on December 25. He dedicated his book to Philip, Earl of Chesterfield, General Governor of the Kingdom of Ireland. Pococke includes plans of Citium and Salamis; we have omitted those plans and his references to them in the text.

[p. 209]

On the twenty-fourth of October, about ten of the clock in the evening, we set sail from Tripoli for Cyprus, on board an English ship, which was obliged to touch at Bayreut in the way. On the twenty-fifth we had little wind all day, and only came up with a small bay called Cabouch, about twenty miles to the north of Tripoli. On the twenty-sixth we came up with Esbele, and sailed close along the shoar under the Castravan mountains; I saw almost all the places we had visited on those hills, and in the evening we arrived in the road of Bayreut, where the supercargo went ashoar; and on his return, we immediately set sail again. On the twenty-eighth we came up with Cyprus, anchored in the evening in the road of Limesol; and on the twenty-ninth went ashoar at that town.

BOOK the Third.
Of the island of Cyprus.

CHAP. I.
Of CYPRUS in general. Of LIMESOL, AMATHUS, LARNICA, and the antient CITIUM

The north part of the island of Cyprus is fifty miles from the Cilician shoar, which agrees with the account of the antients, who making a computation by measuring round the bays of the island, say, that it is about four hundred twenty-eight miles in circumference; but those who computed, probably by travelling round the island by land, make it only three hundred seventy-five miles. Some say, that it was a hundred and seventy-five miles long, others two hundred; but the modern sea carts make it only one hundred and thirty-five in length, and sixty-two miles broad in the widest part.

Cyprus was antiently divided into many small kingdoms, and was conquered successively by the Ægyptians, Phoenicians, Cyrus King of Persia, and Alexander the great; it fell to the lot of the successors the Kings of Ægypt, afterwards was subdued by the Romans, became subject to the Greek emperors, and, whilst it was under them, was laid waste by the Arabs. In one thousand one hundred ninety one, Richard the first, King of England, conquered it, and gave it to Guy Lusignan, king of Jerusalem; and his family continued to govern it until the year fourteen hundred twenty three, when it was taken by a sultan of Ægypt, who permitted their own king to reign over them, on his paying him a certain tribute. In one thousand four hundred seventy three, one of the kings left this island to the republick of Venice, who enjoyed it, paying the tribute to Ægypt, until it was taken from them in one thousand five hundred and seventy under sultan Selim, and it has ever since remained in subjection to the Ottoman port.

There are two chains of mountains that run along the island, one of which begins at the eastern point of it, and extends about three quarters of the length of the island, to the bay which is west of Gerines. The other chain of mountains begins at Cape Pyla, which is to the east of Larnica, and stretches away to the north west corner of the island.

Pliny mentions fifteen cities in this island, and probably in antient times there were as many kingdoms; but at the time of Alexander it was under nine kings, and it is not difficult to discover what cities with their territories, composed these kingdoms, as I shall have occasion to observe in the journey which I made round the island.

Limesol, where we landed, is a small town, built of unburnt brick; there are a great number of mulberry gardens about it, with houses in them, which makes the place appear very beautiful at a distance; the country also abounds in vineyards, and the rich Cyprus wine is made only about this place; the ordinary wine of the country being exceedingly bad. It is one of the cheapest places in the island, which is the reason why ships bound to Ægypt, and other parts put in here to victual. I was told that a small heifer sells sometimes for two dollars, or five shillings: They have built a castle and platform here, to defend themselves against the Maltese. The Greeks have two churches, one of which is a very handsome new built fabric.

We were entertained in a house of the English viceconsul, who was a Greek, and on the same day that we landed we hired mules, and set out to the east. We travelled through a narrow plain on the sea side, and going about two miles came to the river Char, where they keep a guard against the corsairs. When rivers are mentioned in Cyprus, they must be understood only as beds of winter torrents; for I could find but one in all the island that has always water in it. At the end of the plain there are ruins of a low hill, which are called old Limesol; it is about two leagues from the town. This is generally agreed to be Amathus, which is said to have had its name from Amathus, who built a temple here to Venus, called on this account, Venus Amathusia; it is said to have been sacred both to Venus and Adonis. This was probably the capital of one of the nine kingdoms of Cyprus. It is said, that Richard the first of England being hindered by the inhabitants from taking in water on the island, when he was going to the holy war, came to this place on his return, and took Isaac king of Cyprus prisoner, and sent him in silver chains to Tripoli in Syria. There are remains of the town walls, which are fifteen feet thick, and cased with hewn stone.

On the west side there is a building like an old castle, probably on the site of the antient city, which might extend to the east as far as that part, where there are great heaps of ruins, and among them a handsome ruinous church, which may be on the spot where the temple was built to Venus and Adonis, in which the feasts of the latter were annually celebrated. There seems also to have been a suburb to the east, extending to the river Antigonia.

About seven leagues to the east north east of this place, is a mountain called by the Greeks Oros Staveros, and by Europeans Monte Croce, it was called by the antients Mount Olympus, and was compared by them to the human breast; it has the Greek name from a convent on the top of it, dedicated to the holy cross. We went about an hour and a half further, and lay at a Christian village called Menie. On the thirtieth we crossed the hills that make the point which is to the east of Limesol, and having travelled some time we came to cape Malzoto; to the west of it there is a narrow vale, which is a morassy ground; there are many trees and very high reeds growing in it, and I saw some ruins here. Soon after we passed about half a mile to the south of the village Malzoto, which is computed to be nine hours from Limesol, and is directly south of the summit of mount

Croce. Palaea which is mentioned as between Amathus and Citium, might be about this place. We came in an hour to the river Bouzy, where there was a small stream, and in about an hour more to cape Chedè; there are several hamlets about it that go by that name: A rivulet rises out of mount Croce, which is called Creig Simeone, and falls into the sea near this head; it is probably the river Tetius, mentioned between Citium and Amathus. I saw to the north a village called Der Stephanè; in about an hour we came to a large village called Bromlaka, and in half an hour passed over the bed of a torrent, and came to the large lakes, from which they collect every year great quantities of salt; they are filled by rain water, and the soil being full of nitre, produces the salt, when the water is evaporated in summer; but in case there is too much water, occasioned by extraordinary rains, it is not salt enough to harden into cakes, and for this reason the Venetians had drains to carry off the water, which are now neglected. To the west of these lakes there is a small Turkish convent, in which there is only one Dervish; they have a sepulchre there, which is held in great veneration by the Mahometans, it being, as they say, the place where the foster sister of Fatimah, the sister of Mahomet was buried: These salt lakes extend almost to Larnica, and make it the most unhealthy place in the island. When we arrived at Larnica, where the Franks reside, I went to the house of the English consul, to whom I was recommended.

Larnica is situated a small mile from the sea: At the port which belongs to it there is a little town called the Marine; the harbour is naturally well sheltered, but the ships lie off at some distance, and the boats come ashoar on an open beach, and are drawn up to land. Tho' this place is very unhealthy, yet the Franks are settle here, as it is very convenient on account of its situation with regard to Nicosia, where the government resides, it being only six leagues from it.

There is a large antient church at the port, dedicated to saint Lazarus, where they shew his sepulchre; it is a small grot cut out of the rock; they say, that this saint being put into a boat at Joppa, and committed to the mercy of the sea, he was drove to this place, and became bishop of it, and that his body was stolen away by the French and carried to Marseilles; but the French say, that he was drove on their coasts. The ruins of the antient city of Citium are between the town of Larnica and the Marine, which was a capital of a second kingdom in Cyprus. It was famous for the birth of the great philosopher Zeno, and for the death of the renowned Athenian general Cimon, who expired at the siege of it. Ptolemy, the son of Lagus, destroyed this city, and removed its inhabitants to new Paphos; it was about three miles in circumference: There is reason to think that in very antient times the sea washed the south walls of it, though it is now a quarter of a mile distant . . . To the east of the old town there was a large bason, now almost filled up; it served for the security of the shipping, and was defended by a strong castle, as appears by the foundations of it; this must be the inclosed port mentioned by the antients; the walls seem to have been very strong, and in the foundations there have been found many stones, with inscriptions on them, in an unintelligible character, which, I suppose, is the antient Phoenician; and if the city was ever rebuilt, after it was destroyed by Ptolemy, these stones might be put into the walls when they were repaired . . . They have discovered a great number of antient sepulchres in and about the city of Larnica; I saw some built of hewn stone; in one of them I observed the stones were laid along at top like large beams, and others laid over them like a floor; there is another which ends at top in an angle, and both are of excellent workmanship, and finished in the most perfect manner. The fathers of the Terra Santa have a large convent in this town; the capuchins also have a monastery here; and the Greeks four or five very good churches. The republick of Ragusa have a consul residing in this place, as well as the French and English.

CHAP. II.
Of FAMAGUSTA, and the antient SALAMIS.

On the tenth of November we set out from Larnica on mules, under the protection of the consul's janizary, in order to make the tour round the island. We travelled eastward, and came to the bed of a torrent, called Camborounula, which had water in it; I saw mounds near it, which might be the remains of some antient work. In three quarters of an hour we came to the hills that stretch to cape Pyla: That head land must be the antient promontory of Dades; I observed an old tower on it. We came to the vale of Ormilia, where there are several houses and silk gardens belonging to the people of Larnica. We afterwards had a sight of cape Grega, probably the same as that which the writers of the Turkish history call cape Graecia, and was probably cape Throni of the antients, where there was a city of the same name. Going on I was told that we passed within four miles of Trapeza, which, if I mistake not, is to the right, though Blaeu's map puts a place of that name near Famagusta; this probably is a village near the high hill, that was compared by the antients to a table, and was sacred to Venus; I had a view of it on this head of land. This hill was over cape Pedalium, which may be the same as Ammochostus, and I suppose it to be the northern point of that broad head of land, which is now called cape Grega. Pedalium is thought to be a corruption of the antient name Idalium, there having been a town of that name in Cyprus, which was sacred to Venus; the Idalian wood was near it, in which, according to antient fables, Adonis, a favourite of Venus, was killed by a boar, and they feign that she turned him into a flower. There are two ports mentioned between this and Salamis, which are Leucola and Arsinoe; a city also is mentioned with the latter, which might be where Famagusta is at present situated.

We came to a village called Merash, which is half a mile south of Famagusta, where the Christians live who are not permitted to dwell within the city. I was here recommended to a Christian, who assigned me a room, which he had built in his garden, where I was entirely alone, and sent to the town for whatever I wanted. The next day I went with the janizary to see the city; for though I had a letter to the governor, yet I was advised not to send it, as I had no present for him. I went with all freedom wherever I pleased about the town: The governor however was afterwards informed, that I had viewed the town very exactly, and wrote every thing down, tho' I had only copied a short Greek inscription: Upon this he sent orders to the muleteer not to go any further with me, and that they should not permit any Franks to come into the city, on which I sent the janizary with the letter to the governor, who was then very well satisfied, and said he should be glad to see me.

The city of Famagusta is about two miles in circumference, and was well fortified by the Venetians; it is of an oblong square figure; the bastions are all semicircular; on the west side of the town, a rising ground runs along from north to south, on which they took the advantage to build the rampart, which makes it exceedingly strong this way, a fossee being cut into the rock on the three sides to the land; and in that to the west there are covered ways to sally out: This high ground, which is the strength of the west side, exposes the south part of the town to the enemy, for it was from this part that the Turkish general battered the south gate, which is the only entrance from the land; and it is probable, that from the high ground on the north side they planted their batteries against the north east corner to the sea, where there is a strong castle also fortified within. There is a gate from the city to the port, which is well sheltered by several rocks, and the entrance to it, which is at the north east corner, is defended by a chain drawn across to the castle; it was here that the stuffed skin of the brave unfortunate Bragadine was hung up at the yard of a galley, after he had been most inhumanly flay'd alive by the treacherous Turks, against whom he had bravely defended the city. I observed on the ramparts the names of several of the Venetian governors of Cyprus; and near the gate there are two statues of lyons, one of which is very large, they were probably set up on some pillars in the principal parts of the city after the Venetian manner. The antient piazza seems to have been very beautiful; the house of the governor with a portico before it, is on one side, and the western front of the church of saint Sophia on the other; it is a most beautiful Gothic building, now converted into a mosque, but about three years ago two thirds of it was thrown down by an earthquake, together with the greatest part of the city. Before it there is a Greek inscription on a black stone, which might be part of a pedestal for a statue: near the north west corner of the church there are two pillars, which probably had on them the Venetian ensigns; near these there is a coffin of white marble adorned with lyons heads, and festoons held by cupids. It is surprizing to see what a great number of churches there are in this city; St George's, one of the most magnificent, was thrown down by the earthquake; another large one, which, if I mistake not, was dedicated to saint Catherine, is now the principal mosque.

There is very little trade at this place, which is the reason why all provisions are cheap here, the price of a fat sheep being only half a crown: No Christian is suffered to live within the walls, unless it be in confinement, in which condition I saw a Greek patriarch of Constantinople, who being deposed, and intriguing in order to supplant his successor, was banished to this place a few months before; I saw him afterwards in one of the Princes Islands near Constantinople, returned from banishment. They will not suffer a Christian to go in or out of the city, otherwise than on foot; and a European having obtained a firman from the grand signor to enter the city in his chaise, when he sent it to the governor, received this answer in a very cool manner: "That in obedience to the firman he might enter in his carriage, but that he would not permit him to go out of the city in it." The present buildings do not take up above half the space within the walls, and a great part even of those are not inhabited. They have very good water brought three or four miles by an aqueduct, which is carried for the most part in a channel on the ground.

Between the two chains of mountains that stretch along the island, there is a large plain seven or eight miles wide, and between thirty and forty long, beginning about Famagusta; as it is one of the best parts of Cyprus, and most secure from the privateers, so it is chiefly inhabited by Turks, the Christians living more upon the mountains, and near the sea, as they are exempted from that slavery which falls to the lot of the Turks when they come into the hands of these privateers: This plain seems to have been the antient kingdom of Salamis founded by Teucer; the capital of it, which bore the same name, was at the end of the plain on the sea.

The Jews destroyed the old city of Salamis in the time of Trajan; it was afterwards called Constantia, probably from the emperor Constantius; it was again destroyed by the Saracens under Heraclius, and probably it was not afterwards rebuilt. We set out to see the old city on the twelfth, and in half an hour came to a large bason, which is filled by rain water, and in half an hour more to a stream, over which there is a bridge; this must be the antient Pedius. On the north side of it are the remains of Salamis . . . There are still large heaps of ruins on the spot of the antient city, and great remains of the foundations of the walls, which seem to have been between three and four miles in circumference. The port is to the south; it seems to have been made by art, and is almost filled up; the small river Pedius empties itself into the sea at this place. Antient geographers mention two islands of Salamis, which are not now seen. On examining the ground I imagined the sea might have left these islands, and I saw near the port some rising grounds with channels round them, which might formerly be filled by the sea. There appears to have been a more modern city here than that antient one built by Teucer, and there are great remains of the foundations of the walls of the new town, which was about half as big as the old city. The inner walls are supposed to be those of the new town, and the outer ones those of the old city. On that side of the town, which is next to the port, there are ruins of a large church, and also of a small one; and to the north of the town there are some very thick walls, which are also probably the ruins of a church. There is likewise a square plain spot, which might be either a piazza, or a bason for water. On the north of the new town, just within the gate, there are several grey granite pillars lying on the ground, and two or three Corinthian capitals of grey marble cut in a very beautiful and particular manner . . . These pillars seem to have belonged to a temple. This place is now called old Famagusta, and is about four miles distant from the modern town: There are remains of an aqueduct to this city; all the arches which I saw of it were Gothic, and there is an inscription on it in Greek, which makes mention of an archbishop: The antient aqueduct being probably repaired when the new city was built, after the establishment of Christianity in these parts. I saw the arches all along the plain, extending towards the mountains to the north west; on the side of which mountains the water was conveyed from a plentiful source which I saw at Cherkes, thought by some to have had its name from the old Cythera, though that place must have been farther to the south. The Tables place Citari in the road from Salamis to Tremitus, now called Nicosia. Cherkes is six or seven leagues to the west north west in a valley between the hills; it is beautifully improved with mulberry gardens for the silk worms; the plentiful sources of water which supplied this aqueduct are a considerable way in between the hills.

To the west of Salamis there is a small ruined church, and near it a very little church, built and arched over with very large stones, half of it is now under ground; it is dedicated to St. Catherine, who, as they say, was daughter of king Costa, the founder of the present Famogusta, and that the city had its name from him. In this church there is a well, and on one side a chapel built of three stones, the four sides consisting only of two stones, and it is covered with a third, which is angular at top. If I mistake not, they say, this saint was buried in this chapel, and there seems to have been a tomb in it. A mile to the west there is a monastery and a large church dedicated to St. Barnabas, which seems to have been a fine building; the church has been ruined and rebuilt; the foundations of the east end of the old church remain in three semicircles. About half a furlong east of this church there is a descent by several steps to a sepulchral grot cut in the rock, with niches for bodies on three sides of it: Here, they say, the body of St Barnabas was deposited, who was a native of this island, and suffered martyrdom at Salamis in the time of Nero. At the entrance of the grot there is a well of water that is a little salt, and a small chapel is built over the grotto, which does not seem to be of any great antiquity.

CHAP. III.
Of CARPASY, and some other places in the eastern part of CYPRUS.

From Salamis we went on northward, and having travelled about five miles came to the river Deraie, over which there is a long bridge like a causeway, and a high ground to the south of it, which might be the situation of some antient town: In half an hour we came to the river Chour; we then turned to the east, passed over some hills of cape Chaulebernau, and crossing a river, we approached the high hills, on which there is a castle called the hundred and one chambers. These mountains take up almost all that narrow tract, which seems to have been called the Olympian promontory, and probably this highest part of the mountains was called mount Olympus, on which there was a temple to Venus, probably Venus Urania, or the chast Venus; for there was a city in this part called Urania, which was destroyed by Diogenes Poliorcetes, and it was not lawful for any woman to enter this temple, or so much as look on it; all this promontory seems to have been the kingdom of Carpasia. I observed in this part a great quantity of talc in the hills. We arrived at a village called Patrick, where we were well received by the Greek priest. On the thirteenth we proceeded on our journey, and began to cross the hills towards the north side of the island, and came to a village called Galadia, finely situated on a high ground. We travelled on through a very fine country abounding in wood, and passed through Ai-Androniko, where there is a small stream, the sources of which never fail; this village on the south side is inhabited by Turks, and on the north by Christians. All these places are much infested by the Maltese corsairs. We lay in the house of the priest of Yaloufee or Jaloufa on the north side of the island, where there is an antient Greek church; we saw the coast of Cilicia very plainly from this place. On the fourteenth we came to a ruined village, called Mashargona, where they have a tradition that some king antiently resided; soon after we came to a small cape, on which there are ruins of a church dedicated to St. Marina; it is built of fine hewn stone, and the place is called Selenia. Having travelled about four hours, we went to the left of the antient convent of Jaloufa; there is also a bay here of the same name, and as there is a place so called near Scanderoon, which is the bay that had the antient name of Sinus Issicus in Cilicia; this, without doubt, must be Sinus Issicus of Cyprus, which was in this part of the island: This is probably the shoar of the Acheans where Teucer first landed. We arrived at Carpass, and went about two miles northwards to the plain and to old Carpass, called by the antients Carpasia, the capital city of the kingdom of that name, which is now given to all the country: The island here is only three miles and three quarters broad. There are some ruins at old Carpass, especially the remains of a wall near half a mile in circumference, with a pier from it into the sea, at the end of which there are some signs of a tower. The whole seems to have been only a castle for the defence of the port: To the east of it there is a very good church in the Greek style, which belonged to a monastery near called Ain-sphilosè; they call this place also Salamina, and I was told that this name was given it by some religious persons, who began to improve the place not a great many years ago, but were obliged to leave it on account of the Maltese privateers. About the village of Carpas there are a great number of small ruined churches or chapels, which might formerly be built for the use of wealthy families, who might retire to this place. It was on the Carpasian shoars that Diogenes Poliorcetes landed his army.

On the fifteenth we travelled eastward to the village of Asphronisy, where there are ruins of four churches, and it seems to have been some antient town; for I saw on both sides of it ruins of a wall extending towards the sea. We came to the most eastern point of the island, called by the antients the ox's tail, probably from some imaginary resemblance; it is now called the cape of St. Andrew, from a monastery which is cut out of the rock, and dedicated to that saint. Opposite to the north east corner are the isles called Clides by the antients; the largest of which is not a mile in circumference; authors differ about the number of them; those who name but two, probably took notice only of the two largest; there are two more that appear only as rocks, the furthest of which is not a mile from the land; there is another which has some herbage on it, and may be the second as to its dimensions; it is so very near to the land that it may have been separated from it since those authors wrote. At the north east corner there is a grot cut out of the rock, which seems to have been a sepulchre; there are some signs of a large enclosure round it, and higher are several sorts of oblong square buildings of hewn stone, which appear but a very little above the ground, and seem to have had covers over them; I conjecture that they were sepulchres of very great antiquity; one, which is built in a more magnificent manner than the rest, made me conclude that they might be the sepulchres of the antient kings of this part of Cyprus; it consists of three enclosures; there are but two tiers of stone above ground; the outermost building is one and thirty feet square, and the walls are one foot nine inches thick; within it, at the distance of two feet six inches, there is a second, and, at the same distance within that, a third; the top of which is cut with a ledge within to receive a cover. It is possible the two outer walls might be built up higher, and there might have been entrances through them to the sepulchre: The whole is a very particular sort of work, and of such a kind as I never saw in any other place. There are signs of foundations of a building on a little mount, which is a rock of marble of different colours stretching into the sea, and it is a very good situation for a light house, tho' there are some remains on a little point very near it, that have more the appearance of such a building. All this country to the east of Carpass for about twelve miles is almost uninhabited, except that there are a few Turkish herdsman on the south side, where there is a fine narrow plain. The desolate condition of this part of the island is occasioned by the constant depredations of the Maltese privaters, who land more frequently here than in any other part. From the eastern point I saw very plainly mount Cassius near Antioch, and the mountain of Rhossus, now called cape Hog, which is between Kepsè and Scanderoon.

We travelled on southward from this point, and in less than an hour arrived at the uninhabited convent of saint Andrea, in which there formerly lived two or three monks. We went to the south side of the island, crossed the hills, and came to a very large village which is called Mairon, which is about half a mile broad; at the west end of it we began to cross the hills to the north, and saw a cape to the south called Peda. We arrived again at Carpas on the sixteenth, and went to the convent of Jalousa; we passed by Selenia, where I saw remains of pillars four feet in diameter, and came to Jalousa. On the seventeenth we went about two leagues to the south east of Jalousa, near a place called Aimama, and came to a large grot cut into mountain, being very difficult of access; and there is another grot of the same kind two leagues to the east of it, near a village called Galliporno; it is a gallery with four apartments on each side, in most of which there are holes cut down like sepulchres, which are now filled up: On the hills above it, are some small ruins of an antient place, which might be Urania, taken by Diogenes Poliorcetes, and I saw near the grot a great number of sepulchres cut into the rock, many of them being in the manner of graves, which seem to have had stone covers over them: Towards the west end of this promontory the mountains are very high, and the foot of them stretches out in such a manner towards the north sea, that there is no passage on the north side of them; and, I suppose, that these hills were the bounds of the kingdom of Carpasia on the north west side; those to the south west being probably the low mountains, by which there is a narrow pass to the sea. Aphrodisium was situated near the west part of the promontory, and probably on the shoar to the north; it was about nine miles from the territory of Salamis. From this grotto we returned again to Jalousa. On the eighteenth we travelled to the north west and came to Androniga, where part of the village are Turks, who are sometimes under such apprehensions of the Corsairs, that for security they go and lie on the mountains, and they told me, that some of them have even perished with cold in those retreats: We afterwards came to a village of Turks, where one of them holds his lands on the condition of entertaining strangers, and his people came and drew water for our mules; this was in the road from the northern parts to Famagusta. From this place we went out of the road northwards, near an hour to the mountains called Eshbereve; on the highest summit of which is the strong castle of the hundred chambers before mentioned, which is almost entire. We lay at a Christian village on the north side of the hill.

CHAP. IV.
Of Nicosia, Gerines, Lapta, and Soli.

On the nineteenth we travelled westward on the north side of the island, and came to a very pleasant village called Agathon, situated at the beginning of the plain on the sea: There are a great number of cypress and orange-trees about it, and it is probable that Macaria was situated near this place. The plain is a very narrow strip of land not above a mile broad, but extends westward for about thirty miles, almost to the bay where these mountains end; I take this to have been the kingdom of Lapithia, and shall have occasion to make some observations on the supposed capital of it. On the twentieth we pursued our journey, and ascending the hills to the south, visited two small convents, and afterwards the monastery of Antiphonesè; it is famous for the Lignum Cyprinum, of which there are seven trees, there being no others of that kind in the island: It is the oriental plane tree, and is engraved in this volume among the plants which I brought from the east. We crossed over the hill to the south, and came into the great plain between Famagusta and Nicosia, and lay at a Christian village Marashoulou. On the twenty-first we travelled north west to a village called Chyterea by the Franks, of which I have already given an account, and of the river there, which supplied the aqueduct at Salamis.

From this place we travelled to the south west to Nicosia. I went to the house of the consul's broker, and was also recommended to the dragoman of the mosolem; both of them assisted me in seeing that city, which is towards the west end of the plain, and is supposed to be the old Tremitus; it is the capital of Cyprus, where the mosolem or governor resides; it is fortified with very large ramparts, but has no fossee, and consequently is a very indifferent fortification; the ramparts are faced with the hewn stone of the old walls; the circumference of them is about two miles. The walls of the antient city, which were built with semicircular towers, may be traced all round, and they seem not to have been much less than four miles in compass. There are still remaining in the city several very magnificent houses, which are of the times of the kings of Cyprus; some of them have been repaired by the Venetians, according to the rules of modern architecture; and there is a most beautiful Corinthian door-case of a house which, they say, belonged to the Venetian general. The cathedral church, now a mosque, is a large building, and exceeds that of Famagusta in the front, as much as it falls short of it in other respects; there was also a church here dedicated to the holy cross, and another of the Augustinians, which are now mosques. The Greeks have several new built churches in the city, and the Latin fathers of the convent of the holy sepulchre at Jerusalem have a small convent. Though there are very few Armenians, yet they have possession of an antient church here. There is a great manufacture of cotton stuffs, particularly of very fine dimities, and also half sattins of a very coarse sort; they have here the best water in Cyprus, brought by an aqueduct from the mountains.

Two leagues to the north east of Nicosia, on the side of the mountain, is the rich convent of saint Chrysostom, to which we went on the twenty-third; it belongs to the Greek convent of the holy sepulchre at Jerusalem: Over it, towards the top of the mountain, there is a place called the Hundred and one chambers, which consists of several buildings, one over another; the highest is very difficult of access; they have a tradition that a queen of Cyprus, who had the leprosy, chose to live here for the benefit of the air, and that saint John Chrysostom advising her to build the convent below, she followed his counsel, and was cured of her leprosy; others add, that she bathed in a water there, which is still resorted to by persons in that distemper, who find benefit by it. This monastery has been a very large building, though great part of it is ruined; there are two churches, one of which, called saint Helena, is ruinous, the other is covered with a dome, and painted all over within; it is dedicated to saint John Chrysostom: Before it is a handsome portico, from which there are three doors with fine marble door-cases, that do not seem to be very antient; two scepters were formerly deposited behind the folding doors, the figures of which are painted on the wall, and at the bottom there is a place where the crown was kept. All the account they can give is, that they belonged to some queen, and that they were taken away by a pasha of Cyprus. It is possible that the regalia of Cyprus were kept here: This convent is near the road which leads to Gerines.

We crossed the hills again to the north, and lay at a village called Chilta. On the twenty-fourth we went to a most magnificent uninhabited convent, which is almost entire, called Telabaisè; it consists of a very beautiful cloyster; on one side of it there is a magnificent refectory, on the other a fine room up one flight of stairs, which might be a library, and under it there are two very handsome apartments, one of which might be a common refectory, and the other probably served to receive strangers; on a third side, is a church of a more antient and heavy building; all the rest is of a very fine Gothic architecture, and in the cloister they have made a cistern of a beautiful coffin of white marble adorned with bulls heads, cupids, and festoons of exquisite workmanship.

We went about three miles to a ruined port called Gerines, which is the antient Cerynia; the ruined walls are about half a mile in circumference, and seem to be on the foundation of the antient walls, for I observed on the west side, a large fossee cut out of the rock, and the old town might extend further east beyond the present square fort, which is about a quarter of a mile in circumference. Though this place is esteemed to be very strong, yet the Venetian governor, when the Turks were marching towards it, (after they had taken Nicosia) shamefully surrendered the fort, before the enemy laid siege to it. To the west of the town there are a great number of sepulchral grots, and I saw some pillars standing, and remains of the foundations of an antient building. There is one church in the town, which is entire, and two or three in ruins; the priest resides in a convent of Solea, there being not above five or six Christian families in the place: The chief trade here is with Selefki in Caramania, which is the antient Seleucia in Cilicia; the commerce is carried on by two small French vessels, which export rice and coffee to that part, which is brought to Cyprus from Ægypt; and they bring back storax, and a great number of passengers. They also sometimes go over to Satalia, the antient Attalia in Pamphylia; but Selefki is the nearest place to this part of the island, being only thirty leagues off.

We set forward towards the west, and travelled about two leagues to the ruins of antient Lapithos, which I suppose to be the capital of another kingdom. Here I saw several walls that were cut out of the rock, and one entire room over the sea; there are also remains of some towers and walls, but the old name is translated to a village near called Lapta, where there are some sources of very fine water, which seem to be those of the antient river Lapithos. I lay here at the rich convent called Acropedè.

On the twenty-fifth we went on to a bay, and saw a cape beyond it called in Blaeu's map Cormachiti, which seems to be the old cape Crommuon. We crossed the hills to the south, and came into the western part of the plain in which Nicosia stands; for this plain is bounded to the west by some low hills, which stretch from the end of the northern mountains to the southern ones: On the north side is the bay where I suppose the antient city of Soli stood.

When we had crossed the hills, having travelled about six hours, we came to Morpho; they told me this place was eight leagues from Nicosia, probably the city Limenia might be situated here. We went to the magnificent convent of saint Mamma at this place, which appears to have been built on a very grand design; it consists of two courts, the buildings of which are unfinished; they are separated by a very magnificent church, built of hewn stone, and dedicated to saint Mamma, whose sepulchre they show in it. She is had in great veneration in Cyprus, and they have some legend concerning her riding on a lion, in which manner they always paint her. Though the building is not of modern architecture, yet it does not appear to be very antient; I conclude, that it might be built a little before the Venetians had possession of the island; being founded by some noble family of Cyprus: They have a water here, which they say is miraculous.

On the twenty-sixth we went four hours to the north west to a large bay, where, I suppose, the kingdom of Ægea begins, in which the famous Solon took refuge when he was banished out of Greece. It is said that he advised the king of this country to leave the city of Ægea, which was situated between the mountains, and to inhabit a plainer country. I was told that there was a place now called Ege, situated on the hills. At the north west corner of the before-mentioned bay, where the southern hills come to the sea, there are ruins of a very considerable city, which, I suppose to be Soli; on the west and south sides it was bounded by those hills; and to the north and east by the sea, a wall being drawn from the hills to the sea, some remains of which are still seen, as well as of a bason, for the shipping to lye in. The most remarkable ruins of this place are a little way up the side of the hills to the west, where I saw the ruins of a semicircular wall, but could not judge whether it was the remains of a church, or of an antient temple or theatre; lower on the plain are three piers remaining, which are ten feet wide, eight thick, and fifteen feet apart; I could discern that arches had been turned on them; they were adorned on the outside with Corinthian pilasters, the capitals of which were very well executed; it seems to have been a portico to some very grand building. The front is to the north, and on every pier within there is a nich about eight feet high and four feet broad; these niches doubtless were designed for statues: Probably this was the temple of Venus and Isis that was in the city, which had its name from that wise lawgiver Solon; the place is now called Aligora, that is, the sea mart. There is a river falls into the sea at this place, and as the channel of it is not kept open, it makes a morass. This doubtless is the river mentioned by the antients at this place. Some modern writers have placed Soli at Lefca, a village about a league north of this place. The antient cape Calinusa seems to be that point which is to the west of this bay.

Returning southwards to the road, we pursued our journey to the west, and in about an hour and a half came to Lefca; it is a long village built up the side of those hills, which we crossed into the delightful country of Solea, which is a vale about a mile wide, and winds between the hills for seven or eight miles; it is much improved with gardens and buildings, and is very well watered with springs and rivulets. We went to a convent where the bishop of Gerines commonly resides; it is situated on the side of the hills, where there are very rich iron mines which are not now worked.

On the twenty seventh we went along the vale, and crossing the hills came to the small convent of St. Nicholas situated between the hills, where there is such an agreeable variety of fields, wood, water, and cascades, that it is one of the most delightful solitudes I ever saw; two streams come rushing down the hills, and are carried all through the country of Solea in many rivulets. The Asbestus of Cyprus is found in the hills about two leagues to the south east of that place.

We travelled in a very difficult road along the sides of the hills to the convent of St. John. I observed a great number of pine trees, which they destroy by cutting them at the bottom, in order to extract tar. On the twenty eighth we travelled over several hills, and ascended the highest of them, where it is very cold, to the convent called Panaia Cheque, or the Madonna of Cheque, where they have a miraculous picture of the blessed virgin and our Saviour, painted, as they say, by St. Luke, and brought from Constantinople by a king of Cyprus, whom they call Isage. This place is as much resorted to by the

Greeks, as Loretto is by the Latins, and they come to it even from Muscovy. The convent belongs to the Archbishop of Nicosia, and has about seventy monks in it. I was received here with great civility by the superior, who met us without the gate, conducted me to the church, and then to their apartments, where I was served with marmalade, a dram, and coffee, and about an hour after with a light collation, and in the evening with a grand entertainment at supper.

CHAP. V.
Of ARSINOE, PAPHOS, and CURIUM.

On the twenty ninth we travelled over the mountains, and passed by some old iron works; they shewed us a village called Sarama to the east, where they said a part of the mountain had been thrown down by an earthquake: We arrived the same evening at the convent of Aiamone. I had a view of the bay of St. Nicholas to the north west, in which Arsinoe seems to have been situated, where there was a grove sacred to Jupiter. They talk much of the fountain of lovers, but they informed me that there are no ruins about it. They mention also the port of Agama in this part, and some ruins near it, which probably are the remains of the antient Arsinoe, and the present name of it may be derived from cape Acamas, which was the most western point of the island. Opposite to the bay is a small island called St. Nicholas, from which the bay has its name. I was told by the monks, if I do not mistake, that the old name of this island (probably that of the middle ages) was Stiria. Towards the sea to the north there is a village called Bole, where I was informed there were iron mines and hot mineral waters.

On the thirtieth we passed the hills which are on the west side of the island, and went to the south west into a plain, which is about fifteen miles long and three wide: The city of new Paphos, and the port of old Paphos were on this plain. This country probably made another kingdom, of which Paphos might be the capital. We arrived at Baffa, which is situated near the place where new Paphos stood; it is on a rocky eminence in a narrow plain on the sea, which is separated from the great plain by some low rocky clifts, which might antiently be washed by the sea before new Paphos was built. These clifts are now full of sepulchral grots, which doubtless were made for the use of the city. To the west of the town there is a point of land, and the old port was to the south east of it, in an angle made by a small promontory, and was sheltered by piers built out into the sea, some remains of which are still to be seen. The city seems to have been to the east and north of the port; and I observed a very large fossee cut out of the rock to the north of the old town, where probably they dug their stones for building. There are several lofty rooms hewn out of the rock, and many small apartments; one of them seems to have served for a large cistern, there being a hole in the top to draw up the water, and stairs down to it cut out of the rock; it is probable this was filled in winter by an aqueduct from the mountains, of which there are some remains near the town; by this means the city might be supplied with good water in the summer time, of which there is a great scarcity in the island. To the north of the port there are some signs of an antient temple on a ground raised by art: From the manner in which the grey granite pillars lie, and by the disposition of the ground, I judged there was a colonade round it, and a portico to the west with a double colonade; the pillars are about two feet in diameter. Half a furlong to the east of this there are foundations of a smaller building of hewn stone near the corner of the port, which might be either a temple or some other public building. Farther to the east are the remains of a large church, which probably was the cathedral, and seems to have been built on the foundations of a great temple, for there are some very large pillars of grey granite now standing near it; they are about three feet in diameter, and finely polished; it is needless to mention, that both these temples were without doubt dedicated to Venus, for whose worship this city was famous. This place probably began to be considerable when Ptolemy the son of Lagus demolished Citium, and removed the inhabitants to this city; it was almost entirely destroyed by an earthquake, but was rebuilt by Augustus, and called Augusta, in honour of him. Near the cistern before mentioned there is a church under ground cut out of the rock, dedicated to the seven sleepers; and in the town there are ruins of several churches, and houses, most of which are uninhabited. This city is famous in sacred history for being honoured with the presence of saint Paul, and on account of his having here converted Sergius the governor of the island to Christianity. About a mile to the north there is a rocky ground near the sea shoar, cut out into sepulchral grots; many of them seem to have been designed for rooms, and some of them are very large: I saw five or six, which probably were inhabited by families of a superior rank, having a court in the middle, and a colonade of two Doric pillars in front, and three on each side, with an entablature over them, all cut in the rock, and some of the pillars are fluted; one side of these courts is open in front; in each of the other three sides there is a room cut out of the rock, and the door-cases are executed in a beautiful manner.

Half a mile to the east of this place is the new town of Baffa, where the governor resides, new Paphos being now called old Baffa, and is inhabited only by a few Christians, and by a small garrison in a castle at the port. There was antiently at new Paphos a celebrated meeting once a year for the worship of Venus, from which place they went sixty stadia in procession to the temple of Venus at the port of old Paphos, where, according to the fables of the antients, that goddess, who is said to have been born of the froth of the sea, came ashore on a shell. The ruins of the city, called by the antients new Paphos, are now known by the name of old Baffa, where there is a small village of the same name about a mile to the south of Baffa. There is an aga and some janizaries who live at the fort in this place. I was recommended to a brother of the bishop of Baffa, who at that time was imprisoned by the Turks at Famagusta, by the instigation of the archbishop of Nicosia, with whom he had some difference; and I afterwards saw him at Rosetto, when he fled from this place into Ægypt. When I was in my lodgings some janizaries came to me, and afterwards the poor aga of the fort, who were very inquisitive about me, on which I took occasion to talk of my design to wait on the great aga at Baffa, with a letter I had to him. On the first of December I waited on the aga with my letter, and a small present of sugar, which I found was necessary, and could be of no ill consequence, as it was the only present I should have occasion to make on the island. He entertained me with coffee, and sent his falconer along with me, who attended me with his hawk wherever I had an inclination to go.

When I had seen every thing there, we proceeded on our journey; going at some distance from the sea along the plain, in an hour we came to a running water, and saw some ruins of the aqueduct to the right, which here crosses the river on an arch: In half an hour more we came to Borgo Ashedieh where there are remains of a high Gothic aqueduct. Opposite to this place is the first small cape to the south east of Baffa, which might be the old promontory Zephyrium. In half an hour we passed by Ideme, and about the same distance we were opposite to another cape, which might be that of Arsinoe; the port of Arsinoe might be on one side of it, and the port of old Paphos on the other, which was a mile and a quarter from that city; for though I went in search of it, at the cape opposite to Coucleh, where old Paphos stood, and observed the ruins of several aqueducts that way, yet I could see no signs of the port. We ascended to the village of Coucleh, which is situated on a narrow hill extending to the south into the plain. Old Paphos was doubtless here, and there are great heaps of ruins about the place, and remains of the foundations of thick walls; the ruins extend about a quarter of a mile in breadth, and half a mile in length. Some say that this city was built by Paphus, son of Pigmalion, others that it was founded by Cynarus king of Crete, and father of Adonis.

These hills extend quite across the island, and are much lower in this part than they are towards the north; they end here in high white clifts; and where they make a great head of land to the south, they are known to mariners by the name of cape Bianco, part of which might be the promontory called Drepanum by the antients. We travelled over these hills to the east, and in about two hours from Coucleh came to a Turkish village called Alefcora, where we got a place to lodge in with great difficulty.

On the second we went near a large Turkish village called Afdim, which is the same as Audimo or Aitimo. We went on to the other side of cape Bianco, and came to two delightful villages which are contiguous; they are called Episcopi and Colossè. These villages are finely watered, and most beautifully improved with mulberry trees for the silk worms, and also with a great number of orange and lemmon gardens. At the south end of Colossè there is an antient preceptory of the knights of St. John of Jerusalem, which is now in ruins; there are likewise the remains of a very high aqueduct that conveyed water to it, and I saw an epitaph of one of the priors of this place, who died in one thousand four hundred and fifty three. It is the opinion of some that the antient city of Curium was here, but I could not see the least signs of any ruins; but on the hill to the west I observed the foundations of a thick wall, which seemed to have encompassed some antient town, which probably was the city of Curium: And it is not unlikely that the grove, sacred to Apollo near Curium, was where the village of Episcopi now stands, which is a place abounding in water. They think also that the low promontory called cape Gatto was the promontory Curias, from which they threw any one into the sea, who presumed to touch the altar of Apollo; but as this is very low land, it is probable that it was from some point to the west of Curium, where there are high clifts, and might possibly be a part of what is now called cape Bianco. To the east of Episcopi there is a small river, which I should have thought to have been the Lycus of the antients, if that river had not been mentioned as between the town and the promontory. Cape Phrurium is mentioned near Curium, which might be the south east part of this great head of land, as Drepannum was probably that to the north west. The head of land called cape Gatto is to the south of Episcopi; it is a low land, the north and west part of it is a morass, and there is a large salt lake on the east side, which is filled by the winter rains, and is almost dry in summer: The south part of this promontory is a barren rocky soil, and there is a ruinous uninhabited convent on it, called saint Nicholas. They have a ridiculous story, that the monks of this convent kept cats in order to hunt and kill the serpents, of which there are great numbers here; this they say gave rise to the name of the cape; and they add withal, that on ringing a bell the cats used to leave off their diversion, and return home.

To the east of this cape there is a bay, and at the west corner of it Limesol is situated, where I first landed in the island. As I did not meet with any ship there bound to Ægypt, I returned to Larnica, where I found a French ship sailing for Damiata, on which I embarked on the eighth of December. We were obliged by contrary winds to put in at Limesol, where we were detained six days, and I landed a second time in Ægypt at Damiata, on the twenty-fifth of December one thousand seven hundred and thirty-eight.

CHAP. XI.
Of the natural history, natives, custom, trade, and government of CYPRUS.

The climate of Cyprus is not so temperate as that of many other parts in the same latitude; the winds, which blow from the high mountains of Cilicia in the winter, make the island very cold, especially the northern parts; and some of the high hills of the island being covered with snow all the winter, make fires very necessary during the cold season, though they are seldom used in any other parts of the Levant; the clouds also breaking on these hills, often fall down in heavy rains for many days together, insomuch that I was informed it had sometimes rained there for forty days almost incessantly. These mountains and the shallow soil, which is mostly on a white free stone, make it excessively hot in summer, and the island is very unhealthy, especially to strangers, who often get fevers here, which either carry them off, or at least continue for a considerable time, the disorder lurking in the blood, and occasioning frequent relapses.

The soil of Cyprus is for the most part rocky; there are in it many entire hills of talc or gypse, some running in plates, and another sort in shoots, like crystal; the latter is used in many parts, especially at Larnica, as stone for building: They have also in the mountains near that city a very thin marble paving stone, that cuts like chalk with a common saw, and much of it seems to have been laid in the walls in order to bind the stones. Near Nicosia they have a yellowish marble, which, they say, when burnt produces a small quantity of sulphur. At a mountain towards Solea, the Asbestus or Amianthus, called by some the cotton stone, is found in great plenty; it is of a blackish green colour, but runs in veins in such a manner, that the staple of it is not above half an inch long: It is much to be questioned whether they could ever spin it to a thread, but by some experiments tried with it, I have reason to think that an incombustible paper might easily be made of it, like that which they make of the Asbestus of Muscovy. Near Baffa there is a hill that produces a stone called the Baffa diamond; it is very hard, and seems rather to exceed the Bristol and Kerry stones. Cyprus has also been very famous for its minerals, and for many sorts of precious stones, which were probably found in the mines. In going round the island I saw only two iron mines which are not now worked, because in Cyprus they want hands to cultivate the ground; nor is it agreeable to the inclination of the people to be employed in these mines, because they would not be well paid by the officers of the grand signor: One of those iron mines is about half a day's journey east north east of Baffa: the other is at Solea, where there is a large hill that seems entirely to consist of this ore, which is very fine and light, being porous and crumbling, and of a red colour. They have here also the several sorts of earth used by painters, called Terra Umbra, Verde, Rossa, and Jalla; and I was assured, that not long ago a traveller found a very fine azure earth, which is uncommon, and either is not much known, or is found in small quantities, otherwise it would without doubt be exported.

The antients mention three rivers in Cyprus, the Lycus, Tetius, and Pedius, though at the best they deserve only the name of rivulets, and I suppose the water seldom fails in these, though it is generally said that there are no rivers in Cyprus: It is certain they have no fresh water fish, except small crabs, which are in most of the rivers in Asia. All round the island there are beds of winter torrents, which run from the mountains after rains, but during the summer months, when it never rains in these southern parts, they are entirely dry, excepting some few springs which have been rarely known to fail. The water, which is drawn out of wells, is almost all brackish, occasioned by the great quantity of nitre in the soil, which produces the salt in the lakes beforementioned; at Larnica they send above a league for all the good water they drink. The water of the island seems to depend almost entirely on the rain; and when clouds have been wanting either to fall down in rain, or to seed the springs, by lying on the mountains, a great drought has always ensued; and historians relate, that there having been no rain for thirty-six years, the island was abandoned in the time of Constantine, for want of water.

It is said that this island received its name from the cypress trees, which it is certain grow on it in very great abundance, especially on the eastern promontory, and in the northern parts of the island. There is a sort of tree which grows in most parts of Cyprus, which is called by some the cedar, and much resembles it in every thing but its seed, which is like the juniper; it is called in Greek Avorados, and I have been since informed that it is a sort of juniper, and is much like the tree that they call cedar, which is brought from the West Indies, and possibly may be the same, but here it grows rather like a large shrub than a tree. They have also the common juniper on the mountains and pine trees in great numbers, with which they make tar; they have likewise the caroub, called in Greek, Keraka, which is supposed to be the locust tree, the fruit of which in this island exceeds that of any other country, growing like a flat bean, and is exported both to Syria and Ægypt. Most of the trees in the island are ever green, but it is most famous for the tree called by the natives, Xylon Effendi [The wood of our Lord], and by naturalists Lignum Cyprinum, and Lignum Rhodium, because it grows in these two islands; it is called also the rose wood, by reason of its smell; some say it is in other parts of the Levant, and also in the isle of Martinico. It grows like the platanus or plane-tree, and bears a seed or mast like that, only the leaf and fruit are rather smaller; the botanists call it the oriental plane-tree; the leaves being rubbed have a fine balsamic smell, with an orange flavour; it produces an excellent white turpentine, especially when any incisions are made in the bark. I suppose it is from this that they extract a very fine perfumed oil, which, they say, as well as the wood, has the virtue of fortifying the heart and brain. The common people here cut off the bark and wood together, toast it in the fire, and suck it, which they esteem a specific remedy in a fever, and seem to think it has a miraculous operation. They make here Labdanum or Ladanum of a very small balsamic aromatic shrub called Ladany, and by botanists Cistus Ledon, or Cistus ladanifera; it is said that the goats feeding on it in the month of May, a juice sticks to their beards, and makes a sort of a cake, which, being taken off, they purify it, and make the Labdanum: This is in some measure true; but that sort requires much labour in order to clean it, and it is never perfectly sweet, so that in Cyprus they use the same method as in the other islands, and make an instrument which they call Staveros, because it is like a cross; it exactly resembles a crossbow, and they tie pieces of yarn to it about three feet long . . . In the month of May they draw this yarn over the leaves, and the balmy substance sticking to the yarn, they lay it in the sun, and when it is hot, draw it off from the yarn. The common people mix it up with sand, in order to make it weigh the heavier, which is what the druggists call Labdanum in tortis, and in this manner it is commonly sold; but being purified from the sand, it is of the nature of soft bees wax, which is what they call Liquid Labdanum. It is esteemed as a great remedy against many disorders, taken either inwardly or outwardly, and the smoak is good for the eyes, but it is mostly used against the infection of the plague, by carrying it in the hand, and smelling to it. The island produces also cotton and coloquintida, and a root called Fuy, which is a sort of Madder: it abounds also in vineyards, but the common wine is very bad. The rich Cyprus wine, which is so much esteemed in all parts, is very dear, and produced only about Limesol: In some few places indeed they make good red wine.

They plough with their cows, which, as I was informed, they do not milk, looking on it as cruel to milk and work the same beast; but perhaps they may rather have regard to the young that are to be nourished by them. This loss is made up by their goats, which are spotted in a more beautiful manner than any I have ever seen: Indeed a great part of the soil of Cyprus is more fit for goats than for large cattle; they make cheese of their milk, which is famous all over the Levant, and is the only good cheese to be met with in these parts; they are small and thick, much in the shape of the antient weights, and are kept in oil, otherwise when they are new they would breed a worm, and when old soon grow dry. The Turks have such an aversion to swine, that the Christians dare not keep them where they have less power than they have in Cyprus; but from this place the Christians in all parts are supplied with excellent hams, which they cure in a particular manner by salting them, pouring the rich wine on them, and when they have pressed them very dry they hang them up. They have very few horses in Cyprus; they use mules both for burthen and the saddle, of which they have a good breed; the poorer sort of people make use of asses. They have few wild beasts or game, except foxes, hares, and wild goats; and among their birds the chief are a very beautiful partridge, which I believe is the same as the red partridge in France, and a beautiful bird called in Italian Francolino, and in Greek Aftoki-nara, which I have mentioned before. There are a surprising number of snakes here, but few of them venemous, except a small kind; a species, which is generally thought to be the asp, supplies the place of the viper, and is said to have the same virtues; it is called Kouphi (Blind). The largest of them are near two inches thick, and are bigger in proportion than snakes, the head being rather small with regard to their bodies, and it is positively affirmed, that they have been known to swallow a hare whole, which, if true, must be understood of a young one; their bite is exceedingly venemous, but it has been cured by medicines, and by the serpent stone. I have been informed that there is an asp in Italy which is not deaf. It is possible the Psalmist might mean this reptile, when he made mention of the deaf adder, which refuseth to hear the voice of the charmer. They have an exceeding large broad spider, somewhat resembling a small crab; the Franks call it the Tarantula, but I believe it is not the same which is found in Apulia. There is here a brown house lizard called a Taranta, and if it walks over any part of the body, it causes a very great itching, which continues for some time with much pain. I do not find that they have scorpions, which are so common in Syria; but the locusts, when they come, ravage the country in a most terrible manner, destroy whole fields of corn where they alight, and eat the leaves of the mulberry trees, on which their silk depends.

The Cypriotes are the most subtle and artful people in all the Levant, nor have they more veracity than their neighbours, so that their words are not to be depended upon, as they make use of all means that way to deceive. The women are little superior to their ancestors with regard to their virtue; and as they go unveiled, so they expose themselves in a manner that in these parts is looked on as very indecent. They go every Whitsunday in procession to the sea side, which seems to be some remains of the heathen custom of going annually in procession to the sea in remembrance of Venus's coming out of it, which was antiently attended with some other circumstances. They retain here the barbarous custom of the other eastern nations of treating their wives as servants; they wait on them at table, and never sit down with them, unless in such families as are civilized by much conversation with the Franks; for having been under the Greek emperors, and the Venetians, they have come very much into the European customs. They make use of chairs and tables, and lie on oblong square tables, probably to be more free from the noxious animals in the summer, and from the damps occasioned by the great rains in the winter: They make use of carriages with two wheels drawn by oxen. The common people here dress much in the same manner as they do in the other islands of the Levant; but those who value themselves on being somewhat above the vulgar, dress like the Turks, but wear a red cap turned up with fur, which is the proper Greek dress, and used by those of the islands in whatever parts of the Levant they live.

Cyprus, on account of its situation, and the cheapness of all sorts of provisions in the island, is the place where almost all ships touch on their voyages in these parts; and by this way a correspondence is carried on between all the places in the Levant and Christendom: So that furnishing ships with provisions is one of the principal branches of the trade of this island, and they sometimes export corn to Christendom, though it is contrary to their laws. They send their cottons to Holland, England, Venice and Leghorn, and wool to Italy and France. They have a root of an herb called in Arabic Fuah, in Greek Lizare, and in Latin Rubia Tinctorum, which they send to Scanderoon, and by Aleppo to Diarbeck and Persia, with which they dye red, but it serves only for cottons, for which it is also used here; it is called by the English Madder, but it is doubted whether it is the Madder so well known in Holland; they export a red dye for woollen stuffs, which is falsly called by the English vermilion, though that is known to be made of Cinnabar; whereas this is the produce of the seed of Alkermes, called by botanists Ilex coccifer; there is a small hole in the seed, out of which there comes a very fine powder, called the powder of Alkermes, of which the syrup of Alkermes is made, and the seeds afterwards serve for dying, and both are exported to Venice and Marseilles. Coloquintida is cultivated here, and esteemed better than that of Ægypt, which being larger does not dry so well; it grows like the calabash. The seed is sent into England, and to Germany, being much used in the latter for embalming bodies: In Ægypt they fill the shell with milk, and let it stand some time, and take it as an emetic. They prepare a great quantity of yellow, red, and black Turkey leather, which they send to Constantinople; and they export yearly near a hundred thousand pound weight of raw silk to London and Marseilles; for as it is a hard weighty silk, it is much used in making gold and silver laces, and also for sewing. At Nicosia they make fine plain cotton dimities. In a word, it is a surprizing thing to see Cyprus maintain its own people in such great plenty, and export so many things abroad, when one considers the extent of the island, and that half of it at least is mountainous, and much of it near the sea lies uncultivated by reason of Corsairs; nor is the island well peopled, eighty thousand souls being the most that are computed in it; whereas historians say, that in Trajan's time the Jews massacred here in one day two hundred and forty thousand persons, and since that time they have never permitted any Jews to live in the island; so that when this island was well inhabited and cultivated, the produce of it must have been very great.

Two thirds of the inhabitants are Christians, and there are twelve thousand that pay the tribute as such, exclusive of the women and children. They are mostly Greeks; there are indeed near Nicosia some few villages of Maronites, and in the city of Nicosia a small number of Armenians, who are very poor, though they have an archbishop, and a convent in the country; the Mahometan men very often marry with the Christian women, and keep the fasts with their wives. Many of them are thought to be not averse to Christianity; nevertheless the Turks are so jealous of the power of the Christians here, that they will not suffer them to buy any black slaves or others that are Mahometans, which former are frequently brought to Ægypt, and sold to the Turks. The Greeks have an archbishop of Nicosia, and three bishops of Larnica, Gerines, and Baffa; the Greeks are every where in possession of their churches, but cannot repair any that are ruined without a license; they are built in the style of the Syrian churches, but are generally covered with cupolas; they had formerly a custom here, as they have in many other parts, of hanging out flags at the west end of their churches on Sundays and holidays, and I saw some of the stones which had holes in them for that purpose. There are a great number of monasteries in the island; they are to be looked on as religious societies, who go out to labour on the lands that belong to them, with their superior to oversee them; this is their employment all day, and half the night is spent in performing their services: They may be also looked on as places of education, where the youth who labour by day learn to read and chant their offices at night: The lay servants, who are distinguished only by a cap, answer to the lay brothers in the Roman church; but they never take the vow, and may leave the convent and marry; in these respects the eastern churches pretty much agree. There is no nunnery in Cyprus, and I saw only one of the Greek church throughout all Syria, nunneries being very uncommon in these parts, except among the Maronites of mount Libanon. They take only the vow of chastity and obedience, and every monk generally buys his own cloaths, and pays his tribute to the grand signor out of his own purse, which chiefly depends on the charity of those who come to the convents, either for devotion, retirement, or diversion. Where a convent is well situated, the Turks often come and stay in it, and put the convent to some expence, and never make any return; they also serve as inns to which all people resort; but the Christians always leave something at their departure. What a monk is worth when he dies, goes to the bishop of the diocese. The priests here are very ignorant as most of them are in the eastern churches; and though Greek is their mother tongue, they do not so much as understand the antient Greek of the New Testament, tho' the modern Greek differs very little from it; but in Cyprus the Greek is more corrupted than in many other islands, as they have taken some words from the Venetians whilst they were among them; it is notwithstanding a sweet language, but they speak it very fast.

Till within thirty years past Cyprus was governed by a pasha, but now it is under a more inferior officer, called a mosolem. The late grand signor gave this island as a dowry to his daughter, who was married to the grand vizier Ibrahim Pasha, and since that time the island has belonged to the grand vizier: He legally makes of it about seventy five purses a year, each purse being about seventy pounds sterling, but then he has only a share of the harach, and of a tax called the nozoul; and I have been informed that the whole island brings in five hundred purses a year. There are also fees for offences, and upon account of any unnatural death; in the latter case the village pays one purse. The original property of all the lands is in the grand signor, who sells them to the inhabitants and their male heirs, and in default of male heirs, the lands revert to the grand signor, who disposes of them in like manner: The tythe of the land, which doubtless belonged to the church, is granted to two sorts of military bodies; one of them are called zains, of which there are eighteen chiefs, who have the tythes of the lands of a certain district, and are obliged to send a number of men to the war; the others are called timariotes; under the name of Timars lands are granted all over the Turkish empire on the same condition: There is also a poll tax called the nozoul; it is about six dollars a year paid by all those who are not obliged to go to war; both Christians and Turks; and the Christians pay a tribute called the harach, which is universal over the Turkish empire; it is from ten to fifteen dollars a head; there is also a small duty of twenty-two timeens or forty-four medeens a-head, which is about three shillings English, paid yearly to the village where every one is born: The salt and customs belong to the janizaries, who are about a thousand, and have generally an aga sent to govern them once a year from Constantinople. The Cypriotes having their lands at so easy a rate, any one would imagine that they must live very happily; but the mosolem is almost continually harassing the Christians, who often leave the island, and go to the coasts of Cilicia, and very frequently return again, out of that natural love which every one has for his own country: Many of them notwithstanding settle in the sea port towns of Syria, which dispeoples the island very much. Cyprus is now divided into sixteen cadelisks, each having its aga or governor, and cadi or minister of justice; they consist of sixteen towns; and it is probable that among them may be found the capitals of the fifteen kingdoms, into which, some say, the island of Cyprus was at first divided.

Drummond 1745, 1750

[Plates 1–6]

Alexander Drummond, who died in 1769, served as consul for the British government in Aleppo. He documented two trips to Cyprus, one in 1745 and another in 1750, among his many travels, in letters to his brother. The letters were published for him in 1754 by W. Strahan, London, under the title *Travels through different cities of Germany, Italy, Greece and several parts of Asia, as far as the banks of the Euphrates; in a series of letters. Containing, an account of what is most remarkable in their present state, as well as in their monuments of antiquity.* Some of his text on topics not dealing with Cyprus and personal remarks have been omitted.

LETTER VI.

Dear Brother,

In spite of all that vanity which you know I possess in a very eminent degree, I can hardly prevail upon myself to begin a letter, even to you, who have always been indulgent to my frailties, without bespeaking your patience and good nature, in favour of what I am about to write. Such anticipation is an involuntary testimony of that internal conviction by which I stand self-accused of weakness and impertinence. But I have now proceeded too far to think of retreating; and, therefore, must jog on to the end of the chapter.

We sailed from Tripoli on the fourth of March, in the evening; and though we kept a sharp look-out for the French, against whom our minds were embittered with resentment, we reaped no advantage from our vigilance; and, without having met with any adventure or accident in the passage, we arrived in Salines road on the sixth, before noon, when I went up to the town of Larnica, to dine with Mr. Consul Wakeman.

You will, undoubtedly, expect that I should entertain you with a minute account of this little insulary world, which made so much noise in antiquity, and I would willingly gratify your expectation; but I have so few materials, and these so undigested and immethodical, that I am sure you will be disappointed in your hope; though I will so far obey the dictates of my duty, as to transmit every particular which I have been able to learn or observe; I mean those which I think worthy of being communicated.

It is, by many, supposed that this island was a peninsula, joined to Syria, somewhere between Antioch and Alexandretta; and that it was separated from the continent, when the Euxine forced its way through the Thracian Bosphorus, overflowed the Archipelago, and made dreadful havock on the circumjacent coasts. This, however, is a doubtful fact, which the geographers must settle among themselves: at present, I am sure it is an island; and, if ever it was otherwise, it must have been a violent flood indeed, that could sweep away, from twenty-five to thirty leagues of land: for the north-east point of Cyprus, nearest to Syria, is at that distance from the continent, and there is an immense depth of water between them.

Upon the west, north, east, and south of this island, are the Mediterranean, Pamphilian, Syrian, and Ægyptian seas; the length of it is from sixty to seventy leagues, the breadth about eighteen to twenty leagues, at a medium; but, as above one third of the length to the north-east, from hence, is no more than a tongue of land, if I may be allowed the expression, the circumference of the whole will not amount to one hundred and sixty leagues, unless the bays are surrounded, for the figure of it is conical.

Though the natives were always remarkably effeminate and lazy, certain it is, they cultivated the island so as to be enriched by its produce: indeed much industry and labour was not required (though water is greatly wanted) for the soil, in general, is incomparably fertile; not a chalk, as I was formerly made to believe, but an excellent clay, which hard-

ens in summer; yet, by the wretched culture which it now receives from the miserable inhabitants, the earth, where any moisture is left, produces every thing that is sown; and,
though there is not (properly speaking) a river in the whole island, I am fully persuaded,
that, if it were in the hands of the English or Dutch, they would make such advantageous
use of the springs, rivulets, and winter rains, that it would in a little time, become the garden of the east, and exhibit beautiful plantations for the shelter of the cattle and ground.

Cyprus, we are told, was, for a considerable time, divided into nine districts, and
governed by as many princes; then it fell under the Ægyptian yoke, and continued subject
to the sovereigns of that country, until Publius Clodius, famous for his amour with Cae-
sar's wife, as well as for his enmity to Cicero, and his profligate life, conceived a grudge
against Ptolomey, for having refused to pay his ransom to a pyrate, by whom he had been
takèn. In consequence of his resentment, while he was a tribune, he moved the senate for
a decree, declaring Cyprus a Roman province. They did not at all doubt of their being
able to reduce an island, the inhabitants of which were enfeebled by luxury, and im-
mersed in pleasure; and they well knew, that, could they once obtain possession of it,
Ptolomey would neither be able, nor would he attempt to wrest it out of their hands.
They, therefore, without ceremony, sent Marcus Cato to take possession of it; and he, by
stripping individuals of their superfluities, sent immense treasures to Rome.

After the division of the empire, it naturally became subject to the eastern emperor, and so continued until the end of the twelfth century, when Richard the first, of
England, in his expedition to the Holy Land, deprived Isaac Comnenus of the crown, for
his want of hospitality to those sanctified warriors, and gave it to the Knights Templars,
who afterwards sold it to Guy de Lusignan, when he lost his kingdom of Jerusalem: after
his death, it passed through a variety of masters, until it was inherited by Charlotta,
whose bastard-brother James dethroned her and her husband Lewis of Savoy, usurped the
throne, and married Catherine, a Venetian lady, of the Cornara family, whom I mentioned
in a former letter. He died soon after his marriage, and left the kingdom to her, although
she was then pregnant. Some historians affirm, that he was poisoned; and, that his post-
humous son met with the same fate, from the barbarous politics of the queen's brother,
George Cornara, who prevailed upon her to resign the sovereignty in favour of the republic of Venice. After this resignation, which took place about the latter end of the
fifteenth century, she lived retired, in a country house not far from that city, upon a
very moderate income.

If the Venetians obtained this island by such horrid crimes, they shamefully lost it
by the negligence, jealousy, and cursed pride of those to whom the preservation of it was
intrusted; especially of Dandoli, who had assumed the supreme command; and Count Ro-
cas, who was a brave, but empty madman.

About the year 1570, the Turks made themselves masters of all Cyprus, except
Famagusta, which did not surrender until the year following; when the infidels committed
unheard-of barbarities. Twenty thousand were butchered in Nicosia, after the town was
taken; the old of both sexes, with the ugly women, and children unfit for service, were
built up within one funeral pile, in the market-place, and there burned alive: an action
which, in horror, transcends any thing I have seen upon record. All the rest were loaded
with chains, about five and twenty thousand were carried off the island and sold to slav-

ery, and two of the largest vessels were filled with jewels, plate, and furniture, of prodigious value. On board of one of these ships, Mustapha Pasha, who commanded in chief, put the noblesse, and most beautiful of the women, to grace his own triumph, and to enrich the seraglio of his sovereign: but one of the ladies, having procured a lighted match, crept down into the powder-room, and blew up the ship: the fire was immediately communicated to the other vessel: so that both were instantly destroyed, with every person and thing which they contained, except two or three individuals, who escaped with their lives.

I shall give you another instance, from which you may judge what dependance is to be placed upon Turkish faith or humanity.

Famagusta was gloriously defended by Bragandino and Baglione, who inspired not only the soldiers, but all the inhabitants, and even the women, with so much heroism, that whatever their leaders could contrive or command, the others had intrepidity enough to execute; together with a resolution to bear up against all extremities, even such as are almost incredible. Before they surrendered, there was neither cow, horse, mule, ass, dog, cat, or even mouse, within their walls; while the small succours, sent from Venice, loitered four months in Crete, at a time when they knew their fellow-citizens, whose name will never die so long as the records of honour survive, were suffering all imaginable calamities, and struggling with inexpressible difficulties, which they only could have rendered surmountable; for what might not have been expected from the valour of such defendants, had they been seasonably supplied with provisions, arms, ammunition, and a proper reinforcement of the garrison?

Being, at length, reduced with famine and fatigue, to such a degree that they could scarce stagger under the weight of their arms, they were fain to capitulate on these conditions: that the inhabitants should not be plundered, and, that they should have liberty to worship God in their own way; that the garrison should march out with all the military honours, and be supplied with proper vessels to transport them to Crete.

Every thing being ready for their departure, Mustapha sent for Bragandino, who went to wait upon him with Baglione, accompanied by several officers of the first distinction, and such a number of guards as were proper to attend a general upon such an occasion. They were, at first treated, with great ceremony; and, just as they were going away, Mustapha asked for the prisoners. Bragandino, being surprised at this demand, answered, that he never had any from the beginning of the siege: "What! (cried the barbarian) have you murdered the faithful?" So saying, he ordered the whole company, Bragandino excepted, to immediate, and excruciating death: the general he reserved, in order to lengthen out and diversify his tortures; which he bore with the most exalted heroism. His nose and ears being cut off, he was rolled together like a ball, and crammed into a hole scarce wide enough to hold him in that painful attitude; then he was taken out that he might not expire too soon, and forced to kiss the ground upon which the ruffian Pacha trod: they afterwards tied him naked to the yard's-arm in one of their gallies, that he might be exposed to the scoffs and ridicule of the spectators; and, at last, when they found he could not live much longer, he was hung up by one heel and flead alive. During the whole progress of these torments, he was never once seen to shrink: a circumstance which stung the brutal mussulman to the soul. His skin was salted, stuffed, dried, and placed in the arsenal at Constantinople: but the family of this more than mortal man, whose name will ever be revered by all lovers of gallantry and virtue, had the address to convey it from thence; and, I am told, it is now in their possession.

At present, the country of Cyprus is in the same situation with all other places subject to the sway of the grand signior: all industry is discouraged; and, generally speaking, no more ground is cultivated than what yields an easy subsistence to the farmer; for every person who is known to have saved money, may lay his account with being stripped by those in power: for this reason, abundance of wealth is hoarded up through the whole Ottoman empire; though these concealments are chiefly owing to the constitution of their police, in consequence of which, the sultan is heir to all his subjects, whatever number of children they may leave. True it is, this disposition seldom extends to the poor, but all those who have been employed, or die in offices of state, feel the weight of it. Their effects are immediately seized, and their children obliged to the sovereign's bounty for what they are allowed to retain.

Sometimes, if there is a promising boy, he is brought up in the seraglio, and provided for when he comes of age; and the handsome girls are given in marriage to some particular officers: but such care is taken of those only whose parents have been in high favour with the prince, or reigning visier; and this favour can only be obtained by extravagant presents.

A man possessed of great riches, part of which is concealed, may die suddenly, before the hoard is discovered to the son; who is, perhaps, too young to be entrusted with such an important secret: so that the unhappy orphan is left a beggar. Though the son is of age, the father, possibly, dares not make him his confident, lest he should cut his throat, in order to possess his wealth; nor will he venture to unbosom himself to any other person, who might reveal the secret to the sultan, whose vengeance and avarice might overwhelm him and his offspring. In order to avoid these disagreeable risques, the Turks, who are absolute predestinarians, choose rather to leave their hoards to the care of providence, than to that of any friend upon earth: so conscious are they of that falshood and deceit which prevail universally among the followers of Mahomet.

This consideration, one would think, should influence those in office to be just and upright in their functions. When a man is desirous of enriching or aggrandising his family, the devil may now and then get the better of his virtue, and tempt him to play the villain, robber, and extortioner; but, when he knows that all he can amass by rapine and oppression, must contribute to fill the coffers of his superiors, it is surprising that he should take so much pains to render himself odious and detestable by his tyranny and injustice. For every individual governor or officer of the porte, acts uniformly in his station, as if he thought heaven was to be obtained by no other conduct than that which renders his fellow-creatures miserable upon earth: and, that the more he pillages, the higher he shall mount by the favour of his prophet.

Cyprus is ruled by a mussalem, or governor, who is also a muhasel, or collector of the grand signior's revenues, and resides at Nicosia, which is the capital of the island, and stands in a pretty centrical situation. This city, where all the ultimate courts of judicature are held, together with five sea-port towns, where the trade is carried on, constitutes, in effect, all the considerable places in Cyprus. These are Larnica, called, by way of eminence, Cyprus, with its port of Salines, Famagusta, Chirinia, Lemisol, and Baffo; the other towns, though, perhaps, they give names to different districts, are of no note or consequence; indeed, there is more business transacted at Larnica, where I reside, than in all the others I have mentioned. The names given to these places, by the Greek inhabitants, I shall, for the sake of pronunciation, write in the Greek characters, and are Λευχοσια, Λαρνηχα, Αλιχες, Φαμογουστα, Χερινια, Νεμεσον, and Παφου. Famagusta, Salines, and this town of Larnica, which is generally called Κυπρο by the Turks and Greeks, and Cyprus by the Europeans, are the only places of the island which I have yet seen; and, from all I can learn, I believe I shall not stretch my curiosity much farther: for nothing curious or amusing is to be seen, and their method of travelling is not at all inviting. When I went to Famagusta, formerly Salamis, afterwards Constantia, at least the situations seem to agree, I rode upon a mule furnished with a ragged, patched packsaddle, so bulky that I straggled like a beggar upon a woolpack; in lieu of a whip, I was provided with a sharp pointed stick about a foot long, with which I was directed to prick the lazy animal's shoulders when I wanted to quicken his pace; spurs would have been as useless as a whip, for my legs were so expanded, that I could not bring one heel within half a yard of the creature's side. All these circumstances rendered my seat so uneasy, that I was obliged to shift five hundred ways before I finished my journey; which, though no more than twenty-four miles, fatigued me as much as ever I was by riding above one hundred miles a day.

As the Turks permit no Christian to ride into the town, I was obliged to dismount and walk along the bridge. This was no inpolitic precaution with regard to me, who, by the splendor of my equipage, might have made a conquest of some peeping sultana.

We enter the town by a stone-bridge and a draw-bridge laid across a broad and deep fossée; the last is covered with the skull-caps of those who were slain in the siege, and the other is partly paved with grenado-shells. The fortifications have been pretty strong for those times in which military-architecture was not brought to perfection; but the chief strength of the place consisted in the intrepidity, valour, and fortitude of those who defended it. The whole is now in very bad order, and all the fine brass cannon are carried off, except a few, of which not above six or eight are mounted.

In the year 1735, the town was greatly damaged by an earthquake: the cathedral church of Sancta Sophia, which had been converted into a mosque, fell in, and buried in its ruins above two hundred Turks, who were at worship when the shock happened. By what remains of this church, St. George, and some others, I can perceive they were built in the worst gothic taste; the very stones are so bad that almost every one is blown or mouldered by the weather. It is the more surprising that these materials are used, as there are many rocks of marble in the neighbourhood: perhaps this choice was owing to the frugality of the people, though that is very seldom consulted in a religious building, upon which a great deal of work is proposed to be bestowed.

Over the gate of the governor's palace, which has been great but not noble, are the arms of Venice, with an inscription which I could not read, because it was overgrown with shrubs and moss; and these the Turks would not suffer to be cleared away, for they are jealous of they know not what; this, however, was no great disappointment: for, by the few words which I could trace, the purport of it was to signify at what time, and by whom the palace was built. I likewise saw another inscription in gothic characters upon St. Sophia, but it was at such a distance that I could not distinguish the letters. In the front of this church, upon the right, are two granite pillars, detached from it, with capitals and bases of white marble; and between them stands a Sarcophagus, adorned with festoons, but altogether uninscribed; which is a very extraordinary circumstance. Why should such expense be laid out upon a burying-place, when nobody knows to whom it belongs? The gateway that leads to the harbour is under a bastion, over the gate is St. Mark, or the winged Venetian lion, inscribed Nicolao Priolo Prefecto, MCCCCXCVI. It served for a guard-room, and is finely vaulted in form of a cupola. The harbour is good and safe by nature, for no art has been bestowed upon it: from hence into the town, there has been a floodgate, through which they occasionally hauled their gallies into a dock behind the walls, that they might be secure from the efforts of the enemy.

From the inlet of the fossée at one end of the town, to the angle of a bastion at the other, a ridge of rocks stretches around, and forms a kind of oval bason, that may be about a mile one way, and the eighth part of a mile the other; it has no entry but one, which is from forty to fifty feet wide, between the rocks and the angle of a bastion, and across this channel is a chain.

As this is all I have to say about Famagusta, you will readily own it was not worth the fatigue I underwent in going to see it; and, as I am well informed there is not the least vestige of antiquity in the island, in all probability I shall not make many excursions: though I would willingly see Paphos, on account of the character it bore in former times.

Larnica is pleasantly situated at the distance of a little mile from a spacious bay, and, very probably, occupies part of the same ground upon which the ancient Citium stood: be that as it will, there is not one object in it, at present, worth seeing; all the houses here, as well as in other places of the island, are built of mud cut into the shape of large bricks, and dried in the sun; these are neat enough. They never build higher than one floor, in order to avoid some part of the dreadful effects of earthquakes, and these houses last longer than one could imagine, though the architects, joiners, and carpenters, are the most bungling artificers that ever were seen. It is equally astonishing and lamentable to see the ignorance that prevails in those countries, where arts and sciences once flourished to such perfection; and from whence the seeds of learning were scattered through the European world. I believe, I may venture to affirm, that there is not one ingenious artist, or one person who can be deemed a man of learning, in the whole Ottoman empire.

Here the Greeks have three mean churches, as, generally, all their places of worship are. One convent belongs to the Franciscans, and another to the capuchins of Terra Sancta, but neither of them is worth notice.

In this place the French have a factory, and Monsieur Lemaire, consul for that nation, is a polite, well-bred man, with a good share of that vivacity which is peculiar to the French. He has already honoured me with particular attention; but I now shun company and court retirement, because the few hours I can spare from business, I wish to employ in writing to you and some other friends, or in that sort of solitary entertainment which a man can enjoy after he has lost relish for the more sprightly pleasures of society: at present, I am not possessed of that gaiety of temper for which I have been formerly remarkable: my thoughts are more clouded, consequently my conversation must be less desirable; and I have not the same pleasure which I used to reap from the wit and agreeable fallies of other people. Whether this change is the effect of old age, and sourness of temper, which is its usual concomitant, I shall not at present determine; but I hope it will never influence me so far as to render me indifferent to the advances of friendship and sensibility. As the French consul and I are brother masons, we shall, probably, be better acquainted; especially if Mr. Consul Wakeman should become one of the fraternity, which would be very happy in his accession: for no man ever gained so much upon my affection in so short a time. He is consul for the English, Dutch, and Venetians, a man perfectly well acquainted with business, and altogether indefatigable: instead of being rendered fretful and peevish by hurry and fatigue, he seems to take pleasure in his labour, supports the good humour of every body about him, by his chearful disposition, and has acquired the particular love and esteem of all those who are happy in his acquaintance.

At the distance of a short mile from hence, is the port of Salines, where the Turks have a despicable garrison. This port, probably, derives both the Greek and modern name from a very extensive lake, or rather, a cluster of lakes in its neighbourhood, where an immense quantity of salt was annually made, before and after the Venetians were in possession of the island. So sensible were they of the value of this commodity, that, notwithstanding the vast extent of the lake, they or their predecessors surrounded it with a stone or mud-wall, the remains of which are still to be seen in some few places. And well they might bestow such pains upon it; for, according to accounts of the best authority, it yielded a million of piasters, amounting to about one hundred and twenty-five thousand pounds per annum; whereas now it is farmed at the yearly rent of one thousand six hundred piasters, or two hundred pounds. You will think it very strange, that there should be such a prodigious difference between its former and present produce; and, indeed, it can be accounted for no other way, but from the innate indolence and laziness of the people, the insecurity of the property, and the supine negligence of the ministers of the porte, whose whole care is employed in keeping their wives from the eyes of other men, and in extorting money in the most oppressive manner from those who groan under their despotic sway. No care is taken to prevent the salt from being trod upon by man and beast, when it begins to cake, or even when it is fully chrystalized; so that it is mixed with dirt and clay, which renders a great part of it unfit for use. Probably, the Venetians, who had vast territories in these seas, and were a very frugal, polite people, obliged all their subjects to take their salt from this magazine of nature; whereas, the stupid Turks know not how to make such a reasonable advantage of the bounteous gifts of heaven; for other places are now otherwise supplied.

With regard to this lake, various are the opinions of the learned. Some confidently affirm, that the salt is produced from the rain-water which centers here in the winter; and that the exhalations are so sudden, continued, and excessive in summer, during which there is not one shower, that all the saline particles are left in the cake or crust which we see. But I am not at all satisfied with this theory. Rain-water cannot be supposed to be impregnated with such a proportion of salt: and I once observed that the water of the lake had risen since my last visit, although no rain had fallen during that interval. Others imagine there is a subterranean conduit, or communication with the sea: this hypothesis, however, seems to be contradicted by the simplest hydrostatical principle; for, if this was the case, the lake, or bason, would, in spite of the exhalation, be kept as full and high as the surface of the Ægyptian sea. It would, therefore, be more reasonable to suppose, that the banks of the sea, in this place, are of such a porous quality as gently to imbibe the salt-water, which may penetrate into the bason; the water of which, at its greatest height in winter, being nearly equal to the surface of the sea: this water may be distilled through these pores so slowly, as not to supply the effect of the exhalation when the rays of the sun are most intense; so that what remains grows more and more salt. The difference of height, in the water in the lake, may be owing to clouds, or a thickness in the medium, which impede the operation of the sun. The rain-water, which falls after the middle of March, may wash down, from the surrounding land, those saline particles, which have been left by the sea-water which overflowed it in the winter. Nay, I have reason to believe, the earth itself is impregnated with that mineral, the efflorescences of which appear in this spot, as well as in a great many other places. After all, this lake may be formed by a vast collection of salt springs, like those that are found in Cheshire, and other parts of England.

A little farther than this salt-lake is a mosque called Tokée, whither the musselmen repair with great devotion, to offer up their prayers at the grave of Mahomet's grandmother, who, they believe, is here interred; though in what manner the good old lady was transported hither from Arabia, I have not yet been able to learn. Nor are the Greeks destitute of such another pious imposture. At Salines is a church dedicated to St. Lazarus, who was raised from the dead by our Saviour, and afterwards interred in this place. The architecture is such as I never saw before; and now they can only shew the precious hole in which his body was deposited.

This island abounds with a variety of noxious creatures. Tarantulas and serpents are common: of the last species, the most dangerous is the asp; the venom of which, is said to be so deadly as to kill in less than an hour, if the part is not instantly cut out: in order to frighten away these, and other kinds of poisonous reptiles, the reapers, who are obliged to wear boots, always fix bells to their sickles. One serpent I saw in the fields, was about two yards in length, of a blackish hue, with a sort of coronet upon its head, which it carried in a majestic manner, above a foot high, as it waved along. Locusts, which I have seen in incredible swarms, are so prejudicial to the farmers, as to destroy one third of the grain. I am now employed in making a collection of these exotic animals: but, I am afraid, I shall not be able to oblige my friends with any extraordinary trees, shrubs, plants, or flowers; for, though I have made diligent enquiry, I can hear of none worth preserving.

My female friends will, undoubtedly, expect that I should say something of the modern Cyprian ladies, as the ancient dames of this island were so remarkably distinguished; but, as my days of gallantry are now over, and I have otherwise very little connexion with the fair sex, I am very ill qualified to gratify their curiosity on this subject. I shall only observe, that even the Franc, or European ladies, dress in the Grecian mode, which is wantonly superb; though, in my opinion, not so agreeable as our own. Yet the ornaments of the head are graceful and noble; and, when I have seen some pretty women of condition sitting upon a divan, this part of their dress hath struck my imagination with the ideas of Helen, Andromache, and other beauties of antiquity, inspiring me with a distant awe, while the rest of their attire invited me to a nearer approach . . .

I will conclude this dry letter, with telling you, it is likely to be the last of the kind with which you will be troubled, unless I find something in the trade and police of the country worth transmitting. I really wish this may be the case; for, as I have hitherto treated you with nothing but green wine, I would willingly set one bottle of old Cyprus upon the table before we part, "Pour faire la bonne bouche," and send you off with a relish on your palate, so as that you might be agreeably deceived into the opinion that you had enjoyed good liquor during the whole course of the entertainment. Had it been in my power to regale your taste, you know you should have fared daintily; as I have nothing more at heart than to contribute to your happiness, and to convince you that I am inviolably

Your own, &c.

Cyprus, July 18, 1745.

LETTER VII.

Sir,

    . . . I have already told you, that this island is governed by a person who is both mussalem and muhassel, that is, governor and collector of the revenue for the grand signior; though, formerly, it constituted part of the valide, or sultana-dowager's jointure, and with other places appropriated for that purpose, enjoyed great privileges: then Cyprus was ruled by a viceroy, or what they call a pacha, until the late grand signior Achmet, who was deposed, bestowed it as a jointure upon his daughter, who was the widow of visier Ibrahim Pacha: at present it forms part of the revenue of the prime visier, as first-minister, and is farmed to the governor for three hundred and ten thousand piastres, amounting to about thirty-eight thousand seven hundred and fifty pounds, besides presents of considerable value, which he must give to different people in different ways.

    The government is annual; so you may well imagine how the wretched people are fleeced. Muhassel Mustafa Beg, according to the best information I could obtain, has, this last year, extorted as much as will pay his rent, indemnify him for the presents he made, defray the expence of travelling and living, and put in his pocket five hundred purses, amounting to thirty-one thousand two hundred and fifty pounds, exclusive of innumerable things of value, with which his favour has been courted.

    To what purpose has this man oppressed the miserable, and amassed this wealth? Perhaps, in six months after his return to Constantinople, he may not have one asper remaining. For such is the address of a voracious minister, that he can easily conjure up a variety of accusations against him for male-administration; in consequence of which, he may strip him of all his wicked acquisitions.

    This method of raising money, is called Mangiare li denari; that is, to eat, or rather, to devour the coin: and, indeed, every Turkish officer, from the highest to the lowest degree, resembles a creature in Poland of the hog kind, called in the German language vielorass, or the glutton, which gormandizes, in a voracious manner, as long as it can find food, and then getting between two stones, or trees, squeezes itself so as to disgorge what it had swallowed, that it may have the pleasure of eating it again: with this difference, however, that the squeezing of the vielorass is voluntary: whereas that of the Turkish governor is compulsive, and performed by the grand visier, who in a moment transfers the burthen to his own maw . . .

Of the three hundred ten thousand piastres for which the whole of this island is farmed, one hundred sixty thousand are paid for the land-rent, and the rest for the harach, or capitary tribute.

The number of Turks in the kingdom of Cyprus, may amount to one hundred and fifty thousand, and that of the Christians to fifty thousand; I mean Greeks who are subjects of the grand signior; for, as to the Europeans, who live in Larnica or Salines, and no where else, they do not amount to one hundred.

The greatest part of the inhabitants live in Nicosia, Larnica, Famagusta, Carpasso, Baffo, Cerigna, Lemisol, and Salines; but I cannot learn the particular number inhabiting each of these places: for they do not know how to make any tolerable exact estimate, nor do they give themselves any trouble about the matter. In the villages there are about four thousand Turks, who pay contribution; and, of the Greek subjects, about twelve thousand. So that these last constitute by far the greatest part of the labourers in this country.

I told you the salt-pits are let for one thousand six hundred piastres, though, sometimes, they fetch two thousand; for they are annually put up to sale by the tefterdar, or high-treasurer. The money, thus raised, contributes to the subsistence, or rather, is a perquisite of the janisaries: and the farmers, after paying their rent and charges, may pocket five hundred or a thousand piastres, according to the accidents that raise or lower the price of salt. The annual produce must be sold within the year, or never afterwards, unless the annual consumption should exceed the produce; a case that is not likely to happen.

The impositions upon the island are such as you never heard of: namely, the harach, or poll-tax, divided into three classes; the first, called alla, or great, amounting to eleven piastres, raises thirty-eight thousand seven hundred and fifty pounds; the second, eusat, or half, brings in twenty thousand pounds; and the third, called edna, or little, produces eighteen thousand seven hundred and fifty pounds: then there is the maisct, or expence of supporting the governor, for which every man pays five piastres and a half; and nusul, according to their condition or station in life; this tax, by agreement, is generally at seven piastres and a half a man. Those who are rich, of the first class, pay annually of taxes twenty-four piastres each; people of the second class, pay eighteen; and persons of the third rank are taxed at sixteen; besides the other taxes they are obliged to pay: for the furniture of the palace, or seraglio, three piastres; for a murder, a man pays yearly, from one to two piastres; and in like proportion for other crimes, though the pardon is previously purchased with a round sum. All these articles included, a rich man pays for his person about sixty piastres; one of a middling fortune is not quit for less than forty; from a person of the third class, they raise thirty; even the poorest sort are mercifully dealt with, if they are not bastinadoed for not paying that which they are not able to raise: and these taxes are exacted from all persons between the age of fifteen and seventy, that is, from all who are capable of labour.

The method of levying these impositions is very strange: no time is fixed for payment; but when the officer impowered shall make his demand, if the unhappy man cannot produce the money, he must undergo imprisonment, the bastinado, or some other torture: if he is possessed of any effects, houses, lands, cattle, or other moveables, they are instantly sold, at an under-value, to satisfy those cormorants, who set his wife and children a-drift, without remorse or compunction; nay, they even make a sport of their misery.

Infinite are the ways by which those ministers of corruption prey upon their fellow creatures: the most atrocious criminal, if he has address, may buy his impunity; but, without some art, he will lose both life and money. In law-suits, the party who tips the judge highest, will certainly obtain the decree in his favour: but, besides this bribe, he receives as his due, ten per cent. of what is recovered; so that he never finds fault with the exorbitancy of the account. Indeed, nothing can be more absurd than to expect justice in this country, where every office is sold, and the greatest part of these offices conferred without salary: so that the purchasers have no chance for indemnifying themselves but by rapine and injustice. You may judge, from these particulars, with what reason some people affect to prefer the honesty of a Turk to that of their own countrymen.

In this place money is the only basis on which the fortune and honour of every man is founded; and no infamy attends the acquisition, however sordid or wicked the method of acquiring it might have been: of consequence, every man in power is a despotic tyrant by the nature of his office, and all the subjects are miserable slaves; though the Greeks, as a conquered people, are more especially exposed to their cruelty and extortion: they are now become familiarised to oppression, which hath likewise disposed them for villainy, as it were in their own defence; insomuch that they are reconciled to all manner of crimes; and mean dejection, wretchedness, or deceit, is to be read in every countenance. In a word, notwithstanding their silk, cotton, oil, and rich wines, these people will ever be poor and despondent.

> "While proud ambition in their valleys reigns,
> And tyranny usurps their happy plains."

It is impossible for any Englishman of common sense to live in Turkey, without congratulating himself upon his title to the privileges of a British subject; and, perhaps, it would be better for our happy isle, if her representatives had the opportunity of seeing what misery and desolation are the consequences of arbitrary power: the comparison would be a practical lesson, which would sink deep into their souls, and stimulate them to watch with the utmost vigilance over those inestimable rights which are intrusted to their integrity and care.

The officers civil and military, who reside in our capital of Nicosia, where the Mussalem keeps his court, are,

The Mufti, supreme judge, or Mahometan patriarch, by whose decision every difficulty or doubt in the law is removed or determined.

The Molla, who is judge-ordinary, and sub-governor of the city.

The Menakib, who is chief of the race of Mahomet, in this island; a clan who enjoy the honourable distinction of wearing green turbans.

The Mussalem's court is composed of a

Chehaia, who is his deputy, lieutenant and private-secretary.
Divan Effendi, high-chancellor, and secretary of state.
Hasnadar, high-treasurer.
Michurdar, keeper of the seals.
Je Aghalar, grooms of the bed-chamber and pages of honour, who are always near his person.
Iman, chaplain in ordinary.
Imbrohor, master of the horse.
Vechil Hare, master of the houshold.
Katifégee, coffee-maker.
Serbetgee, confectioner, and sherbet-maker.
Bughierdangee, perfumer, and he who carries the perfume of the wood of aloes.
Bas Chiaous, keeper of the prisons.
Alai Chiaous, buffoons, who carry batons tipt with silver, and play a thousand monkey-tricks, fitter for the entertainment of children than of sensible men.
Vené, officers of an inferior rank, who have no particular department, but are fit for many purposes.

The military officers are,

Tefterdar, grand treasurer of the army, or paymaster general, and high chamberlain.
Alai Beghi, general of the horse.
Zaimi, captains, or rather officers of horse, for their degrees are such as cannot be distinguished or understood by our designations and commands: they are thirty-two in number, and, in lieu of pay, rent villages, according to their several degrees of favour or promotion.
Sipahi, horsemen, to the number of three thousand, who are paid from the tythes of the grain, and other produce of the island; but they purchase their sipahilicks, or lands, from the Muhassel, and these lands are for life.
Jeniceri Aghasi, lieutenant-general of the Janizaries or foot-soldiers.
Culchehainsi, lieutenants of the foot-soldiers.
Corbagi, captains of foot, to the number of twenty-eight, who are paid out of the villages.
Jeniceri, infantry, to the number of one thousand, who have no cloathing or regular pay, but subsist upon the produce of certain villages assigned to them, the rents of the customs, the salt-lakes &c.
Serda, high-marechal.
Disdar, or Cale Aghasi, governor of the castle.
    The kingdom of Cyprus, ever since its subjection to the Turks, has been divided into sixteen districts, which derive their names from the most considerable towns or villages in the respective divisions: such as Larnica, Limesol, Piscopi, Ghilan, Afdimo, Cuclia, Crusocka, Baffo, Lefka, Morfu, and Penloia, Cerigna, Famagusta, Messaria, Citrea, Orini, and Carpasso: these are pronounced by the Greeks, Λαρνεχα, Νεμεςον, Πισκ-

οπια, Χιλαν, Αβδιμου, Χουκλια, Χρισοφου, Παφου, Λεφκα, Μορφου καὶ Πενθαγια, Χιρινια, Φαμαφουστα, Μεσαρεα, Χιθρια, Ορινε καὶ Χαρπας.

Any body will at once perceive that these are not the names used by the ancient Grecians, but rather formed by the modern Greeks upon the Italian: but, as I have neither antient geographer nor chart, I cannot favour you with the old names; for, such is the ignorance of every living creature in the island, that they have never heard of Amathus or Urania, or indeed of any circumstance of antiquity: even a bishop scarce knows any other book than his Bible and Ritual, which perhaps he can read, though without understanding more of them than does the mule he rides.

None of these towns and districts have any other officers or magistrates than a cadi, or judge ordinary, excepting Larnica, Famagusta, Cerigna, and Baffo, which are provided with an Alai Beghi, or general of horse; Serdar, a Marechal; Desdor, governor of the castle; Titiban, governor of the islands, vice-inspector; and a Tiumbrackee, or customer.

When any cause of importance falls under the inspection of the cadi, he gives an ilam or report upon it to the mussalem, who, after having considered the circumstances, passes a decree; but both the report and decree depend on the offering, and not upon the merits of the cause. No lawyer is retained, no time fixed for hearing and determining suits, and no place set apart for a court of justice. The divan of the cadi's house is the bench, and every man is his own attorney.

In this kingdom is one archbishop, with three suffragans; he resides at Nicosia, and his see is composed of the districts of Famagusta, Messaria, Citria, Orini, and Carpasso. The bishop of Baffo lives in the town of that name; which, together with Piscope, Afdimo, Cuclia, and Crusocka, or Crisofu, is in his diocese. The bishop of Chitty is sometimes in Larnica, sometimes in Limesol, which two places, and Ghilan, are in his bishopric. The bishop of Cerigna lives in that town, his see comprehending besides, Lefca, Morfu, and Penloia.

Our bishop joins me in the opinion that Chitty is really the antient Citium, or very near the place where that city stood; it appears to have been very extensive, by the old foundations that are daily dug up all round. In ranging about, I found two or three places from whence they dug stones; and, as they were below ground, my curiosity induced me to peep into them. There I found well squared stones, of a prodigious size, neatly laid in good cement: the stupid labourers prop the roofs with pillars, while they undermine the building; whereas, with the hundredth part of the time, toil, and expence, they might have accomplished their aim, by uncovering the whole, and clearing away six or eight feet of earth and rubbish. The wall I traced a considerable way and found it of great breadth; though the labourers had wrought in such an irregular manner, that I could not measure it: from general appearances, however, I am convinced it has been of great strength, and very probably, the foundation of the walls of that city; for we read of none of any consequence in that neighbourhood: and it is at a very little distance from that point of land which now bears the name of Chitty.

The revenue of the archbishop, communibus annis, may amount to ten thousand piastres, which are levied from the towns and villages, in wheat, barley, cotton, and other fruits of the earth; though not by the manner of tythes, but by a certain rate fixed to certain lands: and the other bishops draw their revenues from their own sees. That of Baffo is worth from one thousand five hundred to two thousand piastres, amounting to two hundred and fifty pounds: Larnica, or Chitty, from three thousand to four thousand, equal to five hundred pounds; and Cerigna is equal to Baffo. Their value fluctuates in this manner, because nothing is paid for the lands which are uncultivated; and this is frequently the case, owing to the rapine of a governor, or the extortion of a man in power; for, when an unhappy peasant is plundered of his all, how can he labour his ground? Nay, those savages often reap what he hath sown with the sweat of his brow.

These stipends are very considerable in a country where living is so cheap, and so many fasts observed; yet all the bishops have other expedients for making sums of money: they move from place to place as traders, without bestowing the least attention upon their charge; and frequently the archbishop raises general contributions, under the deceitful veil of employing them in pious uses, or paying some extraordinary avenias, or special assessment of the Turks. For example, in the year 1743, the archbishop for the time being, with the countenance of the mussalem, who shared in the robbery, levied from the poor people no less than forty thousand piastres; but they complained so effectually to the Porte, corroborating their complaints with bribery, that he was stripped of his archiepiscopal robes, dignity, and emoluments. Indeed, there is no difficulty in obtaining this kind of satisfaction; for nothing is more agreeable to those corrupt ministers than complaints, because both plaintiffs and defendants enforce their arguments with presents, which must be renewed every hearing; and, if the plaintiff gains his point so far as to make an empty saddle, the whole profit accrues to these ministers, who not only sell the vacant places to the best bidder, but afterwards share in the plunder of the new purchaser.

The benefices are in the gift of the bishops, who severally receive from each incumbent one hundred piastres, when he is invested with his charge; the bishop likewise raises from every church in the towns within his own diocese, one hundred piastres annually; which are collected from the people of the parish. He exacts from ten to fifteen piastres from every priest he ordains; and one piastre and a quarter for every marriage: but the poor priests subsist almost entirely upon the charity of the parishes to which they belong; this, even in Larnica, never amounts to more than forty or fifty piastres, so that they are obliged to follow the meanest occupations for bread; yet great numbers are brought up at the altar, that they may be exempted from the weight of Turkish taxes; which, as laymen, they would not be able to bear. This being the case, the ignorance of the clergy is not to be wondered at; the very bishops are so illiterate as to believe, that religion consists only in forms, ceremonies, observations of holidays, abstinence from flesh and fasting: in all which they are exceeded by the Armenian church.

The bishops are elected by the general suffrage of the people of the particular dioceses; and, as for the archbishop, he is chosen by a majority of the suffrages taken by the bishop of each diocese; but he must be approved and sanctioned by the patent of the grand signior, who likewise reserves the power of deposition to himself.

Neither the archbishop, bishops, or caloyers of the order of St. Basil, are allowed to marry or eat meat; though, behind the curtain, they indulge all their appetites like true voluptuaries: the other priests may marry, but should they become widowers, they must never again receive the matrimonial yoke.

The trade and produce of this island (as, I believe, I have already hinted) do not amount to the tenth part of what they might yield, were they in the hands of industrious people, governed by just and equitable laws, and the property so secured as that their children should enjoy the fruits of their ingenuity and labour.

I intended to give you a particular account of the import and export of the island, at a medium of three years, with a view of its yearly produce; and, for this purpose, made application to some of the custom-house people, who could not afford me the satisfaction I desired: however, I have reason to think that what follows is pretty exact; because it comes from those who have the best opportunities of knowing every particular. And, indeed, it is scarce worth while to know more than that the island annually produces from thirty thousand to forty thousand okes of silk, amounting to about one hundred and ten thousand pounds English weight, each oke weighing about two pounds three quarters; three thousand quintals of cotton, of one hundred and eighty okes each, which we shall call seven hundred and fifty tuns; and about five hundred quintals, or one hundred twenty-five tuns of sheep's wool; about double the quantity of the dying drug which they call lizarin, and we term madder, unmanufactured; of the brown fossil, called by us, omber, and by them, petran tou troullous, which is used as a ground-paint, there is an inexhaustible store in the mountains, and about five hundred tuns may be yearly exported; of the carobe bean, or chiratzin, five hundred quintals, or one hundred twenty-five tuns are exported to Damiata and Alexandria, whence it is carried to Grand Cairo, and almost every part of Ægypt. All the other merchandizes go to different parts of Europe; namely, Britain, France, Holland, and Venice; what goes to other places is inconsiderable. They likewise export wine to the amount of three hundred sixty-five thousand cooses, or nine hundred seventy-three thousand three hundred and thirty-three gallons, a coose being equeal to two gallons and two thirds: the greatest part of this article is carried to Venice; for the wines of the countries around that city are very bad, and this can be brewed to advantage.

The whole of the wine-harvest, or vintage, may be reckoned at eight hundred thousand cooses, or two million one hundred thirty-three thousand three hundred and thirty-three gallons, equal to thirty-three thousand eight hundred and sixty-two hogsheads, as the worst vintage, barring accidents, yields about seven hundred and fifty thousand cooses, and the best never produces more than nine hundred thousand; so that making the computation at one fourth of a piastre per coose to the farmer proprietor, the value of the vintage will amount to two hundred thousand piastres, or twenty-five thousand pounds per annum: yet, properly speaking, it yields a great deal more to the island, because the longer the wine is kept upon the gross lees, the more valuable it becomes; insomuch that, although I fix it at the rate of one fourth of a piaster per coose, yet immense quantities are sold for double that price, and even for three piastres per coose.

The inhabitants moreover export considerable quantities of hams, bacon, goat-milk cheese, biscuits, vermicelli, macaroni, &c. which it is impossible to ascertain.

Estimate of the export from Cyprus.

365000	cooses of wine,	at P.	1 ½ p.	coose,	P.	547500
40000	okes of silk,		7	oke,		280000
3000	quintals of cotton,		75	quintal,		225000
1000	quintals of madder,		50	quintal,		50000

500	quintals of sheeps-wool,	23	quintal,	11500
500	quintals of carrobe,	2 ½	quintal,	1250
500	tuns of terra ombre,	1	tun,	500
		£. 139468	15	P.1115750

By the laws, all goods ought to pay an impost of three per cent. ad valorem, when imported or exported: so that the duties of the above mentioned commodities should amount to thirty-three thousand three hundred and seventy-two piastres; yet I am well informed that the whole of the customs, free of the charges of management, which are very small, seldom exceeds sixteen thousand piastres or two thousand pounds: but this is not the only duty levied on these goods; for silk pays at the garden one fourth of a piastre per oke; cotton one piastre and three quartets per quintal; and the rest in proportion.

The import consists in broad-cloth, by far the greatest part of which is from France, and some from a new manufactory at Venice; a few bales come from Great Britain, but none, as yet, from Holland; in watches, toys of every kind, cutlery ware, pepper, tin, lead, sugar, all sorts of silk manufactures, and other things of less consequence; but there is no great quantity of any article consumed: for the inhabitants are kept so wretchedly poor, that they cannot indulge their taste for luxury and extravagance, yet they are lazy to an unspeakable degree; and the time which should be employed to some rational purpose, for the benefit of their families, or the common weal, is spent in childish diversions, or in hatching villainous schemes.

They have, indeed, some manufactures in the island, and do not want capacity, were they willing to be rightly instructed. Of cotton dimities, with a little silk, they make about ten thousand pieces, of ten pichi each, the pichi being equal to twenty-seven inches; of cutuni and pesmi, coarse kinds of cotton-sattin, about fifteen thousand pieces; of batani, or broad cotton cloth, about one thousand pieces; of coarse silk handkerchiefs, very bad, twenty thousand pieces; of skimity, which is a kind of cotton linnen, about forty thousand pieces; and of a thin, coarse, cotton shirting, a great quantity, though I do not know precisely what.

Estimate of the manufactures in Cyprus, part of which is exported.

40000	pieces of skimity,	at P.	3 ½ per piece,	P.	140000
20000	pieces coverlids for beds, &c.		12 ½		250000
20000	pieces of handkerchiefs,		6		120000
15000	pieces of cutuni and pesmi,		4 ½		67500
10000	pieces of dimity,		2		20000
1000	pieces of batani,		4		4000
			£. 75187, 10 =		P.601500

exclusive of the shirting.

This country (as I am told) produces a great many medicinal herbs, together with a variety of fossils; but, as I understand nothing of their uses or properties, and have no inclination to dip into that kind of erudition, you shall excuse me from saying anything on these subjects: the truth is, I am so ignorant of these matters, that I scarce know under what species to class the asbestos, of which there is a great quantity near Paphos, I should have said Baffo, but the other name is more familiar to my imagination. This extraordinary production of the earth, in some places, lies in one continued stratum, and sometimes is found here and there in little detached beds; yet, nevertheless, it is dear. The quality of it every body knows, so that I need not expatiate upon that head: here likewise is found vermillion of three different kinds.

* * * * *

In the beginning of this month, I accompanied Mr. Consul Wakeman, and Mr. Boddington, to Mount Croce, which is a pretty high hill, at the distance of about four hours and a quarter, that is seventeen miles, from Larnica, and so remarkable as to be an excellent land-mark for sea-faring people: for this very reason, it must have had some name from the ancients, though now it is not known.

Upon the summit stands a church dedicated to the holy cross, and sanctified by what they imagine part of the wood upon which our Saviour suffered, fixed in a large cross upon the left of the altar. This piece of wood was given to a papa of the Greek Church, by St. Helena, mother of Constantine the great, with liberty to build a church where it now appears. She likewise endowed it with certain lands, which, at present, maintain thirty persons, who serve at, or about the altar; five of them being in priest's orders. The church is very small, and built in the mean manner of the modern Greeks; and the painting is so monstrous, that it would even disgrace a paultry alehouse in our country.

About three miles from this odd fabric, is another chapel and convent, upon the same consecrated lands: here we dined, and our horses were taken care of by the reverend father, who is at once, farmer, innkeeper, and priest.

The consul, and Mr. Boddington, who are extremely obliging, undertook this journey in a good measure for my satisfaction; for, though all around the country is quite parched, without a drop of water, except what is drawn from pits, and that is always brackish, I was struck with the appearance of the place, which, at a distance, resembled our highlands, and seemed to promise a variety of delightful prospects. I was, however, greatly disappointed; though some few pleasant bottoms occurred to our view, and appeared the more agreeable as they relieved the eye from the sight of barren wastes, and introduced a succession of objects. A parcel of low pitch firs are scattered up and down the mountains, though none of the size of timber; while the plains produce some olives, and a good many aromatic herbs. We ranged over many bare hills, and crossed a number of dry channels; so that during the whole excursion, I did not see one pile of grass, or one drop of running-water, except from one sickly, and almost expiring spring. What Briton, of a moderate fortune, would live in such a disagreeable country; where, though the necessaries of life are abundant, and the prices reasonable enough, there is nothing animate or inanimate to entertain your mind, delight your eye, or amuse your imagination! The men are worse than beasts, the women more ugly than fancy can conceive human females to be, especially in an island which was once the seat of beauty and of love; and not the least vestige remains of antiquity, or even of those remarkable objects which the Venetians might be expected to have left upon the island. As for the climate, you may judge of it from the thermometrical table which I shall continue until the year is compleated, and send over as opportunities may occur.

Although I have already trespassed upon your patience, by this dull letter, I cannot help (now that I am talking of the climate) communicating some fresh particulars about the Salines, or inland salt-lakes; though, I am afraid, I have already been too impertinent and prolix upon that subject.

Having often viewed the water in its progression to salt, together with the manner of gathering it, and considered every circumstance with all the attention I am able to bestow, I see no reason for changing my former opinion; but shall add, that the wall built around it, must have been raised with a view to preserve a greater quantity of salt-water than flowed into it by any natural subterranean communication with the sea, between which, and the salt-lake, there is a very distinct canal still to be seen: there the wall has been prodigiously strong, with two sluices to admit or discharge the sea water at pleasure; one of the leaders, or conduits from the sluice, is entire to this day: and what fully refutes that opinion which supposes that the salt is made from the rain-water, the surrounding wall excluded all torrents from the adjacent grounds, for the reception and discharge of which, there was a large ditch or canal round the whole; and over this, at different places, were bridges consisting of two arches, eight or ten feet each, besides the intervening pillar: and there was a good reason for building them of such extent, for all the circumjacent ground declines towards this lake, and there was no level to carry it off; so that as vast quantities fell in the winter, there it lay until it was exhaled by the sun or imbibed by the thirsty soil.

As I walked through the crusted sea, the steam was extremely nauseous, and smelled like putrified fish; the salt, for the most part, was concreted into cakes, like white ice when the water leaves it: and immediately below this, is a coagulated, though not absolutely consolidated water. The surface is taken off with paring shovels, and laid in little heaps, that the watry part may be exhaled or run off; then it is carried on asses to the shore, where it is formed into little mounts: what I call the coagulated water, becomes, in a few days, a solid cake; and thus the people work during the whole season, in which the sun has the necessary influence; this may continue to the end of September, and sometimes longer.

The whole may, probably, produce no more than the two thousand piastres I mentioned by way of myrah, or farm-rent; yet about five thousand cart-loads, of three hundred okes each, are annually made. Of these, the farmer is allowed to make two thousand, but the janisaries make and dispose of the rest at pleasure, though not without paying hush-money: so that the whole quantity will amount to about fifty thousand bushels; whereas it might swell to an infinitely greater proportion. It is, undoubtedly, managed in a very slovenly manner; and when I say so to the inhabitants, they answer, that they make as much as they can consume. But if any man could be properly secured in a lease of it for twenty years, he might make fifty times the quantity, export it in his own shipping, and find sale for it in a variety of markets.

These lakes are a blessing, in one respect, to the country, but a very great curse to this town of Larnica; for, to their noxious vapours, the unhealthiness of this place is imputed: indeed, exclusive of the stench, which must produce foul air from what corner soever the wind blows, the vapours are all impregnated with salt, insomuch that when we went to Mount Croce, in the night (for people cannot travel in the day) the dew upon our whiskers was as salt as the German ocean, though the water of the Salines is, in my opinion, ten times more salt; so that there must be an immense quantity of that mineral in the earth itself. Frequently the milk which is brought for our tea, is so excessively salt that we can not use it with any degree of pleasure; and it is more or less impregnated according to the pasture of which the goats have fed, for there is no such thing as cow's milk to be had on the island, because there is no grass during the summer. This disagreeable taste prevails in spite of all the sugar we can use; and, as all the juices of the human body are salt in a certain degree, what is perspired must certainly partake of that quality; but here it is impregnated with such an incredible proportion, that after the sweat had cooled, I have often rubbed a perfect dry powdered salt from my forehead. Good Heaven! what a country must this be, where a man is pickled alive!

And now, dear brother, as a traveller, I am about to bid you farewell; in that character I shall write no more: but, if ever it shall be my good fortune to return to my own country, you shall have by word of mouth whatever I may have observed in the course of my exile. However trivial, or unentertaining my letters may have been, I will venture to assure you, that every fact I have related has either fallen under my own observation, or been sanctioned by the best authority I could procure . . .

If you read my letters as a critic, I know you will censure them as the friend of,

Dear Sir,
Your ever faithful, and affectionate brother,
Cyprus, Sep. 25, 1745.

LETTER VIII.

Dear Brother,

. . . As I shall probably, in a little time, shift my quarters, you need not be afraid that I shall, after this opportunity, trouble you with any additional remarks upon this island: however, I am resolved to make the most of this occasion, and task my recollection in communicating every extraordinary circumstance of which I have been an eye-witness since my residence at Cyprus.—Well then, our government is changed: and, in lieu of a mussalem, we are ruled by a pacha of three tails; that is, of the highest rank next to the grand visier, but he is provided with the same officers, though in a greater number; so that the country is now subject to a more powerful tyrant, and to him much greater honour is done than to a mussalem, to whom the consuls only send their annual presents; whereas, this viceregent exacts their personal attendance at Nicosia. Accordingly, Mr. Consul Wakeman set out from hence on the sixth of May, to perform this expensive, mean ceremony; which, I think, is unworthy of the crowns of Britain and of France.

The Neapolitan and Ragusian consuls made no attempt to appear magnificent in their retinue and equipage, but the French and Venetians made strong efforts for that purpose, though they excelled us in nothing but number and confusion: our little troop marched with a genteel decency, and every thing was conducted in an elegant manner. The greatest part of the country, until we arrived at the river Peroi, which is about eight miles from Nicosia, is extremely barren; we lodged very agreeably at a village called Margo, from whence we set out next morning, and went to a Greek convent, a little way from town. The pacha had sent his horses very finely caparisoned a la Turquoise, to wait our coming; a very extraordinary compliment: these we mounted, and our little cavalcade began to move in this order. First, the chiavus chilar agasi of the ogiak, or corps of the janisaries; then the muzur of the ogiak, or corps of the spahi; these officers may be understood as majors, adjutants, and sometimes as agents for the respective corps: after them rode the consul's janisaries, the chancellor and first drugoman, Doctor Crutta, the first drugoman's son being a protegeé, the drugoman of the seraglio, the consul, with his zohadars on each side of his horse; Mr. Boddington and your humble servant, together with Mr. Golightly, an English gentleman who was occasionally here, and Mr. Gibson who was followed by the servants in their different degrees.

A little while after we halted at our lodgings, the consul sent to know if the visier pacha would please to give him audience: and the answer was, when it would be most convenient for the consul. We therefore set out for the palace, before dinner, in the order I have already described, and all of us dismounted at the gate, except the consul, who rode into the court of the seraglio, where ten or a dozen fine horses stood gorgeously caparisoned; indeed their furniture was incredibly extravagant. All the guards and officers of the palace were ranged in the court, stairs, passages, and apartments through which we passed to the presence-chamber, and all was silent and still. There we stood until the entrance of the pacha, who clapped the consul on the shoulder, as a mark of high favour and regard, desired him to sit, and several times bad him welcome: nobody sat but the pacha on his divan, and the consul on an elbow-chair of state: the pacha's not being in the room to receive him, and the consul's standing until the other entered, proceeds from this punctilio. A visier, a mussalem, and even those of an inferior rank, think it is too great condescension in them to rise from their seats and salute an infidel; and, on the other hand, a consul will not go into the presence of any officer, whatever his distinction may be, unless he is received standing; so that this method was agreed upon as a salvo for the honour of both: and these preliminaries, with several others, are always settled by the intercourse of the drugoman, before the consul goes to audience.

After some common-place speeches, and hollow assurances of friendship, which gold alone can realize, we were entertained with coffee, sweat-meats, and sherbet, and lastly, with perfumes, which always imply a licence to withdraw. When the consul rose to take his leave, he was presented by the visier with a kurk, or robe lined with fur, which was put upon him by one of the officers. You may imagine this was a distinguishing mark of generosity, but I never heard of that virtue among the subjects of the grand signior; and this vestment had been dearly bought by the presents which the consul had made him in the morning. From the presence-chamber we retreated through the same range of officers, and were favoured with an audience of the khya, or prime minister, conducted in the same manner, though with this difference, the minister is not served upon the knee like his master; thence we returned to our lodgings, with the same order and parade.

The city of Nicosia is situated in the midst of a beautiful plain, between Olympus and another range of mountains, which run from the south-west to the north-east of the island: some geographers, or rather travellers, have distinguished Mount Croce, by the appellation of Mount Olympus, but I am inclined to believe the first to be Mamilla Montis Olympi, which was several miles to the south-east of Olympus; and thus you see how these two mountains bear to each other, as they appear from the road of Salines, where I went on board a ship in order to make a drawing of the bay; *[Plate 1 a.]* which, I think, I cannot exhibit more seasonably than in this place, even though I am talking of Nicosia and Mount Olympus.

With regard to Nicosia, I can not inform you at what period it was built, or whether it had existence while the ancient Greeks possessed the island: some, indeed, assert it is the same as Tremithus, but I rather believe it was near Idalium; for, in a very old charte, which was shewn to me by the French consul Monsieur le Maire, that town is situated near a river called Pedius, upon the banks of which was the famous Idalian grove: this is very near the spot where the Athalas now runs, and not above three miles from Nicosia: yet this is nothing more than conjecture.

The city was well fortified by the Venetians, according to the manner of those times; but all is gone to ruin through the supine negligence and blind security of the Turks. The place is round, and may be about three miles in circumference, but not well inhabited; a circumstance to which it owes its very pleasant and beautiful appearance; for this want of people affords room for a great number of gardens, planted with orange, lemon, cypress, mulberry, olive, and almond trees, which exhibit a most delightful variety to the eye of one who walks upon the ramparts. All the Venetian nobility on the island resided here; therefore the town has been finely built, as appears by the remains of some edifices patched up for Turkish houses, and from the ruins of others that are quite desolate. St. Sophia, now converted to a Turkish mosque, is the only fabric which remains entire, and is of tolerable gothic work; but all the images and figures are defaced by the brutal superstition of the present possessors. One inscription was all I perceived, but I durst not go near enough to read it: no vestige of any thing truly antique is to be seen; for I searched almost every corner, and really I have nothing more to say of this city, but only that its situation is extremely ill judged for a fortified town, there being several hills upon one side of it, from whence the houses might be easily battered down.

The French are a restless people, incessantly employed in working some politic point, to gain which, they use truth and falshood indiscriminately in their insinuations; and, when the deceit is detected, they are never out of countenance. Here they are in continual agitation to promote their own interest, at the expense of their neighbours; but their unfair endeavours are always foiled by the address and known veracity of Mr. Consul Wakeman, whom, notwithstanding their bad success, they still persist in perplexing with their intrigues. It was in order to repair the effects of a dirty mine they had sprung, that I was obliged to set out for Lemisol; a task which I undertook without hesitation. All the country, from Nicosia to that town, is more agreeable than any part of the island which I have yet seen, being diversified with hill and dale, adorned with trees, and refreshed with water, at least, during a certain season; for, in some months, no other than dry channels are to be seen.

Lemisol, though not rich, is a very pleasant place, accommodated with an exceeding good bay for ships; it has a wretched castle, and some small share of trade, yet this small share is greater than that of all the other sea-ports, except Larnica, which being the residence of the Europeans, carries all before it.

About six miles from Limesol, stood the Amathus of the ancients, so celebrated for the amours of Venus and Adonis: it stretched down to the sea, from the face of an hill, where there has been a very strong castle, some of the walls of which are immensely thick, and, probably, were built by some of the Greek emperors: the port has been tolerable; and, from thence to within eight or ten miles of Larnica, the country is neither bad nor disagreeable; but all around this place is, certainly, the worst spot in the kingdom, on account of the salt air, the want of moisture, and the almost total neglect of cultivation. One man ploughs with two oxen, which, though lean as Pharaoh's kine, are strong enough for this purpose: the ground is cut up with an instrument not so strong as a common garden-scythe; and, in lieu of an harrow, a fellow stands upon a short thick plank, drawn by one or two oxen; a method which does not so much break as flatten and press down the earth; yet it produces a better effect than one would at first imagine: for the ground being naturally mellow and tender, is much more easily broke than ours, which is hard and tough; and pressure is necessary to cover the seed, which, otherwise, would be apt to shoot up too soon, with the first shower that falls. I have already observed, that the people of this island reap with sickles furnished with bells to frighten the serpents: their manner of separating the corn from the ear, is this; they nail thick planks together, about three feet square, in which are fastened broken flints or peebles; upon this stage a clumsy fellow sits, or stands, directing an ox or two that drag him round and round a parcel of the grain as it is brought from the field, which he from time to time draws down, as he finds what is under him sufficiently cut or shaken from the ear.

You have, herewith, a thermometrical table of the weather for one year compleat; by which you will perceive a very considerable difference between the heat of this and last year; this, I am told, is of a more natural temperature: the extremes of the other proceeded from intolerable north-east winds, which render the air almost insufferably hot . . .

You will now give me leave to conclude this long letter with the old, and true protestation, importing, that I am unchangeably

Your affectionate Brother.

[Drummond's account of his second trip to Cyprus, April, 1750]

LETTER XIII.

Having, in April last, taken a trip to Cyprus, in order to congratulate my worthy friend Mr. Consul Wakeman and his lady, upon their marriage, I found him pretty much involved in business; which, in some measure, deprived me of the pleasure I expected to enjoy in his conversation. While he was engaged in this manner, I could not resist the inclination I felt to make myself better acquainted with the geography of the country; especially as this inclination coincided with the wishes you were pleased to express in one of your letters, which I received a considerable time ago. Accordingly, I resolved to make the circuit of the island, and should have had the happiness of Mr. Boddington's company, had not he been prevented from taking the tour by an impertinent fever; in consequence of which, I was fain to depart without any other company than that of a janisary, two servants, and a guide, after having provided such stores as are absolutely necessary to one who travels in Turkey.

Though this jaunt did not produce the satisfaction I hoped to have reaped from it, as one can scarce believe, that a country, once so abounding, should now be so barren of antiquities: nevertheless, you may be pleased with knowing the certainty of its present situation, and for that reason, I shall proceed with a detail of my excursion.

My first stage was to Chitty, a village which took the name of Κητε, from its being in the neighbourhood of the point of land formerly called, Dades Promontorium; but, in latter times, distinguished by the appellation of Citium Promontorium, or Chitty Point, because it formed the bay of Citium, and preserved the shipping from the severity of the westerly winds. But to say, that this place derives its name from the antient city of Citium, as some people affirm, from the sole consideration of the affinity of sounds, is altogether absurd; as there is not one reason to support, but many to disprove the supposition: for example, this place is near Dades Promontorium, whereas Citium was not, neither did that city stand upon the banks of the river Tatius, which waters this Village of Chitty, and over which there has been a well built bridge of four arches. Here is no anchorage for the smallest bark, but there was a safe bay for a numerous fleet near Citium, the sea-port of which was called Αλιχες, now Salines, from the neighbouring salt-works. About this village, not the least vestige of antiquity or grandeur is to be found; at Larnica, are undeniable proofs of its having been the ancient Citium; some of these I have already mentioned, and one or two more I found when I was last in that place. Near to the south ruins of the walls, a subterranean vault has been lately discovered; it is nineteen feet in length, above nine feet broad, the walls are near three feet thick; two stones form the roof, which is surrounded with a bold, plain, well wrought cornice. It has two passages at present open, and I call it subterranean, because it plainly appears to have been built into the earth with stones and lime, the walls on the outside being rayled; which could not have been the case, had it been accidentally covered in the general ruin. For what purpose this vault was intended, I shall not take upon me to determine: if as a catacomb, one would expect to see some places for repositories to the dead; and if it had been meant as a sacellum, or chapel, there would, in all probability, have been some place for the statue of the god whose rites were here performed; in either case, niches for lamps would have been necessary; yet none of these circumstances appear: and it could be supplied with no other light than that of portable lamps or candles.

The other piece of antiquity, is laid across what seems to have been a fossee round the city wall; it is composed of two stones, the upper being thirteen feet long, near eleven feet broad, and above six feet thick; the lower I could not measure; but they are cut and joined so as that one has a bed at right angles within the other; and a gateway four feet and three quarters broad, and one foot and an half thick, is cut in the middle, as if the gate had been let down from above, like a portcullis, or the iron gates of a garrison. The use of this contrivance foils my conjecture, unless it has been a sluice to retain the water in the fossee.

For the honour of Bekier Basha, I must communicate an instance of the old gentleman's public spirit. While he was basha of this island, in the year 1747, he formed the noble design of bringing water from the river at Arpera, and occasional springs on the road about six miles from hence, to supply the people of Larnica, Salines, and the shipping. A work worthy of a great and good man, which might have cost him above fifty thousand piastres, or six thousand two hundred and fifty pounds. Accordingly he set down sumpts, or pits, and carried drifts from one to another, to lead the water through the high grounds, and conveyed it in aquaeducts over the hollows: the first of which, from Arpera, is an arcade of fifty arches; two of these are small, the others nine feet wide, the highest twelve feet in height, while the others diminish as the ground rises: the pillars, or peers of the arches, are eight feet broad and three feet thick; and here he has planted fine silk-gardens, with a vineyard, and built a mill, in which grain is ground by the fall of water. The second arcade has twelve arches, each being twelve feet wide, the pillars being five feet broad, and three feet thick, and the highest about eighteen feet in height. The third arcade, which is near Larnica, consists of thirty-one arches, four feet and an half wide, the heighth of the highest being about sixteen feet, each pillar is four feet thick and twelve feet broad.

Here the work stood when he was removed from his bashaleck, and though he left a considerable sum of money in the hands of Christofacco, drugoman of the seraglio, who was murdered when I was last in Cyprus, the villain did not carry on the work as it ought to have been executed, and the basha his successor in office, who knew nothing but the sordid passions of a ravenous Turk, gave himself no trouble about the matter. So that the whole was at a stand until last July, when he sent a person to set it a-going, and by this time, I hope it is compleated.

From Chitty, which is beautified with a number of silk-gardens, to Maroni, the roads are very pleasant, the view being bounded on one side by the hills, and on the other by the sea, and regaled with a great variety of trees, though the greatest part of those upon the plain are carubee, or what we call locust-trees: these, together with olives, adorn an extensive plain, that the eye commands from the village of Maroni, which is delightfully situated upon a rising ground.

We often meet with the channels of rivers which are not mentioned by the antient geographers, with a number of rivulets and brooks that flow plentifully during the rainy season; but, as I performed my tour of nine and twenty days, in the months of May and June, those in the plains were generally quite dry; and the rest, among the hills, had little water, having been almost exhausted for the use of the gardens that are near their courses. This, to be sure, is the best way of disposing them, though they might be used to much better purpose, if the wretched people had any encouragement to be industrious.

Some few miles on this side of Amathus, the country is open and destitute of trees; and to the northward of it, are the Montes Orini, famous for the wines they produce, which are reckoned the best that grow upon the island. From their two high pointed tops, which are very distinct and nearly equal, I should rather choose to distinguish them by the name of Mamillae Montis Olympi, than Monte Croce, were not they almost as high as Mount Olympus, and too much to the westward.

I dismounted at Amathus, and revisited the ruins, together with those of what is called old Limesol by the moderns; and I assure you these are the same, though some make them distinct places. I wish their foolish prince, Isaac Comnenus, had been wiser; or Richard the first of England, more cool in his resentment; for to the one and the other, we owe the utter destruction of Amathus: though, after that period, some mean houses remained, for it was inhabited until of late. I could find nothing upon this my second examination, in which I was so eager and diligent, that I should certainly have found the temple of Venus or Adonis, had the smallest vestiges of any such fabric remained. All, therefore, that I can say upon this subject, is, that St. John the almoner, son of Epiphanius, Governor of Cyprus, first saw the light in this place: in the beginning of the seventh century, he was made patriarch of Ægypt; but he had such attachment to his native spot, that he chose to die in Amathus: and so grateful were the dead, for this instance of his regard, that when he resigned his soul to heaven, and his body to the earth, two bishops, who had been, for some time, in peaceable possession of a magnificent tomb, rose up at his approach, and made way for his more sanctified carcase.

Fatigued and disappointed, I proceeded to Limesol, which was given by Henry king of Cyprus, to the Knights Hospitallers, when they left Palestine; and this, I humbly conceive to be the antient Curium, Carium, or Cumdium: for the geographers of former days bring the river Lycus from two different sources in the Montes Orini, unite them some leagues to the northward of this place, then separate them again into different branches, one of which empties itself into the bosom of the bay, while the other is discharged to the westward of the neck of land hard by the walls of the town. Whereas, I affirm it is one river, issuing from one fountain, and falling into nearly the middle of the bay on the north side; but then I find another river emptying itself into the bottom of the bay, by the south-west side of the town, and coming from the nearest range of hills northwards. I know not how to reconcile these differences, yet I conclude myself right, because my account proceeds from an actual survey, and, I believe, most of my predecessors depended upon hear-say; for almost every one of them is extremely erroneous in laying down the bay of this place: they represent it as a mill-pond, whereas it is a full, open bay, as you see in the chart which I have transmitted. I took the bearings and distances of every thing there inserted, and after having chequed in different ways, I found I had not erred one league in laying down the whole of my circuit.

Upon the neck of land which joins Curium Promontorium to the main, is the village of Agrodiri, which, as well as Mount Olympus, was given to the priests of St. Basil, and the reddendo of their charter was, that they should keep a sufficient number of cats to destroy the serpents, which in great numbers infested the neighbouring grounds: from which circumstance, the Italians bestowed upon the promontory, the appellation of Capo de Gato, which it retains to this day. In all the charts I have seen, this appears as a very long necked peninsula; an error, I suppose, owing to the deception occasioned by the salt-lake which you perceive to the westward; and which one is very apt to mistake for the sea. I myself was deceived when I first saw it; but now the lake being almost crusted, I passed so near as to distinguish it perfectly.

From hence the country is open and pleasant to Colos, which is a fine village, where there was formerly a commanderie of the Knights Hospitallers. Lewis de Magnac, grand commander of Cyprus, built, in this place, a plain, square, and strong tower, which still remains; the front exhibiting this appearance. It is about seventy feet high, and fifty-four feet broad, adorned with coats of arms at those places where you see the letters *[Plate 2 a.]*; but the great gate is buried in some vile house, so that I could not see it: yet part of the convent, which has been large, is still to be seen.

This place I take to be the Treta of the ancients, because a river runs between it and Piscopi, and Treta was situated east of a fine river. But I find it impossible to reconcile the ancient geography with what I saw, and what I may reasonably suppose from appearances and the traditions of the country. Piscopi is a beautiful large village, resembling those of Great Britain; the adjacent grounds are watered by an aquaduct from the river; broken fusts lie scattered around, and some grand ruins are still visible. Here, or in the neighbourhood, was a nemus sacred to Apollo; and one of those ruins somewhat resembles a temple: the people say it was the palace of one who taught music; and, from this tradition, we may conjecture it was dedicated to Apollo; though, to me, it seems to have been the palace of the superior, or lord of the manor: for it evidently appears, that the buildings around it have been intended for the sugar works which were carried on in this place; and I could find neither figure nor inscription which might have ascertained the nature of the whole.

Having proceeded some miles beyond this village, I entered the hilly country, exhibiting, for some way, nothing but bare rocks towards the shore, which is bold; but afterwards I found the ground covered with woods. In one place I saw the effects of an earthquake which happened a considerable time ago, and was seized with horrour at the sight. Vast profound chasms opened to my view; and, into these, huge, split rocks had been hurled: mountains, which were rent, seemed to gape to the very center; while others, still more frightful, hung menacing, as if in the very act of tumbling, with such an enormous weight, as (one would think) might shake the earth to its foundation.

Having viewed these wrecks of nature with astonishment, I went forward to Livathi, which stands upon the river Aphdiem, not far from what is at present called Capo Bianco; and here I find Arsinoe about two leagues north from this shore; yet we see it always laid down west of Paphos Antiqua: perhaps another of the same name may have stood in that situation, but now no vestige of it remains. This cape I suppose to be Phrurium; because it is the first we meet with to the westward of Curium, which has any considerable projection, and the rest are rather points than capes.

Through cursed rocky roads, I passed the mountains about Pisouri, and then obtained a better view of a bluff head, which, according to my geographical system, ought to be Zephyria, though there is no Paphos nor river to the eastward, but Chapatomi to the west. Couclia I substitute in the place of Arsinoe upon the ancient charts, partly for the above reason, and partly because it is, at this day, known, and sometimes called by the name Παληκυθερα. It is a charming place, and, from some fragments of antiquity, appears to have been of note; or, according to the language of the country, a favourite of queen Aphrodite. If this is granted, then Lesata, or Mandraka, or both, must be Hierocepia, and Xero will answer exactly to the river on which that town was built.

Let us now consider the celebrated Paphos, which, we are told, was built by Cinyras king of Assyria, who had Adonis and others by Metherme, daughter of Pygmalion, king of Cyprus. Some say the founder was Paphos, son of Pygmalion, by the statue which Venus animated; and thence the island derived its name.

"Illa Paphum genuit de quo tenet insula nomen." Ovid.

But this is a question of no great importance. At present, we shall only mention the temple which is said to have stood upon the spot where the goddess landed, when she was wafted on shore by the gentle waves from which she sprung, and to have been dedicated by Cinyras. It was one of the three sanctuaries belonging to the island, and noted for divination, which was introduced by Tameras of Cilicia, who agreed that the rites should be performed equally by his descendants, and those of Cinyras; but, at length, that honour was entirely ceded to the Paphian royal race. Here the votary had the choice of the victim, which was always male, as being most acceptable to the goddess, whose figure was round, broad at bottom, and terminating in a point: a form, the reason of which nobody has been able satisfactorily to explain. The greatest faith was given to the entrails of kids; the altars were never stained with blood; nothing but pure fire was offered upon them; and, though they stood in the open air, and the rites were performed in all seasons, no rain extinguished, or even approached the sacred flames. This miracle may be easily accounted for: in a place where it rains so seldom, they might easily defer the sacrifice until the clouds were drained; for, in a little time after they appear, down they pour in a deluge, and then all is over.

This place is likewise remarkable for an horrid scene acted by the royal family, when Ptolomey reduced Cyprus. Nicocles at that time reigned in Paphos, and, hoping to shake of the yoke, made an offensive and defensive alliance with Antigonus, king of Syria; but Ptolomey was informed of their scheme, and defeated it before it could be brought to maturity: he pronounced sentence of death upon Nicocles; but that prince prevented the execution by making away with himself. Axithea, his unhappy queen, followed his example, after she had, in despair, slain her own daughters: the same frenzy seized the royal sisters, who likewise put an end to their lives; and their husbands added to the funeral pile, by setting fire to the palace, and perishing upon the bodies of their beloved wives.

What I have farther to say will rather involve us in new doubts, than extricate us from those which have already occurred: however, if I was not satisfied in every particular I wanted to know, I was, in consequence of the kind letters of recommendation which I received from Mr. Consul Wakeman, treated in every place with uncommon marks of civility and regard. Here Christians and Turks vied with each other in giving me assistance and information; and the aga sent an old man, reckoned the best antiquary in those parts, to conduct me to every remarkable place, and gratify my curiousity to the best of his knowledge: yet all I could learn amounts to very little.

Old Paphos or Erythra I, in my map, removed from Zephyria; Arsinoe I found, and still set down, near that place, for the reasons I have already advanced, and because Ptolomey Philadelphus consecrated a temple on the Zephyrion Promontorium, to his wife Arsinoe, under the name of the Zephyrion Venus; but of this nothing now remains. I fix old Paphos at the port of Baffo; Cythera I have already left behind me, and in its place I take the liberty to put Paphos Nova, or Baffo, as you will see they exactly answer to each other, when you compare the old chart I sent home with this which I now transmit: but that you may not think I am too dogmatical in my assertions, I shall communicate my reasons for alterations I have made.

No place in this island ever bore the name of Old Paphos, except the sea-port, which nature has formed into an harbour; and the town of Baffo is handed down, from father to son, as a place that was built long after the town, at the port, which is capable of receiving small vessels; yet these were esteemed large, when navigation was in its infancy. At or about Zephyria there is no place for the reception of any boat whatever; let us therefore lay aside fable and appeal to truth. Venus is said to have risen from the sea, and landed in Cyprus near Cythera: true it is, the island Cythera, now Cerigo, contended for that honour, though the greatest probability is in favour of Cyprus; for that goddess was first worshipped in Phaenicia, and this worship was communicated to the different nations with which they had commerce: the vessels they first used consisted of small pieces of wood, bended across each other, bound with wickers, and covered with hides; consequently their navigation could not be very distant; so that we may more naturally suppose Cyprus to have been their first discovery, than that they launched out into a wide sea, in order to find trade in Peloponnesus, or any of the adjacent islands. Cyprus they could see from their hills, and this prospect probably invited them to venture from their shore; and though the west end was the most distant, their landing in that part might be owing to the accident of contrary winds. When they approached the coast, it is to be supposed, they crept along it until they found a place of safety for their vessel; and if they missed Limesol Bay, they could find no other convenient shelter until they arrived at the place which I imagine to have been the ancient Paphos; and indeed to me it appears very improbable that Paphos should be built at either of the capes which I make Phrurium and Zephyria, and there is not another until we reach Drepanum.

In Baffo or Paphos Nova, which is now a large, agreeable town, there are no remains of antiquity; but many ruins of christian houses are built upon by the Turks: the churches have been very numerous, not only here, but also through the whole island: insomuch, that though I intended to mark them singly on my chart, they swelled so fast that I was fain to drop my project, otherwise it would have been a map of churches. The port, or Paphos Antiqua, according to my conjecture, has been large, and contained many noble buildings, as appears by the ruins at this day, particularly by those of the churches Agioi Solomoni, and Chrisoupolitisa; but they are so demolished that a drawing of them would yield no satisfaction. Great numbers of broken columns are scattered up and down; and of the temple of Venus, which stood on a high place, three subterranean vaults still remain: the traditional account of this temple, taken from an old manuscript, which they told me was stolen by a gentleman-traveller some years ago, imports, that it was a palace built by one of the queens, called Aphrodité, who, being extremely beautiful and excessively lewd, allured all the young men to the court, and bestowed her favours upon all those who pleased her fancy. Her example was followed by all the women around; and this disposition soon spread over the whole island. After her death it was consecrated as a temple, and rites were performed to her as to a divinity, because nought but pleasure was known during her reign. It was thrown down by an earthquake, rebuilt about one thousand four hundred and ninety-five years before the birth of Christ, and finally destroyed by Saint Barnabas, in the fortieth year of the christian aera. This account agrees tolerably well with the story of Venus; though it is not at all probable that the temple was demolished by the influence of Saint Barnabas, during whose life it was in very high repute, whereas the christians, at that time, had very little power and authority: at any rate, if it was actually thrown down, it must have been reared again by the votaries of the goddess; for it was an asylum in the reign of Tiberius, and Titus Vespasian consulted the oracle in this very place, upon his return from Corinth, after having heard of Galba's fate; and in consequence of the response repaired to his father in Syria; so that its last destruction, in all probability, has been in the fourth century, when the general earthquake changed the course of many rivers, and, by swallowing up many others, occasioned an excessive drought. It was upon this occasion (say they) that Saint Helen restored water to the island, by virtue of the wood of our Saviour's cross, which was in her possession. Having found this in the Holy Land, she gave one half of it to the priests of Jerusalem, and brought the other along with her, to sow, as it were, its sanctity through the east and west. Accordingly an infinite number of miracles were performed by this hallowed timber; and had not she thrown one of the nails of it (which our heralds call passion-nails) into the sea, when she was overtaken by a dreadful storm in Satalia Bay, her imperial majesty would undoubtedly have gone to view the wonders of the deep; but the holy nail bore down the waves, smoothed the surface of the sea, and procured her a safe landing. Though I do not find that either she or any of her beatified historians tell us whether or not the nail, after having knocked down the tempest, was pleased to return to its former station.—I can recollect nothing else to say about this Paphos, but that here Elymas the sorcerer was struck blind, and Sergius Paulus the proconsul converted by Saint Paul.

Near Baffo, to the westward, are what they call their Diamond-mines, where, in some places, the spar seems to be crystalized, and pellucid stones are found, like those in the western and northern mountains of Scotland, though not near so good in quality. A muhassel, some time ago, deceived by the name of Diamond-mines, sent thither twenty or thirty men to dig for what he imagined would soon enrich him; but he was grievously disappointed; for all that he got was a few rock-crystals, at the expense of three or four hundred dollars. At Poli di Chrisofou he expected, or pretended to expect, to find solid iron; and having employed his people to dig, without success, he laid a tax upon both places, granting to the christians of Baffo the privilege of the Diamond-mines, for four hundred and fifty dollars, and to others that of the Iron-mines, for three hundred and fifty dollars per annum; so that he exacted eight hundred dollars annually for nothing from those poor, oppressed people, and his successors have ever since religiously followed his example.

From Baffo I took my route northwards through the mountains, from some of which I took the bearing, &c. of the land about Acamas, where flows the celebrated spring called the Fountain of Love: but I had no curiosity to taste of the water, the effect of which upon old people like me, is said to be that of making the spirit willing while the flesh continues weak.—The roads are very rugged, extending through several precipices which are dangerous for the traveller: the woods are thin, the hills very bare, the intermediate grounds tolerably good; but the grain was as green as if it had been sown ten degrees north of the plains I had left a few hours before: but about Stroumbi the fields have a better aspect; for in the neighbourhood of the village, which is pleasant and well peopled, one might easily perceive that more industry had been used in the agriculture: and indeed, through all Cyprus, the soil is such as will well reward the labour of the farmer.

When I entered the village, I was surrounded by almost all the people both young and old, few of whom had ever seen a person in my habit: I gratified their curiosity by standing amongst them, and amusing myself with their pretty children, after I had viewed their church. The poor little creatures were shy at first, but soon flocked round me at sight of a Para; so natural it is, even for children, to be allured by money.

In my progress forwards I arriv'd at Poli di Chrisofou, which is beautifully situated in a bottom among hills; and its vicinity to the sea adds to the agreeableness of its situation. Though there is no trade worth mentioning any where but in Larneca, where the Europeans live, yet a variety of creeks for small craft are to be found all around the island, particularly a bay near this place, formed by the Acamas land, which would be of infinite service to the inhabitants, in manuring their grounds, were they freed from oppression, and secured in their properties; but those blessings seem to be at an infinite distance from them, for the misery of the people is at present inconceivable, occasioned by a total want of rain, whereby vegetation was in a manner choaked up in the earth: what little did appear above ground, was in many places almost totally destroyed by innumerable swarms of locusts, which covered the island, and devoured every thing that had the least verdure, so suddenly, as to have destroyed, in one night, a field which would have given bread to fifty thousand men for a week, besides fodder for the cattle: nay, a farmer-priest told me, that of three hundred scala of wheat (each consisting of about forty-five yards square) which he had sown, he had not reaped twenty. All these circumstances of distress, one would imagine sufficient to drive those poor people to despair; but the government is of another opinion, and never indulges them with the least compassion or forbearance: those who were obliged to depend upon the produce of their lands for the subsistence of their families and payment of their taxes, must sell every little moveable in their possession for that purpose; and those who could not thus pay the exactions of the governor, were under the fatal necessity of quitting the island, or obliged to run the risque of dying under the torture of the drubbing-sticks: many thousands have therefore fled into other countries, while those who remained were compelled to make up the deficiency of the fugitives, as if they had been all joined together in a general co-partnership. Their professing the christian religion was a sufficient cause for subjecting them to such horrid tyranny and damnable injustice! such as must inevitably end in the ruin of the kingdom, unless the locusts are removed, and the thirsty soil plentifully supplied with rain, for the nourishment of the seeds and roots that are now in the ground, as well as of those that may be sown next winter and spring.

At the distance of an hour from the village are what they call the Iron-mines, though this is no more than the place where their furnaces and forges were erected: the ore was undoubtedly found amongst the hills, for here is nothing that resembles it: wood from the mountains might easily be transported hither for smelting; and for this purpose, in all probability, the adjacent hills have been left bare of their covering, for scarce a tree is to be seen upon them, while those at some distance are covered with as good pines as any the country affords.

In my progress from hence I found myself engaged in a very deep gutt, upon the rocky sides of the river Simbula, between two impending hills, from whence the rocks and trees seemed to stretch themselves horizontally to cover us: I might have travelled two hours farther, but I was so charmed with the romantic wildness and delicious coolness of the spot, which nothing but the meridian rays could invade, that having dismounted, I indulged my people with an holyday till two o'clock next morning. Here I amused myself the whole evening in wandering through the woods and surveying the sea-shores far and near, which produced variety of reflections foreign to our present correspondence. To this place I must take the liberty to give the name of Jovis Lucus, because I find it exactly answers the situation of one consecrated to that deity, near which a river fell into the sea. Next morning, after four (for two hours are scarce sufficient to put our caravan in motion) I left this pleasant retreat, and, in the course of three or four hours, rode along a good many different precipices, one of which had well-nigh deprived you of this tedious epistle, for my mule made a false step upon the face of a rock, and down we came together: had this accident happened a few seconds sooner or later, I should have been crushed to pieces before I could have reached the bottom; but we were providentially saved by a bit of rock, which served as a natural parapet; so that I escaped for a contusion on the hip-bone, and a hurt on the elbow; and, after having made some wry faces, proceeded on my journey.

Near the river Piaerga I dined in a delightful grove of tall spreading trees, hard by which is a very extraordinary rock, almost perpendicular, with a ruined christian chapel on the top: this grove is said to have been planted, and the chapel built, by one of their queens, together with what they call a grand palace in the mountains in this neighbourhood. Indeed, all their castles and palaces have been raised by the ladies, if we may depend upon tradition; but they have not been so just to the memory of these benefactresses, or so obliging to the curious, as to preserve their names, either in records or inscriptions . . .

The fabric has been extremely mean, being only sixteen feet high, and, as it were, intentionally irregular in the elevation.

Four sorry arches adorn the front; there are five little windows above, in the right wing, two only in the other, and there is neither letter, figure, or ornament upon any part of it. Among the mountains I found many broken fusts where I saw no vestige of building; and at some distance from this place, in my way to Lefca, I observed, near an headland, two small perpendicular rocks in the sea, about which the natives tell the following story. A brother and sister being enamoured of each other, fled hither from some neighbouring part of the country, in order to indulge their guilty passion; but, just as they arose from the sea, in which they were bathing, they were changed into these rocks, by the offended deity; and their piteous moanings are often heard to this day. —Probably the inhabitants of this corner of the island have heard some confused story of the Propetides, from which they have derived this fable.

After having endured much fatigue through the day, I arrived at night at Lefca, having passed what is called its port, and a river which I take to be the Satrachus. The port, I presume, is the ancient town of that name, or the port of Solos, for it is surrounded by many foundations of houses: the town is prettily situated about an hour from the port; a variety of gardens, the meanders of the river that wind about it on the south, and the adjacent grounds, that lie in the form of a theatre, concur in beautifying the scene. In the morning I crossed the river Cunara, and entered a deep gutt between the mountains, which are covered with large pines or pitch-firr, and of these they make a considerable quantity of tarr, pitch, and rosin: the river one must often cross, ascending and descending precipices which are frightful to the view; but the mules are generally so sure-footed, that the danger is not great. I have no where seen a more surprising prospect than that which presents itself to the eye, from the top of a mountain near the river Gambo; the numerous hills around rise either in the form of sugar-loaves or sharp wedges; some are covered with tall pines, and others with small firrs, interchangeably; but the most agreeable view is where the verdure is more diversified, and these verdant pyramids afford great variety; such as prodigious sycamores or platanes, a name we borrow from the Greeks, who call them πλατανοι; καρουπη, or the locust, which name they have from the Italians, for καιραζηα is the proper Greek word; σκλιθρον, which I take to be our elm; οσφιλια, a tall thorn; very large καριδια, or walnuts; almonds; which have two names, μιγδαλλα or αθασια; περιγνια, a kind of alder, the leaves of which shine like a green orange; the backs of them, when young, are yellow; but as they grow old, they turn brown: ανδρουκλια, which I do not remember to have seen in Europe; the leaf is pretty broad; it bears a small fruit, in clusters, and annually changes the bark, which is extremely thin and smooth; the old is of a fine red colour, but the new coat is white: ζηζηφια has a narrow leaf, and bears a small fruit not larger than a cherry, but of the apple species. There was a great number of others, which I cannot name; but the whole was sweetly wild and agreeable.

About an hour from Gambo were the first vineyards I had seen in those parts; a circumstance that surprised me not a little; for nature almost every where affords proper grounds for this purpose. From hence, for a considerable way, I travelled through a lane of natural perfumes, such as roses, the first honey-suckles I had ever seen in this country, and a great number of other fragrant plants and shrubs. On my arrival at the famous Madonna di Chekka, I was received with great courtesy by the papa, who among them is not much inferior to a bishop in point of dignity. The convent is well ornamented in their way; but none of the particulars are worth mentioning, except that the architect has forgot to make an entry to the church from the west: yet no body had perceived this deficiency until I took notice of it, and then they were greatly surprised, because it is such an uncommon omission; for at their first entrance, they ought to see the great altar, that they may cross themselves and bow to it: hence judge of their simplicity. In one apartment of the convent is a wretched piece of painting (which however they highly esteem) representing a Caloyer on the cross; on his left hand is a gay figure of a man on horseback, at full speed, holding a cup of wine in steady poise, and surrounded with palaces, groves, cascades, &c. and on the other side, is an oddly-imagined hell, with monsters among flames, devouring the wicked, while our Saviour in the clouds, pointing to the martyr, offers him a crown of glory. On each side of this emblematical performance are explanatory verses, which I shall give you, in small Greek letters, not for their poetical excellency, but to evince their taste in writing. On the right of the picture are these lines. *[Plate 1 b.]*

My learned and valuable friend, the reverend Mr. Crofts, gives this verbal translation.

Behold here fairly pictur'd the life of a true monk,
How absolutely he is crucified to the flesh and to the world.
The cross expressively typifies mortification,
The lamps truly represent the splendor of the virtues.
The shutting of the eyes, that he is not to regard at all,
The vain and unstable objects of this false world.
The silence of the mouth, that he should not speak unseasonably
The contumelious and filthy language of the present age.
The nails in the feet, that he must not at all walk

In the broad path, nor indulge in intemperate delicacies;
But, with charity, silence, and purity of life,
Shine visibly to the world beyond the sun's lustre;
And wage perpetual war with the deceitful world,
The lusts of the flesh, and the malicious devil:
For the Lord of the universe, with his angels,
Is near him for his assistance,
And holds in His hands a crown and a diadem,
That, if he prove victorious over the lusts of the flesh and the world,
He may, according to his merits, crown his brow,
And admit him into the kingdom of heaven.

July.

1742.

In the evening I walked about the place with intention to give you a perspective of it from some proper spot; but, as I could find no point of view either uncommon or tolerably agreeable, I put up my pencil, and dropped my design. Yet, notwithstanding its mean appearance, the revenues are sufficient to maintain three hundred of the fraternity, besides those who manage their farms, if they lived under any government less savage than that of Cyprus; whereas, when I was there, the number of the brothers did not exceed threescore.

The Valley of Sollia or Soglia I think the finest in the island; Massaria indeed is a rich, extensive, and would be a plentiful country, were it not wholly destitute of trees and villages, which the other has in plenty, together with abundance of water and wood from the adjacent hills.

When Solon, the famous Athenian law-giver, came to Cyprus, he lived some time with Philocyprus, one of the kings, whose capital, Apeia, was built, in the mountains, by Demophoon, son of Theseus; it was strong, because almost inaccessible, but the circumjacent lands were barren and bare, though near the river Clarius; the sage advised him to remove from these naked rocks into the fertile plains, where he might build a larger and fairer city; his majesty relished the advice, and left the management of the whole to Solon, who, in a little time, raised a large, noble, and well-fortified town, which, from the pleasantness of its situation, the rich produce of its soil, and the equitable laws which he had instituted, drew all the inhabitants from Apeia, which was left quite desolate, and soon allured the best men from every corner, who came to dwell under his paternal sway; so that he became more opulent and powerful than all the neighbouring princes. In gratitude to the author of such felicity, he bestowed upon his infant city the appellation of Solos, which we may suppose it bore, without corruption, until the Italians got possession of the island, and converted it into Soglia, which has a more Italian termination. There was one inevitable inconvenience which attended this concourse of people from different parts: the language became so proverbially corrupt, that to speak barbarously, and to speak like those of Solos, were deemed synonimous phrases; hence comes the word Solecism, rather than from the Soli, who settled in Cilicia—I need not observe to you the absurdity of the old maps, in laying down the situation of this town, which had certainly a port and river. Had they placed it in a spot where there either is, or ever could have been, a bay or harbour, I should have approved of the site, because agreeable to history, so far as relates to the port; but they have carried it into the district of Morfou, far from that which bears its name to this day; and represented it upon a place from whence a shallow beach extends a great way. I therefore presume to say, the port was near Satrachus, Clarius, or the river that runs between them, which probably, in those days, bore the name of the city.

Morfou is a very chearful place, about a league and an half from the sea, and its church is the handsomest building of its kind in the whole island: the court is finely walled with hewn stone, about fourteen feet high, extending to two hundred and fifty two feet in front, one hundred and fifty-six feet on each side, with forty-five feet for cloysters, &c. It was almost finished, in a kind of Italian taste, when the Turks conquered the island. I here give you the elevation of the front, because it is the first and only instance of the improvement of their gout: but this was nipped in the bud by the irruption of the barbarians, and they returned to their old manner. They have built a mean corridore in front, which has never been intended by the first architect, and is far from being of a piece with the rest, so that I would not draw it; but, from the projecting stones, at C and D *[Plate 2 b.]*, I imagine, he designed a portico, which might have added to the beauty of the fabric.

Saint Mamas, to whom this church is dedicated, performed abundance of miracles while he lived upon earth, and even now affords daily matter for astonishment. When alive, he either could not or would not pay his carache, or poll-money, and the collectors were always restrained, by the operation of some praeternatural power upon their bodies and spirits, from using him in the savage manner in which they treated others, who were deficient in their payments. The prince, being informed of this extraordinary circumstance, ordered him to be hunted out from the hollow rocks, caves, and gloomy woods in which he always lived, and brought into his presence; and Saint George and Saint Demetrius, hearing of his being taken, followed, overtook, and accompanied him in his captivity. During his journey to court, seeing a lion rush out of a thicket and seize a lamb, to the terror and astonishment of his guards, he ordered the beast to quit his prey, and his command was instantly obeyed by the lion, who fawned and wagged his tail, in token of submission. The good man, being tired with walking, took the lamb in his arms, and mounting the wild beast, rode forwards to court, to the amazement of all who saw him. He presented himself, in this equipage, to the king, who, being apprized of these circumstances, accepted the lamb, generously remitted the caraches he owed, and gave orders that the Saint should live without paying any tax for the future: thus favoured he came hither and built a little church, in which at his death his body was deposited. This is one way of telling his story, which is varied by every papa whom you consult on the subject. As I have related one of his performances while in life, I will now communicate one of the feats he has acted since he went to the other world. Just above the place where he lay interred, a marble sarcophagus was placed, and on the wall is a picture representing him riding on the lyon, with the lamb in one hand and shepherd's crook in the other: upon his right is Saint George, and on his left Saint Demetrius, both on horseback. The Turks, expecting to find a treasure in this sarcophagus, broke it up; and ever since, through two little holes, which were then made, water is continually conveyed into a hollow, being supplied from the sweat that issues from the face of the above picture, which is never dry, though those of his brethren saints, who are close to him, shew no signs of moisture. I know the Greeks, who are naturally credulous, gave faith to traditional miracles; but, if I rightly remember, this is the first I have ever known them impose upon mankind.—So much for miracles, and indeed for this place, of which I shall take my leave with telling you that several marble capitals, &c. are here very injudiciously sited.

About six or eight miles hence, I was pleased to see the industry of the people, who make the most of the springs from above, by collecting them into reservoirs; and distributing them to the fields below; yet almost all the grounds, for a dozen if not twenty miles together, though rich and capable of improvement, lye quite uncultivated, except in the neighbourhood of these springs: a circumstance which I partly attribute to the lazy, trifling disposition of the Greeks themselves, and partly to the tyranny of the government under which they live.

In a former letter I said so much of the city of Nicosia, that it will be needless to add another word on the subject, because I did not find, in this last tour, the least change either for better or worse, though I walked all around it, in order to refresh my memory; I shall therefore proceed to the northern mountains, where the first object that attracted my attention, was a hanging rock; by the side of a charming rivulet that runs murmuring through a long, narrow vale; and this I chose for the place of my noon repose. I had not long solaced myself under this impendent rock, when, looking up, I was agreeably surprized to see that all above me had been once a wood of noble trees, the roots of which, now petrified, formed a curious projecting canopy: of these I brought away some pieces; and, being much pleased with my acquisition, remounted, and soon reached the plains near the sea, from whence I had a very agreeable ride to Lapitho. This town is said to have been built by Belus, and stands agreeably situated on the rocks of the shore, whence the harbour seems to have run far to the westward; but it has no river, and yet all the grounds of the slope from the mountains are fertile and pleasant, bearing great numbers of natural and planted trees, with fine crops of grain: so that I do not wonder it should be formerly called Amabilis Lapithus. At present there is not a tolerable house in the place; yet, by some remains, I could perceive there had been once good edifices, and some grand buildings, particularly one, the foundations of which I partly traced: the wall was two feet thick, and fifty-seven feet long; the front thirty-six feet broad, and in the center of the west side was a space of six feet, where no foundation was to be seen; I therefore suppose this to be the width of the gate: the flooring is mosaic, very neat work. Perhaps another person would have found out a temple in this vestige; but I chuse to represent only what I saw, and leave you to your own conjectures. In the church of Saint Acheropeto I found the monumental stone, the drawing of which we have at No. 2. *[Plate 3 a.]* The work is so extremely low, that it cannot even deserve the name of basso relievo; and perhaps you may not think it of much value, yet I would willingly give you specimens of every thing by which you may judge of Cyprian taste: as for this performance, it is but about two hundred years old.

Next morning I set out, elevated with the hope of seeing some valuable things upon the top of a neighbouring mountain, with which my expectation had been regaled. Passing through the village of Elia, I observed, over a well-built gate-way, two coats of arms inclosed within a wreath of fruitage: on one was the imperial eagle, on the other the Venetian Saint Mark, or winged lion seyant, holding the evangelists in his dexter paw; whence I conclude, they must have belonged to some public edifice, the whole being very neatly cut in bas relief, upon a stone of white marble. Here were the first cypress-trees I had seen in the journey; but from hence there is plenty of the different kinds along the shore to the eastward.

As we approached what is vulgarly called Agios Largos, but properly Saint Hilarion, which is on the summit, we found the west side of the hill so steep that our beasts could not mount it; I therefore left my luggage at Carmi, and with eight mules took a turn to the eastward, in order to find an easier access. When I came to the rock on which it stands, I dismounted, and, having refreshed myself, sate down to make a sketch of its extraordinary aspect, which I now give you, No. 3. *[Plate 3 b.]* then taking my stick in my hand, I ascended as well as I could, and walked through all the different parts of the castle. It has certainly been strong, both from its site and fortifications; but I found no beauty nor inscription, not even the year, upon any one part of the ruins; so that, being disappointed and heartily tired, I walked down the west side, and you will have some notion of the difficulty of the descent, when I tell you that I spent thirty-five minutes in reaching the foot of the rock upon which the castle stands. This extraordinary place is said to have been fortified by one of their queens, but by which of them I could not learn: however I think it must have been Charlotta, who, with her husband, was obliged to take shelter in the castle of Cerinia, when James the Bastard was established on the throne by the Egyptian power: there he besieged her for a considerable time, but was obliged to quit his enterprize, and left her a great while at liberty; in which interval, we may suppose, she built this castle, to secure the hilly country, as that of Cerinia gave her command of the plains below; till the poor unhappy royal pair, after tedious and fruitless solicitations, receiving no succour from their friends in Europe, and the bastard making new preparations to extirpate them, they fled to Rhodes, and put themselves under the protection of the grand master, who received them with all the honour due to their birth and dignity.

Heartily fatigued and scorched, I, in about two hours, reached the port of Cerinia, which was probably built by Cyrus, and is reckoned the best on the north side of the island: the harbour seems difficult to strangers, and is only fit for small vessels; the entrance hath been in some measure guarded by a fortification on each side, built on the rocks, and is absolutely secured by a very strong quadrangular castle on the land: two of the opposite angles of this fort are furnished with square, and the rest with round bastions. No European is allowed to enter or even to approach it; so that I can only judge, from its appearance, that it may have been fortified by king Henry, at the same time with Famagusta and Nicosia; and that probably the whole work was repaired by Savorniani, who, in the year 1525, demolished the old works of these places, and refortified them: on such an occasion we cannot suppose this important place to have been forgot and neglected, especially as we find the military architecture of all three in the same stile. The town has likewise been very well walled, and strengthened by towers, bastions, and a fossée: of these fortifications we may judge by the immense quarries which have been dug on both sides of the town, as they could have no use for the stones elsewhere, every place being more than sufficiently provided. These quarries they have wrought in such a manner as to form communications with the fortress, and make several noble granaries for their grain.

My next excursion was to see the ruins of a very magnificent structure, called Dela-Pays; it is said to have been a monastery, but no circumstance that I have seen gives me reason to be of that opinion. I rather suppose it to have been the grand commanderie of the island, for it is built in the palatial stile of those days; and its Italian name, Della-Paese, though a little corrupted, seems to confirm my conjecture. I could find nothing that resembled the cells of the monks; the apartments are all a little more knightly: the court is a square of an hundred feet; the corridore round it fifteen feet within, vaulted, and supported by clustered corinthian pillars: on the right is the refectory, an hundred feet by thirty; and on the left, the church, which is by no means equal to a monastic edifice of such a superb form: behind, on the ground-floor, are two spacious rooms; but, immediately above, is the grand sale, of an hundred feet by thirty, and thirty feet high, arched in clusters, from six pilasters on each side. Over the gate of the refectory are three coats on a marble architrave; that of Jerusalem in the centre, Jerusalem and Cyprus quartered on the dexter, and Cyprus on the sinister. The same bearings are likewise in other parts; and just by the gate of that dining-room stands a beautiful marble fountain, from whence the company have been supplied with water: on each side of it is a boy bearing up festoons of fruitage; and in the bendings thereof are lions heads, and bulls heads on the angles, all well executed: but, that you may have a more distinct notion of this structure, I send you a drawing of it, No. 4. *[Plate 4]* Just by the church door is this inscription, on a tombstone, in old French of the thirteenth century, which however I cannot understand. *[Plate 6 a.]*

It must seem very strange to all thinking mortals, that a set of men, professing an order which was instituted in the year 1099, with intention that the members should live in poverty, subsisting on the charity of their fellow-creatures, which charity should not exceed a bare sufficiency to supply them with arms, ammunition, and the necessaries of life; that these men, I say, after having been expelled from the Holy Land, should be in a condition to build sumptuous palaces, and support one prince against another. But that wonder will cease when we consider that mankind were, for some centuries, so drunk with superstitition as to be deceived by the grossest imposture. As for those knights, although they vowed poverty, chastity, and temperance, yet, in forma pauperis, they held above nineteen thousand lordships among the deluded christians; and, being possessed of such wealth, enjoyed every delicacy that could be procured, wallowed in unnatural lusts, and even dictated to sovereigns: in a word, they lived, inter scorta et epulas, regardless of every consideration that merited the name of virtue. However, this I will say in favour of the Hospitallers, that they were outdone, in all manner of wickedness, by the Templars, from whose fate they learned some caution.

From this delightful retirement I went to Agios Phanentis, the rocks of which are washed by the sea, and there I found several human bones and teeth petrified. The country people, who, you know, abound in legends, say that a vast number of foreigners, called Allani, who came from a savage country to subdue and seize their fruitful lands, were here shipwrecked and perished; their bones, as a punishment, and monument of their crimes, were turned into stone, as we now see them; though some of them, being converted to the christian faith, lived happily in the island and became saints. Of this number was Saint Mamas, of whom such honourable mention hath been made; yet some say he was a native of the island, while others affirm he was born upon the main.— Ridiculous as this fable may appear, there is certainly some foundation for it. We know the Goths invaded Greece, and visited some of the islands; and though I do not remember the circumstance in history, some of them may have made an attempt upon Cyprus; else how should the inhabitants become acquainted with the word Allani, and transmit it from father to son? I never saw a vegetation of stone-bones, stone-teeth, &c. yet I have such petrifactions in my possession; and heads, fingers, and toes have been found; whence I conclude that a great many people, in the early or distant ages of the world, have been wrecked upon this little point, and their bodies, when washed on shore, indurated by the natural means of petrifaction.

On my road from this place nothing occurred worth mentioning until I re-crossed the hills and came to Citraea, which is one continued chain of gardens and summer-houses of vast extent; everything was in the highest bloom and gayest verdure, being watered by living streams, conveyed to every field through little channels.

In my way to Saint Chrysostomos I crossed a field where perpendicular strata of stones run along the surface like so many foundations of walls. The convent of which this saint is protector, I found a large though mean building; some parts are of good marble, well wrought, and tolerable mosaic of variegated stones, with a great deal of gilding and painting; but nothing is of a piece.

The superior had no records, which indeed none of them have, but he told me it was founded by the king's daughter, who built the Spitia tis Regina, upon the top of an almost inaccessible rock, two miles farther up in the mountains; the drawing of which you have, No. 5. *[Plate 5 a.]* If it proves agreeable to you I shall be pleased; but, I assure you, I should neither trouble you nor myself with so many sketches of this sort, did not some people talk of them as so many valuable remains of antiquity. Now you may judge for yourself, as I have given the most favourable views of them, and endeavoured to do them justice.

This night I lodged at Palaecitraea, about three miles from Citraea. It had been one of the ancient Cytheras or Cythereas, of which there were several in the island; but I saw no vestige of antiquity: indeed I was conducted to a place where the foundation of a temple, sacred to the queen of love, remained about a foot high some years ago; but the cadi, in order to save the expense of working a quarry, ordered the stones to be removed and employed in building an house for his women. I should not be sorry to hear they had tumbled down upon this barbarous Goth, and crushed him in the embraces of his favourite concubine, provided the innocent girl could escape unhurt.

I have already said something of the country of Massaria, anciently Macaria, through which I now travel, and it affords nothing new to communicate.

About four miles N.N.E. from Famagusta appear the ruins of the famous Salamis, built by Teucer, of which I have taken some notice in a former letter. I saw a great many foundations, which I conceived to be the remains of different fabrics; but I shall mention none except those of the celebrated temple dedicated to Jupiter Salamine, for they are so distant that I cannot well mistake them. It is an hundred and ninety-two feet in length, seventy-two in breadth; the walls are four feet thick, besides cloisters for the priests, their apparatus and attendants, which run the whole length of the temple on the south side, and are in breadth twenty-one feet within walls, with an entry different from that of the temple. Nothing is now to be seen but the vaults below, which supported the temple, and some parts of the walls above: the vaults are uncovered, and it appears that twelve rows of arches have run from side to side, and four from one end to the other; which must have formed a very firm groupe, and was their manner of building, in order to prevent the effects of earthquakes. Part of the pedestal that supported the statue remains in the east end:

the grand court is six hundred and sixty by three hundred and ninety feet, and hath included other buildings besides the temple, but of what kind I will not presume to say. One part, on the north of the square, I take to have been a circus; great numbers of broken fusts are scattered about, some being three feet and a half in diameter, so that they must have been very high: they lie near the temple, among some foundations which probably belonged to the palace, as one person was both king and high priest. The city has been large, about half a mile from the sea; but I cannot perceive that they had any safe or convenient harbour, as there is no great depth of water near the place. I need not observe, that the temple, being one of the three sanctuaries, maintained the priests in affluence, and drew many people within its confines; or, that this city, in the time of Evagoras, was reckoned the capital of the island.

For the same reason I gave you at Nicosia, I say nothing of Famagusta, but that I took up my quarters under a tree in a garden; a kind of lodging I always prefer to an house, though they would have opened the gates for me at any time.

Sancta Nappa is much admired by the people of the country, though for what I do not know: the convent is rendered agreeable within, by a fountain of water, round which the people can sit and solace themselves under a large cupola; but there is nothing beautiful in or about the place. Here I found a Latin inscription, on a marble stone of this figure: [Plate 6 d.] by which it plainly appears to have been a Roman convent: and I found a place called the Latin chapel, under the same roof with the Greek church, part of which is dug out of a rock.

Near the convent is a pretty little harbour, which I take to be Leucola Portus; and from hence the poor people employ themselves in fishing, with boats of a very particular texture, consisting of a few sticks bound together, with some very small ones laid in the hollow, where the fisherman sits managing his tackle, and steering his machine with a paddle.

From this place I returned to Larneca, through lands which, though naturally good, are quite disregarded; and I shall finish the journal of my tour with this observation.

We are told that Ptolemey Soter destroyed the city and kingdom of Malum: and indeed not only the remains of the city are thought to be lost, but the very kingdom itself is gone. May not the ancient geographers, who were very inaccurate in many things, have erred in laying down its situation? Malum, we know, lay east from Citium; now, if Chitty be the Citium of the ancients, Malum must have been situated where there is nothing but sea; and Ptolemey, instead of razing it to the ground, must have tore away the land itself, and sunk it in the deep: a piece of history which hath not as yet fallen in my way. But if Larnaca be the ancient Citium, which I suppose it to be, there are many places even to Cape Greco, extremely proper for the situation of a city; nay, there cannot be a nobler site in the whole island than that very point, which seems to be cut out by nature for the purpose; and on the road to Sancta Nappa many ruins are to be seen.—You will say this is a bold conjecture; but, from all these circumstances taken together, I pronounce it to have been the seat of the ancient kings of Malum.

At my return to Larneca I concerted with Mr. Boddington, who was quite recovered, another tour through the province of Carpass, which we very soon put in execution. On the 15th of June we directed our course towards the river Peroi, the ancient Giallias, not Athalas, as I formerly called it, upon wrong information, on the banks of which was the famous Idalian grove; for the old chart gives the name of Pedius to this river, leaving the real Pedius to find a name for itself; thus Idalium cannot have been where Nicosia now is, but somewhere down this river eastward, near the grove; and by comparing what you find in my former letter with the map I now send, you will perceive what difference there will always be between informations and an actual survey.—As Mr. Boddington had never been to the northward, we took my former route through the mountains, of which I have nothing further to say.

From Malandrina we went towards the bay of Limeone, where vessels from the east come to an anchor when they cannot fetch Cerinia; and if the ground is clean and good, it has the appearance of a place of safety. About two or three miles farther is a bluff-head, on which are the ruins of Sancta Marina, which has not been a mean place, for several broken fusts, &c. are to be seen lying scattered around it. Probably it was Macaria, the situation of which should be hereabouts: the soil is very good, but so much disregarded as to be covered with shrubs and underwood.

The village of Agathou, on the skirts of the mountains, is extremely pleasant; but we saw nothing else worth regarding till we came to Zdavlo, where we found a pretty good bay, with a rock on each side, and ruins which possibly may have been Aphrodisium, as this was the first thing like a port which we met with in the division of Carpass. From this place we mounted a very steep hill, in order to visit the castle of Cantara, the buildings and fortifications of which, we were told, remained almost entire. We accordingly dismounted, at the foot of the rock on which it stands; and, after a very difficult and fatiguing search, ascended to a gate, through which we entered; and viewing the whole, found it as much out of repair as any we had seen. You have a sketch of it, such as it is, at No. 6. *[Plate 5 b.]*

The greatest part of the country is extremely pleasant, particularly from Estabomi to Platonissa, where rising grounds covered with wood, and opening glades, form an agreeable contrast: from the tops of the hills about Liornarissa the plains and gardens delight the eye; and there is a great deal of rural sweetness in the neighbourhood of Agios Andronicos, even to Galousa, from which, directly north about a league, is a large, broad bluff head, with a little rocky island both at the east and west point. In the morning we went to survey it, and passed through many ruins with two churches, about a mile from Galousa: upon the east side of this head we found what they call the harbour, though a little to the north west is another much better: the first has a rising ground on each side; that on the west of the head, has been covered with buildings, one of which, being round, may have been a temple, dedicated to the goddess of love; and the whole I suppose to have been the Achaeorum Littus, but I cannot allow the harbour a west situation, which the old geographers say it had: indeed the old chart-makers seem to be very fond of giving their bays and harbours a western exposition, even when nature has made them easterly; for what reason I know not: but, be that as it may, this is a very bad harbour; and, in my opinion, none can be safe which are not sheltered from the west.

About half a dozen miles from hence we struck off to the southward, to see a ruinous village, where we were told we should find magnificent remains: the place has, I believe, been of note; and, by the cutting of the stones, which lie scattered up and down, seems to have been well built: two square towers, embattelled with a neat little chapel, are still standing; the portraits of some saints are undefaced, and two large cisterns not yet ruined; but no figures in sculpture or letters are to be seen.—In the bay of the Carpasian

Promontory the Golgi inhabited, not unlikely where we found a large, modern cistern, with old foundations of houses.

The modern Carpass is by no means so fine a town as I expected to see: it consists of a parcel of vile, scattered houses and gardens; and I did not see one handsome woman in the place, which hath been always famed for beauties. Here is a new church, built after the mean vulgar form, though the wooden carved work of the choir is better than what I have observed in any Greek church, and must have belonged to some other, for it is very old.

About two miles eastward are fine ruins of a village, which they call Athendrae, though I cannot find it in any map I have seen: however, in many circumstances it answers the description of the ancient Carpasia, built by Pygmalion; and I have taken the liberty to mark it as such in my chart. The island is very narrow in this place, from whence we ascended to the top of Mount Olympus, where Venus had another fane, in lieu of which we found, just on the summit, the ruins of a little, wretched Greek chapel. From this spot, which is a great deal higher than any other part in the neighbourhood, I took the bearings of the country to Cape André, or Clides Prom., and we found the air intolerably cold, and so moist, that a vellum paper-case that was in my pocket parched and shrivelled up with the heat, in a few minutes felt humid, and soft as my glove. From hence to the point are little plain spots interspersed with bushy hillocs, but altogether uninhabited.

We returned through a variety of good and bad, beautiful and bleak grounds, until we arrived at the convent Canakarga; where, recollecting that it would be proper to give you an idea of a Greek church in their true taste, I pulled out my pencil and made the sketch, No. 7. *[Plate 6 b.]* to save myself the trouble of drawing and measuring, and you that of considering, an ichnographical plan: I shall only inform you that it is built exactly according to the mode of the ancient Greek churches, which, you know, consisted of a νάρθηξ, or porch, πρόναος or outward chapel, ναος, body or nave, βημα, the chancel, and θυσιαστήριον, the altar.

About three miles from hence we passed some rocks of talc, then descended into a delightful bottom, where stands the village of Rosala, surrounded with corn-fields, gardens, gentle swells, pretty tufts of trees, and a natural fence of little hills. Half an hour farther we came to Komatougalou, which is prettily situated, and the fields are well laid out near the sea: it was once so extensive as to contain fourteen churches; but now five-sixths of it lie in ruins, among which is the church of our Lady, where I found the following inscription upon a stone, accidentally laid on the four pillars of the altar-table. It is written in old French, like that which I sent you from Dela-Pays: I can read every letter, and many words I understand; but I cannot oblige you with an explanation of the whole, which I therefore leave to your own investigation. *[Plate 6 c.]*

Through a number of delightful spots we came to Famagusta; and from Castro, where there are still cisterns, with the remains of a town and fort upon a little hill, I traced a causeway, made in the Roman manner, the whole way to Salamis, where we lost it for a while, and found it again, proceeding almost as far as the garrison, which we reached at noon, having travelled above nine hours that morning, with intention to stroll about the city after dinner. But the silly people of the country, being alarmed at my taking notes and making sketches, and especially at my looking often upon my compass, which they took to be a sort of divination, began to imagine we were people sent to reconnoitre proper places for descents, and observe where their greatest strength or weakness lay. These notions are circulated with incredible rapidity; and, like snow-balls, gather as they roll along: nay, they produced such a clamour at Cerinia, that the cadi sent a message, desiring to know our business, and whither we were going. Our answer to this impertinent address, was, that we were in search of our pleasures, and he had no business to ask what they were.—This wise magistrate was weak enough to inform the muhassel, that we were employed, by the Venetians, as spies; and that we had made drawings of the harbour, town, and castle: in consequence of this impeachment, the muhassel sent for Signior Crutta, chief drugoman to the British nation, who happened to be at Nicosia, and questioned him touching this important matter; which Mr. Crutta explained so much to his satisfaction, that he could not help laughing at the officious fool who had sent such intimation. Besides this accusation, we were exposed to other dangers; for people were actually sent to way-lay us; but one of them, having more consideration than his fellows, diverted them from their purpose, by representing that we were British subjects, and friends to the government.—These circumstances, simple though they seem to be, together with an expression which was dropped by a fellow as we passed by the side of the fossée of Famagusta, made us determine to avoid the risque of being insulted in the town, which both of us had seen before: we therefore turned aside into the garden, where I had formerly lodged; there we refreshed ourselves with good meat and drink, and cooled our half-burnt carcases in the shade, from whence we did not stir that whole afternoon; but next morning set out for Larneca, where we arrived in safety, without having seen any other thing worth mentioning; except large tracts of fine land, which lie quite uncultivated.

Thus I finished a tour of about six hundred miles, with less fatigue perhaps than that you will undergo in reading the account of it; for I had already written so much to my friends concerning Cyprus, that the little matter it affords was in a good measure exhausted. This letter, however, you will be so good as to receive by way of testimony of that esteem and affection, with which I continue to be,

Dear Sir

Alexandretta,
Nov. 13. 1750.

Your most obedient servant.

       The water is now brought
       into the city of Larneca.

Ives 1758

Edward Ives was the surgeon of Admiral Charles Watson's ship, and of his Majesty's Hospital in the East Indies. He wrote of travels to India, his observations about that country and its neighboring states, and of travels back to England from Persia. He details his visit to Cyprus on that latter trip from October 5 to October 31, 1758. He earlier mentions having read Consul Alexander Drummond's *Travels*. Ives' *A Voyage from England to India, in the Year 1754: Also, a Journey from Persia to England by an Unusual Route* was published in London by Edward and Charles Dilly in 1773.

[p. 386]

At eleven I embarked on board the *Elena Fortunata* brig, *Giovanni Taddei* master. Mr. *Nun,* an *Irish* gentleman is the mate, and Mons. *Rey,* a *Frenchman* the pilot. The brig carries eight hands, and two guns, half-pounders. At twelve we set sail for *Cyprus,* with a fair breeze from the east. At sunset the next day, twelve minutes before six, the island of *Cyprus* was seen by our people; and at twelve at night the day after, we came to an anchor in *Saline's-bay.*

October 5. About eight in the morning, I went on shore at *Larnica,* and found Mr. *Turner* with his chaise at the water's side, waiting to conduct me to his house. I was soon visited by Mons. *Cruter* (father to *Jasper Cruter Dragoman* at *Latichea*) and by many other gentlemen, and some few ladies.—This evening came in the *Swede* from *Scanderoon* bound to *Leghorn;* a few hours however too late, for the *Italian* hath been beforehand with her, and engaged the whole of her intended freight.

This island of *Cyprus* is situate between 33 and 36 degrees of east longitude, and 34 and 36 degrees of north latitude, opposite the shores of *Syria* and *Cilicia.* It extends in length from east to west 220 miles, and is in circuit about 550. The air is so pleasant, the soil so fruitful, and the hills so abounding with metals, that the ancients called it *Macaria,* the *Happy Island;* and the inhabitants thereof being a lewd, lascivious people, it was thence consecrated to *Venus,* who is frequently stiled *Venus Cypria* and *Dea Cypri.* The first inhabitants were the *Cilicians,* who yielded to the *Phenicians,* as they did to the *Greeks. Ptolemy* the last king of this island, knowing that *Cato* was sent against him by the *Romans,* put an end to his own life. It continued in the hands of the *Greek* emperors till 656, when it was conquered by the *Saracens.* In 807, the *Greeks* recovered it; but *Richard* 1st, King of *England,* going to the holy war in 1191, and being ill treated by the inhabitants, conquered it, and gave it to *Guy Lusignan,* whose successors were dispossessed by the *Templars* in 1306. In 1472, the *Venetians* possessed themselves of it; and in 1560, *Selim* the *Grand Seignior* took it, whose successors have enjoyed it to the present time.

October 6. This evening I took a ride with Mr. *Turner,* to the *Salines,* or natural *Salterns;* an accurate description of which Mr. *Drummond* hath already given to the public.

October 7. To-day we went together to the *Basha's* garden, and took a view of the aqueduct, by which *Larnica* is supplied with water from a spring at the foot of a mountain, six miles off.

October 10. Mr. *Turner* and I dined this day with our consul, and rode out as usual in the evening. We visited a small village called *Chitty,* supposed to be built on the same spot as the *Citium* of the ancients. The mornings and the evenings are sharp, but the middle of the day is yet warm . . .

October 18. At five this morning, I set out on horseback for the top of Mount *Croce* or *St. Crux,* in company with Mr. *Turner,* and his clerk Mr. *Michael Clamson, Alexander McIntosh,* and two other servants. We rode about W. by S. for an hour and half through a plain, having passed in our way the last set of stone arches belonging to the aqueduct, and which consists of 31 to the best of my remembrance. At six we left the village *Vastrio* our right, and in half an hour, *Vudia.* We then began to ascend a rising ground, and after riding two or three points to the northward of the west, we got at half past seven, to a small *Greek* church and convent dedicated to St. *Athanasius,* situated between two hills; where, in the rainy season and for some months after, is a great run of water from the mountains (called by Mr. *Drummond,* the river *Tatius*) but the bed of it is at present dry. On the sides of both those hills, are the ruins of many buildings, in appearance very ancient. Some of them are of brick, others of stone, and they are several miles in extent. We also passed by some ruins of a more modern date, seated on another hill to our right. The inhabitants frequently dig up stones, marble, &c. among the ruins.

We continued riding on till half past eight, still ascending, and passing between mountains covered with the pine, oak, olive, locust (or *Carubee*) and walnut-tree. Here were also the hawthorn, myrtle, blackberry, vine, oleander, and other bushes and shrubs in great plenty. From half past eight till a quarter after nine, we continued to ascend *Monte Croce;* then we came to another convent, where we dismounted to rest our horses. In this convent we found two or three *Papas* or priests, one of whom was making a pair of shoes. They readily gave us all the assistance in their power, nor did they think it beneath them to take care of our beasts; such was the real, or at least seeming humility of these holy men. We made free with the *Papas* kitchen utensils to dress the victuals we had brought with us.

At eleven, leaving our horses behind for greater safety, we mounted on mules to visit the *Holy Cross,* a church placed on the very summit of the mountain, and reached it in about half an hour's riding. We found there another *Papa,* and a little boy. The church is small, and its walls are build of an iron-stone found in the neighbourhood. Tradition says, that this edifice was erected at the expence of St. *Helena* the mother of *Constantine,* 1400 years ago; though it plainly appears to have been rebuilt since that time, for not a third part of the ancient wall now remains. They shew you a large cross, before which a silk curtain is drawn, and if you will believe the priests, it is inlaid with a part of that very cross on which our Saviour was crucified. Devotees never fail coming here once a year, to offer up their devotions at the *Holy Cross.* From the top of this mountain we had a most delightful and extensive prospect over the greatest part of the whole island. We clearly saw the following places.

		Hours
Corno	distant	1 and ½
Isha or Isiah		3
Dali (the antient *Idalium*)		5
Nicosia		7
Famagusta		11
Livadia		5
Larnica		5
Chitty		3
Aspera		3

About one o'clock we quitted the top of the mountain, and in half an hour got to the lowest convent; where we alighted, refreshed ourselves, and at half past three set out for *Larnica,* which is about 15 miles from the summit of the mountain, where we arrived a little after seven, very much fatigued.

Both in going and returning, Mr. *Turner* and I thought it necessary to dismount and walk over some particular places, the road being narrow, and the precipices dangerous. We made the *Papas* at both convents a small present, with which they appeared very well pleased. He, who resided in the last convent, took our *Douceur* so kindly, that, mounting his ass, he gratefully accompanied us for a considerable way, and shewed us the best turnings in the road . . .

October 22. The marriage ceremony was this day performed between two young persons, who were *Christians*. It was intended to have been a public affair, but afterwards changed to a private one, as the point of precedence could not be settled between the *British* and *French* consuls.

Mr. *Turner* was so obliging as to trouble himself about my sea-stock, and procured me an hogshead of old *Cyprus* wine. All the wines almost of this island, have in them a peculiar taste of tar; this is owing to the vineyards lying on the sides, or at the foot of the mountains which are covered with pine trees, whose juices washed down by the rains, impart this flavour to the grapes.

October 24. The wind blew this morning from the N.E. which brought the coldest weather I have know for some years, and obliged me to have a fire.

October 26. This afternoon, four of the *English* gentlemen from *India*, Messrs. *Gregory, Tottingham, Bailey,* and *Pasley* arrived here, having left one of their party behind at *Aleppo;* and at five o'clock they paid me a visit.

October 27. I returned their visit this morning, and made them an offer of the use of the great cabbin with me, provided they were inclinable to go in the *Leghornese* vessel. They expressed themselves greatly obliged to me, and agreed with the captain for a passage for themselves and servants. They left *Bengal* in *February* last; touched at *Karec* and *Bassora,* and brought a letter from *Baron Kniphausen* addressed to Mr. *Doidge* and me.

* * * * *

In the evening we rode out, and visited those other remains of antiquity, mentioned in Mr. *Drummond*'s travels . . . We went also to the marine town, and saw the church of *St. Lazarus*. The *Papas* told us, it is now 1722 years since he was buried here. This saint is he, whom our Saviour raised from the dead. They shewed us the end of his coffin under ground, and desired us to take notice of some scraps of rags and ends of thread brought hither by those who have been favoured with the assistance of the saint. The end of what they call the coffin, has been pitched or besmeared with some bitumenous substance, designed to impose upon the ignorant and credulous, as moisture issuing from the saint's body. The church belongs to the *Greeks;* but the *Romans* on *St. Lazarus*'s day, never fail to perform divine service at one of the altars.

Thank God! I am now in perfect health, which is more than I have been able to say for ten months past. I spent some hours this day in taking leave of the several families I am acquainted with. I met by accident with the *French* consul, went with him to his house, and for the little time I tarried, was entertained very politely.

Monday. October 30. We agreed with a cook to go with us to *Leghorn,* and to continue in our service during the quarantine we shall be obliged to perform there. The terms are 50 dollars, and ten or twelve more to be paid him by way of *Buxie* (or present) on his good behaviour. This last sum is meant to defray his expences back.

October 31. To-day the cook sent us word, that his wife will not let him go: however we soon hired another, who is to have 60 *Cyprus* dollars, and *Buxie* on the same footing as was agreed on with the first.

We paid our farewel compliments to the consul in the morning, who with his *Chancellor,* returned the visit a few minutes afterwards; and we went aboard.

My very worthy and obliging friend Mr. *Turner* made us a visit on board the *Elena Brig,* and finding the captain not inclined for sailing, insisted on taking us ashore again. We yielded, and in our way paid our respects to the consul, but spent the day with Mr. *Turner*, who at our request, procured for us two hogsheads of water, some charcoal, and other culinary necessaries, which we on examination thought the vessel wanted, though the captain and pilot both insisted on the contrary. Mr. *Turner* accompanied us on board in the evening, and after supping with us, left the ship about nine; when we wighed anchor, took leave of the island of *Cyprus,* and put to sea, steering the proper course for the port of *Leghorn* in *Italy.*

Bruce 1768

James Bruce, also known as Bruce of Kinnaird, undertook a series of travels over a period of years to trace the origins of the Nile River. His book, aptly named *Travels to Discover the Source of the Nile in the Years 1768, 1769, 1770, 1771, 1772 and 1773* was published by Archibald Constable and Co. and Manners and Miller in Edinburgh, and by Longman, Hurst, Rees and Orme in London. This excerpt is from the second edition published in 1805 in seven volumes. The first edition was published in 1790 by G. G. J. and J. Robinson, London.

This brief stop at Cyprus was made on the way to Egypt in 1768, Bruce's first voyage of his searches in the headlands of the Nile.

[Vol. I, p. 79]

On Saturday the 15th of June, 1768, I sailed in a French vessel from Sidon, once the richest and most powerful city in the world, though now there remains not a shadow of its ancient grandeur. We were bound for the island of Cyprus; the weather clear and exceedingly hot, the wind favourable.

This island is not in our course for Alexandria, but lies to the northward of it; nor had I, for my own part, any curiosity to see it. My mind was intent upon more uncommon, more distant, and more painful voyages. But the master of the vessel had business of his own which led him thither; with this I the more readily complied, as we had not yet got certain advice that the plague had ceased in Egypt, and it still wanted some days to the festival of St John, which is supposed to put a period to that cruel distemper.

We observed a number of thin, white clouds, moving with great rapidity from south to north, in direct opposition to the course of the Etesian winds; these were immensely high. It was evident they came from the mountains of Abyssinia, where, having discharged their weight of rain, and being pressed by the lower current of heavier air from the northward, they had mounted to possess the vacuum, and returned to restore the equilibrium to the northward, whence they were to come back, loaded with vapour from Mount Taurus, to occasion the overflowing of the Nile, by breaking against the high and rugged mountains of the south.

Nothing could be more agreeable to me than that sight, and the reasoning upon it. I already, with pleasure, anticipated the time in which I should be a spectator first, afterwards an historian, of this phenomenon, hitherto a mystery through all ages. I exulted in the measures I had taken, which I flattered myself, from having been digested with greater consideration than those adopted by others, would secure me from the melancholy catastrophes that had terminated these hitherto unsuccessful attempts.

On the 16th, at dawn of day, I saw a high hill, which, from its particular form, described by Strabo, I took for Mount Olympus. Soon after, the rest of the island, which seemed low, appeared in view. We scarce saw Lernica till we anchored before it. It is built of white clay, of the same colour as the ground, precisely as is the case with Damascus, so that you cannot, till close to it, distinguish the houses from the earth they stand upon.

It is very remarkable, that Cyprus was so long undiscovered; ships had been used in the Mediterranean 1700 years before Christ; yet, though only a day's sailing from the continent of Asia on the north and east, and little more from that of Africa on the south, it was not known at the building of Tyre, a little before the Trojan war, that is, 500 years after ships had been passing to and fro in the seas around.

It was, at its discovery, thick covered with wood; and what leads me to believe it was not well known, even so late as the building of Solomon's temple, is, that we do not find that Hiram, king of Tyre, just in its neighbourhood, ever had recourse to it for wood, though surely the carriage would have been easier than to have brought it down from the top of Mount Libanus.

That there was great abundance in it, we know from Eratosthenes, who tells us it was so overgrown that it could not be tilled; so that they first cut down the timber to be used in the furnaces for melting silver and copper; that after this they built fleets with it; and when they could not even destroy it this way, they gave liberty to all strangers to cut it down for whatever use they pleased, and the property of the ground when cleared.

Things are now sadly changed. Wood is one of the wants of most parts of the island, which has not become more healthy by being cleared, as is ordinarily the case.

At Cacamo (Acamas), on the west side of the island, the wood remains thick and impervious as at the first discovery. Large stags, and wild boars of a monstrous size, shelter themselves unmolested in these their native forests; and it depended only upon the portion of credulity that I was endowed with, that I did not believe that an elephant had, not many years ago, been seen alive there. Several families of Greeks declared it to me upon oath; nor were there wanting persons of that nation at Alexandria, who laboured to confirm the assertion. Had skeletons of that animal been there, I should have thought them antediluvian ones. I know none that could have been at Cyprus, unless in the time of Darius Ochus, and I do not remember that there were elephants even with him.

In passing, I would fain have gone ashore, to see if there were any remains of the celebrated temple of Paphos; but a voyage, such as I was then embarked on, stood in need of vows to Hercules rather than to Venus, and the master, fearing to lose his passage, determined to proceed.

Many medals (scarce any of them good) are dug up in Cyprus; silver ones, of very excellent workmanship, are found near Paphos, of little value in the eyes of antiquarians, being chiefly of towns, of the size of those found at Crete and Rhodes, and all the islands of the Archipelago. Intaglios there are a few, part in very excellent Greek style, and generally upon better stones than usual in the islands. I have seen some heads of Jupiter, remarkable for bushy hair and beard, that were of the most exquisite workmanship, worthy of any price. All the inhabitants of the island are subject to fevers, but more especially those in the neighbourhood of Paphos.

We left Lernica the 17th of June, about four o'clock in the afternoon.

Journal 1779

In 1784 an anonymous journal of 155 pages was printed in Horsham, England, by A. Lee and sold by J. F. and C. Rivington. *A Journal kept on a journey from Bassora to Bagdad over the little desert to Aleppo, Cyprus, Rhodes, Zante, Corfu, and Otranto, in Italy, in the year 1779 by a Gentleman, late an officer in the service of the Honourable East India Company* has been variously attributed to C. Eversfield or to Samuel Evers. The author arrived at Famagusta on June 30, 1799, and embarked on July 22, and finally cleared the island on July 28.

Friday, June 28.

Having procured a convenient boat to carry us over to Cyprus, we embarked this evening, and on the morning of the 29th got under way, and sailed out of the harbour; by noon we were in sight of the island of Cyprus, but the wind proving contrary, we were driven to the leeward of it, which obliged us to keep beating to windward the whole day, during which time several vessels passed us, bound for Latichea and the Syrian coast.

CYPRUS. *June 30.*

About sun-set we anchored off the town of Famagusta, formerly the capital of this island, when the Venetians had the possession of it, at which period it was a most beautiful flourishing city, and remarkable for its stately cathedral church, which at present is made use of as a Turkish mosque. The fortifications were certainly very strong and extensive, and maintained a siege of six months before the town surrendered to the Turks, who although it capitulated with the honours of war, cruelly caused the governor to be flead alive, and put the rest of the inhabitants to the sword.

This beautiful place, once so much admired, is now entirely neglected; its stately edifices are all in ruins, and inhabited by Greeks. The Turkish governor has his seat at the city of Nicosia, (now the metropolis) in the middle of the country. The European merchants who reside on this island, live at Larnica, a town about twenty miles distant from hence, which has a more convenient harbour, and is consequently better situated for traffic.

Thursday, July 1.

In the evening we weighed anchor, and sailed for Larnica, and arrived about noon of the 2d at the Marine, a mile distant from the town; we went immediately on shore, and being conducted to the consular-house, found Mr. Burford in a very indifferent state of health, and likewise learned that the consul Mr. Devezin had been seized that morning with a violent fever. He, however, soon came out to receive us, and gave us as kind and genteel a reception, as could be expected from a person in his situation, and we are all accommodated with lodgings at his house.

In the evening we paid a visit to Mr Rizzini, a merchant of this place, and brother to the Venetian consul of Aleppo, and also to the lady of the latter, who lives at present at the house of her brother Mr. Capara, the Venetian pro-consul. We met with a very polite reception, and found the lady sensible and accomplished; she was very agreeable in her person, but being an Italian, and of French education, she was very partial to their manners.

Saturday, July 3.

We set a-part this day to view the town, which consists of regular streets and fine houses, belonging to the consuls and merchants of different nations, and to the principal Greeks. Few of the Turks live in the town. It is by no means healthily situated, being surrounded by low lands and salt marshes, which considerably infect the air; these added to the heat of the climate, in the summer season, subject the inhabitants to continual fevers, that carry numbers of them off. Most part of the inhabitants of the island are Greeks, the lower class of whom are generally employed in tilling land, and dressing the vine-yards. The island produces great quantities of grapes, from which excellent wine is made, and sent to all parts of Europe. Great quantities of cotton are likewise cultivated here, which appears of a much finer quality than any I have ever seen in India. In short, the soil is exceedingly luxuriant, and the farmers would be immensely rich, but for the heavy taxes levied by the Porte, and the rapaciousness of the Turkish governors, who are continually plundering them, till they have reduced them to a state of wretched poverty. Our time, for about ten days, was spent in one continued scene of gaiety and amusement, at the different villas of the European gentlemen; but we now began to find our healths much impaired by the unwholesomeness of the climate, and every one of us were seized with a violent fever, which had such an effect on the head as to render us almost distracted. The doctors advising a change of air, we removed to a country house belonging to the Venetian consul, ten miles from Larnica, where we remained a few days, when, finding ourselves getting worse, we were obliged to return to the town for assistance. Every medical attempt to establish our health proving fruitless, it became necessary for us to leave the island as fast as possible, but a French frigate coming into the harbour, we were obliged to be very cautious about the mode of our departure, for fear of being made prisoners. We agreed with the captain of a Sclavonian vessel, bound to Venice, for the cabin of his ship, for which we were to pay sixty pounds sterling, which, though exorbitant, we joyfully gave. The French frigate sailing the next day for Acria, we shipped on board a proper quantity of provisions, and taking leave of our good and generous friends, who had shewn us so much civility during our stay on the island,—on the 22d, in the evening, we embarked on board the vessel, in very infirm states of health, and early the next morning sailed out of the harbour. Our situation on board was truly deplorable; we found a very dirty vessel, and so crouded with cotton bales upon deck, that we had not room to move ourselves; and to compleat our misfortune the captain and crew spoke a language we did not understand.

The island of Cyprus is situated on the most easterly part of the Mediterranean, sixty miles south of the coast of Caramania, and thirty west of Syria; and is supposed to have taken its name from the great number of Cyprus trees growing in the country. Its circumference is about 250 miles. The air of this country is for the most part hot and there are but few springs or rivers in the island, so that if the rains do not fall plentifully at the usual seasons, the inhabitants are much distressed by the scarcity of water. Ancient tradition says, the whole island was consecrated to Venus, and she is represented by the poets as taking a particular pleasure in visiting this country, and to have holden her court there. Be this as it may, very few of her representatives are there to be found at present. This island was conquered by Richard I. king of England, on his way to the Holy Land. The trade is considerable; their chief commodities, besides wine, are oil, cotton, salt, silk, and turpentine.—For some days past nothing particular has transpired. On the 28th we found we had compleatly weathered the island, and lost sight of land.

Sibthorp 1787

Dr. John Sibthorp (1758-1796), a respected botanist, earned four degrees at Oxford including an M.D. When his father resigned his professorship at Oxford, Sibthorp, though he was appointed in his father's place, went on to receive a doctor's degree from Gottingen, and then set out for Greece to determine the plants named by Dioscorides. He and Ferdinand Bauer, an artist who was to illustrate Sibthorp's works, traveled through Italy and spent the summer of 1786 in Crete, before proceeding to other islands, and finally to Constantinople. In March 1787 he sailed, stopping at islands and the coast of Asia Minor, to Cyprus where, for five weeks, he studied the fauna and flora. Disturbances in Greece prevented him from completing a study journey there, though he visited a few sites in 1787. After devoting himself to the preparation of a flora of Oxfordshire, he started again for Greece in March 1794 and spent a year gathering the information for his ten-volume publication *Flora Graeca*. He became ill on his return to England in 1795, and died the next year at the age of 38.

Sibthorp's following observations on Cyprus were reported in his unpublished papers, which Robert Walpole excerpted and published in *Memoirs Relating to European and Asiatic Turkey*, London: Longman, Hurst, Rees, Orme and Brown 1817, and in *Travels in Various Countries of the East*, by the same publisher in 1818.

Sibthorp's lists of flora and fauna in Cyprus, now superceded by modern scientific study, has been omitted. His other comments are included here as they appear in the two volumes of Walpole.

[Walpole, *Travels* pp. 13-27]

April 3.—Early in the morning we had a very distant view of Cyprus. Our sailors caught a small species of lark, the Alauda spinoletta of L., which probably lighted upon our vessel in its passage. We were becalmed in sight of Cyprus the whole of the next day. We shot the Charadrius spinosus flying near our ship; this singular bird Linnaeus makes mention of, as an inhabitant of Egypt; Wheler saw it in Greece. We caught also two species of Motacilla, the sylvia and trochilus of Linnaeus.

April 8.—We anchored in the bay of Larnaka in Cyprus; the consul being absent, we engaged lodgings at the house of Sr. Natali, an Italian, pleasantly situated on the beach at the Salines.

April 9.—I walked out to botanise, along the eastern coast, and returned by Livadia. The crops of corn had been much hurt by hail and a severe winter; the orange groves or gardens were quite destroyed.

April 10, 11.—I staid at home that my painter might have time to design the plants collected in my walk to Livadia, and several birds that were shot by a Chasseur whom we had employed as a guide. Our situation at the Salines was one of the most favourable in the island for the botanist and ornithologist. Several little pools invited a number of Grallae to its neighbourhood. Near Larnaka was one of considerable extent, and the salt lake was scarcely a mile distant. Cyprus, situated between Asia and Africa, partakes of the production of both; sometimes we noticed the birds and plants of Syria and Caramania; sometimes those of Egypt. Many of the Grallae we saw were probably birds of passage.

April 12.—We made an excursion to the mountain of the Holy Cross. We passed by the aqueduct of Larnaka, and after four hours ride over an uneven plain enlivened with varieties of the Ranunculus Asiaticus, now in flower, we dined under a carob tree. Several little rivulets crossed the road, skirted with the Oleander. These were frequented by the beautiful Merops apiaster, one of which we shot. Numerous Jack-daws burrowed in the holes of the free-stone rock near the rivulet; and the Roller, which after short flights pitched frequently before us, rivalled the Merops in the splendour of its colours. After dinner we lost our way in the mountains covered with the Pinus pinea; we arrived late at a hamlet belonging to the convent; and about one hour distant from it. The ascent was steep and difficult; and the sun set soon after our arrival. Disappointed at finding the convent quite deserted, and no habitation being near, we resolved upon attempting an entrance by force. The different instruments we had brought with us for digging were employed: but without success. At length a Caloyer arrived with the key, and having opened the door of the church, we discovered some straw mattresses; these were drawn before the altar, and we lay down to repose.

The mountain, a bluish grey argillaceous rock thinly covered with earth, furnished but few plants; a species of Astragalus, which I do not find mentioned by Linnaeus, called by the Greeks ἀγριόκυτζος, grew in abundance. I saw the Valeriana tuberosa, which is certainly the Mountain-nardus of Dioscorides, on the summit, with the Ziziphora capitata, and a species of Cucubalus and Thymus, neither of which I find described. On the walls of the convent I observed the golden Henbane growing plentifully.

April 13.—At eight we left the convent; the Pinus pinea was less frequent as we advanced in our descent. I observed a new species of Gladiolus, G. montanus, and Thymus tragoriganum, frequent. Arrived at the bottom, we stopped at a village to refresh ourselves; we then passed through a more level country covered with different species of Cistus, the Onosma Orientalis, and Lithospermum tenuiflorum. I observed among the scarcer plants the Brassica vesicaria and the Salvia ceratophylloides. Swarms of locusts in their larva state often blackened the road with their numbers, and threatened destruction to the crops of corn now almost ripe. Near the aqueduct we observed several hawks hunting in troops; Falco tinnunculus was the most frequent species in the island, called by the Greeks κύτζος. We shot two other species; one with a blue tail, named Mavromati, and another, something like a buzzard, called a φαλκόνι.

April 17.—We set off at eight in the morning for Famagusta; after riding four hours through a rising plain we reached Armidia, a village pleasantly situated about half a mile from the sea. Near the roadside I observed the Scabiosa prolifera, and a species of Arum, unnoticed by Linnaeus, called by the Greeks ἀγριοκολοκάσια, and a rare species of Linum with a red flower, the Linum viscosum of Linnaeus. The low hills round Armidia were covered with the Cistus incanus now in flower. On the beach I gathered the Scorzonera Tingitana and a new species of Geranium. We shot also a bird of the Gralla kind, the Haematopus ostralegus of L. After a ride of four hours over an extensive plain, we reached at sunset a small convent in the outskirts of Famagusta.

April 18.—Early in the morning we walked to Famagusta, a melancholy place now almost depopulated: in the time of the Venetians the fairest city in the island; and renowned for the brave defence they made in it against the infidels. The lines of the fortification which are very considerable are still sufficient to show the extent and former strength of this place: they are now suffered by the Turks to moulder away in ruins. Some cannon, with the arms of Venice, were lying dismounted on the ramparts; the Lieutenant of the fortress pointed to them with an air of triumph. In the enceinte grew among the rubbish the Aloe vera, the Iris Germanica, and Florentina in great abundance. Leaving the fortress we passed through the streets now deserted, a melancholy picture of Turkish desolation; the gateway by which we returned to the convent was paved with cannon balls. At noon after a ride of five hours we arrived at Upsera. About a mile from Famagusta, we observed some small lakes to our right and left: these were frequented by different species of Grallae: we had shot the Ardea alba, which flew over the convent, in the morning. The desolation we had observed at Famagusta extended itself along the country we now traversed. We passed by the mouldering ruins of several Greek villages, and slept at a Greek cottage at Upsera. This like other villages we had passed seemed by the desertion of its inhabitants to be hastening to ruin: it was pleasantly situated on the side of a hill: a fertile vale stretched beneath it, bounded by the approaching mountains of Antiphoniti.

April 19.—At eight in the morning we left Upsera, and passing through the vale below, gradually ascended into the mountain of Antiphoniti. At noon we arrived at the convent, most romantically situated, having a view of the sea and a distant sight of the high land of Caramania. I was come here on the authority of Pococke to see the Lignum Rhodium; this the Greeks call Xylon Effendi. The Hegoumenos of the convent, a very old man, offered himself as my conductor, and leading me a few paces below the convent into a garden now covered with rubbish, pointed out a tree which on examination I found to be the Liquidambar Styraciflua. The trunk of it was much hacked, and different bits had been carried off by the curious and superstitious, as an ornament to their cabinets and churches. This was probably the same tree that Pococke had seen. To ascertain the Lignum Rhodium has been much wished by the naturalists. An American tree growing in the swamps of Virginia seems to have little claim to be considered as that which should produce it. The name of Xylon Effendi and the tradition of the convent testify the reputation in which this tree had long been held in the island; it was probably at first introduced by the Venetians during their possession of it. I could not discover, either from observation or enquiry, that it was to be found in any other part of Cyprus; nor do I recollect that the

Styrax liquidambar has been mentioned by any botanist as an oriental tree. Whether the Lignum Rhodium of the shops is the wood of this tree, or not, I am doubtful; the Aspalathus primus of Dioscorides I think is certainly the Lignum Rhodium of the ancients; he describes it as a thorny shrub, probably a species of Spartium, which the Cypriotes still call Aspalathi; his Aspalathus secundus, which also grows in the island, is certainly the Spartium spinosum. The Pinus pinea, the Cypress, the Andrachne are the principal trees that grow in this mountainous track. In the crevices of the rocks I found a few curious plants. Scutellaria peregrina, Ononis Ornithopodioides, Polygala Monsp.; and a species of Valeriana with an undivided leaf, which seems distinct from Val. Calcitrapa. In the environs of the cloister we shot two species of Loxia; one which I have called L. Varia; the other L. Cinerea.

April 20.—At eleven we left the convent of Antiphoniti and descended the mountain to the sea-coast. In our journey I observed the Papaver somniferum with a small blue flower growing in great abundance: the plant which we find sometimes in waste ground and in corn-fields in England has probably escaped there from the garden. We now coasted along the shore, rocky, and much indented. I here observed several curious plants, Arenaria Cerignensis, Scabiosa Cerignensis, Cheiranthus littoreus, Teucrium Creticum.

Leaving the shore, we entered into a more difficult tract of country called Bel Paese; a ridge of mountains running from north to south, terminated in some rising hills, which, sloping towards the sea, were richly cultivated with corn. Near Cerignes, where we arrived rather late in the evening, I discovered a beautiful species of Salvia, S. Cerignensis.

April 21.—Having employed the morning in drawing, and putting our plants in paper; we rode out after dinner to the monastery of Lapasis, a fine remain of an old Gothic structure. In the court below was a sarcophagus; but of bad workmanship. We were told, that on the summit of the mountains to the left of Lapasis were the ruins of an ancient temple: our guides who had excited our curiosity refused to satisfy it, by risking their mules on the steep road which led to them. Captain E. and myself attempted on foot to reach the summit of this distant mountain. The sun shone with uncommon force; nor did the least breeze mitigate the fervour of its rays. After a very hot and fruitless walk, we came back, finding the summit too distant to reach it, and return before night. We joined our companions at the monastery of Lapasis, situated in a beautiful recess, surrounded by corn-fields and vineyards, and shaded by trees, whose foliage is kept green by several purling rills, that watered the environs of this romantic spot. I collected a few plants in this excursion: the Hedysarum saxatile grew on the mountain; and the Styrax officinale was frequent in the hedges near the monastery.

April 22.—We left Cerignes at nine, a paltry town with a port, which carries on a small commerce with Caramania: we passed the mountains of Bel Paese by a narrow defile; on the sides of which grew the Moluccella fruticosa; descending, we entered the plains of Messaria; and about two arrived at Nicosia. On the mountains we observed several large birds which our guides told us were Eagles, Ἀετόι; I was not so fortunate as to procure one of them during my stay in the island, but from their flight I should suppose them to be Vultures; near Nicosia, I observed the Salvia Argentea. In the evening, we visited a small convent of Spanish friars, under the protection of France and Spain; and slept at the house of the Danish dragoman, for whom we had brought a letter.

April 23.—The governor of the island being informed of my arrival, sent a message, that he wished to see me; he was a venerable old Turk, with no other complaint than that of age, and its companion, debility and loss of appetite. He received me with great politeness: our ambassador, Sir R. Ainslie, had procured me letters for him. Having felt his pulse, and prescribed for his complaint, he offered us his firman; and ordered his dragoman to prepare a magnificent dinner. A Gazelle, a species of Capra called by the Greeks Αγρεινο, was brought to me for my painter to take a drawing of. I was assured it was an inhabitant of Mount Troas; though this animal had been sent to the Governor as a present from the coast of Syria. There was nothing in the palace which indicated the magnificence and dignity of the Governor of so large and rich an island; but unfortunately for Cyprus, it is the appanage of the Grand Vizier; who obliges the Governor by measures the most oppressive to remit an annual revenue much exceeding the force and strength of its inhabitants under the present distressing circumstances. The poor Greeks pay a charatch of forty or fifty piastres; and annual emigrations of large numbers are the consequence of this oppressive despotism. The Greeks have at first, perhaps, from necessity been induced to practise some low tricks of lying and knavery; and from frequent repetition these may at length have become habitual among many of them. One of our guides had secretly made an agreement with a Turk, that two of our horses should carry his corn to Larnaka; tempted to this dishonest proceeding with the hopes of gaining a few paras. Had I mentioned the circumstance to the Governor, the poor fellow would have lost his head; I hinted it only to the dragoman, who immediately sent an officer to inform him, he should answer for his conduct in the most exemplary manner, in case of any further complaint from us. The fellow frightened became, from the most obstinate, the most docile creature in the world on our journey to Mount Troas.

Our dinner was served after the Turkish fashion; a great variety of dishes well dressed, gave us a favourable idea of the Turkish cookery, and the Governor's hospitality. I had counted thirty-six, when the dragoman made us an apology for the badness of the dinner; and that he had not assistance enough to prepare it. The Governor expressed an anxious wish that I should see the medicine prepared, which I had prescribed for him, expressing a great want of confidence in his physician at Larnaka. Upon my making my promise to him, and wishing that it might relieve him, all the persons in waiting exclaimed, Ish-Allah. It was late when we left Nicosia, and after eight hours we arrived at our lodgings at the Salines.

April 27.—We set out on an excursion to Mount Troas. Leaving the Salines of Larnaka, we passed through a vale in which were some ruins at a place called Cetti; being alarmed at the appearance of a thunder storm, we stopped at a small village, Magado, to dine, four hours from Larnaca. In our way to Mouni, I observed the Linum Nodiflorum, and shot a beautiful species of Fringilla with a yellow breast, and a black head, called by the Greeks Σκάρθαλις. This bird sings delightfully, rivalling the Nightingale in its note; we observed it frequently in the evening perched on the top of some bush or tree.

April 28.—We left Mouni eleven hours from Larnaka, and after four hours' ride arrived at Limesol. On the road we passed the ruins of the ancient Amathus; I observed the Scabiosa Syriaca growing among the corn, and on the sea-sand a species of Anchusa. Limesol is an inconsiderable town, frequented only on account of its corn, and the neighbourhood to the vineyards of La Commandería. The bay is deeper than that of Larnaka, and ships approach nearer the shore to take in their lading. Our vice-consul, a Greek, treated us handsomely; and uncommon for a Greek, lodged us in his house without making a bill. At Nicosia, the Danish dragoman brought in a most shameful charge for a supper, to which he himself had invited us. We here found our companion Mr Hawkins, who had been to Soulea and the Panagía of Cicci.

April 29.—At seven we left Limesol; having travelled two hours in a plain, we passed a little rivulet; the country was covered with Cistus and Mastic; among these we heard the frequent call of the Francoline. Having crossed the rivulet, we entered into a wild mountainous country, and stopped to dine at a Turkish fountain, five hours from Limesol. After dinner, we soon entered into a more cultivated district: the sides of the hills were planted with vineyards; little brooks watered the vales below, which were sown with corn, yet green. The mountains of Troados covered with the Pinus pinea stretched themselves out, and terminated the vale. I observed the Styrax tree frequent in the hedges; and the Anagyris foetida in the outskirts of the villages. At sun-set we arrived at the convent of the Holy Cross: this is regarded as the second monastery in the island, and was probably more flourishing under the pious care of Maria Theresa. It is situated in a Greek village, where we observed an appearance of greater affluence than in most of those we had yet seen. Mountains are indeed generally the last retreats of liberty.

April 30.—At seven we set off from the convent of the Holy Cross for Troados. Our road led us through a steep tract of country, well wooded. The Pinus pinea, the Quercus Ilex, and Arbutus Andrachne covered the higher part of the mountain; in the vales below grew the plane, the Cretan maple, the black poplar, the white willow, and the alder. After two hours of very difficult road, we arrived at the convent of Troados; a Greek Papas, whom we had taken as a guide to conduct us to the snow on the summit of the mountain, brought us to this miserable cloister. As we were now told it was impossible to reach the snow, and return, we passed our day with much disappointment at the convent. I picked up but few plants: Smyrnium perfoliatum, Imperatoria Ostruthium, Alyssum campestre, Cheiranthus Cyprius; and among the rocks, Euphorbia Myrsinites, and Turritis glabra. We discovered the jay by hoarse screams, hopping among the branches of the Pinus pinea; and we shot the Parus ater, picking the buds of the fruit-trees below the convent; and the Muscicapa atricapilla busily employed in catching the flies.

May 1.—Having taken a goatherd for our guide, at seven we began our ascent from the convent. After two hours' climbing with our mules over steep and dangerous precipices, we arrived at the summit, where we found a small quantity of snow lying on the north-east side: the pine-tree and the cypress grew on the heights with the Cretan Berbery. The mountain, composed of grünstein, with large pieces of hornblend, and but slightly covered with earth, disappointed my botanical expectations. A species of Fumaria, an Arabis, A. purpurea, with the Crocus vernus growing near the snow, were almost all the plants I observed on the mountain. We now descended rapidly over rocks of serpentine veined with amianth, and in three hours arrived at the bottom. The trunks of the old pine-trees were covered with the Lichen purpuraceus.

We now entered the vale of Soulea, the most beautiful we had yet seen in the island; well watered and richly cultivated. Green meadows contrasted with the corn now ripe, hamlets shaded with mulberry-trees, and healthy peasantry busily employed with their harvest, and the care of their silk-worms, enlivened the scenery. Having travelled two hours in this delightful vale, I stopped at a Greek village. My guide conducted me to the house of the Papás; a bed was prepared for me in the vacant part of a chamber, where silk-worms were kept. In a little morass, in passing through the vale, I had picked up the Lobelia setacea, and Pinguicula crystallina. My draughtsman stopping to sketch these plants was the cause of my losing my companion, who slept at a neighbouring monastery.

May 2.—We left the village at six; the country now became more barren; the hills were covered with the Cistus Creticus, from which they collect the Ladanum: some land was sown with corn; but this was almost devoured by the locusts, which had now their wings, and flew in swarms destroying every green plant. No vegetable escaped their ravages, except some prickly cartilaginous plants of the thistle tribe. After five hours we arrived at Peristeroani, where I found my companions waiting for me. I had collected some grasses in my road; Poa aurea, Cynosurus durus, and Avena Cypria. Leaving Peristeroani, we travelled over a plain for five hours, and at sun-set arrived at the convent of the Archangel, at a small distance from Nicosia. Near the convent I observed the coriander and the garden-cress growing wild among the corn.

May 3.—At seven we left the convent of the Archangel, and after a ride of eight hours through an undulated plain arrived at our lodgings at the Salines; near Agios Georgios we observed immense beds of petrified oysters, Pectines and Balani. Our chasseur shot a very rare bird of the Tetrao kind, T. Alchata, called by the Greeks παρδαλός. This is a bird of passage, visiting the island in the spring and retiring in the autumn. We shot also on this plain the stone curlew, Charadrius Oedicnemus.

May 8.—At six in the evening, embarked on board the Providence, a small vessel, for Rhodes . . .

May 11.—We anchored about eight in the morning, about five miles to the east of Bafo. The town now presents a melancholy ruin; few of the houses being inhabited. In walking through it, we entered the inclosure of a modern Greek church, where we discovered three pillars of the most beautiful Egyptian granite: at four feet from the ground they measured ten feet four inches in circumference; and from the present surface, which evidently had been much raised, fifteen feet in height. At the distance of about forty yards were two smaller pillars; one of them was fluted. This was probably the site of an ancient temple of Venus: near it stood the ruins of a small Gothic chapel, probably Venetian. From Bafo we passed over some fields to a beautiful village called Iftinia, where the Governor of the district resided. We produced our firman; and his dragoman, full of promises, offered his services. The bishop, who had been informed of my arrival, wished to consult me. Like the Governor, I found him with no other complaint than that of old age and a weakened vis vitae. We were offered pipes, and entertained with coffee, liqueurs, and perfumes. From Iftinia we walked to what our guide called the Diamond Hill: these diamonds we found to be nothing but common quartz crystal. Hence we descended to the beach, to some ruins under ground. We found there several buildings; and from the architecture we were led to suppose them catacombs, or repositories for the dead. They occupied a very considerable tract of ground; and offer a curious and interesting field of research to the antiquary. On removing some stones I discovered two species of lizards; the Lacerta Chalcides, and Lacerta Turcica: on the sand I observed the Sea Eryngo, the Sea Samphire, and the Prickly Cichorium: the Silene fruticosa, the Cyclamen Cyprium, and the Ruta graveolens grew on the rocks: on the road from Bafo to Iftinia, and upon rubbish ground on the outskirts of the town, the Aloe vera, the Sempervivum arboreum, and the Physalis somnifera: the Galium Cyprium on the diamond rocks: the Crucianella Ægyptiaca, the Teucrium pseudo-chamedrys, and the Teucrium pseudo-polium on the plain below. It was late when I returned to the ship, where I found a Turk, to whom I had offered a suitable reward, waiting for me, with a specimen of the formidable Κούφι.

May 12.—We went on shore, and after waiting three hours at Iftinia for horses, set off at eleven on an excursion to Fontana Amorosa. Riding three hours through a fine cultivated corn country we crossed a rivulet, and dined under an olive tree; among the corn I had observed the Bupleurum semicompositum and Ruta linifolia. After dinner our road led us over a rough steep mountain whose sides were cultivated with corn; we then traversed a stony plain, and in three hours' time arrived at a large Greek village. We now descended towards the beach, having a view of the distant coast of Caramania. The Cistus Monspeliensis was frequent on different parts of the road: the leaves of this species are used by the Cypriots as a substitute for the Mulberry leaf: we met frequently with peasants conveying home horse loads of this plant for their silk-worms. After riding for some time in the dark, we arrived at Poli; the Aga of the village, a venerable man, received us with much politeness, and having spread before us a frugal repast of Yaourt and rice milk, he left us and retired to his harem.

May 13.—At six we set out for Fontana Amorosa, which our guides informed us was little more than an hour distant from Poli. We descended towards the coast; and passing near the shore by a narrow and difficult road, and having turned a considerable mountain, arrived in four hours at a small spring: this we were informed was the famous Fontana Amorosa, which had so greatly excited our curiosity. Among the stones of a ruined village we observed the Lacerta Stellio, the same which Tournefort had found among the ruins of Delos; and on the sides of the mountain I gathered the Centaurea Behen, and the Cynara acaulis, and the Thapsia foeniculifolia; and under the shade of some trees hanging over a rivulet the Osmunda Cypria. Our guides, who had contrived to mislead us, after eight hours brought us back to Poli; they now refused to set forward for Bafo, alleging, their horses were tired. The Aga of Poli was absent when we came back: and a black slave supposing us hungry brought a bundle of bean stalks, and threw them down before us, saying, *there* was something to eat. As we had promised our captain to return, we continued our journey with our guides. The little owl, Strix Passerina, hooted mournfully among the rocks; and at sun set, we were left in an unknown and dangerous country. We arrived at a Greek village about an hour from Poli in the dusk of the evening; and the Papas having furnished us with a guide, we travelled all night, and reached the shore of Bafo at daybreak.

May 14.—We embarked at six in the morning.

[Walpole, *Memoirs* pp. 77-83]

We find in Cyprus a much smaller number of quadrupeds than we should expect from the size of the island. The domestic animals, if we except the camel, are nearly the same as those of Crete, and the other Greek islands; and its wild quadrupeds, when compared with the neighbouring coast of Asia, are very few. It possesses neither the lynx, nor the wolf, nor the jackall, inhabitants of the opposite shore of Caramania; and the weasel tribe is wholly wanting, of which we find some species in Crete. The wild boar inhabits Cape Gatto, and the Gazella, the higher parts of Mount Troados. Hares are scarce, and seem to confine themselves to the mountainous tracts of the island. The hedge-hog, I was also informed, was an inhabitant. The large bat was mentioned, but I only found the common species. Asses, I heard on good authority, were found in a wild state at Carpaso, and that it was permitted to any person to hunt them; but that, when caught, they were of little value, it being almost impossible, from their natural obstinacy, to domesticate them.

The naturalist, disappointed in finding so small a number of quadrupeds, is surprised on observing the great variety of birds which migrate to Cyprus at different seasons of the year. The birds of the thrush tribe, inhabitants of the northern climates, visit it only during the depth of winter. At the first appearance of spring they retire to the higher mountains of Caramania, where, the snow preserving a constant humidity, they find food and a proper habitation. Great numbers of Grallae pass over in the spring from Egypt and Syria; these retreat further, in proportion as the salt pools near Larnica are evaporated by the sun. The Francolin and red partridge reside throughout the year; the Pardalos and the quail visit the island in the spring, and retire in the autumn. Immense flights of ortolans appear about the time of the vintage; these are taken in great quantities, preserved in vinegar, and exported as an object of commerce. The swallow, the martin, the swift, the Melba, the Pratincola, which frequent in numbers the pools in Larnica, visit also the island in spring and leave it in the autumn. Those large birds which frequent the higher regions of Troados, called by the inhabitants Ἀετοι, I should suppose from their flight to be a species of vulture. The Falco Tinnunculus breeds here, but the difficulty of procuring the birds of this tribe prevented me from ascertaining the number of species with more precision. The raven, the hooded crow, the jackdaw, the magpye, are common. The jay is found but rarely in the pine-woods of Troados. The little owl, though a nocturnal bird, flies frequently by day among the rocks. The great horned owl, which I did not see, is found in the mountainous parts of the island. The roller, the bee-bird, and the oriole are not uncommon; and we often heard the hoopoe and the cuckow. I observed the rock-pigeon on the cliffs in the western extremity of the island: the wood-pigeon and the turtle-dove in the groves of Bel-paese. The Calandra and the Crested lark are the most common species of the lark tribe, and these inhabit the island probably throughout the year. The two species of Lanius confine themselves to the pine-woods, with the black titmouse. Different species of the Motacilla are confounded under the general name of Beccafica. Of the Fringilla tribe, the house-sparrow is the most numerous; and the beautiful Scarthalis, perhaps the Fringilla flaveola of Linnaeus, rivals the nightingale in the charms of its song, and is sometimes confounded with it under the general name of Ἀηδόνι. Among the domestic birds, I observed a few turkeys in the convent of the Archangel; geese and ducks are kept, but not in great numbers. Fowls and pigeons are the principal domestic birds. During my stay in the island, I used every possible means to procure its birds, and succeeded in obtaining the greater part of them. Of the rarer species of these my drafts-man has taken drawings. I have been also fortunate in procuring most of the Greek names: but it is much to be regretted that Cyprus has hitherto wanted an ornithologist, who being stationary here might observe with more exactness the migration of the differ-ent birds of the Levant.

On observing the list of amphibia, we are surprised at finding the Testudo Caretta, mentioned by Linnaeus as an inhabitant of the West India islands, and no notice of the Testudo Aquatilis common through Greece and Asia Minor. The genus Coluber and Lac-erta are both rich in the number of their species; of these, fortunately for the island, the Κούφι is the only venemous species. The black snake, whose colour is indeed suspic-ious, is perfectly harmless, and I was informed by the physician of Larnica, that among the country people it is even an object of affection; that they suffer it to twist and twine itself in the hair round the heads of their children, as a remedy for the Tinea capitis. I searched in vain for the Lacerta aurea, said by Linnaeus to be the inhabitant of Cyprus; but I am perfectly convinced from a very attentive inquiry after the tribe, that it is not to be found in the island; an inaccuracy in the information of the collectors must probably have led Linnaeus into this mistake. The Testudo Caretta is not only an inhabitant of the Cyprian sea, but is the most common species in the Mediterranean, and the Lacerta aurea is not an inhabitant of Cyprus, but of the south of France, Germany, and Italy. Of the six species of Coluber which we find in the island, I can scarcely refer any of them to the Linnaean species.

The classical ichthyologist receives a particular pleasure from comparing the modern Greek names of the Cyprian fishes with those of Oppian, Aristotle and other writers. The Scarus, which the Swedish naturalist affirms to be *piscis hodie obscurus,* is known to every Cyprian boy. Belon, guided by the Cretan fishermen, found it on the rocky shores of Crete. These fishermen are much better commentators on the Greek ich-thyologists than their learned editors, who, by their unfortunate conjectures, more fre-quently confuse than clear a doubtful text. The striking agreement of the modern Greek names with those of ancient Greece is nowhere so evident as in Cyprus. Here we still find the words Μόρμυρος, σπάρος, σκάρος, σαργός, σάλπα, μελάνουρος, πέρκα, όρφος, and others, precisely the ancient names of Oppian and Aristotle. They are very properly re-tained by Linnaeus for trivial names. The shores of Cyprus receive a great number of Mediterranean fishes; some of these confine themselves to its rocks, and seldom emigrate into more northern latitudes. In river fish, it is, as we should expect to find it, deficient; the rivulets few in number, and inconsiderable in their size, generally dried up in summer, do not lead us to expect a large catalogue of river fish: and upon repeated inquiries I found that the eel was their only inhabitant. My list of Grecian fishes was already very considerable when I arrived at Cyprus; the market of Constantinople had furnished me with those of the Thracian Bosphorus and the sea of Marmora. I had still, however, hopes of discovering some other species in the more southern latitude of the Mediterranean. Cyprus did not deceive my expectation: I added several species of Labrus and Sparus to my collection, among these the Labrus Cretensis, which, from its more vivid colours, and the superior elegance of its figure, carries off the palm of beauty from the L. Iulis, cited by Linnaeus as *Europaeorum facile pulcherrimus.*

The greater number of the Grecian islands have been examined by a botanist of the distinguished merit of Tournefort. Cyprus, from its situation and its size, gives us reason to expect a peculiarity as well as a variety in its vegetables, and it is with surprise that we find an island so interesting in its natural productions has been little examined. Hasselquist visited it on his return from Egypt, at a season of the year when its annual plants, which form the greater number of its vegetables, were burnt up by the summer sun; and Pococke, a better antiquary than botanist, has given us only a scanty account of some of them. A view of its Flora, and comparison of the modern and popular uses of the plants with those of ancient Greece, gave me hopes in an island so near to Caramania, the native country of Dioscorides, of ascertaining several of the more obscure plants of this author. My expectations have in some measure succeeded; the modern names, though greatly corrupted, still retain sufficient resemblance to those of ancient Greece, to enable us to determine many plants with certainty; and the superstitious and popular uses of many still remain the same. My inquiries were frequent among the Greek peasants, and the different priests whom we met. From the physician of Larnica I collected some information relative to their medical uses.

I crossed the island in different directions. Cyprus, though possessing several of the Egyptian and Syrian plants, yet, from the scarcity of water, the great heat of the sun, and the thin surface which covers the upper regions of the mountains, can scarcely be considered as rich in plants; and when compared with Crete must appear even poor: the sides of whose mountains, those for instance of Ida and Sphakia, are watered with streams supplied from the perpetual snows that crown their summits. Notwithstanding the character of woody given to it by Strabo, when measured by a northern eye, accustomed to the extensive woods of oak and beech that we find in some parts of England, or the sombre pine-forests of Switzerland, Cyprus appears to have little claim to the appellation of woody. The higher regions of Troados are covered with the Pinus Pinea; this, mixed with the Ilex, and some trees scattered here and there in the valley below of the Quercus Ægilops, are the only trees that can be regarded as proper for timber. The carob, the olive, the Andrachne, the Terebinthus, the lentisc, the kermes oak, the Storax, the cypress, and oriental plane, furnish not only fuel in abundance for the inhabitants, but sufficient to supply, in some degree, those of Egypt.

[Walpole, *Memoirs* pp. 284-285]

The Ferula, or νάρθηξ of Prometheus.

Near the convent of the Holy Cross I observed the golden Henbane in abundance: and when we had descended, a peasant brought me a pumpkin with water; it was corked with a bush of Poterium Spinosum, which served both as a coverlid and a strainer, and prevented the entrance of flies and other insects. It preserves in most of the Greek islands its ancient name Στόιβη. The stools on which we sate were made of the Ferula Graeca; the stems cut into slips and placed crossways were nailed together. This is one of the most important plants of the island in respect to its economical uses. The stalks furnish the poorer Cyprian with a great part of his household furniture, and the pith is used instead of tinder, for conveying fire from one place to another. It is now called νάρθηκα, the ancient name somewhat corrupted.

Κούφι of Cyprus. An veterum Aspis?

The reapers were busy in the harvest, and the tinkling of the bell fixed to their sides expressed their fears of the terrible Κούφι. A monk of Famagousta has the reputation of preventing the fatal effects of the venom of this serpent by incantation; and from the credulity of the people had gained a sort of universal credit through the island. We were frequently shewn as precious stones compositions fabricated by artful Jews; these were said to be taken out of the head of the Κούφι; and were worn as amulets to protect the wearers from the bite of venomous animals.

Carlyle 1800

Joseph Dacre Carlyle (1759-1804), an Arabic scholar and Cambridge professor, accompanied Lord Elgin's mission to Constantinople in 1799 as chaplain. He toured Asia Minor, Palestine, Greece and Italy with stops in Cyprus in February and October 1800. A book of his poetry, *Poems Suggested Chiefly by Scenes in Asia Minor, Syria and Greece*, was published in 1805 after his death by W. Bulmer for J. White, London, but the excerpts here about Cyprus are from his letters to the Lord Bishop of Lincoln published by Robert Walpole in *Memoirs Relating to European and Asiatic Turkey*, London: Longman, Hurst, Rees, Orme and Brown, 1817.

[Walpole, *Memoirs,* p. 154]

The isle in which we now are seems to have suffered less from the blighting influence of Turkish power than most other parts of the empire, but I cannot think that it contains at present one-fourth of the inhabitants it is capable of supporting, and I fear these are rapidly diminishing in number.

[Walpole, *Memoirs,* p. 168]

Upon quitting Cyprus, where the plague raged violently, the Greek captain of our little vessel was seized, as all on board believed, with the disorder; for two days in which we were shut up with him in the skiff, we expected his death every moment; he however recovered, and providentially no one else caught the contagion. I confess, my Lord, I have been much disappointed in being thus obliged to give up a favorite scheme, from which I had expected considerable instruction, and for which I had taken some pains to prepare myself.

Leake 1800

Colonel William Martin Leake (1777-1860), who studied and wrote extensively on the antiquities and topography of Greece, made a brief trip across Cyprus and back in 1800. It is recorded in *Journal of a Tour in Asia Minor with Comparative Remarks on the Ancient and Modern Geography of that Country,* London: John Murray, 1824.

CHAPTER III.
CONTINUATION OF THE JOURNEY FROM KóNIA.

. . . Feb. 11.—We land this forenoon at Tzerína, called by the Italians Cerina, and by the Turks Ghirne. It is a small town with a Venetian fortification, and a bad port on the northern coast of Cyprus; it is reckoned by the Greek sailors to be eighty miles from Kelénderi, but is probably less than sixty English. The town is situated amidst plantations of oranges, lemons, olives, dates, and other fruit-trees; and all the uncultivated parts of the plains around are covered with bay, myrtle, and lentisk. On the west side of the town are extensive quarries, among which are some catacombs, the only remains of the ancient Ceryneia. The harbour, bad and small as it is, must, upon a coast very deficient in maritime shelter, have always ensured to the position a certain degree of importance. The natural formation of the eastern part of the north side of Cyprus is very singular: it consists of a high rugged ridge of steep rocks, running in a straight line from east to west, which descend abruptly on the south side into the great plain of Lefkosía, and terminate to the north in a narrow plain bordering the coast. Upon several of the rocky summits of the ridge are castles which seem almost inaccessible. The slope and maritime plain at the foot of the rocks, on the north, possess the finest soil and climate, with a plentiful supply of water; it is one of the most beautiful and best cultivated districts I have seen in Turkey.

Feb. 12.—Finding it impossible to procure horses in time to enable us to reach the gates of Lefkosía before sunset, at which time they are shut, we are under the necessity of remaining at Tzerína to-day. I visit a large ruined monastery, in a delightful situation, not far to the eastward of Tzerína, at no great distance from the sea. It contains the remains of a handsome Gothic chapel and hall, and bears a great resemblance to the ruins of an English abbey.

Feb. 13.—From Tzerína to Lefkosía, six hours. At the back of Tzerína the road passes through a natural opening in the great wall of rock I have already described, and descends into the extensive plain of Lefkosía. This is in some places rocky and barren, and is little cultivated even where the soil is good. Like most of the plains of Greece, it is marshy in the winter and spring, and unhealthy in the summer. On the west and south are the mountains which occupy all that part of the island, and the slopes of which produce the wines exported in so large a quantity from Cyprus to all the neighbouring coasts. In the centre of the plain is Lefkosía (Λευκοσία), called Nicosia by the Italians, the capital of the island and of the province of Itshili, of which Cyprus is considered a part, though the government is now always administered, like that of the other Greek islands, by a deputy of the Capudán Pasha. The ramparts of the Venetian fortifications of Lefkosía exist in tolerable preservation; but the ditch is filled up, and there is no appearance of there ever having been a covert way. There are thirteen bastions: the ramparts are lofty and solid, with orillons and retired flanks. In the town is a large church converted into a mosque, and still bearing, like the great mosque at Constantinople, the Greek name of St. Sophia: it is said to have been built by Justinian; but this may be doubted, as Procopius, in his work on the edifices of that emperor, makes no mention of it; and its Gothic style seems rather to mark it for the work of one of the Frank kings of Cyprus. The flat roofs, trellised windows, and light balconies of the better order of houses, situated as they are in the midst of gardens of oranges and lemons, give, together with the fortifications, a respectable and picturesque appearance to Lefkosía at a little distance, but, upon entering it, the narrow dirty streets, and miserable habitations of the lower classes, make a very different impression upon the traveller; and the sickly countenances of the inhabitants sufficiently show the unhealthiness of the climate. At Lefkosía we were very hospitably entertained by an Armenian merchant, of the name of Sarkís, who is an English baratli, and under that protection has amassed a considerable property, and lives in splendour; he and his relations seem to occupy all the principal offices of the island held by Christians, such as those of interpreter and banker to the Motselim, or deputy of the Capudán Pasha, of collector of the contributions of the Christians, of head of the Christian community, &c.

Feb. 14.—From Lefkosía to Lárnaka, eight hours. The first half of the distance was a continuation of the same plain as before; the remainder lay over rugged hills of soft limestone, among which we cross some long ridges of selenite. At Lárnaka we found Sir Sidney Smith with his small squadron: he had just signed a treaty for the evacuation of Egypt by the French.

Feb. 15.—We pass the day on board the Tigre, where we find General Junot, afterwards Duke of Abrantes, and Madame Junot and General Dupuy: the latter, next to Kleber, the senior general of the army of Egypt. They were taken by the Theseus, Captain Styles, in attempting to escape from Alexandria.

The town of Lárnaka stands at the distance of a mile from the shore, and has a quarter on the seaside, called Ἁλικαίς by the Greeks, and Marina by the Italians. In the intermediate space are many foundations of ancient walls, and other remains, among the gardens and inclosures. The stones are removed for building materials as quickly as they are discovered; but the great extent of these vestiges, and the numerous antiquities which at different times have been found here, seem to leave little doubt that here stood Citium, the most ancient and important city in this part of Cyprus.

March 2.—After having remained several days at Lárnaka and Lefkosía, we arrive to-day at Tzerína, on our return to Constantinople. The purity of the air on the north coast of Cyprus is very sensibly perceived, after leaving the interior plains and the unhealthy situation of Lárnaka. The Turkish troops are already arriving in large bodies, on their way home, in the faith that the war of Egypt is concluded.

Wittman 1800

In 1798 the British government sent a military team, part by land and part by sea, to Constantinople to assist the Turks in their conflict with France. William Wittman, M.D., of the Royal Artillery and a member of the Royal College of Surgeons in London, was assigned to this British military mission acting with the army of the Grand Vizier. He sailed from England on the transport ship the New Adventure in early April 1799. After a celebration of the King's birthday hosted by Lord Elgin, the British ambassador, the mission left Constantinople to join the Turkish army. After many stops, they came within sight of Cyprus on May 26, 1800. This excerpt is from Wittman's *Travels in Turkey, Asia-Minor, Syria, and across the Desert into Egypt during the years 1799, 1800, and 1801, in company with the Turkish Army, and the British Military Mission*, London: Richard Phillips, 1803.

[p. 115]

On the 25th we had light winds from the south-east, the weather being at the same time extremely warm. We expected to make Cyprus in the course of the day, but were disappointed. When the evening came on, we had nearly lost sight of the land, which we afterwards contrived to approach, and passed Cassel de Roso during the night.

On the morning of the 26th the land was out of sight, and we were nearly becalmed; but a gentle north-west breeze springing up at noon, we were shortly after enabled to descry the land, which was, however, at a great distance from us. In the course of the afternoon we saw several strange sail, one of which, an English snow, bound to Rhodes, hoisted her colours. At five o'clock we perceived the low land of Cyprus.

At eight in the morning of the 27th, we were close in with Cape Biancho, steering with a light breeze for Limesol, in Cyprus: at noon we came to anchor in seven fathom water off that place, which had a pleasing appearance from the ship. We were informed that the inhabitants of Limesol were free from the plague; but that at Nicosia, situated in another part of the island, it was then making great ravages, insomuch that fifty individuals perished daily. It was agreed that we should make a short stay here, to take in ballast, and recruit our stock of provisions.

On the 28th we went on shore early, and paid a morning's visit to the consul of Limesol, Signor Demetrio Nicolo Frankuli, with whom we dined, and afterwards walked in the town. The houses are white, and flat-roofed, being built of clay and straw, intermixed with stones. Withinside, the ceilings of the apartments are arched and lofty, to render them as cool as possible. The inhabitants consist chiefly of Turks and Greeks. The appearance of the part of the island in which Limesol is situated, was, at the time we were there, somewhat dreary: this, we were told, had been occasioned by the dreadful havoc made by the locusts some weeks before, at which time, we were assured by the consul, these devouring insects were strewed on the ground, in some places, nearly a foot thick. They had eaten the foliage of the orange and lemon trees, and had destroyed all the herbage in the vicinity of Limesol. In certain years they visit the island at a stated period, to renew their destructive ravages.

The shrub which bears the caper grows wild at Cyprus, and has a very pretty blossom. Among other vegetable productions, we saw medzanes, okers, cucumbers, gourds, and melons, the three latter extremely large. Provisions, vegetables, fruits, and wine, which are in general sold at a very moderate price in this island, were become dear on account of the havock which locusts had made. Cyprus wine of a good quality cost us from four to five piastres the measure, which contains eight okes, or nearly eleven English quarts.

After having paid a visit to the Aga, who made us a present of several sheep, we purchased the different articles of which we had need, and among others a good store of green almonds and apricots, the former of which, as well as mulberries, grow wild in abundance. During our stay at Limesol, we were incommoded by the excessive heat, which was augmented by the reflection of the sun from the white buildings. In returning to the transport in the evening, we met with the captain of a vessel who had left Jaffa, the place of our destination, three days before, and who had seen there, at the time of his departure, Sir Sydney Smith, and the Capitan Pacha. We also fell in with a considerable number of Turks, who had deserted from the army of the Grand Vizier at Jaffa, and were on their way to Constantinople.

We weighed anchor, and bore away on the following morning at half past eleven, with a south-west wind; and on the 30th, at noon, found, by our dead reckoning, that we had run a hundred and three miles since our departure from Limesol, in the space of somewhat more than twenty-four hours. We were then in the latitude of 32 degrees, 56 minutes, and without sight of land. During the night the wind was scanty; and this occasioned us to experience a very unpleasant motion from the rolling of the transport.

Clarke 1801

The journeys of Edward Daniel Clarke are recorded in his *Travels in Various Countries of Europe, Asia, and Africa. Commencing January 1, 1801* published in several parts and sections. Cobham notes that quarto volumes, "sumptiously printed and illustrated" were issued between 1810 and 1828. The Reverend Clarke, a professor at Cambridge University, visited Cyprus from June 6 to June 16, 1801 as described in Part the Second, *Greece, Egypt and the Holy Land*, Section the First. This excerpt is taken from that work published in New York by Whiting and Watson, 1813. This trip encompassed Constantinople, Troy, Troas, Rhodes, the Gulph of Glaucus, Egypt, Cyprus, Syria and Jerusalem. His extensive footnotes are not reproduced here.

[p. 157]

About six o'clock in the evening of June the third, we made land, north-east and by east. It fell to my lot to give the first intelligence of its appearance, being aloft, upon the look-out, in the phuttock shrouds. Cape Blanco, antiently *Curias* Promontory, then hove in view, (to use the language of seamen,) and soon after the whole island was seen indistinctly looming amidst thick fogs. It appeared very high and mountainous. We had such light breezes and frequent calms, that we did not reach *Salines* Bay until 3 o'clock, P.M. on Saturday the sixth of June. We had coasted the whole island, from its western extremity, and so near to the shore, that we had a distinct survey of the features of the country. We saw the fortress and town of Baffa, antiently Paphos, backed by high mountains. The coast towards the west much resembles the southern part of the Crimea; the villages and cultivated places being near the shore, and all behind craggy and mountainous. From Baffa to Limassol, near the spot where the antient city of *Amathus* stood, the coast appears very fertile, and more so than any part of the island that we afterwards visited. Towards the southwestern district the country is well covered with forest trees, and particularly the neighborhood of Baffa. Limassol produces the finest muscadine wine of Cyprus; some of this pours like oil, and may be kept to a great age. The wine called *Cammanderia* is, however, held principally in esteem among the natives.

As we sailed into *Salines* Bay, antiently that of *Citium*, now called ʹΑλίκες, from a cluster of salt lakes near the sea, the town of Salines appeared covered with that white fog, so much dreaded, and so well known in Italy, by the name of *mal-aria*. The mountains behind the place were partially concealed by this unwholesome vapour. It rose from the shore and buildings like smoke. Whenever this appearance is presented, the heat upon the island is excessive. Few of the natives venture out of their houses during mid-day; and all journeys, even those of caravans, are performed in the night: the dews are then neither abundant nor dangerous: in this respect Cyprus differs entirely from Egypt, and from all the neighbouring shores. Its ports are more sultry than any other in the Levant. Salines, and the towns situated on the eastern and north-eastern coasts of the island, are subject to such dangerous temperature, that, in the months of June and July, persons fall victims to the afflicting malady called a *sun-stroke*, or *coup de soleil*, if they venture out at noon without the precaution of carrying an umbrella. The inhabitants, especially of the lower order, wrap their heads as if exposed to the rigour of a severe winter; being always covered with a turban, over which, in their journeys, they place a thick shawl, many times folded. The great heat experienced upon the eastern coasts of Cyprus is owing to two causes; to the situation of the island with respect to the Syrian, Arabian, and Lybian deserts; and to its mountainous nature, preventing the cooler winds, the west, and north-west, from the low shores to the east and north-east.

We had scarce entered the bay, when we observed, to the north-east, a lurid haze, as if the atmosphere was on fire; and suddenly, from that quarter, a hurricane took us, that laid the Ceres upon her beam-ends. At the time of this squall, I endeavoured to ascertain the temperature of the blast. We found it so scorching, that the skin instantly peeled from our lips; a tendency to sneeze was excited, accompanied with great pain in the eyes, and chapping of the hands and face. The metallic scale of the thermometer, suspended in a port-hole to windward, was kept in a horizontal position by the violence of the gale; and the mercury exposed to its full current, rose six degrees of Fahrenheit in two minutes, from eighty to eighty-six; a singular consequence of north-east wind to Englishmen, accustomed to consider this as the coldest to which their island is exposed. All the coast of Cyprus, from Salines to *Famagosta,* antiently *Salamis*, is liable to hot winds, from almost every point of the compass; from the north-east; from the east; from the south-east; from the south; and south-west. The north-east coming from the parched deserts of Curdistan; the east, from the sands of Palmyra; the south-east, from the great desert of Arabia; and the south, and south-west, from Egypt and Lybia. From the west, north-west, and north, the inhabitants are shut, by high mountains, lying open to the beams of a scorching sun, reflected from a soil so white, that the glare is often sufficient to cause temporary blindness, without even the prospect of a single tree, beneath which one might hope for shade. In the middle of the day, few animals are seen in motion, except the lizard, seeming to sport with greatest pleasure where the sun is most powerful, and a species of long black serpents, abounding in Cyprus: one of these we killed, four feet three inches in length. Sometimes, also, a train of camels may be noticed, grazing among dusty thistles and bitter herbs, while their drivers seek shelter from the burning noon.

We found at anchor, in this bay, the Iphigenia, Captain Stackpole, from the fleet, with several transport-ships, waiting for supplies of cattle and water. On the following morning, June the seventh, about ten o'clock, we landed, and carried our letters of recommendation to the different Consuls residing at *Larneca*, about a mile from Salines, towards the north. Here the principal families reside, although almost all commercial transactions are carried on at Salines. We dined in Larneca with our own Consul; collecting, during our walk to and from his house, beneath the shelter of umbrellas, the few plants that occurred in our way. In our subsequent visits, we soon found that the *mal-aria* we had witnessed from the deck of the Ceres, veiling all the harbour with its fearful mist, could not be approached with impunity. Our lamented friend, and exemplary commander,

Captain Russel, was the first to experience its baneful influence; being seized with a fever, from which he never afterwards recovered. Indeed, the fevers of Cyprus, unlike those caught upon other shores of the Mediterranean, rarely intermit; they are almost always malignant. The strictest attention is therefore paid by the inhabitants to their diet. Fortunately for them, they have no butter on the Island; and in hot weather they deem it fatal to eat fat meat, or indeed flesh of any kind, unless boiled to a jelly. They likewise carefully abstain from every sort of pastry; from eggs, cream, and milk. The island produces abundance of delicious apricots, from standard trees, having a much higher flavour than those of Rosetta, but equally dangerous to foreigners, and speedily causing fever, if they be not sparingly used. Those of *Famagosta* are the most celebrated. They are sent, as acceptable presents, to *Nicotia*, the capital. The apricots of Larneca are also fine, and may be purchased in the market at the small price of three shillings the bushel. Many different varieties of the gourd, or pumpkin, are used in Cyprus for vegetables at table. The young fruit is boiled, after being stuffed with rice. We found it refreshing and pleasant, partaking at the same time the flavour of asparagus and artichoke. We noticed also the beet-root, melons, cucumbers, and a very insipid kind of mulberry, of a white colour. The corn of the island, wherever the inhabitants have courage or industry enough to venture on the cultivation of the land, in despite of their Turkish oppressors and the dangers of the climate, is of the finest quality. The wheat, although bearded, is very large, and the bread made from it extremely white and good. Perhaps there is no part of the world where the vine yields such redundant and luscious fruit. The juice of the Cyprian grape resembles a concentrated essence. The wine of the island is so famous all over the Levant, that, in the hyperbolical language of the Greeks, it is said to possess the power of restoring youth to age, and animation to those who are at the point of death. Englishmen, however, do not consider it a favourite beverage, as it requires nearly a century of age to deprive it of that sickly sweetness which renders it repugnant to their palates. Its powerful aperient quality is also not likely to recommend it, where wine is drunk in any considerable quantity, as it sometimes causes a disorder of the bowels even after being kept for many years. When it has been in bottles for ten or twelve years, it acquires a slight degree of effervescence; and this, added to its sweetness and high colour, causes it to resemble Tokay more than other wine. This, however, is not the state wherein the inhabitants of Cyprus drink their wine. It is preserved by them in casks, to which the air has constantly access, and will keep in this manner for any number of years. After it has withstood the changes of a single year, it is supposed to have passed the requisite proof, and then it sells for three Turkish piastres the *gooze*. Afterwards, the price augments in proportion to its age. We tasted some of the Commanderïa, which they said was forty years old, and was still in the cask. After this period it is considered quite as a balm, and reserved, on account of its supposed restorative and healing quality, for the sick and the dying. A greater proof of its strength cannot be given, than by relating the manner in which it is kept; in casks neither filled nor closed. A piece of sheet lead is merely laid over the bung-hole; and this is removed almost every day, whenever persons visit their cellars to taste the different sorts of wine proposed for sale. Upon these occasions, taking the covering from the bung-hole, they dip a hollow cane or reed into the liquor, and, by suction, drawing some of it, let it run from the reed into a glass. Both the *Commanderïa* and the *Muscad* are white wines. When new, they have a slight tinge of a violet hue: but age soon removes this, and afterwards they retain the colour of Madeira. Cyprus produces also red wines; but these are little esteemed, and used only as weak liquors for the table, answering to the ordinary "*Vin du Pays*" of France. If the people of Cyprus were industrious, and capable of turning their vintage to the best account, the red wine of the island might be rendered as famous as the white; and perhaps better calculated for exportation. It has the flavour of Tenedos; resembling that wine in colour and strength; and good Tenedos not only excels every other wine of Greece, but perhaps has no where its rival in Europe.

This island, that had so highly excited, amply gratified our curiosity by its most interesting antiquities; although there is nothing in its present state pleasing to the eye. Instead of a beautiful and fertile land, covered with groves of fruit and fine woods, once rendering it the Paradise of the Levant, there is hardly upon earth a more wretched spot than it now exhibits. Few words may forcibly describe it; Agriculture neglected— inhabitants oppressed—population destroyed—pestiferous air—contagion—poverty— indolence—desolation. Its antiquities alone render it worthy of resort; and these, if any person had leisure and opportunity to search for them, would amply repay the trouble. In this pursuit, Cyprus may be considered as yet untrodden. A few inscribed marbles were removed from Baffa by Sir Sidney Smith. Of two that the Author examined, one was an epitaph, in Greek hexameter and pentameter lines; and the other commemorated public benefits conferred by one of the Ptolemies. But the Phoenician reliques upon the island are most likely to obtain notice, and these have hitherto been unregarded. The inhabitants of Larneca rarely dig near their town without discovering either the traces of antient buildings, subterranean chambers, or sepulchres. Not long before our arrival, the English Consul, Signor Peristiani, a Venetian, dug up, in one place, above thirty idols belonging to the most antient mythology of the heathen world. Their origin refers to a period long anterior to the conquest of Cyprus by the Ptolemies, and may relate to the earliest estab- lishment of the Phoenician colonies. Some of these are of *terra cotta*; others of a coarse lime-stone; and some of soft crumbling marble. They were all sent to our Ambassadar at Constantinople, who presented them to Mr. Cripps. The principal figures seem to have been very antient representations of the most popular Divinity of the island, the PANTAMORPHA MATER; more frequently represented as *Ceres* than as *Venus,* (notwithstanding all that Poets have feigned of the Paphian Goddess,) if we may safely trust to such documents as engraved gems, medals, marbles, and to these idols, the authentic records of the country. Upon almost all the intaglios found in Cyprus, even among the ruins of Paphos, the representations are either those of Ceres herself, or of symbols designating her various modifications. Of these, the Author collected many, which it would be tedious to enumerate . . . Among the gems found in Cyprus, we noticed intagliated scarabaei with similar symbols; and obtained one whereon Isis was exhibited holding the quadruped, precisely according to the appearance presented by the statue dis- covered at Larneca. Since these antiquities were found, the inhabitants have also dug up a number of stone coffins, of an oblong rectangular form. Each of these, with the exception of its cover, is of an entire mass of stone. One of them contained a small vase of *terra cotta,* of the rudest workmanship, destitute of any glazing or varnish. Several intaglios were also discovered, and brought to us for sale. We found it more difficult to obtain an- tient gems in Larneca than in the interior of the island, owing to the exorbitant prices set upon them. At Nicotia, the goldsmiths part with such antiquities for a few *paras*. The people of Larneca are more accustomed to intercourse with strangers, and expect to make a harvest in their coming. Among the ring stones we left in that town, was a beautiful intaglio representing Cupid whipping a butterfly; a common method, among antient lapidaries, of typifying the power of love over the soul. Also an onyx, which there is every reason to believe one of the Ptolemies had used as a signet. It contained a very curious monogram, expressing all the letters of the word ΠΤΟΛΕΜΑΙΟΥ.

[p. 167]

The signet stones of Cyprus, although cut in a variety of substances, were more frequently of red carnelian than of any other mineral. Some of the most diminutive size were finely executed in red garnet, the carbuncle of the Antients. Others were formed of plasma, onyx, blood-stone, topaz, jasper, and even of quartz. Of all these, the most antient had the scarabaean form.

CHAPTER XI.

It will now perhaps be interesting to ascertain from what Phoenician city the antiquities discovered at Larneca derive their origin; and if the reader will give an author credit for the difficulties he has encountered, in order to ascertain this point, he may perhaps spare himself some trouble, and render unnecessary any ostentatious detail of the volumes it was necessary to consult. The antient geography of Cyprus is involved in greater uncertainty than seems consistent with its former celebrity among enlightened nations. Neither Greeks nor Romans have afforded any clue by which we can fix the locality of its Eastern cities. Certain of them, it is true, had disappeared in a very early period. Long prior to the time of Pliny, the towns of *Cinyria*, *Malium*, and *Idalium*, so necessary in ascertaining the relative position of other places, no longer existed. Both the nature and situation of important land-marks, alluded to by the antient geographers, are also uncertain. According to Strabo, the *Cleides* were *two* islands upon the north-east coast; Pliny makes their number *four*; and Herodotus mentions a promontory that had the name given to these islands. If we consult the text of Strabo, his description of Cyprus appears to be expressed with more than usual precision and perspicuity. Yet of two renowned cities, *Salamis* and *Citium*, the first distinguished for the birth of the historian Aristus, and the last conspicuous by the death of Cimon, neither the situation of the one nor of the other has been satisfactorily determined. D'Anville assigns a different position for these cities, and for the present towns of Famagosta and Larneca; although Drummond, "*Vir haud contemnendus*," as he is styled by a late commentator upon Strabo, and also Pococke, whose proverbial veracity is beyond all praise, from their own ocular testimony reconcile the locality of the antient and modern places. "At Larneca," observes the former of these writers, are undeniable proofs of its having been the antient Citium. Perhaps the antiquities now described may hereafter serve to confirm an opinion of Drummond's, founded upon very diligent enquiry, and repeated examination of the country. During the time he was Consul at Aleppo, he thrice visited Cyprus, and upon every occasion industriously surveyed the existing documents of its antient history. The sepulchral remains occupying so considerable a portion of the territory where the modern town is situated, appear to have been those of the Necropolis of Citium; and this city probably extended from the port all the way to Larneca, called also *Larnec*, and *Larnic;* implying, in its etymology, independently of its tombs, "*a place of burial.*" Descending to later authors, we find this position of Citium strongly confirmed by the Abbé Mariti, who discovered very curious testimony concerning it, in a manuscript preserved at Venice. From his very interesting account of Cyprus, we learn that the erroneous notions entertained with regard to the locality of the city, originated with Stephen de Lusignan; who was deceived by the name of a neighbouring village, called *Citi*, from a promontory at present bearing that appellation. Mariti places Citium between Salines and Larneca, upon the authority of the manuscript before mentioned, and the ruins he there observed. It is, as he remarks, of some importance to determine the true situation of a city once so renowned, on account of the celebrated men it produced, and the splendid actions of which it was the theatre. Yet it is singular, that this writer makes no mention of its Phoenician origin. Concerning this fact, so well ascertained, a few observations may therefore suffice.

Citium, from whose ruins we shall now consider both the modern towns of Salines and Larneca to have arisen, was founded, together with the city of *Lapethas*, by a Phoenician king, of the name of Belus. Its inhabitants, according to Cicero, were originally Phoenicians. Cyprus, from its vicinity to their country, and its commercial advantages, was the first island of the Mediterranean that came under this dominion. Eusebius observes, that Paphos, a Phoenician city in Cyprus, was built when Cadmus reigned at Thebes. It is moreover affirmed by the learned Bochart, that before the time of the Trojan war, Cinyras, king of Phoenicia, possessed this island of Cyprus, having derived it from his ancestors. To this monarch, Agamemnon, according to Homer, was indebted for his breast-plate. The cities of *Urania* and *Idalium* were also founded by the same people; the former received its name from *Urania Venus*, whose worship, as related by Herodotus, was transferred to Cyprus by the Phoenicians from Ascalon. Citium derived its name from the Hebrew appellation for the Island, CHETIM; the *Chittim*, or *Cittim*, of the Holy Scriptures. It was famous as the birth-place of Apollonius, a disciple of Hippocrates; and of Zeno, who, being shipwrecked upon the coast of Attica, from a Phoenician merchant became founder of the Stoics, and had for his illustrious followers, Epictetus and Seneca. According to Plutarch, it was with the sword presented by a king of Citium that Alexander triumphed over Darius. This weapon was held by him in such estimation, that he always wore it upon his person. The same author also informs us, that at the siege of Citium, Cimon, son of Miltiades, received the wound whereof he died. It is quite uncertain when this city was destroyed. Mariti believes that event did not take place later than the beginning of the third century. In 1767, an excavation being made to procure from its ruins materials for building, the workmen discovered a marble bust of Caracalla, some medals of Septimius Severus, Antoninus Caracalla, and Julia Domna, with Greek inscriptions. Upon their obverse sides were exhibited the Temple of Paphos, with the legend ΚΟΙΝΟΝΚΥΠΡΙΩΝ. Some of them had the image of Caracalla on one side, and that of Geta on the other. There were also others, with the head of the Emperor Claudius.

Many circumstances concurred to excite our curiosity concerning the interior of the island; although we despaired of being able to penetrate as far as *Baffa*, the antient *Paphos*, on account of the plague, then raging over all the western part of Cyprus, and particularly at Baffa. The ruins and other antiquities of this place, are numerous. Sir Sidney Smith removed some inscriptions already alluded to; and the English Consul at Larneca presented me the hand of a colossal marble statue, found there, of the most exquisite sculpture. We also hoped to enrich our collection of plants, and make some observations concerning the minerals of Baffa, especially a beautiful variety of crystallized quartz, as diaphanous as the rock-crystal of the north of Norway, called *Yeny Maden* or *Madem* by the Turks, and sold by Armenian merchants in the Crimea for diamonds. Before we left that peninsula, Professor Pallas had particularly requested information with regard to the locality of this stone. Among the substances offered for sale as false diamonds, there is nothing more common, all over the Mediterranean, than highly-transparent quartz; hence the various names of "*Gibraltar* diamonds," "*Vesuvian* diamonds," "*Baffa* diamonds," and many other. We have also, in our own country, the "*Bristol* diamonds." All natural resemblances of the diamond have, however, been lately eclipsed by a very different mineral, the White Topaz of New Holland. This stone, when cut and polished, with the exception only of the white Corundum, possesses a degree of lustre and limpidness superior to every other, excepting the real diamond. The antient mines of Cyprus, now entirely neglected, appear to have been situated towards the Paphian extremity of the island; for if the natives exhibit any mineral substance remarkable for its beauty, utility, or hardness, they name it by way of eminence, "a *Baffa stone*." Amianthus of a very superior quality is found near Baffa, as flexible as silk, and perfectly white; finer, and more delicately fibrous, than that of Sicily, Corsica, or Norway. The Cypriots call this mineral "*the Cotton Stone*."

Early on the morning of June the eighth, having procured an order for mules and asses, and a *firmàn* to authorize the expedition, we left the Ceres, and set out for *Nicotia*, the *Leucusia* or *Leucosia* of the Greeks, and present capital of Cyprus. We were detained at Larneca until the evening, by the hospitality of the English Consul, Signor Peristiani, who had prepared a large party of ladies and other inhabitants, all eager to represent to us the danger of travelling during the day; and to gratify very reasonable curiosity—for a sight of strangers, and for news from Egypt. Among the party was the English Consul from Berytus, from whom I obtained a silver tetradrachm of Tyre, in the highest state of preservation. The interesting costume presented in the dress of the Cyprian ladies ought not to pass without notice. Their head apparel was precisely modelled after the kind of *Calathus* represented upon the Phoenician idols of the country, and upon Egyptian statues. This was worn by women of all ranks, from the wives of the Consuls to their slaves. Their hair, dyed of a fine brown colour, by means of a plant called *Henna*, hung behind, in numerous long straight braids; and, in some ringlets disposed near the face, were fastened blossoms of the jasmine, strung together, upon slips from leaves of the palm-tree, in a very curious and pleasing manner. Next to the Calmuck women, the Grecian are, of all others, best versed in cosmetic arts. They possess the valuable secret of giving a brown colour to the whitest locks, and also tinge their eye-brows with the same hue; an art that would be highly prized by the hoary courtezans of London and of Paris. The most splendid colours are displayed in their habits; and these are very becoming to the girls of the island. The upper robe is always of scarlet, crimson, or green silk, embroidered with gold. Like other Greek women, they wear long scarlet pantaloons, fastened round the ankle, and yellow boots, with slippers of the same colour. Around the neck, and from the head, were suspended a profusion of gold coins, chains, and other trinkets. About their waists they have a large belt or zone, fastened in front by two large and heavy polished brass plates. They endeavour to make the waist appear as long as possible, and the legs, consequently, short. Naturally corpulent, they take no pains to diminish the size of their bodies by lacing, but seem rather vain of their bulk; exposing their bosoms, at the same time, in a manner highly unbecoming. Notwithstanding the extraordinary pains they use to disfigure their natural beauty by all sorts of ill-selected ornaments, the women of Cyprus are handsomer than those of any other Grecian island. They have a taller and more stately figure; and the features, particularly of the women of Nicotia, are regular and dignified, exhibiting that elevated cast of countenance so universally admired in the works of Grecian artists. At present, this kind of beauty seems peculiar to the women of Cyprus; the sort of expression exhibited by one set of features may be traced, with different gradations, in them all. Hence were possibly derived those celebrated models of female beauty, conspicuous upon the statues, vases, medals, and gems of Greece: models selected from the throng of Cyprian virgins, who, as priestesses of Venus, officiated at the Paphian shrine. Indefinite as our notions of beauty are said to be, we seldom differ in assigning the place of its abode. That assemblage of graces, which, in former ages, gave celebrity to the women of Circassia, still characterizes their descendants upon Mount Caucasus; and with the same precision that enables us to circumscribe the limits of its residence, we may refer to countries where it never was indigenous. Foremost in the list of these, may be mentioned Egypt. The statues of Isis, and the mummies, exhibit, at this hour, the countenance common to the females of the country; nor did the celebrated Cleopatra much differ from the representation thus afforded, if the portrait given of her upon Mark Antony's medals may be considered as authority. There are some countries (for example, Lapland) where it might be deemed impossible to select a single instance of female beauty. Here, it is true, the degraded state of human nature explains the privation. But among more enlightened nations, a traveller would hardly be accused of generalizing inaccurately, or partially, who should state that female beauty was rare in Germany, although common in England; that it exists more frequently in Russia than in France; in Finland, than in Sweden; in Italy, than in Greece; that the Irish women are handsomer than the Spanish; although learned antiquaries would assure us that both were originally of Pelasgian origin.

The gardens of Larneca are very beautiful, and constitute the only source of delight the women of the place seem to possess. They are, however, no ornament to the town, being inclosed by high walls. Almost every house has its garden: the shade and verdure thus afforded is a delightful contrast to the glare of a white and dusty soil, everywhere observed around. In these gardens we noticed two sorts of jasmine, one common in European countries, and the other derived from Syria: the double-blossomed pomegranate, a most beautiful shrub; also lemons, oranges, plums, and apricots. The *Phaseolus Caracalla*, kept in the green-houses of the Seraglio gardens at Constantinople, flourished here in the open air. They had also the *Arbutus Andrachne*, growing to an enormous size.

We left Larneca in the evening, and found a very good road to Nicotia; travelling principally over plains, by a gradual and almost imperceptible ascent, towards the northwest. Mountains appeared in the distant scenery, on almost every side. The soil everywhere exhibited a white marly clay said to be exceedingly rich in its nature, although neglected. The Greeks are so oppressed by their Turkish masters, that they dare not cultivate the land: the harvest would instantly be taken from them if they did. Their whole aim seems to be, to scrape together barely sufficient in the course of the whole year, to pay their tax to the Governor. The omission of this is punished by torture, or by death: and in cases of their inability to supply the impost, the inhabitants fly from the island. So many emigrations of this sort happen during the year, that the population of all Cyprus rarely exceeds sixty thousand persons; a number formerly insufficient to have peopled one of its towns. The Governor resides at Nicotia. His appointment is annual; and as it is obtained by purchase, the highest bidder succeeds; each striving, after his arrival to surpass his predecessor in the enormity of his exactions. From this terrible oppression the Consuls and a few other families are free, in consequence of protection granted by their respective nations. Over such a barren tract of land, altogether desolate, and destitute even of the meanest herbage, our journey was neither amusing nor profitable. It might have suggested reflections to a moral philosopher, thus viewing the horrid consequences of barbarian power; but when a traveller is exposed to the burning beams of an Eastern sun, mounted on a sorry mule dislocating his very loins, fatigued, and breathing hot pestilential vapours, he will feel little disposition to moralize. We rejoiced indeed, when, in a wide plain, we came in view of the little huts where we were to pass part of the night, previous to four more hours of similar penance.

The venerable pair with whom we rested in the village of *Attién,* were the parents of our mule-drivers, and owners of the mules. They made us welcome to their homely supper, by placing two planks across a couple of benches, and setting thereon boiled pumpkins, eggs, and some wine of the island in a hollow gourd. I observed upon the ground the sort of stones used for grinding corn, called *Querns* in Scotland, common also in Lapland, and in all parts of Palaestine. These are the primaeval mills of the world; and they are still found in all corn countries, where rude and antient customs have not been liable to those changes introduced by refinement. The employment of grinding with these mills is confined solely to females; and the practice illustrates the observation of our Saviour, alluding to this custom in his prediction concerning the day of judgment: "Two women shall be grinding at the mill; the one shall be taken, and the other left."

In these little cottages we found very large establishments for bees, but all the honey thus made is demanded by the Governor; so that keeping these insects is only considered as the means of an additional tax. The manner, however, in which the honey is collected, is so curious, and so worthy of imitation, that it merits a particular description: the contrivance is very simple, and was doubtless suggested by the more antient custom, still used in the Crimea, of harbouring bees in Cylinders made from the bark of trees. They build up a wall formed entirely of earthen cylinders, each about three feet in length, placed, one above the other, horizontally, and closed at their extremities with mortar. This wall is then covered with a shed, and upwards of one hundred swarms may thus be maintained within a very small compass. Close to this village grew the largest Carob-tree we noticed in all our travels. It is, by some, called St. John's bread-tree; the *Ceratonia Siliqua* of Linnaeus. It was covered with fruit, the pods being then green, and had attained the size of our largest English oaks. We could neither discover nor hear of antiquities near this village; except one large reservoir for water, pointed out as an antient work, although probably of Venetian origin. This is still in a perfect state, lined with square blocks of stone, about twenty-five feet deep, and fifteen feet wide. It is situated in a field close to the village.

Two hours before sun-rise, we again set out for Nicotia. The road lay through an open country; but high mountains were every where in view, as on the preceding evening. Some of these, as we drew nearer to them, exhibited very remarkable forms, standing insulated, and with flat tops, like what are usually called table mountains. On our right, we observed one that arose out of a fine plain, having a most perfect conical form, except that its vertex appeared truncated parallel to its base. Upon the road we noticed distinct masses of the purest transparent selenites, or crystallized sulphat of lime, as diaphanous as the most limpid specimens from Montmartre, near Paris. It seemed as if they had been dropped by caravans passing the road; although we could learn nothing, either of the place whence they were derived, or the purpose for which they were intended. A ridge of mountains bounded all the view in front of our route; at length, at the distance of two hours and a half from Attién, we beheld the city of Nicotia, situated in the middle of one of the fine plains common in this part of the island, at the base of one extremity of the mountain barrier. As we advanced towards it, we were struck with the magnitude of its fortifications: these, although neglected, still remain nearly entire, surpassing, in extent and beauty, those of almost every other city. The moat is half a mile wide; it is now dry, or at best, an unwholesome swamp. Beneath the walls, the bed of this moat abruptly terminates in a deep and wide fosse. The ramparts are still mounted with a few pieces of artillery. The road winds round the walls towards the gate, which had once a portcullis. We found the entrance filled with beggars. The guard demands a toll from all Greeks passing through. As we rode into the town, we met a long train of women, dressed in white robes, the beautiful costume of the capitol, filling the air with their lamentations. Some of these were of the middle age, but all were handsome; as they came on, they exposed their faces and breasts to public view, tearing their hair, and weeping piteously. In the midst of the procession rode a Turk upon an ass, smoking his pipe in the most tranquil manner, and wholly indifferent to their cries. Upon inquiring the cause of this tumult, we were told that these women were all prostitutes, whom the Governor had banished the city, and whom they were therefore conducting beyond the gates. Their dress was modelled after a very antient form, and highly elegant; it consisted entirely of fine white linen, so disposed as to veil at once the whole figure, unless when purposely cast aside; and it fell to the ground in long graceful folds.

We went to the house of Mr. Sékis (the English *Dragoman,* as he is vulgarly called) a rich Armenian merchant, who enjoys the English protection for transacting whatsoever business their nation may have with the Governor. His house was in all respects a palace, possessing the highest degree of Oriental magnificence. The apartments were not only spacious, but they were adorned with studied elegance: the floors being furnished with the finest mats brought from Grand Caïro, and the divâns covered with satin, set round with embroidered cushions. The windows of the rooms, as in all Oriental houses, were near the roof, and small, although numerous, and placed close to each other. They had double casements, one being of painted glass, surrounded by carved work, as in the old Gothic palaces of England. These perhaps derived their original form from the East, during the Crusades. So many instances occur to strengthen the opinion, that I may be liable to unnecessary repetition, when allusion is made to this style of building. The custom of having the floor raised in the upper part of a chamber, where the superiors sit, as in our old halls, is strictly Oriental: it is the same in the tents of the Tartars. We were permitted to view the Charem. This always consists of a summer and a winter apartment. The first was a large square room, surrounded by divâns; the last an oblong chamber, where the divâns were placed parallel to each other, one on either side, lengthways; and at the upper extremity was the fire-place, resembling our antient English hearths.

About half an hour after our arrival, the worthy old Armenian came home; and throwing himself at full length upon the divân, began to fan himself with a bunch of coloured feathers, while his secretary opened and read to him our letters. Refreshments were instantly served, and pipes brought by his attendants: soon after this, he proposed that we should accompany him to the Governor's. As we descended, he shewed us his beautiful garden, filled with standard apricot-trees laden with ripe fruit, and our wine, as he said, for dinner, already cooling in marble fountains, beneath the shade of orange, citron, lemon, fig, vine, and pomegranate trees. We entered the court-yard of the Governor's palace, and observed several beautiful horses, richly caparisoned, standing without any attendants, each fastened by a chain to its fore leg, and to a spike in the ground. This custom exists, as a kind of parade, in almost all the palace-yards of Pachas who are governors, and are called *Mussuleem*. We were conducted first into the chamber of the Dragoman, or interpreter, where we found a crowd of persons assembled upon business. Here again pipes were brought, while our firmâns were examined, and some questions put, concerning the state of affairs in Egypt, the death of the Emperor Paul, and the victory gained by Nelson over the Danes. We were then led through several passages, until we came to the Governor's apartment, who having heard our names and business, desired us to be seated upon the divân opposite to him. As this man affected all that haughtiness with which Franks were formerly received, in times when the English name was not quite so much respected as it is now in Turkey, I shall particularly specify the ceremony attending our visit. The custom shewn in the reception of strangers, is the same over all the Ottoman empire; and in all countries the punctilios of hospitality are best exercised by proud men. It is only our equals who lay aside ceremony.

The Governor of Cyprus was no Pacha, nor had he any other rank than what his wealth had procured in his temporary station at Nicotia; an honour annually purchased of the Capudan Pacha, as before stated, by the highest bidder. One short year of dominion, wholly dedicated to the exercise of a vain ostentation, and to unbounded rapacity, was therefore all that awaited him, in return for the expenditure whereby the post had been obtained. It was truly amusing, therefore, to see the manner of displaying his new sovereignty. Our credentials were of a very superior nature; because, in addition to our firmân, we carried with us letters from the Capudan Pacha, and the Commander-in-chief, both of the fleet and of the army. At sight of these, however, his new-made Excellency affected to turn up his nose, muttering between his teeth the expressive word *Djowr,* with considerable emphasis, and taking up the skirts of his pelisse, (as our venerable friend the Armenian kneeled before him, to act as our interpreter,) that they might not be defiled by the touch of an infidel. This insolence was the more remarkable, as the Turks, except when in a state of open rebellion, generally salute the Grand Signior's firmân: even the haughty Pacha of Acre always made sign of obeisance when it was produced. After thus endeavouring to make us feel our inferiority, he next strove to dazzle our senses with his splendor and greatness. Having clapped his hands, a swarm of attendants, most magnificently habited, came into the room, bearing gilded goblets filled with lemonade and sorbet, which they presented to us. A high priest of the dervishes then entered, and prostrated himself before the Governor, touching his lips with his fingers, crossing his hands upon his breast, and raising his thumbs afterwards to his ears. All these marks of reverence ended, he rose and took his station upon the divân, on the left side of the Governor. Next came a fresh party of slaves, bringing long pipes of jasmine wood with amber heads, to all the party; these were suddenly followed by another host of myrmidons in long white vests, having white turbans on their heads, who covered us with magnificent cloths of sky-blue silk, spangled and embroidered with gold. They also presented to us preserved fruits and other sweetmeats; snatching away the embroidered cloths, to cover us again with others of white satin, still more sumptuous than before. Then they brought coffee, in gold cups studded with diamonds; and the cloths were once more taken away. After this, there came slaves kneeling before us with burning odours in silver censers, which they held beneath our noses; and finally, a man, passing rapidly round, spattered all our faces, hands, and clothes, with rose-water—a compliment so little expected at the time, and so zealously administered, that we began to wipe from our face and eyes the honours which had almost blinded us. The principal dragoman belonging to the Governor next presented each of us with an embroidered handkerchief; "gifts," he said, "by which Infidels of rank were always distinguished in their interviews with his Master." The handkerchief consisted of embroidered muslin, and was enclosed in a piece of red crape. These presents we in vain solicited permission to decline; adding, that "as private individuals, meanly habited, in the view of travelling expeditiously through the island, we hoped he would not form his ideas of Englishmen of rank either from our appearance or pretensions." Upon further conversation, we found that all intercourse with Baffa and the western side of the island was cut off by the plague, which had begun to shew itself even in the neighbourhood of Nicotia: we therefore resolved to return to our more humble host in the village of Attièn the same night; when, to our great surprise, the Governor requested that we would spend a few days with him; and, as we stated this to be impossible, he even threatened to detain the frigate at Salines for that purpose. We were however resolute in our determination; and therefore representing to him the illness of our Captain, and our utter inability to remain an instant after the Ceres had got her cargo on board, we took our leave; accompanied by an officer of his guard, whom he permitted to attend us among the goldsmiths of the place, in search of medals and other antiquities.

   It is to these artificers, bearing the name of *Gûyûmjee*, almost universally in Turkey, that the peasants of the country, and lower order of people in the towns, carry all the pieces of gold or silver they may chance to find in the soil, to be exchanged for modern trinkets. They are generally men in a small way of trade, sitting in a little stall, with a crucible before them, a touchstone, and a handful of very ordinary tools. Their chief occupation consists in making coarse silver rings, of very base metal, for the women, and in setting signets for Turks of all denominations. There is hardly a Mahometan who does not bear upon one of his fingers this kind of ornament. The Turkish signet is generally a carnelian stone, inscribed with a few words from the Korân, a proverb in Arabic, or a couplet in Persian. We found, as usual, ample employment among these men; and were so much occupied in the pursuit, that we even neglected to visit the Cathedral of St. Sophia, built in the Gothic style by the Emperor Justinian, when he raised the edifice of the same name in Constantinople. We have the testimony both of Drummond and Mariti for the architecture exhibited in this building. The cathedrals both of Famagosta and Nicotia are described as Gothic. If it be true, therefore, that the Nicotian church was erected by Justinian, we have authority for the existence of that style of architecture, in a high degree of perfection, so long ago as the middle of the sixth century; six hundred and forty years before the conquest of Cyprus by Richard the First; and certainly long anterior to the introduction of any specimen of the architecture called Gothic in Great Britain. Other instances of still higher antiquity exist in Egypt and Palaestine.

Our success in collecting gems was so great, that the number of our acquisitions in Nicotia exceeded the total of what we had been able to procure since our departure from Constantinople. We found also silver medals of Antoninus Pius, Severus, Faustina, and of the Ptolemies. The bronze were all of late date, and almost all after the time of Constantine. We also made diligent enquiry concerning the *Yeny Madem* crystal. Some detached and very ordinary specimens of crystallized quartz were shewn to us, by the name of *Baffa stones*; but the inhabitants were unable to polish even these. All the stones found in the island, capable of being polished, are sent to Grand Caïro for this purpose. This fact, while it serves to shew the wretched state of the arts in Cyprus, also conveys a proof of their flourishing state in the present capital of Egypt, beyond the notions usually entertained of that remote city. Among our intaglios were numerous representations and symbols of Isis, Ceres, and Venus; a very beautiful gem representing Mercury leaning upon a sepulchral *stêlê*; of Anubis, kneeling with the dove upon his left hand; and one of very diminutive form, but of exquisite beauty, meriting a more particular description; it is a highly transparent garnet. The subject engraven represents a colossal statue, whose two arms extended touch the extremity of the stone. Before this figure is seen a person kneeling, in the act of worshipping the idol. This corresponds so accurately with the descriptions given of the statue of Jupiter Serapis at Alexandria, whose two hands touched the sides of the temple, that it is probable the gem was intended to preserve a memorial of the image. It has no resemblance to the appearance of any Grecian Deity; the *calathus*, or rather the *pileus*, upon its head, is like that seen upon Indian or Chinese Idols; and this further coincides with the history of the worship of Serapis, transferred by one of the Ptolemies from Asia to Egypt.

In the evening we mounted our mules, and again returned to Attièn. Our good friend Mr. Sékis had laden an ass with all sorts of provisions for our journey, but we would only accept a basket of his fine apricots. These he said were nothing in comparison with the apricots he received annually from Famagosta, yet they were the finest we had ever seen. We met caravans of camels in our way to Attièn, marching according to the order always observed in the East; that is to say, in a line, one after the other; the whole caravan being preceded by an ass, with a bell about its neck. Camels never seem to seek the shade; when left to repose, they kneel down, exposed to the hottest beams of the sun. Trees, however, are rarely seen in this part of the island: the inhabitants relate, that eastward of Nicotia, towards Baffa, the country being more mountainous, is also well covered with wood. The rivers of Cyprus are dry during the summer months. Sudden rain swells them into torrents. Some fell during the second night we passed at Attièn. In the morning, two hours before sun-rise, we set out for Larneca; and, having to cross a bridge, found it shaking so violently with the impetuosity of the water, that we feared it would fall. The antient Cypriots pretended, that their Paphian altars, although exposed to the atmosphere, were never wetted by rain. Probably they would not have escaped drenching during the showers which had caused this inundation. We reached Larneca at eight o'clock, and were on board the Ceres before ten. Captain Russel's fever had much increased. The apricots we brought for him seemed to afford a temporary refreshment to his parched lips and palate, but were ultimately rather injurious than salutary. The symptoms of his melancholy fate became daily more apparent, to the great grief of every individual of his crew.

During our absence, the English Consul had been kindly endeavouring to procure for me other reliques from the interesting vestiges of Citium. Before I left the island, he obtained, from one of the inhabitants, a small, but thick, oblong silver medal of the city; considered, from its appearance, as older than the foundation of the Macedonian empire. A ram is represented couched in the front. The obverse side exhibits, within an indented square, a rosary or circle of beads, to which a cross is attached. Of these rosaries, and this appendage, as symbols, (explained by converted heathens at the destruction of the temple of Serapis), having in a former publication been explicit, it is not now necessary to expatiate. That the soul's immortality was alluded to, is a fact capable of the strictest demonstration. The Consul from Berytus also presented to me a magnificent silver tetradrachm of Tyre, with the inscription "OF . TYRE . HOLY . AND . INVIOLATE"

ΤΥΡΟΥΙΕΡΑΣΚΑΙΑΣΥΛΟΥ

. . . We left Cyprus on the sixteenth of June, steering for the coast of Egypt, and first made land off Damiata.

Hume 1801

This selection is from pages 246-248 of *Travels in Various Countries of the East, London: Longman, Hurst, Rees, Orme and Brown,* 1818, edited by Robert Walpole. Walpole found this record of a visit to Cyprus in 1801 in the journals of a Dr. Hume. Elsewhere in the book is a reference to "J. R. Hume, Esq. who was on the medical staff of the British army in Egypt." We have not been able to determine if this is John Robert Hume (1781-1857) or Joseph Hume (1777-1855), both of whom were medical officers in the British army, or some other Hume of the same period.

We landed at the sea-port or Marina of Larnaka, called by some authors Salines from the salt-pans in its neighbourhood. It stands at the bottom of the bay: it is a small place; but contains a mosque, a church, baths, coffee-houses, and well filled shops. In these we observed plain and striped cottons, mixed stuffs of cotton and silk, silk purses, tobacco-pipes, hard-ware, books in modern Greek. Some of the streets are rendered cool and pleasant in summer by a canopy of vines. Larnaka is situated about a mile to the east of the Marina, and is a fine village; but owes all its beauty to the delightful gardens in the neighbourhood; the walks of which are overhung with the jasmin, the evergreen rose, and particularly by the nerium oleander, or rose-bay. This grows here with great luxuriance, and is remarkable for the clusters of pale crimson flowers; and forms the chief ornament of the gardens. In the fields adjoining the town, we observed the caper-bush in flower, as well as the lycopersicon or love-apple.

From the accounts we had received of the unhealthiness of Cyprus we were under considerable apprehensions on our arrival; and were cautious at first: but such is the effect of habit, that in a short time we walked about in the middle of the day. Among the natives not a creature was stirring abroad at that time; but in the morning and the cool of the evening there is a considerable bustle among them. Except the oppression produced by excessive heat, I remember no unpleasant effect from the air of the island; in summer, however, strangers are apt to be affected by a *coup de soleil*, often the forerunner of fever or death. The fevers of Cyprus are in general so rapid in their course, that there is little time for remission; but in one case I saw almost an intermission: the patient walked about and said he was in perfect health; but from the appearance of his eyes and hurried manner, it was too evident this was not the case. Those men who died of the fever on board of the Ceres had slept all night on shore. The sick belonging to the Thisbe were landed at Limosol; and kept in a tent during the ship's stay there; and though the surgeon's conduct in this instance appears to have been rash, I did not hear that any bad consequences followed it.

There seemed to be no want of schools at Larnaka. In the courts of private houses, I have seen the elder boys teaching the younger to read; and not from manuscript, but printed books. Of these they have a considerable number; but most of those I examined related to religious subjects: they have also translations from the European languages.

The church of St. Lazarus at the Marina is a large heavy building; instead of a steeple, it has merely a circular rising, or rude dome, on its roof; the use of bells being prohibited to the Greeks by the Turks. The church is large and spacious inside; is ornamented with much carving and gilding; and has some paintings ill executed. A part of the building being more elevated than the rest, and separated from it by wooden lattices, is appropriated to the women: but it has no kind of ornament. From the area, or ground-floor, which at the time of our visit was kept remarkably clean, a flight of steps leads to the relics and pictures, which are all placed in that part of the church opposite to the female lattices. Our guide took care to point out the most valuable relic, the great toe of St. George, who at one time was held in great reverence on the opposite coast of Syria. The grand object, however, of our guide's veneration was the tomb of St. Lazarus. It is in a vault under ground, and said by the Cypriotes to be possessed of sovereign virtue, being able, in their opinion, to restore even the dying to perfect health, if they be laid upon the tomb. In passing to this, our friend cast an approving glance upon a picture of a huge saint, with a dog's head, which had the name ΧΡΙΣΤΟΦΕΡΟΣ written above it. The representation resembled extremely the common figures of Anubis. In the neighbourhood of this church is the burying-ground for Protestants; and here I took notice of the tombs of several Englishmen, who had all died in the summer, when the heat is excessive.

The Mahometan burying ground in this part of the island is full of grave-stones; but inscriptions are not common. When the body is deposited in the grave, an arch is built over it with lath and plaster, and then covered with earth: we saw the grave open in places where this had given way.

In our observations on the domestic habits of the Cypriotes, we found them hospitable and obliging: in whatever house we entered, we were received with kindness. The inhabitants, in general, are well clothed: the shops are well filled; and the women of the middle classes have rich dresses. There seemed to be no want of provisions; they have sheep and fowls in great number; the gardens abound with vegetables, and the vines hang almost every where in the villages with luxuriant clusters. The desserts on their tables consisted of the finest fruits, musk and water melons, apricots, &c. The musk-melons we seldom tasted, on account of their supposed tendency to produce disease, but the water-melons afforded an agreeable beverage, peculiarly grateful in a hot climate.

During the month of July, 1801, we were twice at Limosol: this place is situated in the southern part of Cyprus, in N. lat. 34°. 39´, E. lon. 33°. 30´. It stands at the extremity of an open bay, and is a long straggling town intermixed with gardens, inclosed, for the most part, by stone walls. It is much cooler in summer than Larnaka. I observed in the fields near the town the wild poppy in flower, a branchy species of hypericum, with small yellow blossoms, a species of orobanche with violet-coloured flowers, and the convolvulus. The gardens seemed to be equally productive with those of Larnaka.

We went to Limosol for the purpose of procuring wood and water: the latter was obtained from a well by means of a Persian wheel of rude construction, turned round by an ass. The well was in a sequestered situation, to the west of the town, overshadowed by a variety of trees, among which were the Palma Christi, or Castor-oil Shrub, and the Morus alba.

The plain of Limosol is perhaps one of the most fertile districts in the island; and where the ground is not cultivated there are clusters of the olive and locust tree, and the evergreen Cypress. No tract of country perhaps affords a finer variety of thorns and thistles; and there, as well as at Larnaka, the caper-bush grows luxuriantly. Some small fields near the town were covered with tobacco and cotton plants; and in this plain the sugar-cane is said to have at one time abounded. I found the olive on the banks of a river, the bed of which was now dry; and on the borders of other streams a number of trees were in bloom, such as the Mimosa, the Oleander, the Pomegranate, and the Jasmin. The fruit of the locust-tree is very astringent, when green; but as soon as it ripens, it becomes sweet and pleasant, and in the winter-season constitutes the ordinary food of the sheep and goats. In the hedges, that beautiful shrub, the Palma Christi, is quite common, and its ripe fruit is sometimes used by the natives medicinally; but I do not know that they have ever extracted the oil as an article of commerce. The vine is seen growing in almost every courtyard, and its fruit is of exquisite flavour; but the richness of the red grape brought to Limosol in little hampers, from the interior, is perhaps unequalled.

Browne 1802

William George Browne was born on July 25, 1768, the son of a respectable London wine merchant. In ill health as a youth, he was privately tutored until entering a classical curriculum at Oxford. After the University he began a study of law only to abandon that for a broad study of literature, languages, sciences and travel accounts, especially of Africa. His first excursion was to Alexandria in 1791, when he intended to visit the interior of Africa. War in upper Egypt prevented him from journeying south at that time; he then traveled widely in lower Egypt until he was able to join a caravan to the country of Dar-fûr in 1793. The first European in that country, he was treated harshly and not allowed to leave for three years. From Cairo the next year he traveled throughout Palestine, Syria, and Asia Minor. Although some of his most valuable registers and journals were lost, he published his remaining materials in *Travels in Africa, Egypt and Syria from the Year 1792 to 1798*, London: T. Caddell and W. Davies, 1806.

Browne continued his travels and observations interspersed with periods of intense study. A trip to the Levant in 1802, which included his stop in Cyprus, added to his reputation as an Orientalist. The excerpt below from his unpublished papers was published by Robert Walpole on pp. 138 and 140 of his book *Travels in Various Countries of the East; Being a Continuation of Memoirs Relating to European and Asiatic Turkey, &c.*, London: Longman, Hurst, Rees, Orme and Brown, 1820. In 1813 Browne set out from Tabriz to Teheran through an area controlled by the Persian army and was reportedly murdered by "banditti," although it has been suggested that the Persian shah may have instigated the act.

I embarked in a small boat with several passengers for Larneka in Cyprus, which in Turkish is called Tûsla from the adjacent salt works.

. . . On the morning of the seventh day from our departure, we landed at Larneka. The heat of this part of Cyprus is very intense; and the north-east wind, which is said to be the most hot and oppressive, blew at the time of my arrival. Caleshes, in other places used as a luxury, are here almost necessary; for though the town be but at a small distance from the sea, yet exposure to the rays of the sun in passing thither, is seldom hazarded with impunity. Agues and complaints of the eyes are common; and none of the natives have the appearance of robust health.

The bread made in private houses in Cyprus is unequalled, except perhaps by that which is prepared for the table of the Sultan, at Constantinople. It is composed of what is called "*fiore di farina*" The flour is divided into three parts, to obtain the kind which is proper for manipulation. The first separated is the coarse and husky part; the next, the white impalpable powder; after which operation remains the *fiore di farina*, which is neither very finely pulverized, nor remarkably white, and is by far the smallest quantity of the whole mass. This is found to contain the purest part of the wheat, and to make the finest bread.

Mayer 1803

Luigi Mayer arranged to publish a series of exceptional color drawings that had been collected by Sir Robert Ainslee, British ambassador to Turkey. To these drawings Mayer added a commentary on his own travels to the lands depicted in the drawings in a volume titled *Views in the Ottoman Empire, Chiefly in Caramania a part of Asia Minor hitherto unexplored: with some curious selections from the islands of Rhodes and Cyprus, and the celebrated cities of Corinth, Carthage, and Tripoli: from the original drawings in the possession of Sir R. Ainslee, taken during his embassy to Constantinople*, London: R. Bowyer, 1803. The text presented here retains Mayer's peculiar orthography.

[p. 17]

This fine and rich island, situate near the head of the Mediterranean, has been celebrated on various accounts from very remote antiquity. Covered with woods when first visited by the phenicians, part of the timber served to smelt the ore with which it abounded; part furnished it's maritime visitors with materials for building ships; and both these employments being inadequate to the purpose of thinning it's forests sufficiently to

render the island habitable, much was cut down and destroyed by persons, who retained
the ground they cleared as their own property. It was perhaps before any great progress
had been made in rendering the land fit for cultivation, that the island was stigmatized as
insalubrious, for some modern travellers give it a different character. Pococke indeed
considers it as still unhealthy; and ascribes this to the intense heat in summer, the sun
being reverberated from the lofty mountains, and the shallow soil lying chiefly on a white
freestone; while some of these mountains are covered with snow all the winter, which
renders the island much colder at that season than any other part of the Levant, and frequently occasions deluges of rain of long continuance. Be this as it may, it was renowned
in ancient times for the worship of Venus, of whom this was supposed to be the favourite
abode; and for it's wines, which still retain their celebrity. Not that all it's wines are
equally good; that produced in a district called the Commandery, from occupying part of
the great commandery of the templars and of the knights of St. John of Jerusalem being
the best. This wine, when of sufficient age, and properly managed, is of exquisite flavour;
but, as deception is too common in trade, the wines of Cyprus in general, whatever their
quality may be, are commonly sold under the name of wines of the commandery.

To make the best Cyprus wine, the grapes are not gathered till they are fully ripe,
and they are then laid carefully on covered terraces to the depth of a foot and a half.
When the juice begins to flow from them, they are taken up with shovels, and carried into
a cellar paved with marble, or covered with a solid kind of plaster, and the floor of which
is made sloping toward one side. Here they are bruised with a flat mallet, and squeezed
three or four times under small presses. The juice that issues from them is sweet and viscous, and flows into a large vessel, out of which, as it fills, it is taken, and conveyed in
small pitchers to a large earthen jar half buried in the ground, and of a conical shape at
bottom. In this vessel the wine is left to ferment for twenty days, it not being filled to the
brim, lest the liquor during the effervescence should run over. Some keep the vessel uncovered during this period; others stop it up, merely leaving a small air-hole. At the end
of forty days, the vessel is stopped close with a lid of similar ware. As the wine clarifies,
it deposits at the bottom of the vessel a fat viscous matter, which the cypriots call manna,
and which, instead of being injurious to the quality of the liquor, contributes greatly towards bringing it to perfection: hence vessels that have been already used, and containing
these lees, sell for four times the price of new ones. The greeks have still a custom, derived from remote ages, of burying large vessels full of choice wine, and closely stopped,
when they have a child born; and this remains in the ground till the marriage of that child,
for the celebration of whose nuptials it is appropriated. As persons in easy circumstances
generally bury more wine than is consumed on such occasions, merchants have sometimes an opportunity of purchasing a part, and this is superiour in flavour to any.

The city of Amathus in this island was once celebrated for a temple dedicated to
Venus and Adonis, in which was reported to be preserved a rich necklace of gold and
precious stones, the work of Vulcan, and a present to Hermione. On the ruins of this city
arose another called Limisso, now likewise destroyed, and distinguished by the epithet of
ancient from the present Limisso, a wretched place in it's vicinity, built of unburnt brick,
full of ruins and rubbish, though it's harbour is much frequented, and occupying the site
of what was Nemosia. In the neighbourhood of this city Mr. Mayer discovered an ancient
vase, thirty feet in circumference, and nine inches thick. It is of stone, and it's external

surface is very hard, but on the inside the sandy particles easily rub off on the finger, and emit a smell resembling petroleum, as is the general case with the stone of this island. This vase stands in a very lonely spot, occasionally visited only by persons in pursuit of game, to whom the bull that appears in the hollow of one of the ears has sometimes served for a mark to shoot at for wagers, or as a trial of their skill.

In speaking of Egypt we had occasion to notice the ignorance and want of taste, that it's present inhabitants display in architecture; but even the greeks of the present day appear little superiour to them in this respect, though they enjoy the advantages of more perfect models. Here, as on the shores of Africa, we find fragments of columns finely wrought by the skilful artists of former times jumbled together; capitals of all orders side by side, and a piece of a plain doric shaft supporting or supported by another of a fluted corinthian, sometimes of a greater diameter, sometimes of less, to eke out what is called a pillar. Surely in places where sculptured fragments lay scattered with so much profusion, something more approaching to symmetry might have been obtained, were not the ignorance and indolence of the builder extreme.

Smyth 1810–1824

Rear-Admiral William Henry Smyth commenced naval operations in the Mediterranean in 1810 carrying out scientific measurements that made a contribution toward "a complete Sailing-Directory for the whole Inner Sea." He was one of the Board of Visitors of the Royal Observatory and officer of several scientific organizations of London, Boston, Washington, New York, and Italy. Smyth felt that his book *The Mediterranean: A Memoir: Physical, Historical and Nautical* offered the "present exposition of the state of our knowledge of the Mediterranean Sea . . . at the close of the year 1824." It was not published until 1854 in London by John W. Parker and Son.

[p. 82]

In the north-east part of the Levantine Sea, at ten or twelve leagues south of the coast of Karamania, and about twenty leagues to the westward of Syria, is the large and once famous island of Cyprus (Κυπρος); once an important kingdom, now a mere appanage of the Sultan's Grand Vizier. Its length is 140 miles, by 50 at its greatest breadth, narrowing gradually to the east; it is traversed from east to west by a range of woody mountains, of which Oros Troados (*Olympus*), the principal summit, is 6590 feet above the sea. It possesses the ports of Famagusta (*Arsinöe*), Limasol, Baffa (*Paphos*), Larnaka, and Ghyrna (*Ceryneia*), of which Famagusta is the chief. But though the range mentioned extends through Cyprus, the greater part of the island consists of fine plains, of which the soil is excellent; and even under imperfect cultivation yields corn, wine, oil, carubbas, and other fruits; and among its exports are also silk, cotton, wool, morocco-leather, soda, salt, coloquintida, gum, laudanum, madder, cochineal, turpentine, tar, and pigments. The resources of the island are, however, sadly depressed by misgovernment, the Grand Vizier acting only by proxy.

* * * * *

[p. 107]

Severe earthquakes are ever accompanied by an agitation of the neighbouring seas, as was specially noted during the tremendous calamity at Lisbon in 1755: and the fact was observed and recorded very early, for Herodotus (*Urania*, § 64) mentions a convulsion of the earth which was felt out at sea, by the fleet of Eurybiades; and I myself have felt such shocks on several occasions. Eruptions from the bottom of the sea, so far as I could learn, exhibit their phenomena exactly as from those subaërial vents which open at once into the atmosphere: subject only to the modifications produced by the greater density of the surrounding medium, and the greater external pressure caused by the weight of the overlying column of water, which then becomes an element of the repressive force. Professor Pallas mentions that in September, 1799, a submarine eruption took place in the Sea of Azof, 150 fathoms from the shore, opposite Temruck, accompanied with dreadful thundering, emissions of fire and smoke, and the throwing up of ashes and stones; after which an isle—'like a great sepulchral hillock'—rose from the bottom; but which sunk again, before he could visit it. In 1814, another new island was raised on that spot, by volcanic explosions: and both were accompanied by earthquakes in the vicinity. On the 13th of August, in 1822, when Aleppo was destroyed by a terrific earthquake, which instantly buried thousands of the inhabitants under the ruins of their houses, two rocks arose from the sea in the vicinity of Cyprus (*Journal of Science,* vol. xiv., page 450), an island ever partaking in the disasters of Syria.

*   *   *   *   *

[p. 282]

The island of Cyprus affords an epitome of the usual Levantine weather, as the action of the breezes is confined to a comparatively circumscribed space. In the general progress of its seasons, the heats increase as the summer advances, and would be altogether insupportable were it not for the cooling imbatto, which begins to blow at 8 A.M. the first day of the season, increases as the sun advances till noon, when it gradually declines, and at 3 P.M. entirely ceases. Nothing is more easy to comprehend than the cause and course of this wind: between 8 and 10 A M. the land is sufficiently heated to rarify the atmosphere over it greatly,—the cool air upon the sea consequently expands and forms a strong current to the land. Towards sunset, the sea being thus heated, something like an equilibrium takes place. About an hour after sunset, the imbatto generally dies away: an almost dead calm ensues, and at about 1 or 2 A.M. a light air springs up from the land, which continues for about an hour after sunrise. But before these winds terminate for the season, they become extremely violent. This imbatto is considered as a sea breeze on the north-west of Cyprus, and a land one on the south-east. The falling of the wind is usually succeeded by moisture, which renders the air somewhat heavy; but it is dissipated in the evening by a breeze springing up daily at that time. In summer this wind blows till four in the morning, in autumn and winter not till day-break, while in spring it does not continue longer than midnight. Those winds which arise in the beginning of summer, cease about the middle of September: and this is the period of the most intense heats, there being no breeze to attenuate them. Fortunately, however, they are not of long duration; and about the middle of October they sensibly decrease, as the atmosphere then begins to be freighted with watery clouds. The north winds, though possessed of some good characteristics, are disagreeable in summer, on account of the injury they inflict on the cotton plants, which are sometimes withered thereby to the very roots; and coming from the high mountains of Asia Minor, they are often very cold. But the principal cause of failure in the crops of Cyprus is drought, for the earth is often parched up—as it were—from the end of April till the middle of October.

Bramsen 1814

John Bramsen recorded an extensive journey in 1814 in *Letters of a Prussian Traveller; Descriptive of a Tour through Sweden, Prussia, Austria, Hungary, Istria, the Ionian Islands, Egypt, Syria, Cyprus, Rhodes, The Morea, Greece, Calabria, Italy, The Tyrol, the Banks of the Rhine, Hanover, Holstein, Denmark, Westphalia, and Holland,* published in 1818, in two volumes, by Henry Colburn, London. The following extract is from Volume I.

LETTER XXIII.

Mr. Taitboult, the French Vice-Consul, having informed us that a brig under Russian colours was shortly to sail for Cyprus, we thought it best to negociate for a passage, and succeeded in obtaining it, although at the enormous sum of three hundred piastres, better than thirty pounds English. The captain was a Greek, from Corfu, and the greater part of the crew were of the same nation. The day before our departure the French Consul introduced us to a Christian in the Levantine costume, who during the late war acted as interpreter to Sir Sidney Smith, and is now major-domo to Lady Esther Stanhope, who for several years past has been travelling in the Levant. He informed us that she was in a convent near the Druse mountains, where she had been confined by indisposition, from which, however, she was fast recovering. When this lady visited Saide she wore a Turkish dress, and rode an Arabian charger, to the astonishment and admiration of the Turks, who hold her in the highest estimation, and we heard in many places that she was actually imagined to be an English Princess.

We took our leave of Mr. Taitboult, from whom we experienced every civility during our residence in Saide, embarked on board the brig, and sailed with a fair breeze. We soon found that our vessel was very old and leaky, and at the same time a very dull sailer. Though the distance from Saide to Larneca is only from eighty to ninety English miles, yet, incredible to relate, we were no less than six days at sea, being driven about by contrary winds, and having a strong current against us. On the sixth day we dropped anchor in this harbour, which is esteemed by no means secure, it leaving vessels much exposed to the heavy gales, which at particular seasons set in regularly at a certain time of the day. It is now about a fortnight since we anchored in this port, during which time only three days have been exempted from the violent gales. On more than one occasion we have seen vessels drifting from their moorings, and running foul of other ships, but we heard of no serious accident.

On our arrival we sent our Greek on shore with a letter of recommendation to Mr. A. Vondiziano, who is a native of Cyprus and acts as English Consul. He returned very shortly with the information that the island was extremely unhealthy, and that a malignant fever was raging there with such violence that hardly a house was exempted from its destructive influence. We heard with sorrow that the Consul, together with his wife, four of his children, and several servants, lay infected with the malady. He advised us to consult our own safety, and to quit the island as soon as we could find an opportunity. We were informed that a brig under English colours from St. Maura, loaded with cotton, was to sail in a few days for Malta. We made an agreement with the captain for eighty Spanish piastres (about twenty pounds), stipulating that he should put us on shore at the island of Cerigo, and that we should be permitted to live on board his brig during our stay here, in order to avoid sleeping on shore and exposing ourselves to the infection. We were assured that many ships in the harbour had the fever on board, and that several sailors had fallen victims to it. We were also sorry to hear that many European vessels were prevented from sailing, the greater part of the crews being sick or disabled.

We shifted our quarters from the Russian brig to one named the Mahomed, Captain Spiro Patrizio, where the accommodations were considerably better. The following day we were invited to dine with the English Consul; we rowed on shore and found his cabriolet waiting for us. This species of vehicle is much used by the inhabitants; it is drawn by one horse, and has an awning over it to keep off the scorching beams of the sun: the driver is seated at the feet of the passengers, so as not to incommode them. The Consul received us very politely; he lives at about an English mile from the *Dogana*, or Custom-house, in which quarter all the Consuls and most of the respectable inhabitants reside. His house is large, and though but one story high has abundant accommodation. He reserves the front part for the use of such travellers as are recommended to him, and it is not difficult to see that he shows a marked attention to those of the English nation. He is well educated, and speaks French, Italian, and modern Greek with almost equal fluency. Though most of the Consul's family were invalids, we escaped all contagion by proper precaution and by smoking tobacco. [*The last sentence is footnoted:* M. Vandiziano showed us the rooms occupied by Colonel Rook, who died at Baffa, a port in this island. It may be well for his relatives to know that he had left a variety of trunks, &c. in his apartments.]

We were also well received by Mr. Howel, an English merchant, who has married a lady of the island, and lives near the *Dogana*.

We paid a visit to the French Consul, an engineer officer, who was appointed to this office at the time Buonaparte landed in Egypt; he is a well informed man, but appeared to be of a melancholy disposition. We could not help noticing the immense old military cocked hat which he wore even in the house, and which had a singular appearance contrasted with the other part of his dress. He lives on very good terms with the Bey, and had influence enough to prevail upon him during the war to interdict the exportation of corn to Malta. There is but little on the island of Cyprus to make the traveller regret his not touching at it, although there are a great many antiquities around Larneca, yet the jealous Turks will not permit any person to make researches. Besides the climate is very dangerous, and the passage to Europe very long and tedious, in consequence of the strong currents and the westerly winds, which set in from May to November, followed by very sudden easterly gales, which are always boisterous. It would be much more advisable for the traveller to keep a direct course for Europe; but should chance bring him to this island, he had better not embark before November, but take up his residence either at the English consul's or at the house of Mr. Howel's mother-in-law, who speaks a little Italian. The latter house is spacious and well built. It is kept on the plan of a boarding house; cleanliness is tolerably well attended to; the general accommodations are good, and the hostess seems solicitous to contribute to the comfort of all who are her inmates.

Larneca, or Larnec, is the most healthy port of the island. Baffa, Famagusta, and Nicosia, are highly dangerous to the European, who is very likely to find his grave there, if he visits these places during the sickly season, which is from June to October. The view of the town from the bay is very picturesque: it spreads out in the form of a crescent, and has a great variety of beautiful scenery in the neighbourhood. The houses are built close to the wharf, which is a central situation of much bustle and business. Here are two coffee-houses, a billiard-room, and a variety of shops mostly kept by Europeans, who are all dressed in the European manner, as is the case with most of the Christian natives of the islands. It recalled pleasing associations to us to see hats again, instead of the turban, to which we had so long been accustomed. The female part of the inhabitants generally adopt the Grecian costume; they wear their fine long black hair according to the fashion already described, and are habited in long dresses of yellow or green silk, trimmed with gold or silver lace; the old women wear short sleeves with a profusion of ruffles; but the young ones cover their arms and do not use these ornaments: they wear white muslin or silk petticoats, and red or yellow shoes. Yellow halfboots appear to be a kind of distinguishing mark between the higher and lower classes. The women of this island, once consecrated to love and celebrated for beauty, are generally tall and well shaped, but of a pale complexion; they are conspicuous for their fine blue eyes and well turned hands and arms, and are graceful in their persons, though the stoop they have in walking takes from the elegance of their carriage. They wear less covering on their bosoms than a European eye could reconcile with decency. They marry very young, and it is remarked that after this a few years are sufficient to blight their beauty; they then begin prematurely to look old, and grow careless of their persons.

A few days ago we were present at a wedding of the servant of the English Consul, a native of Larneca, with a pretty looking girl of the same place. There was some disparity of years between them, as the bridegroom was about forty and the bride only eighteen. We had no sooner entered the room, than we were presented with a large wax taper, with which most of the guests, who sat on benches round the room, were provided. Coffee and wine were handed round; and shortly after our arrival the ceremony began. Two Papas (the name given to regular Greek priests) with burning tapers proceeded round the room, and lighted those given to the most distinguished guests: we observed that many of them blew theirs out again and took it home with them. The bride was dressed in a green silk robe trimmed with silver lace; the covering on her bosom left but little for the imagination to indulge upon, and was ornamented with a large nosegay; a long white veil concealed her face, but her taper hand and arm remained uncovered. The bridegroom was very plainly dressed, and from the large nosegay which he wore in his breast, appeared to be as great an admirer of flowers as his bride. After a form of prayer the rings were exchanged, and the bridegroom kissed the cheek of his bride, who wept during the whole ceremony. When the priests were changing their rings, the parents and relations of the married couple threw small sugar plums at them, and *paras*, a small silver coin, at the priests. These reverend gentlemen seemed to think it no insult to be pelted in this way, but coolly deputed some of their attendants to collect the pieces of money, and put them in a plate, which was held for that purpose. Pipes and coffee were then brought, and the guests sat down to a supper prepared on the occasion.

The language of the country is the Romaic, or modern Greek; it may be necessary to observe that the parent tongue is scarcely understood. The inhabitants are generally poor, and even the better classes are so selfish in their dispositions, that scarce a single trace remains of the boasted hospitality of their ancestors. Some days since, a vessel touched here for provisions on her way to Jaffa; she was under Spanish colours, and was filled with pilgrims for Jerusalem, to which place she was carrying forty thousand Spanish piastres (about ten thousand pounds sterling), fifty boxes of Havannah sugar, ten thousand pounds of coffee, and several cases of cordials, as presents from the court of Spain to the principal convent there, which is in a great measure supported by that government; and it may be a matter of doubt, whether these presents will prove most gratifying to the monks of the convent or the Bey of Jerusalem.

LETTER XXIV.

The town of Larneca is very irregularly built, and chiefly consists of wretched houses one story high. There are, however, some very large buildings with spacious court-yards and fine gardens; as for example, the houses of the English, French, and Prussian Consuls, and those of some eminent merchants. The streets are narrow, dirty, and not paved. A considerable part of the town is surrounded with stagnant water, waste land, and salt marsh, which during the long continuance of the dry season, which lasts from May till October, renders the air very insalubrious. The inhabitants have an idea that this unwholesomeness of the air arises from another cause. They pretend that these pieces of stagnant water are rendered putrid by the bodies of immense quantities of locusts, which are destroyed by the intense heat and the want of verdure.

A great quantity of salt was formerly made in the island, but at present the pits are quite neglected by the Turks, and the quantity that is yearly made is very inconsiderable. The soil is not naturally sterile, and if property managed would abundantly repay the labours of the cultivator; but industry is not among the virtues of the inhabitants, and little or no attention is paid to the agriculture of the island.

The French Consul has a large country-house and a fine garden, five miles from Larneca, near a small town called Chiti, formerly Citrum, which is pleasantly situated at a short distance from the sea, and though but small, produces abundance of orange and lemon trees, grapes, apples, and other fruits and vegetables, which is a sufficient proof of the goodness of the soil. Cotton of a very superior quality is also cultivated in this neighbourhood. We visited the country-house of the Neapolitan Consul, which is but a short distance from that of the French consul, and has a garden well stocked with abundance of fruits and vegetables.

The principal branches of trade on this island are cotton and cotton-seed, wine, honey, turpentine, salt, and corn. The latter article is prohibited from being exported in any but Turkish vessels; this prohibition is however constantly evaded, and great quantities are exported in a clandestine manner. The avarice of the custom-house officers easily gets the better of their scruples; they have an accommodating habit of shutting their eyes, at the same time that they open their hands, and if the latter are well filled the former remain instinctively blind. It was even hinted, that the Turks, during the war, were sometimes obscured in the same way and that considerable quantities of corn were exported to Malta. The wine is of a superior quality and very cheap, not more than about three pence the bottle. The Greeks bring it to the market in leathern bags, of which it always retains a certain taste, not the most agreeable to the palate. Butter and cow's milk are, as in Egypt, very scarce. The breed of horses is very inconsiderable, but there are great numbers of asses, oxen, goats, sheep, and hogs. It was here, for the first time since I quitted Europe, that I saw a plough drawn by oxen, and in the use of it the Grecian peasant appeared tolerably expert.

It was about the end of September when our captain got under weigh, with the land breeze, which regularly sets in towards evening, but we had scarcely cleared the channel when it began to blow directly contrary. The captain immediately determined to return to port, but this we did not effect without difficulty, as the sea ran very high and the ship laboured hard. At length, on the following morning, we dropt anchor once again in the port of Larneca, where we were detained the whole day. Next morning we sailed a second time with a fair breeze, and the day after passed Simacosta, under full canvass, and the second day Baffa, both ports in the island of Cyprus. The latter place has lately been much thinned by a malignant fever, and many European sailors became victims to its destructive influence. We heard of instances, when ships have been detained there, as in Larneca, several months for want of hands to work them. We soon found that our captain was but half master of the brig, and that the mate and his two brothers, who were sailors on board, did what they pleased. We likewise discovered that our gallant tars made no scruple of sleeping very composedly during their watch, and leaving the helm lashed the greater part of the night. We could scarcely credit the circumstance, when we were first informed of it by our Greek interpreter; but the following night we had a practical proof of the correctness of his assertion, for we were on the point of running foul of an English brig, though the moon was shining in full lustre. On hearing the noise I hastened on deck, where the captain was vociferating and swearing in the most violent manner. I enquired the cause of his anger, and he assured me that not only the whole watch had been asleep, but even the steersman, a Frenchman, who was the carpenter of the ship, lay snoring beside the helm; that we had narrowly escaped running foul of an English brig, and that had the wind been high and the night dark, our situation might have been perilous in the extreme.

Kinneir 1814

A visit to Cyprus by John Macdonald Kinneir, a captain for the East India Company between January 2 and 24, 1814, was described in his *Journey through Asia Minor, Armenia, and Koordistan, in the Years 1813 and 1814; With Remarks on the Marches of Alexander, and Retreat of the Ten Thousand*, published in London by John Murray in 1818.

Kinneir said that his object in presenting this material was to contribute to the general knowledge of geography. He had intended to visit the lands through which a European army might travel in attempting an invasion of India. Illness prevented the latter portions of such a trip, but he left England for Gottenburg in early 1813 "intending to proceed through Sweden and Russia to Constantinople. But the disastrous retreat of Napolean from Moscow having in the mean time opened a more direct road, I joined the head quarters of his Majesty the Emperor Alexander, then in pursuit of the French, and from Dresden resumed my journey to Turkey by Vienna."

He was able to visit the Middle East, Persia and, of course, Cyprus where he was advised to go "for the benefit of his health."

[p. 176]

I hired a boat to carry us to Famagusta, in the island of Cyprus, where we landed on the 2d of January, after a voyage of fifteen hours. The entrance into the harbour is not, I should suppose, more than eighty, or a hundred yards wide, defended on one side by a bastion of the works, and on the other by a ruined tower. This port could once admit vessels of a considerable draft of water; but since the conquest of the Turks, sand and rubbish have been suffered to accumulate in such a degree, that none but small vessels can now enter it with safety. I had scarcely put my foot upon the shore, before I was beset by a tribe of Custom-house officers and other vagabonds, imperiously demanding buckshish; but, without attending to their clamours, I entered the sea-gate, and walked about a quarter of a mile through deserted streets and decayed churches, to a small coffee-house in the inhabited part of the town. Famagusta, which is said to have derived its name from Cape Amochostos, is situated above five miles to the S. of the ancient Salamis, now called Eski Famagusta, and is said to have been founded by a colony from Constantia, fortified by Guy of Lusignan, and afterwards embellished by the Venetians. It stood a long and memorable siege against Sultan Selim, and appears to have been a fortress of considerable strength; its works, which are now dismantled, cover a circumference of about two miles, and consist of a rampart and bastions, defended on the land side by a broad ditch hewn out of the rock. In the centre of the town, which is inhabited by a few Turkish families, and which, for the number of its decayed churches, might be compared to old Goa, although not on so superb a scale, stand the remains of the Venetian palace near the Cathedral of St. Sophia, a respectable Gothic pile, now in part converted into a mosque.

As I could not procure a lodging within the walls, I hired a small room in a Greek village, about three quarters of a mile off, and in the morning went to look at the ruins of Salamis, or rather of Constantia; for the former was entirely overwhelmed by an inundation of the sea. These ruins consist of the foundation of the ancient walls, about three or four miles in circuit; old cisterns for collecting rain water, broken columns, and foundations of buildings, which lie scattered along the sea shore and near the mouth of the Pedaea, the ancient Pedaeus. The country around Famagusta, and the ruins of Constantia, is sandy, bleak and rocky, for the most part uncultivated and overspread with a small weed resembling the camel's thorn on the deserts of Arabia.

4th. I hired one horse, four mules, and a jackass, to carry myself and attendants to Larnica; but it had rained with such violence the preceding day and night, that I would not have quitted Famagusta had I not found myself most uncomfortably situated in a miserable hut, scarcely water proof, and filled with fleas, bugs, and vermin of every kind. The morning was fine and we mounted about eleven o'clock, but we had not gone a couple of miles before the rain again fell in torrents. It blew a furious gale from the west; the roads were so deep and slippery that the cattle were stumbling at every step; and the surrounding country was so bare and desolate, that there was not a single object on which the eye might repose with pleasure. I saw neither villages nor trees, nor even shrubs, excepting the small thorn before mentioned, which covered a vast and dreary flat, over which we travelled for thirteen miles to the village of Ormidia. It being reported to me, when we had gone about half way, that one of my servants, who was mounted on the jackass, had disappeared; I dispatched the muleteer in search of him, but he was no where to be found, and did not again join us until the next morning. He had lost his way on the heath, and as his poor beast was too jaded to proceed, he had been reduced to the necessity of passing the night in the fields. Thoroughly drenched to the skin, I took shelter in a Greek house in the valley of Ormidia, and as it was now nearly dark, and the storm continued to rage with increased violence, I resigned all thought of reaching Larnica that night. In the house where I halted, several Greek mariners were making merry round a large fire in the middle of the hall, and, on our entering, opened their ring to afford room for us near the fire; but as this apartment was the only accommodation the house afforded I inquired whether or not it were possible to hire a room in some other part of the village, which consisted of a number of scattered huts built along a range of heights overlooking a bay of the sea. I was informed that there was at some distance, close to the sea shore, an old house belonging to the English dragoman, where the Greek believed I might be accommodated, as it was only inhabited by a man and his wife, who had the care of it. I sent for this man, who said I was welcome to pass the night in the house, and that he would shew me the way. It was excessively dark, but after following him for about a quarter of a mile, through pools of water, and over hedges and ditches, we entered the hall of a large and ruinous building, filled with broken chairs and tables, worm eaten couches, and shattered looking glasses.—In this uncomfortable place I settled myself for the night, and notwithstanding my carpet, as well as my clothes, was quite wet, lay down to rest, and slept soundly until break of day.

5th. In the morning we pursued our journey along the shore, and through a flat and marshy country, rendering the approach to Larnica difficult on this side. I saw but one village, situated close to a range of low hills, running from W. to E., and distant about four miles from the sea. I remained nine days at Larnica, at the house of M. Vandesiano, the British consul in Cyprus, and during that period made several short excursions into the neighbourhood, although there was but little to attract admiration or call forth remark.

The island is one hundred and forty miles in length and sixty-three in breadth; at the widest part a range of mountains intersects it from E. to W., terminating towards the E. in a long promontory called Cape St. Andrew (ancient Denaretum,) and rising in a lofty peak called St. Croix, (Mount Olympus,) bearing nearly N.W. of Larnica. The soil is naturally fruitful, and although a very small proportion of the land is under cultivation, the merchants of Larnica annually export many cargoes of excellent wheat to Spain and Portugal. The population does not exceed seventy thousand souls, and is said to be daily decreasing; half of this number are Greeks under their archbishop, and the remainder Turks, with the exception of the Franks at Larnica. The evil consequences of the Turkish system of government are no where more apparent than in Cyprus, where the governor, who is appointed yearly by the Capudan Pasha, the ex-officio proprietor of the island, has recourse to every method of extortion; so that the Turks would labour under the same grievances as the Christians, were not the latter, in addition to the demands of the government, compelled to contribute towards the support of a number of lazy and avaricious monks. All affairs connected with the Greeks are under the superintendance of the Archbishop and Dragoman of Cyprus, (an officer appointed by the Porte,) who are accountable to the Mutesellim for the contributions, miri, &c. The most fertile, as well as the most agreeable parts of the island, are in the vicinities of Cerina and Baffo, the ancient Paphos, where, according to Tacitus, Venus rising from the waves was wafted to the shore. Here we find forests of oak, beech and pines, groves of olives and plantations of mulberries. Cyprus is remarkable for the fineness of its fruits, wine, oil and silk; the oranges are as delicious as those of Tripoli, and the wine, which is of two kinds, red and white, is sent down the Levant, where it is manufactured for the English market. The silk is also of two kinds, yellow and white, but the former is preferred. The wheat is of a superior quality, and rice might be cultivated in several parts of the island, were the agriculturist permitted to accumulate a sufficient capital to enable him to clear and prepare the land; but the Greek peasantry, who are the only industrious class, have been so much oppressed by Turks, monks and bishops, that they are now reduced to the extremity of indigence, and avail themselves of every opportunity to emigrate from the island. The governor and archbishop deal more largely in corn than all the other people of the island put together; they frequently seize upon the whole yearly produce, at their own valuation, and either export or retail it at an advanced price; nay, it happened more than once during the war in Spain, that the whole of the corn was purchased in this manner by the merchants of Malta, and exported without leaving the lower orders a morsel of bread. The island abounds in game, such as partridges, quails, woodcocks and snipes; there are no wild animals excepting foxes and hares, but many kinds of serpents, and, amongst others, that of the asp, which is said to have caused the death of the renowned Cleopatra. All sorts of domestic fowls, as well as sheep and cattle, are bred in Cyprus, where it is the boast of the natives, that the produce of every land and climate will not only flourish but even attain the highest point of perfection.

Larnica is situated on the site of the ancient Citium, the native city of Zeno, the philosopher, and at the head of a bay, constituting the best roadsted in the island. It is the second town in Cyprus, the emporium of its commerce and the residence of innumerable consuls from the different European powers, who parade the streets with as much self-importance as if they were ambassadors. Larnica consists of an upper and a lower town, both together containing a population of five thousand souls; of which number forty families are Franks, and the remainder Greeks and Mahomedans. The houses being built of mud are mean in the extreme, but those of the Franks are comfortable within, and most of them are adorned by a lofty flag-staff, where, on Sundays and holidays, they hoist the colours of their respective nations. The upper town contains the convent and cathedral of St. Saviour, the residence of the bishop, and the Marino or Port; the chapel of St. Lazarus, a very old structure, without beauty or magnificence, but consecrated by the Greeks, as the spot to which Lazarus fled for refuge from the rage of the Jews. A stone coffin or sarcophagus, in a vault, is said to have once contained his ashes until they were carried off by the French to Marseilles. At a short distance from the chapel of St. Lazarus stands the castle, an edifice originally erected by the Princes of the House of Lusignan, but now crumbling to ruins. The exports are wheat, barley, cotton, silk, wine and drugs; the imports rice and sugar, from Egypt, and cloth, hardware and colonial produce from Malta and Smyrna. This traffic is carried on by Levantine ships under English colours; there is no harbour, consequently the ships lie at a considerable distance from the shore, but the anchorage is tolerably good, and accidents seldom happen. The prevailing winds blow from the N.E. and S.W., the latter being in general accompanied by heavy falls of rain.

An adjacent cape is still denominated Chitti, whilst the ruins of Citium are recognized in heaps of tumuli and hillocks of rubbish; from which bricks of a superior quality and medals are frequently dug up by the natives. Between the upper and the lower town is an elevated spot, on which a building appears to have been erected, and immediately at the foot of this mount is the ancient basin of the Port, the mouth of which is now blocked up with sand and gravel; so that the water becomes stagnant in the summer. Traces of the fosse as well as of the aqueduct may be discovered; for Larnica has no good water in itself, and is still supplied from a distance by an aqueduct constructed by a Turkish emir about half a century ago.

The military force of Cyprus amounts to three hundred men, immediately about the person of the governor, and four thousand janissaries, without courage, arms or discipline, dispersed over the different parts of the island. (*The last sentence is footnoted:* The possession of Cyprus would give to England a preponderating influence in the Mediterranean, and place at her disposal the future destinies of the Levant. Egypt and Syria would soon become her tributaries, and she would acquire an overawing position in respect to Asia Minor, by which the Porte might at all times be kept in check, and the encroachments of Russia, in this quarter, retarded, if not prevented. It would increase her commerce in a very considerable degree; give her the distribution of the rich wines, silks, and other produce of that fine island; the rice and sugar of Egypt, and the cotton, opium, and tobacco of Anatolia. It is of easy defence; and under a liberal government would, in a very short space of time, amply repay the charge of its own establishment, and afford the most abundant supplies to our fleets at a trifling expense.)

I bade adieu to Larnica, and its motley inhabitants, without a sigh of regret, and on the morning of the 14th of January set out for the capital. For the first three miles I travelled through a dreary and uncultivated plain, having the bay on my right hand, and the mountain of St. Croix, with the ridge of Olympus, to the N.W.; crossing at the fourth mile a streamlet, I entered a range of low rocky hills, and at the ninth mile saw the lofty chain which bounds the plain of Nicosia, on the N. This range branches from Olympus, first towards the N., and then, turning towards the E. and W., terminates on the W. at Cape Epiphany, and on the E. at Cape St. Andrew. At the twelfth mile descended into a noble plain, bounded on the N. by a low branch of Olympus; and at the fourteenth, halted to refresh our horses at the Greek village of Atteno. If we except a few fields in the immediate vicinity of Larnica, the country, during the whole of the journey, was in a state of nature; the soil was marly, and covered with the weed so often mentioned before. After an hour's repose we again mounted our horses, directing our course across a plain, thickly overspread with large pebbles; which I was informed increased the fertility of the land by preserving a certain degree of moisture, and at the same time protecting the rising grain from a blighting wind common to this island. At the fourth mile crossed, on a stone bridge, the southern branch of the Pedio, flowing gently through a valley interspersed with groves of olive trees; the first we have seen. From the bridge we ascended an eminence, and entered upon an extensive table land, intersected with low hills, of a singular appearance and formation; they are composed of a gravelly substance, some of them square and others round, with flat summits and vertical sides: the nature and appearance of the country, in other respects, the same as that between Larnica and Atteno. At the tenth mile was a small hamlet; and at the fourteenth, the city of Nicosia, the ancient Tamasis, broke upon the view, at no greater distance than five or six hundred yards: it made a fine appearance, and bore a striking resemblance to Shiraz in Persia, when that beautiful city is first seen on issuing from the gorges of the mountains, behind the tomb of Hafiz. Like the capital of Fars, it is situated in a noble plain, bounded by the lofty mountains, tipped with snow, whilst its numerous spires and minarets are seen to rise in the same manner above the branches of the trees; but the fine cathedral of St. Sophia, towering over the heads of all the other buildings, combined with the extent and solidity of the walls and bastions, gives an air of grandeur to Nicosia which Shiraz cannot emulate.

I entered the city by the gate of Larnica, and was conducted to the episcopal palace through a number of narrow lanes, where my horse was nearly buried in mud and filth. The archbishop, dressed in a magnificent purple robe, with a long flowing beard, and a silk cap on his head, received me in the vestibule, and ordered an apartment to be prepared for me in the palace, a large and straggling building, containing upwards of a hundred chambers. These are all required for the accommodation of the bishops, priests, and their attendants; for the archbishop, both in power and affluence, is the second personage on the island. All affairs connected with the Greeks are under his immediate cognizance and management; and, consequently, when the governor is desirous of making a new arrangement regarding that class, or of levying contributions, he has recourse to the archbishop, who has lately usurped the whole authority, and seldom even deigns to consult the dragoman. From the humble situation of an obscure deacon, he raised himself, by extraordinary means, to the episcopacy: he borrowed immense sums of money from the rich, which he lavished on the poor; securing, in this manner, the votes of his creditors, that they might be repaid, and those of the others in expectation of future reward. He pressed me to remain with him for a short time, promising, on this condition, that he would procure the mutesellim's boat to transport me from Cerina to Kelendri; and as he was prepossessing in his manners, and far superior to the generality of Greek priests, I consented to postpone my departure for a couple of days. At seven o'clock supper being announced, he took me by the hand, and led me through a gallery into the refectory, a long and dirty hall, where about thirty priests and bishops sat down to table. The wine and provisions were excellent and abundant, and the bread, which was white as snow, and baked with milk instead of water, was the best I remember to have tasted.

During my stay at Nicosia, I visited every thing worthy the attention of a traveller; amongst the rest, the cathedrals of St. Sophia, St. Nicolas, St. Catherine, and St. Dominique: the former is a handsome Gothic structure, but the others are small, and do not merit any particular description. Three of them are now mosques; that of St. Nicholas is converted into the Bezistein, and that of St. Dominique contains the tombs of many princes of the house of Lusignan, who held their court at Nicosia. The mutesellim resides in the ancient palace of the kings of Cyprus; but it is now so much altered and disfigured, that it is not possible to form any idea of its original appearance: the gate is however entire, and over the arch, in basso relievo, is the figure of a griffin, the crest, I believe, of Lusignan. From the palace I directed my course to the ramparts, round which I walked in about an hour and a quarter; they are built, or probably only faced, with hewn stone, flanked with large oblong bastions: the ditch is dry and shallow, but so broad that it now yields a considerable quantity of corn; the rampart is also in some parts cultivated, and of great breadth, as all the earth and rubbish from the interior of the town appears to have been transported thither in order to add to its solidity. The batteries are en barbete, and I counted but four small pieces of artillery without carriages and completely honeycombed, a matter however of no consequence, as this city could never stand a siege, being entirely commanded by the heights to the S. of it. Nicosia, or, as the Turks call it, Licosia, contains, according to the account of the archbishop, two thousand families of Mahommedans, half that number of Greeks, forty of Armenians, and twelve of Maronite Catholics; four public baths, eight mosques, (all of which were once churches,) six Greek chapels, and one Catholic convent, besides the episcopal palace, and a large caravanserai now falling to decay. The remaining part of the town consists of brick and mud huts, many of which have been erected on the foundations of the old edifices. The bazar, although tolerably well supplied, is not even arched, but roofed with reeds and mats, which admit the rain in all directions. The city is entered by three gates, namely, those of Larnica, Cerina, and Paphos, of which the latter is most deserving of notice; the circumjacent plain is filled with Greek convents, and the white peak of mount Olympus bore about S.W. by W.

16*th*. In the morning the dragoman paid me a visit, and in the evening I returned it: he was a Greek, of a good family at Constantinople, and formerly attached to the English army in Egypt. It was not difficult to perceive that a jealousy subsisted between him and the archbishop, whom he accused of avarice and ambition, and a desire of intermeddling in matters that did not concern him.

On the 19*th* I bade adieu to Nicosia, and set out for Cerina, where I intended to embark for the opposite coast of Caramania. I directed my course through the plain in a N.W. direction, and about a mile and a half beyond the city wall, crossed the northern branch of the Pedio, a small stream flowing to the E. At the fourth mile we entered a range of low brown hills, through which we travelled until the ninth mile, when we descended into a narrow flat, running along the foot of the lofty chain of mountains before mentioned: this flat had the appearance of great fertility, but it was neither inhabited nor cultivated. At the eleventh mile we reached the foot of the range; when changing the direction of our course to the N.E. we entered a cleft or opening in the mountains, the sides of which were clothed with myrtle, a variety of other evergreens, and sweet-scented flowers. Our route, for about three miles, led through this defile; when, on turning the point of a rock, we had a view of the distant coast of Cilicia, and the finest part of Cyprus I have yet seen: a narrow belt of land, covered with shrubs and trees, confined on one side by the sea, and on the other by the mountains, extended to the E. and W. as far as the eye could reach. The little town of Cerina, or, as the Turks call it, Gerinia, with its ancient chateau, was discerned immediately under us, reflected in the water; and on the right hand the stately towers of the convent of Bella Paisa rose amidst the wooded cliffs of the mountains: we were nearly an hour in descending, and at three in the afternoon reached Cerina, the whole distance being, according to my computation, about eighteen miles.

I had no sooner arrived than I was informed by the Zabit, that the boat had sailed only a few hours before for the opposite coast, and was not expected back for two or three days;—a circumstance which occasioned me some uneasiness, as I foresaw that I should be detained in a place where it was impossible to procure even a habitable apartment. I had brought a letter of introduction to Signor Loretti, the captain of the boat; but he was gone in command of the vessel, and I was therefore necessitated to cultivate the acquaintance of the Zabit, who invited me to dinner, and regaled me with abundance of wine and a Cyprian concert, consisting of two blind fiddlers, accompanied by a boy who sang and played upon the lute. In the morning, the Signora Loretti, an old dame with a very long waist, entered the court of the hovel where I resided; and dismounting from her mule observed, that she was come to carry me to her country-house, where I could remain until her husband returned from Kelendri. I accepted, with gratitude, her kind invitation; and promising to be at her house in the evening, she departed, saying that she would go and make preparations for my reception.

Ibrahim, who had never perfectly recovered from the effects of the Latakia fever, was once more taken ill, and in the course of a few days, reduced to extreme weakness. I left him under the care of the Zabit, and set out with a guide to look at the old and magnificent monastery of Bella Paisa, situated on the declivity of the mountains, about four miles S.E. of Cerina; from the town to the monastery, which was founded by a princess of the house of Lusignan, I passed under the shade of olive, myrtle, and orange trees. A Greek priest stood at the gate to shew me the ruins. Several cows were grazing in the outer court, from which we passed into a decayed cloister, and thence into the chapel; which, for the lightness and elegance of its architecture, might be compared to the cathedral of Salisbury: it has six windows facing the north, and commanding a delightful prospect of the adjacent country, sea, and coast of Caramania: it is forty-three paces in length, and fourteen in breadth; but of all its ornaments a stone pulpit alone remains. On the E. side of the cloister, the ceilings of two gothic chambers have fallen in; and immediately above there appears to have been a hall of the same length as the chapel, decorated with six handsome pilasters on either side, and two noble Gothic windows opening towards the sea: there are several other apartments in ruins; and on the south side of the cloister, another Gothic hall has been converted into a Greek chapel. Above are the cells of the monks, and beneath the monastery is a prodigious subterraneous cavern, completely arched, and now used as a cowhouse and stable. The ground, for some distance round the monastery, is covered with the remains of other buildings, appendages no doubt to the former establishment, which has more the appearance of a prince's palace than a place of religious retirement. It is difficult to imagine a situation more convenient or delightful; lofty mountains and hanging cliffs, clothed with wood and verdure, rise immediately behind, and continue to extend in successive ridges both to the E. and W.; a fertile plain spreads to the channel, formerly called Aulon Cilicius, which is bounded by the rocks of Mount Taurus, mantled with snow. I quitted this pleasing spot with regret; and bending my course along the foot of the mountains, reached, at four in the evening, the habitation of Signora Loretti, a neat little cottage, standing on an eminence about three miles to the S.W. of Cerina. The old lady was ready to receive me at the door, and conducted me to my apartment, which was distinct from the other part of the cottage, and stood in the middle of the garden. Captain Loretti had purchased this estate, consisting of several hundred acres of excellent land, for twenty piastres, or about a pound sterling, and had amused himself in improving it, by planting olive trees, which yield a large profit in a short time.

The town, or rather village, of Cerina, the ancient Cerinia, was formerly defended by a strong wall; but the greater part of it has fallen down, and the port has been nearly filled up by the ruins. On the east side of the harbour stands the castle, a fortress erected, it is said, by the Venetians; it is of a square form flanked at each corner with round towers, washed on the N. and E. by the sea, and defended on the S. and W. by a deep ditch: the walls are lofty, and built of an excellent kind of stone; it has one gate in the west face, and there are, I believe, four small brass swivels mounted in the works. The harbour, which is small, is exposed to the north wind, and cannot admit a vessel of more than a hundred tons burthen; but the trade is inconsiderable, there not being above fifteen families in the place.

22*d*. Captain Loretti arrived from Kelendri during the night, and reached his habitation early in the morning, mounted on a mule without a saddle: he was a native of Dalmatia, and appeared to be bordering on sixty years of age; tall and muscular, and dressed partly as a Turk and partly as a Frank: he pretended to much learning, but was ignorant of the most common occurrences; and although he boasted of being able to speak ten different languages, it was with exceeding difficulty you could understand him in any. He was vain, rude, and presuming; but kind, hospitable, and attentive; and altogether the strangest compound of a man I had ever met with. He wished me to spend a week with him, saying, that the boat could not sail before the treasure intended for the Capudan Pasha should arrive from Nicosia; and when I urged the necessity of my immediate departure, he laughed so loud that he might have been heard at least a mile off, adding, that the boat should not move from her anchorage before the time specified. After a warm dispute I wrote a letter to the Zabit, who sent an order that the boat should sail whenever I thought proper. The captain, upon receiving this message, broke forth into a furious torrent of invective against the poor Zabit; but I at last assuaged his wrath by stating, that he might himself remain quietly at home, and send his mate, a Greek, to see me fairly across the channel. He liked the proposal, and said that the boat should depart with me in the morning.

Light 1814

[Plate 7]

Henry Light, a captain of the Royal Artillery stationed in Malta, kept a journal and sketches of his travels and offered them for publication to Robert Walpole, who declined. Light then had them published by Rodwell and Martin, in London in 1818 as *Travels in Egypt, Nubia, Holy Land, Mount Libanon, and Cyprus in the Year 1814.*

[p. 238]

I had endured much inconvenience in the last seven months, and on board the different coasting vessels had never been under cover; yet my patience had not been exhausted: here, however, it was lost; and, as I knew my voyage to Constantinople [*from Beirut*] would occupy at least three weeks, I determined to disembark at Cyprus, where the vessel touched to take in provisions for the voyage; and accordingly, after three comfortless days and nights on board, I landed at Larnica on the 26th of September, having seen the shore appearing on the east in a tract of low land, and in the west in a range of high mountains, the evening before.

Here, in expectation every day of obtaining a passage in a vessel where the accommodations would be better, I was detained three weeks; and was at last, from so much time having elapsed, obliged to give up the thoughts of my expedition, and determine on taking the first conveyance to Malta.

My residence at Larnica was not uninteresting. I had apartments in a detached pavilion of the vice-consul's, who was a Zantiot, and had amassed a considerable fortune from his office during the latter periods of the war, when every vessel coming to Cyprus bore the British flag.

Though Larnica gives the name to the road in which vessels anchor, yet it is distant from the shore nearly a mile, and is detached to the east from the town which may be called the port, and bears the name of La Scala, about the same distance. This place contains the custom-house, and is the mart for trade. It consists of a long street, chiefly a bazar, where common necessaries of life and articles of dress are sold; is inhabited by Greeks and Turks; the latter commonly employed in the affairs of the custom-house, the former in trade. The houses are low, built partly of mud and partly of stone, whitewashed.

The space between La Scala and Larnica is barren, as indeed is the greatest part of the plain at the foot of the mountains, which for several miles east and west of La Scala is either uncultivated or marshy land, intersected by salt lakes. The foundations of an ancient town are often found between La Scala and Larnica. The effects of the marshy land are evinced in the countenances of the natives, who suffer every year from agues and fevers, that diminish the population, and regularly appear in the hot months of June, July, August, and September. When the Venetians had possession of the island, care was taken to drain the marshes and confine the water to the salt lakes, which produced an immense revenue; but, like all other sources of riches of the Turks, are neglected, though still productive enough to be a considerable article of trade.

Though the language of Cyprus is said to be more corrupt than of any other part of the East where Greek was once spoken, yet I could not but be pleased to hear ancient Greek words used for figs, cheese, and milk, by the market-people who passed me; and I was conducted to the vice-consul's house by a Cypriot, to whom I made use of an ancient Greek phrase, pronounced as the modern Romaic. On my arrival I was shown into a house fitted up in the European manner, though built partly in the Eastern style; and on presenting my letter of recommendation from Colonel Misset, and stating my determination to wait for another opportunity for Constantinople, was settled in the apartments I have before alluded to: they had been occupied by Lieutenant-colonel Rooke, who had died at Baffa, the ancient Paphos, a few days before; a gentleman whose memory seemed to be held in great respect at Cyprus, and whose inclination for travel had kept him for a long time in the East, where he lavished large sums in objects of research and in acts of generosity, endearing him to the natives of the countries he visited.

Thus settled at Cyprus, I was left to my own resources for employment, and obliged to remain at Larnica for the chance of any unforeseen occasion to quit it. I became one of the family of the vice-consul, and conformed to the unwholesome custom of making a heavy meal at mid-day. The mornings and evenings I passed alone.

I was often amused by the assumed dignity of the different representatives of European nations at Larnica, where the Austrian, Neapolitan, French, and Spanish consuls had their residence, and where etiquette of precedency was pushed to a degree not known in our own country. All except the French consul were engaged in trade; and of course their own interest prevailed over that of the country they represented. The only English merchant on the island resided at La Scala: he had to contend with the united phalanx of Levantines, who had no inclination to admit a competitor in trade. An Englishman wishing to settle there will be exposed to much opposition, and will only succeed by having large funds to meet every exigency to which he is liable. Much of the trade is contraband, particularly corn: and it is necessary to keep on good terms with the aga and officers employed at the custom-house by presents, the best and only means of ensuring favour in any competition with Levantines.

In the cemetery of the convent of St. Lazarus at La Scala, I saw the tombstones of English who formerly resided at Larnica; but their date is not later than 1750.

The sickness that exists in the country during the hot weather caused the presence of a vast number of medical men, whose abilities may be appreciated when the reader hears that one of the most eminent of them took me on one side to question me relative to the effects of James's powder, which I had recommended and given in a slight case of fever. I was asked, with great seriousness, whether it was not composed of pulverized cranium of the human head. It was a medicine not known except by report amongst them.

To guard against the effects of the *mal aria,* a European must leave the plains in the month of June, seek the mountains, and not quit them till October: without this precaution he must inevitably be seized with illness, and often is carried off by the fevers that rage with great violence during the hot months.

The superstition of the Levantines of this island may be imagined by my mentioning, that I observed the nurse who attended the consul's children burn incense under their nose every evening at sun-set, to prevent the effects of the evil eye. On my smiling at this ceremony, I was told it was common; perhaps, indeed, my presence, as a stranger, rendered it essential.

Larnica contains two or three wide streets, and has one mosque. The principal Levantines and Franks inhabit large houses in the outskirts of the town: amongst the most considerable is a palace of the archbishop of Cyprus; where, during my stay at Larnica, I went, on the occasion of some particular ceremony, to pay my respects to the archbishop. All the Franks and Levantines, under their respective consuls, were assembled. The canons of the church received them in an antechamber. Coffee and refreshments were handed about; and, as the archbishop had been taken suddenly ill, only a few of the principal visitors were introduced to him, amongst whom I was one. He was lying on a crimson bed of state, in full costume; and, if the length of beard was intended to add to dignity, his must have been increased for that purpose. He only spoke Romaic; but asked me some few questions by the help of his nephew, who had been studying medicine at Padua for some years, and seemed an intelligent young man, ardent in the pursuit of science, and apparently very little pleased at being doomed to bury himself in such a place as Cyprus; where, he told me with a sigh, he should be obliged, in a year or two, to fix his residence.

The costume of the Franks is, for the men, generally that of Europe. The consuls have an uniform, which they make as rich as possible with embroidery. I saw them all in grand gala on the birth-day of the Emperor of Austria, whose consul received a visit of ceremony from all the others. The costume of the women is Greek, and almost similar to that which the late travels in Greece have rendered so familiar to all readers. The descendants of the Venetians still preserve their dialect, though purer Italian is spoken by many of the Franks.

This island, which is said to have been divided, in former days, into nine populous kingdoms, is now reduced to between eighty and ninety thousand inhabitants; which, according to common report, is daily diminishing. The produce of the island is still considerable in corn, wine, oil, and silks, notwithstanding its neglected state. A considerable quantity of salt is collected in the neighbourhood of La Scala, in an extensive lake into which the sea water passes. The salt is produced by simple evaporation from the rays of the sun, and collected in heaps at the east end. The north side is confined by rising ground, where is a beautiful mosque, built in honour of one of Mahomet's relations. The mountains of the Holy Cross appear to rise behind it. Towards sun-set, its rays, verging on the lake, produce a bright red, on which were reflected the figures of the carts, horses, and passengers traversing it: this, combining with the mosque and the tints on the overhanging mountains, produced a beautiful picture.

The government is an appendage to the Captain Pasha, who vests it in the person of a mosallem or governor, nominally appointed for three years; the present one had, however, contrived to remain longer. The seat of government is at Nicosia, where the chief Turkish population resides. The island is divided into sixteen districts, each under a lieutenant, who bears the title of Cadelesquiere. The Grand Signor, at the commencement of a war, demands four hundred men from Cyprus, who form part of the Timariots. The Greeks are, as usual, oppressed. The dignitaries of the church are protected by the governor, who obtains contributions easily through their influence. They consist of one archbishop and three bishops: the former with an income of forty thousand dollars: the latter have much less; and, in an excursion I made for a day in the mountains, a return of money for hospitality shown was thankfully received by one of them.

The Roman Catholics have a considerable establishment at Larnica. The convent of the Propaganda is a large building, where I should recommend travellers to endeavour to gain admission, as they will be more independent, and enabled by payment to make a recompense for the treatment they receive; which, however freely granted by the Levantine agents, yet is considered a tax on them; and they take care to let you understand the British government does not pay for it.

Unfortunately for me, so few military men had been seen as travellers in the East, that I was supposed employed by my government. I became an object of suspicion to the Franks and Turks, and of extortion to the Levantines. From this latter circumstance, I lost two opportunities of leaving Cyprus, by not acceding to the enormous demands made for my passage, and began to feel the effect of *mal aria*. To counteract this, I joined a party, on the 8th of October, in an excursion into the mountains west of Larnica. The road lay at first through a plain in a dry gravelly soil, producing only olives, growing to a larger size than those I had seen in other parts of the Mediterranean: after continuing in the plain for three hours, we ascended very gently for three more to the convent of Sta. Thecla, where I slept during the night. I had in vain looked for cultivation: briers and olives were the only produce of the ground. A few rhododendrons flourished in the water courses we passed. A miserable stone cottage now and then showed itself, where fig trees and vines were to be seen.

The peasantry is ill looking. The men were dressed in a white canvass vest over a waistcoat of the same material, and a white linen turban on their heads. They wore the Albanian petticoat, similar to the Highland kilt, or the usual sharaweel or breeches of the Turks, and high boots, used, as I understood, to avoid the fatal venom of the serpents of the island.

I found only an old Greek priest at the convent of Sta. Thecla, who from his dress I imagined was a peasant: he had two or three attendants with him. The convent was undergoing a repair, for the reception of an additional number of priests, and for a feast that was to take place in a few days in honour of the saint. I had supplied myself with provisions, and therefore did not intrude on him. He was an old man, of about sixty years of age, perfectly ignorant of all except his missal, which he could not read; he had learnt it by heart; it was all that was necessary. He was proud of his chapel, and pointed exultingly to the wretched daubs that adorned it. He left his pipe, to repeat evening prayers; and having finished them, took to it again. This seemed his only occupation. Though I had an interpreter with me, I could gain no information as to the state of the peasantry in his neighbourhood: what I saw was wretched.

Our party slept on boards; we rose early, continued our excursion towards the summit of the chain we had proposed to reach. In a short time, we were amongst myrtles in full bloom, and fir trees: there was nothing else to interest me for two hours, till we arrived at a space of ground cleared of wood, where was a square range of buildings belonging to one of the bishops, who literally kept a *table d'hôte* for some of the rich inhabitants, who had left the unwholesome plains to breathe the pure air of the hills. I was introduced to him, was invited to remain, and I dined with his party at twelve o'clock, without anything worthy of remark passing. After which our party was increased by some of his, and we ascended to the summit of the mountain of the holy cross, where stood a small convent shut out, as it were, from the rest of the world; inhabited by two or three monks, who seemed to have no other occupation beyond saying their mass and watching the precious deposit of a small piece of the cross on which our Saviour was crucified. From the terrace of a small garden, in the rear of this convent, is an extensive view of part of the south side of the island, seen as a map; broken on all sides into gentle undulations of ground, highly appropriate to the growth of vines.

The capability of cultivation is easily observed; but large tracts remain neglected. My attention was directed towards Limason, where the richest wines are made; and I was led to understand, that the thinking part of the population looked forwards to the remainder of the island becoming equally fertile, by the presence of some European government, who would at least abstain from oppression, if it did not encourage industry.

Having showed my respect for the relic, which was uncovered in honour of my arrival, by a small present to one of the monks, I returned to the bishop's house, where I slept more luxuriously than on the preceding night; and having given a suitable remuneration in money, returned homewards; where, to my great delight, I found a small schooner bound to Malta, freighted by some Moorish merchants; on board which, as the stormy season of the year was approaching, I took my passage, being without chance of proceeding to Constantinople, except by land; first to the coast of Cyprus opposite Asia Minor, and thence again proceeding by land.

With regard to the mode of going to Constantinople or Smyrna in the way above alluded to, the traveller must understand, that though in Cyprus he is tolerably secure from insult or danger, yet in Asia Minor he is at the mercy of the different agas and chiefs of the country through which he passes, for whom he must provide himself with presents. He must wear the Turkish dress, and accustom himself to Turkish manners; the roads are rarely free from banditti, or from the passage of troops; and he will not be exempt from plague. The vice-consul mentioned an English gentleman who had undertaken this journey, and finished it with safety. He occupied a few days in traversing the island to the port opposite the coast of Asia Minor; whence, having passed the sea, he arrived in a fortnight at Constantinople. I had neither time nor means of performing this interesting journey.

I had some difficulty in obtaining the consent of the Moors to my embarkation, as two of them had their female slaves on board: it was only on condition that I did not enter the cabin during the voyage. This being agreed on, I was allowed to embark; and was struck by the singularity of my adventure, in being as badly off in point of accommodation, at the end of three weeks, as when on board the vessel from Beirutte.

I went on board on the 15th of October, and, on the 2d of November, anchored in Marsamuscetta harbour at Malta.

[p. 255]

Military defenses . . . and political remarks.

LARNICA.

A small casemated battery, level with the water, defends the approach to the beach of La Scala. Of the other parts of the island that are fortified, I am not able to speak. Famagusta is celebrated for the siege it stood against the Turks, and for the barbarous treatment its governor endured from them after its surrender. It is still called a fortified town. Nicosia the capital is walled round, but neither would stand a regular siege.

Before I conclude this chapter, I shall add a few words on the political state of the possessions of the Turks in this quarter of the world. Could the interests of Great Britain be ensured, the delivery of Syria and Cyprus from the Turkish rulers, by any European power, would be an advantage to the world: that power is now looked for in the shape of Russia. Prophecy, still existing in the East in full force, bids the Mahometan beware of Russia, who is to swallow up all that the Turkish government possesses, and to plant its colonies in Syria. The jealousies and fears of all the chiefs in that country are directed against Russia; and they appeared to dread the overthrow of the French ruler, whose power prevented her from turning her arms against the Turks. Lord Bacon, in his Essay on Prophecies, says, "they are not to be despised, for they have done much mischief." When he wrote, the state of Europe was not so enlightened as it now is: he considered it involved in ignorance, and subject to enthusiasm. In that condition Syria remains. If the emir of Mount Libanon be not first induced to become a tributary to Russia, it might be possible to assist him in such a manner as to induce all the Christians to flock to his standard; and by enabling him to become a powerful and independent prince, the Turkish power might be greatly reduced in that quarter. Of the consequences I cannot presume to judge.

. . . The possession of Cyprus might easily be acquired by any government having a navy. If it were wrested from the Turks, with a certainty of not being given up at a peace, it would soon become a flourishing country: the population would be increased by swarms of Greek emigrants from Asia Minor, who would gladly fly to an asylum from the tyranny of their oppressors; and if their industry were encouraged, would soon fertilize the barren waste overrunning one half the island. The unwholesomeness of the air may be remedied by draining the marshes that cause it. In the time of the Venetians this was done, and the *mal aria* was not felt. Circumstances may hereafter oblige Great Britain to strengthen herself in the Mediterranean; and, for the richness of soil and general advantages to be derived from it, Cyprus may be considered more valuable to her than either Syria or Egypt.

Turner 1815

William Turner was attached to the British Embassy in Constantinople. He traveled in Greece and Albania and adjacent islands, and in 1815 stopped in Cyprus on the way to and from Palestine and Sinai. Turner was in Cyprus from March 11 through March 22 and from October 3 until he boarded a ship on November 8 and finally lost sight of the island on November 21, 1815.

Turner's *Journal of a Tour in the Levant* was published by John Murray, London, 1820 in three volumes. The following selection is taken from Volume II. Turner said he kept no regular journal during his three years in Constantinople but jotted down "such occurences as seemed to me to illustrate the character of the government, or the manners of the people." He maintained that the rest of the journal was written for himself with no intent to publish.

Some of his footnotes have been incorporated into the text. Others that seemed speculative and perhaps inaccurate have been omitted. We have also omitted a few words in Greek, usually the names of villages, which are often orthographically peculiar and add nothing to the narrative.

[p. 31]

Saturday, March 11th.—At day-light, to our indescribable happiness, we found we were close to Cyprus. It was nearly calm in the early part of the morning. At ten o'clock we were under the south-west coast of the island, gazing on the celebrated Paphos, which now bears the name of Baffo, though there are no remains of it but the small hill on which it stood, and (I was afterwards told) sixty-two subterraneous chambers, probably of the temple, not yet filled up, as are a great number of others near. In the afternoon there sprung up a breeze, which carried us at six knots an hour along the coast; it is much lower land than I was used to see, and very marshy, which in the heat of summer produces fevers, and renders the island a very dangerous residence. I did not see the coast to-day in its beauty, as it was raining very hard ashore. In the evening it began to blow very strong, and all night there was quite a gale, from which we sought shelter in the large bay of Limesole, where we anchored at half past six, too late to enjoy the prospect of the village and its environs, which the last glimpse of day-light just enabled us to perceive.

Sunday, March 12th.—Three hours after midnight we weighed and left Limesole. When I went on deck at eight o'clock, I found we were but just turned round a point which hid that village from our view, and were in a dead calm. The whole of the coast that we passed to-day was very verdant, and varied by moderate mountains and rich valleys, which at intervals contained most delicious meadows. At eleven o'clock a breeze sprung up, that carried us first at three, and afterwards increasing, at five and seven knots an hour. In the afternoon we passed Cape Citti, whence we saw the pretty village of the same name, (built, it is said, on the site of the ancient Citium), and at ten miles' distance, the Marina of Larnaca, before which we anchored just at sun-set, and were delighted with the neat appearance of its houses, with its verdure, and its palm trees. We went immediately ashore, and I was pleased on landing to be accosted by a Turk, who spoke a little English, which he had picked up when a boy, from the ships employed on the expedition to Egypt, that anchored here. We walked immediately to Larnaca, about a quarter of a mile distance from the Marina, where I went to the house of the English consul, to whom I delivered dispatches from Mr. Liston, and who received me with the greatest hospitality, and put me into a very neat room, where I soon forgot the fatigues of my voyage in a good bed, which was the more acceptable, as I had slept on boards in the boat without pulling off my clothes. Mr. Vondiziano, my host, is a man in easy circumstances, (a native of Cephalonia), whose family consists of a wife and five daughters.

And most heartily glad we were to escape from a boat, in which there was no subordination, and each man had equal command; and besides the danger from their ignorance, most of them were Candiotes, which is saying all that is bad of them, as the Candiotes are, without any exception, (if the palm be not disputed with them by the inhabitants of the Seven Islands), the most atrocious scoundrels of the Levant, so fruitful in villany . . .

Monday, March 13th.—When I rose in the morning, I was happy to find myself in the house of a British consul, who keeps up the dignity of his character. He has the King's Arms over the door of his house, at which two Janizaries are stationed.

From the 13th to the 16th, I employed myself in writing with ink my journal, which I kept in pencil as I came along. Indeed the streets of Larnaca being unpaved, are so miry that there was little temptation to walk. From my window I had a view of a flat plain, bounded by mountains, which being all marsh land, must be fatally unwholesome in summer. I was glad to make acquaintance with Mr. H., an English merchant, living at the Marina, who introduced me to his wife, a native of the island: he strolled with me about the bazaars, which are mean and unprovided; and showed me the Greek church, a heavy building of the Low Empire, and the English burying-ground, where are interred many Englishmen, some of whom have handsome tombstones over them, dated the beginning of the last century, when the English factory here consisted of fifteen or sixteen houses. The burying-ground is now, however, falling to decay, as the Greeks also are interred there, and many masons have been working on the tombs, by which they have quite effaced the inscriptions of the flat ones. The Marina consists of warehouses, and a few houses and huts, in which live some merchants, Europeans and Greeks, porters and boatmen.

Friday, March 17th. (Thermometer 55.)—Cyprus, Mr. V. tells me, is nearly 600 miles in circumference; an extent which would require at least a population of a million to cultivate it so well as the excellency of the soil deserves; especially as, unlike the other islands of these seas, it is chiefly laid out in fine plains, a very small part of it being mountainous.

The population has, however, been reduced by the tyranny of the government, to between 60,000 and 70,000 souls; of whom about 40,000 are Greeks: of these there are in Larnaca, including the Marina, between 5 and 6,000; and in Nicosia (which, under the Venetians, contained 80,000) 15,000. These are the only populous towns of the island, the others being almost desert. Imperfectly as it is cultivated it abounds in every produc-tion of nature, and bears great quantities of corn, figs, olives, oranges, lemons, dates, and indeed of every fruit seen in these climates: it nourishes great numbers of goats, sheep, pigs, and oxen, of which latter it has at times exported supplies to Malta. Its principal commerce consists in cotton, wool, provisions, (of which it sends supplies to Syria and Egypt, and particularly did so to our expedition there) and silk, of which latter the trade was 150 years ago so considerable as to attract here an English factory. The following is the state of its commerce, delivered from the Custom-house about ten years ago; being the annual amount of the exportation:—

COTTON,—average quantity 3,000 cantars; (the cantar here is 180 okes, four times that of Constantinople); average price 280 piastres a cantar: nearly all this goes to Europe.

WHITE SILK,—average quantity 10,000 okes of 400 drachms each; average price 15 piastres an oke: nearly all goes to Egypt.

YELLOW SILK,—average quantity 5,000 okes; average price 31 piastres: nearly all goes to Egypt.

WOOL,—average quantity 600 cantars; average price 90 piastres: formerly all went to Europe, latterly all to Syria.

CATTLE and SHEEP,—from 8,000 to 10,000 head.

CORN,—in an abundant harvest, from 200,000 to 250,000 killoes of Constantino-ple (our Winchester bushel); average price from 2 1/2 to 3 piastres a killoe: all goes to Europe and Turkey.

BARLEY,—in a good harvest, 300,000 to 350,000 killoes; average price from 35 to 40 paras a killoe: all goes to Europe and Turkey. Double, or even treble this quantity would, it is said, be produced, but for the mischief done by cattle and horses.

OIL,—some years it is imported, there not being enough in the island for its own consumption; in other years there is enough and to export: average price from 32 to 40 paras an oke.

CAROBA, (called by us the locust tree, and producing a sort of bean); average quantity 6,000 cantars; average price 9 paras the cantar: most part goes to Egypt, some to Syria and Constantinople.

WINE, of a year old,—average quantity 65,000 *cuse,* (a *cusa* is eight okes); aver-age price from two to three paras the *cusa:* most part goes to Venice, some to the Black Sea.

OLD WINES,—from ten to twelve paras the *cusa.*

COMMONEST RED WINE,—average quantity 40,000 *cuse*: great part is consumed in the island, for drinking and making rackee; the rest supplies European ships touching here, and is sent to Turkey: average price 40 to 50 paras the *cusa*.

RACKEE, (weak, white brandy)—from 100,000 to 200,000 okes; average price 15 to 20 paras the oke: great quantity is drank in the island, the rest is sold to European ships and sent to Turkey.

COLOQUINTIDA, (the bitter apple),—from 30 to 40 cantars; average price from 180 to 200 paras the cantar: all goes to England.

MADDER,—average quantity 600 cantars; average price from 80 to 100 paras the cantar: nearly all goes to Europe, very little to Turkey; sometimes it will sell at 130 paras the cantar; in 1803 it sold from 200 to 230 paras the cantar, being a bad crop.

TERRA D'OMBRA, (an earth used by painters) immeasurable quantity,—average price two paras the cantar.

SALT,—There are two considerable salt-pits, one near Larnaca, (the best in quality) and one near Limesole. These produce annually 4 or 5,000 *araba* (a measure of 1,000 okes each), which is sold from ten to fifteen paras an araba. It is sent to Syria and Constantinople, but there is not a market for the whole.

There is besides a quantity of *Sesame*, from which is extracted an oil, consumed in the island; and some small manufactories of silk and cotton mixed, and of printed calico, also consumed in the island.

Of wax and honey there is hardly enough for the island, which imports, in case of necessity, a small quantity from Caramania.

Such is the state of an island, which, under the Ancients, and even under Venetian oppression, was so rich and flourishing. The consul tells me that its whole trade now does not clear it above two millions of piastres. It diminishes yearly, because the population is yearly diminished. And it was lately, like Rhodes, or even more, because nearer, ruined by the Turkish fleet and army off Satalia, the Captain Pasha who commanded, forcing the island not only to furnish him gratis with all sorts of provisions and fruits, and even to pay the freight of them, but to buy the ships he took at his own price.

It is the property of the Captain Pasha, and is governed by a Musselim appointed by him, who farms it, and of course squeezes it more than it can bear. [*To the last sentence Turner adds the following footnote:* There were formerly three Pashas in Cyprus; one of three tails at Nicosia, and two of two tails at Fam Agosto and Larnaca; but seventy years ago the inhabitants wrote to Constantinople that the island every day became poorer, and that the expense of these Pashas' establishment was too heavy on it: the Porte attended to their complaint, and gave the island as an appendage to the dignity of Captain Pasha, who keeps a Musselim in it to govern in his name. The peasants of Cyprus work only for themselves, there being superabundance of land for the population in the island since its decline. Those who cultivate the Sultan's farms have no other pay than their food, and exemption from the miri, or land-tax.] He resides in Nicosia (called by the Greeks Λευκοσία,) but comes annually to Larnaca to receive the visit of the consuls, when it is the custom of them to present him with gifts to the amount of 500 piastres, in return for which he gives an old benisch (outer robe) to the dragoman, and an embroidered handkerchief of Constantinople, valued at 20 piastres, to the consul. His administration is very strict, and keeps in good order the Turks who, as they drink very hard, would otherwise be very disorderly; but Signor V. very earnestly absolved them from the charge of being so bad as the Candiotes, which I had heard. The Greeks are better than the Turks, and the latter have no greater privileges than the former, at which they are constantly expressing great discontent.

The cheapness of living in Cyprus is extraordinary, considering the declining state of the island. M. Vondiziano, with all the expenses of the consulate, a wife and five children, a large house, six servants, two janizaries, a carriage, horse, and mule, spends only 5,000 piastres a year. Servants' wages (men-servants the dearest) a few years ago, were only from fifty to sixty piastres a year; but now they are generally ten, and sometimes even twenty, piastres a month.

In the morning I went with Signor Vondiziano, (who put himself in grand state, with a large cocked hat which he always wears, even in the house, a gold-headed cane, and preceded by a janizary,) to visit the Austrian consul, who lived in a good house near us. He has lately married a young lady of the country, who was tolerably pretty. He was now much frightened by a report brought two or three days ago by a ship from Constantinople, that Austria, in conjunction with Russia, had declared war against the Porte; from which fear I delivered him. I afterwards walked to the Marina, where I bought two or three little trifles, of which I stood in need, as almost all the magazines and bazaars are there. Being caught here in a most furious storm of hail and rain, I ran for shelter to the house of Mr. H., but it lasted so long that I staid and dined with him (the consul's hour being past) on some salt-fish, and some delicious small artichokes; for as it was the Greek Lent, no meat could easily be had. As I saw there was no chance of the storm ceasing, I was forced to walk to Larnaca in the middle of it, and went to call on Dupont, whose house, after a long search, I found: he was not at home, but I was very civilly received by his mother and sister, the latter of whom I thought very pretty, perhaps because she was like an English woman, having light hair and blue eyes. Both of them were ill with the fever, from which they said they had never been totally free for four years past. Indeed I cannot wonder at it, for besides the marshes and the mud in the streets, which is so deep, and smells so offensively, that it is hardly possible to pass, the room where they sat, as is the case in all the houses here, was paved with stones about four feet long, and two and a half broad, through some of whose crevices water was coming up. In the evening the rain being moderated, I returned to Signor V.'s house.

Saturday, March 18th. (Thermometer 61.)—The traveller certainly sees in Cyprus that he is in a more civilized spot than he must often expect to find in Turkey. Larnaca, the second city of the island, contains about 1,000 houses, and the Marina consists of about 700 more. Though the streets by the depth of mud which they present, evidently shew themselves to be Turkish, yet one meets in them carts drawn by oxen of a much better construction and workmanship than I have hitherto seen in the Ottoman dominions; and every family in tolerable circumstances keeps a calesh, like our one-horse chaise when the covering is up, but not quite so high (drawn by a single horse), which they bring from Tuscany. The country is so flat, that they can go with these as far as the capital (Nicosia), though, as the roads are bad, and the Cypriote race of horses small and not strong, this journey, between seven and eight hours, requires one change of the horse. In the morning I went with Signor V. to visit the Spanish consul, a man respectable for having resisted all the temptations and threats held out to him to induce him to declare himself a partisan of Joseph Buonaparte; and who, having in the earlier part of his life been in London, still speaks tolerable English. Though he lived only a few doors off, it required a pretty long walk to reach him, for the houses in Larnaca are so far asunder, that in spite of the fewness of their number, it is a three miles' walk round the city. We did not find him at home, but we saw his wife, a fat dame, who being near fifty, last year brought him a son. One would think there was something prolifick in the air of Cyprus, for the Russian and English consuls are in the same circumstances, though the Greek women are generally old at thirty and thirty-five. After dinner I went with the consul in his *carroza*, again in consular state to visit M. Peristiani, the Russian consul, who was also Swedish (a precaution that saved him from the necessity of flying during the last Russian war), who lives on the Marina. On our way, I observed among the marshes through which we passed, many pools of water of some depth, which being close to the sea, I thought were filled from it; but Signor V. told me that they were all rain-water, and being of consider-able extent were formerly joined, and formed a small port for boats, to which was cut a communication with the sea, now choked. How poisonous must their exhalations be in summer, and, in a soil that would so well pay the labour, how easy would it be to drain them under any other government than that of the Turks. We found the Russian consul at home, in a good house, crammed with the arms of Russia; he received us in a very large apartment well furnished, and introduced us to his wife, a comely matron of no common size. I had seen Mr. Peristiani two years ago, when he visited Constantinople on consular business. In the room was an old deaf Greek priest, who kissed me very affectionately, and who I was told was the Ἀρχιμαντρίτης (Archimantrite) second in clerical authority to the archbishop of the island, who is in fact the governor, having by ancient privilege great power, and keeping the public treasure, which it is his business to supply. By the bye, his financial talents will now be exercised, for a letter is to-day arrived, by an ex-press Tatar, from the Porte to the Musselim, peremptorily demanding 50,000 piastres as the contribution of Cyprus for repairing the fortifications of Constantinople; and the Tatar says, that messengers are going over all the country to collect troops, so that Mr. P. is afraid of a Russian war; but I should rather suppose that it is designed against the Waha-bees, who it is reported have lately defeated the Pasha of Egypt with great slaughter, and made the Porte fear for Mecca and Medina. [*To the last sentence Turner adds the follow-ing footnote:* The reports of this defeat I afterwards found were not true, being spread, it is supposed, by the Pasha of Egypt himself, to avoid sending contributions to the Porte.] This Tatar brought an account of the suppression of the late tumult among the janizaries, at which the Musselim (who is a creature of the Captain Pasha, and must fall with him) was so delighted, that he invested the Tatar with a caftan (robe of honour). After stopping an hour with Signor P. we returned home. The west wind blew tremendously all day, and at night brought the croaking of the frogs in the marshes, always excessively loud, to my window, with such incessant noise, that it required the exertion of all my great talents of sleeping to save me from being disturbed by them.

Sunday, March 19th. (Thermometer 66.)—In the morning the Russian consul and his wife came to visit me in all consular glory. He was glittering in an embroidered coat, and the largest possible cocked hat: he apologized for having been prevented by a severe cold and swelled face (flussione), from paying me a visit before; and in answer, I assured him, very sincerely, that I regretted his having had the trouble now. He was accompanied by the Greek priest whom I saw at his house, and whom I suppose to be the spiritual comforter of the family, as Madame was very assiduous in brushing dust off his robes, &c. This priest was to return to-day to the archbishop at Nicosia; I found him by far the most candid Greek ecclesiastic I have seen, as he confessed to me that he did not think there was any spiritual use in the numerous fasts of the Greeks, but held them sacred rather from custom than from religious motives. He told me that the Turks here are much more mild, and less bigoted, than in other parts of Turkey, many of them in private even eating pork, and all of them being very sociable and friendly to the Christians. As I certainly did not come to Cyprus to pay or receive visits, I was glad, when the Russian consul was gone, that all such ceremonies are past, I being under no obligation to call on the French consul, as he has shown me no civility since my arrival, and is moreover a great Buona-partist (having accompanied his idol to Egypt), and consequently, even declaredly, no great lover of the Bourbons, or the English. At noon I went with the consul in his carroza to dine with Mr. H. at the Marina, where we fared sumptuously, in company with three Maltese captains. There are now in the road here (for there is no port) seven Maltese, and five French, vessels. These bring here articles of English or German manufacture, (the greater part of which go to Syria,) and carry back the productions of the island. The road-sted is defended, or rather pretended to be so, by a small Venetian castle, now falling to ruins; of which, the only interest is, Shakspeare's having supposed it to be the post of Othello. To-day being Sunday, the consul's flags were all flying. On our return from the Marina, we saw numbers of female Christian pilgrims from the Archipelago and Carama-nia, on their way to Jerusalem, who are distinguished by a large linen veil that covers their whole body. I paid a visit to-day to the Franciscan friars, offering to carry any letters for them to the Holy Land. I entered while they were performing service in a small neat church, where, on pretence of its being Palm-Sunday, the French and Austrian, the only catholick, consuls, were stuck up in state. There is not near such a passion for full dress at Constantinople, as here; the uniform is mounted on every trivial occasion. In the evening I called on Dupont, whose sister I found in a sort of hysteric fit, to which she has been rendered very subject by the state of weakness to which fevers have reduced her. The west wind continued very high to-day, but now in the evening is calmed.

Monday, March 20th.— Mr. H. having been kind enough to lend me his horse, a small grey of the country, with an English saddle, at a quarter before seven I set off with Ibrahim, one of Mr. V.'s janizaries, mounted on a small mule, to visit the site of the ancient Idalium, famous for the death of Adonis. It is now a small village, five leagues' (hours') distance from Larnaca, a little more than half way between that town and Nicosia. Our road lay through an extensive plain of a dry but fruitful soil, not one-tenth part of which was cultivated, and that by a miserable wooden plough, drawn by two oxen or mules. The plain is bordered by mountains very insignificant in height, which bore a singular appearance from their tops being naked and of a sandy white, while their base was covered with brown moss. Along the road, which, however, was in general too stony to need or admit any care, I observed some remains of a brick pavement, probably Venetian. In an hour we came to the village of Ἀραείπου, (Araeipou,) consisting of about twenty-five houses; and we passed two others, Γότζι, (Gotzi) containing about ten, and Λουριτζ-ίνα, (Looritzena,) about thirty houses. Near Gotzi was a mountain in shape a complete sugar-loaf, which contained on its peak a small Greek church, of the lower empire, (of which construction there are several Greek churches about the island) that had a very picturesque effect. At half past ten we arrived at Idalium, (a small village of 100 houses, still to my great delight called Δαλι, *Th*ali,) which is situated in a plain better cultivated than the surrounding country, being very fruitful in corn, grapes, (whence they make the common red wine of the country, sold for eight paras an oke,) beans, and cotton, and sur-rounded by small mountains near it, whence, perhaps, issued the boar fatal to Adonis. We went to the house of a peasant, who admitted us very cordially, and his wife shook hands with us on our entering, contrary to the custom of countries in the Levant, which is either to kiss hands, or to carry the hand to the forehead. They gave us some eggs, which, with bread and cheese and wine brought by Ibrahim, made me a good dinner. The master of the house and his family made themselves so serviceable, and were so civil, that I sup-posed them Greeks, and was astonished when he told me he was a Mussulman, as well as his wife and six children. He went to Constantinople four years ago, he said, to fight against the Russians; and after serving six months in the Turkish army, received 70 pias-tres as pay: his wife was weaving cotton, which, in its raw state, sells here for 3 1/2 pias-tres an oke. His cottage was neat and clean, and consisted of only one room with mud walls and a mud floor, of which one half was raised above the other. After dinner the peasant offered to conduct me to a very fine antique building in the neighbourhood, and on my assenting, led me about two miles through rich fields full of the productions be-fore-mentioned, and shaded by long rows of olive trees, and watered by a small river: the *tout ensemble,* with the mountains round, made a pleasing prospect. On my way my guide complained bitterly of the tyranny of the government, who exacted from each cottager 150 piastres annually. When we came to the antique he had boasted of, I found it was a small Venetian building, on which I left it immediately, and he led me to the site of the ancient Idalium, which is about a quarter of a mile to the north of the village, between two small mountains, part of which it covered: here he said, according to a tradition in the village, stood a large city formerly, and though there were no walls standing, yet the tra-dition was supported by an amazing number of stones scattered about the fields and the mountains, and by two small stone water troughs that appeared ancient. I had not been able to borrow at Larnaca any volume containing Bion's Idyll on the death of Adonis, but fortunately my pocket Anacreon contained, among some few pieces of other poets, the ode of Theocritus "To the dead Adonis," which I read on the spot with enthusiastic pleas-ure. From the site of the ancient city, I had a very advantageous view of the modern vil-lage, with its small mountains, behind which were others in the distance of a considerable height: but it is infested by the curse of modern Cyprus, pools of stagnant water, which were drying and brewing fevers apace. At a quarter past three I left *Th*ali, rather disap-pointed at not having been able to find a single antique. We met several peasants on the road driving large flocks of sheep and goats: their prevailing dress was a white turban, white jacket, and white shalvars, (trowsers); that of the women was the common Greek dress, with a large white veil to shade them from the sun. When we were about half way, Ibrahim made me turn aside from the road, a narrow pass between two rocks, to look at the tomb of a poor Greek who had been found dead on the road, having been ill with the fever, and, it is supposed, drank too copiously of a pool of water near which his body was found. The rocks that we passed were very white, and scooped out into natural basins by the rains. We passed a little after sun-set the village of Araeipou, where I got some delicious milk, warm from the goat, the flocks being just returned. Hence we proceeded by glimpses of the moonlight, which was at intervals obscured by clouds. When we were drawing near Larnaca, we met four Greek peasants on donkies; as the first in passing us saluted us with "καλ᾽ ἡσπέρα" (good evening,) Ibrahim struck him with the switch in his hand, returning his salute with "Anasseny sikdem" (the common Turkish expression of anger or contempt); immediately he and the other three alighted with great expedition: when I asked Ibrahim why he struck the man, he said it was because he had not alighted in passing me; and I found, on enquiry, that every Rayah here is forced to alight whenever he meets a Turk of rank. I, of course, charged Ibrahim, who had insisted on the same respect being paid to me, not to be so punctilious on my account in future.

At half past seven we reached Signor Vondiziano's house. I could not observe my thermometer at noon to-day, but at nine in the evening it was at 56. We passed on the road several camels, which attain here their full size and perfection; my horse was not like the Grecian horses of old, either frightened or disgusted by them.

Tuesday, March 21st. (Thermometer 78.)—Cyprus is no longer famous for the beauty, or infamous for the immodesty, of its Women. The Turkish women of Nicosia are, I am told, in general pretty, but not to any extraordinary degree; and one half of their charms is destroyed by the relaxation of the system consequent on their frequent use of the bath, the enemy of female attractions throughout the Levant. But after seeing the rigour with which they are guarded at Constantinople, I was astonished to see the familiarity with which they enter the houses here, even of the Franks, divested of either ferredjee or yatchmak. [*To the last sentence Turner adds the following footnote:* the ferredjee is a large cloak that entirely envelopes them. The yatchmak, a veil that hides all the face but the eyes. The Turks, who think that nothing but extreme restraint can secure female virtue, lay it down as a principle, that a woman cannot, without a crime, let her face be seen by any other man than her husband, father, brother, uncle, and father-in-law (the four latter only at stated festivals); and that two persons of different sexes cannot be innocently alone together for a moment.] The winds that blow most commonly in the island are the west and south-west during summer, and the north in the months of December and January. The best white wine in the island is made on the mountains near Limesole. Cotton is cultivated in the greatest plenty in the north of the island. In the morning there came in here a small Sta. Mauriote vessel, of about twenty tons, put in here on her way from Alexandria home, owing to tempests, by which she had been very roughly handled, having lost her masts, and been forced to throw her cargo overboard. In the evening I went to call on Mr. H., whom I found heartily tired, having been up half the night loading wheat, which, though permitted by the government here, must be done secretly, owing to the severe orders of the Sultan that no corn should be exported, except to Constantinople. H. told me that the island, after supplying its own population, can furnish corn enough to load sixty or seventy vessels. I walked to the Marina to look for a ship, and found a large three-masted one going for Jaffa as soon as the wind should change, which, since my arrival, has blown so strong from the west and south-west, that no ship has ventured to leave the island.

Wednesday, March 22nd.(Thermometer 66.)—Last night a Turkish (Barbary) ship came in, being twenty-four days from Malta, which being a large vessel of 330 tons, and the captain a good-natured and civilized Barbaresque, I determined to take advantage of. It was bound for Barout, where I now resolved to go, as the bad weather had kept me too late for the Catholick Easter. In the morning I paid a visit to the Franciscan Convent, where I found a Monk, who arrived yesterday from Jerusalem. He left Cyprus four months ago on his way there to be President of the Holy Land; and by his speedy return, it is supposed the priests there refused to receive him in that capacity. I was lucky enough to find a servant at the convent, a young and destitute orphan Greek, about fifteen, speaking Greek and Arabic, of whose fidelity I was assured by the fathers who had brought him up, and at whose request I agreed to give him sixty piastres a month, an extravagant rate of wages for this country. In the evening I packed up, and after having taken leave, with many thanks, of the Consul and his family and of Mr. H., went on board with George, my new servant, at half past seven, in a shore boat. The captain received me very kindly, and gave me his own bed. We sailed soon after.

* * * * *

[p. 527]

Monday, October 2nd.—Again a dead calm all the morning. We could see the mountains of Cyprus, but with difficulty, as the weather was very hazy. Indeed during all our voyage, the air has been excessively cloudy, and in consequence very cool. At two we got a breeze from the west, which carried us all the rest of the day between two and three knots an hour. At sun-set we were fifteen miles south-east of Cape Gatta.

Tuesday, October 3rd.—All night a dead calm. All the morning light breezes from the north-east till eleven; from eleven to two again dead calm. We then got a light breeze, which carried us along the shore, and, freshening at three, brought as to an anchor in the roadsted of Larnaca at five. I went immediately ashore, and found all my Cyprus friends quite well. I stationed myself again in the house of the consul. . . There has, I am glad to find, been very little fever in Cyprus this year.

Wednesday, October 4th. (Thermometer 82.)—This being the fête-day of the Emperor Francis, I went with Signor Vondiziano and the few English subjects here to pay a visit in form to the Austrian Consul, and to the monks of the convent of Terra Santa. At the convent I saw my servant George, who went with me through Syria, and whom I sent back from Alexandria: he told me that he had had a most unfortunate voyage to Cyprus, having been driven by storms on the coast of Caramania, gone two days without provisions, and having been fifteen days in the passage, after narrowly escaping drowning. At noon I called on Mr. Vietti, dragoman of the French Consulate in Aleppo (whence he is now on his way to Constantinople), whose wife is a daughter of Mr. Escalon, a very respectable old French merchant of my acquaintance in Constantinople. After writing part of the afternoon, I called on Dupont, whom I found ill of the Cyprus fever, as well as all his family. I passed the evening at the Marina with my new Aleppo friends, at whose house I was agreeably surprised to find Mr. Monge, the young Marseillois, whose acquaintance I made in Acre, and who is now on his return to France . . .

Friday, October 6th. (Thermometer at half-past 6, A.M. 66.)—This being the fête-day of St. Thecla, to the village bearing whose name the Greek peasants flock from all parts of the island, I was glad to accept an invitation from Signor Peristiani, the Russian Consul, to dine with him at his country-house there, and see the amusements of the festival. I set off at seven with Mehemet, the same janizary that accompanied me seven months ago to Δάλι (*Th*ali). For the first hour and a half we rode over a high plain, covered with heath and thistles, and entirely uncultivated, having our road now and then varied by a stony path lying between low heath hills. Our last two hours lay over low mountains of naked sandy-coloured earth, in part clothed with heath, and through valleys of rich soil utterly uncultivated, but full of heath, wild flowers, and thistles. What little cultivation there was in the neighbourhood of a village, was only that of vines, with a very few olive-trees, and there were scattered along our road some few bushes of laurel. We passed three villages on the road,—Kalon Khourgon, St. Anna, and Psefgas. Through the latter lay the passage of a considerable mountain-stream, now dry, there having this year been very little rain in the months of April and May, fortunately for Cyprus, as its fevers proceed from the exhalations of the marshes filled by those rains. Owing to the want of rain, all the land (which, when I saw it in February was quite green) is now burnt up by the sun. At eleven we reached Thecla, where I was heartily welcomed by Signor P. into the Greek convent, in which I found also the old deaf Greek priest, whom I saw at Signor P.'s house at the Marina, seven months ago, and all Signor P.'s family,—wife, two sons, and two daughters,—dressed out in gala. This convent was built by Sta. Helena, but has been renewed and repaired several times since its original construction. The country round Thecla was beautiful: it was a valley full of olive, fig, and mulberry trees, and laid out in gardens, through which ran a small mountain-stream, whose banks were every where covered with olianders in flower. The mountains around of grey rock and of earth, of different, and some of very lofty, height, were well clothed with brushwood, and plentifully scattered with wild pines. This rural amphitheatre was crowded with Greek peasants (about 1,500), in their best clothes of different colours, sitting to dine and drink, playing on their mandolina (a sort of guitar), singing, and dancing. About 500 were gone to their homes this morning, of whom we met many on the road. One of these peasants had taken such ample and repeated draughts of rackee, (white brandy of the country) that it gave him an oppression which his friends round thought betokened death; and by making him swallow a draught of warm water, which greatly relieved him, I got the reputation of being a learned doctor. After dining at the convent, and taking an hour's sleep, I set off with Signor P. and his family for the convent of St. Barbara, which was higher up the mountain, on the road to the summit of Sta. Croce, the ancient Mount of Olympus: we reached it at a quarter-past five, after just an hour's riding through a fine hilly road covered with wild pine bushes, tamarisk bushes, and brush-wood, but very little cultivated, and that only in vines, of which there were but few fields. St. Barbara is a recently-built convent, small, but beautifully situated at the foot of Sta. Croce, and surrounded by the richest land, which the caloyers cultivate and lay out in vineyards. I ascended the mountain immediately, being decided to return to Larnaca to-morrow morning. The road was steep and abounded in precipices, but wildly beautiful, being covered with pine bushes and brush-wood; and the valley below, which, in the rainy season, is the bed of a stream, abounds in laurel and oliander: it produces, too, many wild herbs, which in any other country would be of medical utility: I reached the top in three quarters of an hour. On the summit stands a convent built with great solidity, though small, by Sta. Helena. Under it are subterraneous chambers, of which three have been opened and found to contain rich priestly habits; of these the Turks took possession; there remains a fourth unopened, of which the priests conceal their knowledge till they shall find an opportunity of opening it, unknown to their tyrants: the door of the convent is guarded by a portcullis; the church is small and mean; I found it full of about 150 Greek peasants, who were bowing and praying to a cloth, on which was embroidered a cross. One of the women fell down in a fit, which she was in the habit of doing, and the foolish Greeks laid her down in the church before the picture of a saint, stuffed the cross into her mouth, and so pressed round her, that I wonder she was not stifled by the heat. All remonstrances were in vain, for the only answer that I could get was that the cross would certainly cure her. The terrace of the convent commands a fine view, extending about twenty miles on every side. The evening was rather misty, but I could, with my glass, plainly discover Larnaca to the east, six hours distant, and Nicosia, eight hours off, lying north by east. The sea lay visible to the east, south-east and south: Limesol is visible in clear weather. The view consisted of plains, burnt up by the sun, interrupted by low round hills, and bounded by high pointed mountains. Very little cultivation was visible, and that only of olive trees and vines: the mountains were generally naked, but those round Sta. Croce were clothed with pine bushes, and other wild verdure: the convent is built on an isolated precipice of grey rock, which overhangs the mountains below. I descended the mountain after sun-set, and amused myself asking questions of my peasant guide, who inveighed bitterly against his Mahometan oppressors, whom he named always ὁ Τούκος ὁ σκήλος, (the dog of a Turk): I reached St. Barbara by moon-light, and there found a good supper prepared for us by the Caloyers, and slept in a tolerable bed provided for me by Signor Peristiani.

Saturday, October 7th. (Thermometer 85.)—Mehemet and I set off at day-light, and rode with a guide through the delicious country, at the foot of Sta. Croce, of which the wild beauty that appears in precipitate crags of grey rock, in pine bushes, tamarisks, and brush-wood, is occasionally contrasted with a few cultivated vineyards, and a small grove of olive trees. At the foot of the mountain near St. Barbara, is the small village of Stavros—the cross. We dismissed our guide at Psefgas, whence we returned by our yesterday's road to Larnaca, which we reached at ten o'clock.

Monday, October 9th. (Thermometer 83.)—I passed all the morning writing in my room, and in the evening went with my friends, to the fête of a Catholick marriage at the Marina, where we remained dancing till near eleven; most of the better class of inhabitants were there, all dressed *a la grecque*, without any variation from the common costume. The Romäika was danced, not as I have usually seen it in a ring, but by two only, who scarcely moved from one place, but confined their activity to raising and bending their arms, making *des petits pas* with their feet, and wriggling their bodies with more voluptuousness than grace . . .

Thursday, October 12th. (Thermometer 96.)—Having arranged this morning an excursion to Famagosto, I set off at seven o'clock with Ishmael, the brother of Mehemet, who had accompanied me to St. Thecla, and who found himself ill in consequence, he said, of the violent exertion of that five hours' journey. In two hours we reached the mountains, (not very high to the east,) that bound the plain on which stands Larnaca. This plain though of the richest land is, except in the immediate environs of the town or of the neighbouring villages, utterly uncultivated, but covered with rich long grass, heath, palm, and tamarisk bushes. We then rode an hour close to the sea, having to our left low rocks which overhang the sea, and are perforated by time and weather, and naturally formed into stalactite shapes. The land round us through the whole of the journey was of the same description as the plain of Larnaca, displaying, that is, the greatest richness in its abundance of brush-wood, and the length of its grass; but I do not believe that in the whole of our ride there were fifty acres of cultivated land, and that was all laid out in vineyards. I have as yet seen little or no corn in Cyprus. In the neighbourhood of a village one sees a few olive-trees and vines, but beyond its precincts all is barrenness. We saw but four villages on the road. The first of these was Ormi*th*ia.

When Cyprus was yet considerable in the hands of the Turks, and an English Factory resided here, Ormi*th*ia was their favourite village, at which most of them had their villas, and it owed this distinction to its situation on the banks of the sea, and the consequent salubrity of its air. Between Ormi*th*ia and Avgorou is the convent of Ayia Nappa (St. Nappa, this is the name of the spot; the convent is devoted to the worship of the Παναγία—Virgin). This convent is remarkable for having a large church cut out of a grotto in the rock: but as I have seen several of these grotto churches, and it was two hours out of my road, I did not turn off to visit it. I saw on the road two or three isolated Greek churches, which, from the clumsy solidity of their construction, appeared to be of Byzantine date, but they were small and insignificant. The distant view of Famagosto which we first saw about an hour off, is strikingly pretty. The ruins in the city, particularly the high one of the church of Sta. Sophia, the high mountains behind, the capacious bay, on whose banks stand the city, and the gardens near it, form in their combination a fine *coup d'oeil*. Near the city is a village inhabited by Christians, who are not excluded from the city, but prefer living in the village of which each house has its garden. This village contains about 100 low houses, mostly of mud, but some of stone. I went to the house of Signior Benedutzi, a Greek merchant there, to whom Mr. H. had promised me a letter, but forgot to send it to me. I did not, however, feel the want of it, for he received me with the readiest hospitality. I arrived at half-past one, and after dinner, went with Ishmael on two excellent mules of Signor B. to the city, which is about a quarter of an hour north-east of the village. Famagosto was the strongest place the Venetians had in Cyprus, and was the residence of most of the nobles. Its importance is well attested by its amazing strength. It then contained from 15,000 to 20,000 houses, and the extraordinarily disproportionate number of 365 churches. Its siege was most obstinate and bloody, and at last want of provisions only caused its fall. It was accordingly most terribly battered in the attack, and its ruin was completed by an earthquake (to which this part of the island, is, I am told, very subject) in 1735. The walls which remain uninjured, are immensely thick and strong, and are fortified by a fosse, in many parts hewn from the rock, about eighty feet wide, and twenty-five deep, into which the sea was formerly admitted, but it is now dry. The only gate is defended by a draw-bridge and portcullis. Three years ago the Turks would allow no Christian to enter it but on foot, but they have lately abated this insolence, though I was assured that I should have found a difficulty in riding in, if I had not had a janizary with me.

From the gate to the port there is a subterraneous passage which the Turks leave unexplored. I rode through streets of levelled palaces, choked up with ruins and rubbish to the house of the Aga, of which one half was choked up by the fallen stones of the other. He was a meanly dressed Turk, who received me very civilly, and sent a chiaoux with me to shew me the place. I first entered the principal church of Sta. Sophia, now converted into a mosque, and surmounted by a broken minaret. It is very large, and built in the Gothick style, mixed with Venetian ornament, the arches of the door and window being overtopped by a large triangle sculptured in high relief. I found a small stone at the door with a Greek inscription, of which I made out the following words.—In first line, ΑΝΤΡΑΙΑΝΟΝΚΑΙΣΑΡΑ; in 2nd, ΓΕΡΜΑΝΙΚΟΝΥΙΟΝΘΕΟΥ; in third, ΒΑΣΤΟΥΗΠΟΛΙΣ.

The interior, which is about 120 feet by 90, and about 80 high, is disposed in three aisles, divided by thick round columns, which rise into arches. The windows were neatly fretted, and a recess for the altar was made at the top of the middle aisle. As is usual in Turkish mosques, its walls are now entirely naked, and it is furnished only with a few lamps and mats, and a small pulpit. On the floor are a few tombs with inscriptions written in a language which, though to me illegible, I believe to be Gothick. I copied a line of it *Plate 7 b.]* . . . From Sta. Sophia I walked to the citadel, which is at the eastern extremity of the city on the sea-shore, and is immensely strong, being surrounded by the thickest walls, and defended by a separate fosse, a drawbridge, and portcullis. Over the entrance were the arms of Venice (which are very frequent in the city,) and the inscription "Nicolas Foscareno Cypri Præfecto, 1492," in Roman letters.—On crossing the drawbridge, we ascended by a stone staircase to a defended passage leading to the sea, at the end of which was a strong tower overlooking, and completely commanding, the port. The thickness of the walls, and their domineering situation, show this passage and tower to have been formerly of prodigious strength, but there now remain on it only eight bronze guns (the rest were carried to Constantinople) which are almost rusted, and without serviceable carriages. The port was admirable, being about one quarter of a mile in length, and something less in breadth. It is sheltered by low rocks, connected where necessary by a strong mole. It has only one entrance, about sixty feet wide, close under the tower, from the bottom of which, to the opposite extremity of the mole, crossed a strong chain upon occasion. The port is now mostly choked up, nor will the Turks clear it, or permit it to be cleared (the Franks once offered to do it, at their own expense) suspecting, as usual, that the bottom contains treasures, of which they may be cheated.

From the citadel I walked to another massy round tower near it, from which a gate opened on the scala of the port. This gate was guarded by a portcullis, and over it are the arms of Venice, and the inscription in Roman characters of "Nicolas Paolo Prafecto, 1496." There were five boats of a large size in the port, which are employed in carrying corn from Famagosto to the ships at Larnaca. But ships that stop during the winter in Cyprus, still come for safety to anchor in Famagosto. There is another gate opening to the port, which the Turks have closed up. The Ducal palace was near Sta. Sophia, and is now completely crumbled to ruins. Under it are some subterraneous chambers, full of cannonshot. There is here, too, one chamber, in which are deposited some old sabres, guns, and armour, taken with the city, but this is guarded most rigorously, and no Frank is permitted to enter it. It is, said the Chiaoux, under the care of twenty-eight Belou Bashis, all of whom must be united to open it, and this is only done twice a year at Ramadan and Bairam. It is hardly credible that a city so lately flourishing should be so completely ruined as is Famagosto; of its numerous palaces and churches, not one remains entire. It is now inhabited by not more than 100 souls, almost all Turks, for there are only three Greek families. These live in crumbling palaces, which they patch up to make habitable, and the only room in which they can live is blocked up by the fallen materials of the rest. The streets are in many places hardly passable, from the heaps of stones that choke them. But the city might easily be restored, for the walls and fortifications yet remain entire. To walk round the outside of them requires a little more than an hour. A few fig, olive, and mulberry trees, are the only vegetation within the walls. The ruins have the same yellow hue as those of Athens.

As there are no hands to cultivate it, the fine plains which surround Famagosto present on every side nothing but a scene of heathy barrenness. The gates being regularly and rigorously shut at sun-set, I returned in the evening to the house of Signor Benedutzi where I found a good supper and bed. The next day I returned to Larnaca by the same road . . .

Sunday, October 15th. (Thermometer 94.)—In the evening I went to the fête of a marriage (of which there are three here to-day) at which I danced till nine o'clock. I went also to pay a visit to a lying-in Cypriote lady. We found her sitting-up in bed, and in good health and spirits, though it is only the second day since her delivery. She was gaily and splendidly dressed, and wore a garland of flowers round her cap (at Constantinople the costume in these cases is a small embroidered white handkerchief on the head): the only sign of her indisposition was the room being darkened . . .

Tuesday, October 17th. (Thermometer 90.)—At half-past seven I set off on a poney of Mr. H. with my companion, the Maltese flag captain of the vessel which brought me here from Alexandria, and Ishmael, on two excellent mules of the country, whose owner accompanied us as guide on a donkey. In an hour and a quarter we passed the northern extremity of the plain of Larnaca which was covered with heath, and brushwood, and burnt grass. We then rode over and between round hills, naked and white, in general like sand hills, in the valley of which we followed for an hour the course of a mountain stream, now dry, and covered with the finest olianders and sistus, and large trees of brush-wood, but bearing no marks of cultivation. After leaving these hills, we came to a plain, on the beginning of which, at half-past ten, we stopped at the village of Athiainon, consisting of a few houses of mud, and a neat Greek church. It is four hours (of distance) from Larnaca, and half way to Nicosia. Round it are a few fields of corn, and some insignificant gardens of olive and mulberry trees. This being the village of our guide, we dined here off some eggs cooked for us by his wife, and at noon set off again, our haste not permitting us to consult our comfort, which was attacked by a burning sun. All the rest of our road to-day lay along a very rich plain entirely uncultivated (except in the immediate neighbourhood of a village,) covered with long grass, brushwood, heath, and thistles, and occasionally varied by low round whitish hills, sometimes of earth, and sometimes of stone. At one we crossed a mountain stream, now dry, but in winter considerable, over which lay a good stone bridge of six arches, built by the Venetians, and to the left of which was the village of Beroi, and to the right (in going) that of Margon. At half-past three we entered Nicosia, round which, in sight of it, are the villages, all inconsiderable, of Athalassa, Aklangiar, Palgiogothizar, Kaimaklee, Aimalouthaeis, St. Themeetrie, Mayionissa, and Strovilion.

Nicosia (which has been supposed to occupy the site of the ancient Tremitus) is situated in a low, rich, extensive plain, of which the moisture is shewn by the quantity of rushes it bears, and which accordingly causes constant fevers in summer. Behind (to the north of) the city is a line of high, brown, pointed mountains, which completely domineer it; and all round it, on the plain, are a number of low round hills; the city must, therefore, have been either formidably strong or ridiculously weak; strong if the Venetians had forts on these hills and mountains, which would command the plain, and assure a constant supply to the city; and, in the contrary case, absolutely untenable for any length of time: I rather believe the latter, as I saw no remains of forts in the vicinity. It is surrounded by walls which form (as far as I could see, and as I was told) a hexagon: they are very broad, being double, and having the middle space filled with trodden earth; the upper half slopes like a pyramid, and at intervals, some parts project to defend the others: they are of unequal height; in some parts of thirty, and in some of forty, feet, are irregularly built, as the pyramidical slope is often continued to the bottom (where it was so I saw dogs running down them) and have no fosse. [*To the last sentence Turner adds the following footnote:* The walls of Nicosia extended further under the Venetians, as is still attested by ruins of them outside of the present city. Crows round Nicosia are uncommonly numerous; they are called the partridges of Nicosia, for the poor eat them . . .] A few Venetian cannon remain on the ramparts, and these are immoveable from the ruined state of their wooden carriages. The ground of the city is very unequal, being in some parts elevated to the height of the walls within, and in some a deep valley: this is, perhaps, caused by the earth taken out to fill up the space between the walls. As every house has a large or small garden attached to it, the first view of the city is very pleasing from the contrast which this cultivation affords, with the dark mountains behind. The Greeks told us, that to encompass the city requires an hour and a half on horseback, which would give it the, not improbable, circuit of four and a half miles. The gardens within the walls are well cultivated, and abound in fig, olive, mulberry, orange, lemons, and pomegranate, trees, &c.

Immediately on arriving, we rode to the Greek convent, which, though irregularly built, is large and commodious, and delivered a letter, with which Mr. Vondiziano had furnished us to the archbishop, who received us very hospitably: he is the primate of the island, and is so respected by the Greeks, that he shares the supreme power with the Aga. His enemies in Constantinople having declared, that his tyranny and rapacity rendered his name odious to the Cypriotes, the Porte has sent two Turks (whom we found with him) to inquire into the affair; but he has escaped from the snare by procuring a declaration from the Greeks, that they are content with him, and by giving presents (without which no declaration would avail him) to the messengers. He told me that he was entirely independent of all the four patriarchs, for the following cause:—In the time of the latter Byzantine Emperors of Constantinople, the church there having no authentick copy of the Gospel of Saint Matthew, issued orders for the seeking of one throughout the Empire. The priest of a convent near Famagosto dreamed that if he dug under his church in a spot pointed out, he should find it. Next day he obeyed the injunctions of the Angel who had appeared to him in a vision, and found the tomb of Saint Barnabas, with the Gospel of Saint Matthew laid on the bosom of the dead saint. The Archbishop wrote this to Constantinople, whence the royal galleys were immediately sent, on board of which he carried the treasure to the capital, and in return for his present he was made independent, and presented with a red vest, (which he still has the prerogative of wearing,) and allowed the privilege of writing with red ink, which he has ever since continued. He has a third privilege, that of bearing the arms of the Greek church (very like the Russian Eagle,) on his chair, like a Patriarch. After sitting and smoking half an hour with the bishop, we went to look at the church of Sta. Sophia, (built by the Venetians, and now converted into a mosque,) which stands about the centre of the city. It is built in the Gothick style, (corrupted by the same triangular ornaments as I observed in that of Famagosto,) in an oblong form, with a pentagonal projection at the end opposite the entrance, for the reception of the altar. It is already much ruined, and the Turks have broken the wall in three or four places, to make doors. The interior is laid out in three aisles, divided by clumsy white-washed Corinthian columns.

There is another insignificant Venetian church in the city, also converted into a mosque. It is astonishing how few Venetian remains there are in Nicosia. A few foundations, and half walls of palaces, over which the Turks have raised their wretched houses, are all that is to be seen; but it would be easy to restore the city, whose walls and fortifications are all entire. All the present houses are of mud, which, (like those of Larnaca,) require yearly reparation to keep out the rain. On the two belfries of Sta. Sophia, the Turks have built two high and handsome minarets. We then walked round part of the walls, which are still entire and strong. The streets of the city are without pavement, and, in general, between ten and fifteen feet broad; they are now decently clean, but in winter are almost impassable. We returned to the convent and supped with the Archbishop, whom I was astonished to see, contrary to the custom of the East, sit himself at the head of a long table in a great armchair covered with red cloth. He said that there are 5,000 houses in the city, but we were not inclined to believe there are more than 3,500, and many of these are so wretchedly small as to be little better than hovels. All the information we got, however, agreed that two thirds of these are Turks. We slept well on the divan, which the Greeks made into a tolerable bed for us.

Wednesday, October 18th. (Thermometer 88.)—After loading the mules and charging them with some provisions, with which the Archbishop had been good enough to furnish us, we left the city at seven, by the western gate; it has three gates.

The porter at first would not let us pass, alleging that he had orders to stop all the Greeks to work at the clearing of a mountain stream, for which service he wanted to press our guide. I tried fair words, and pleaded my firman, as long as my patience lasted, but finding them of no avail, I forcibly pushed aside the young soldier who opposed our passage, who forthwith ran away; and as the porter himself sat all the while quietly smoking his pipe, while he issued his decrees, we met with no further obstacle. We rode in a northerly direction over the plain of Nicosia, which extends on this side to the sea. The land immediately in the vicinity of the city is sown with corn, (we have as yet seen no vines on our road,) and the flatness of the plain is occasionally interrupted by low hills sometimes of earth and sometimes of rock. At half-past ten we alighted, and dined under a few mulberry-trees, near which were the ruins of an arched cistern, whose water flowed in small streams over the plain. Leaving this pretty spot, we proceeded at eleven along the plain, and at noon saw the sea to the north of the island, having to our left a high ridge of brown mountains, and behind us those of Nicosia. At half-past twelve, we crossed a mountain-stream, considerable in winter, though now almost dry; and at one stopt to dine at the village of Kakotopia. Except in the immediate vicinity of Nicosia, and of one or two villages which we had passed, the plain was utterly uncultivated, and overgrown with heath, brushwood, and long grass, though the land was of the richest nature and frequently of a reddish colour. Our road had been frequently either a sheet of rock or masses of stone fixed in the ground. At Kakotopia (translated, it means an unlucky spot,) we stopped in a mud cottage, which we left at half-past three, after devouring a couple of fowls. Just as we set off we were attacked by a tornado, which covered us with dust and thistles, and was so violent that we found it impossible to face it, but turned our backs to it, and even then could hardly keep our seats: this lasted an hour, and was attended with a very little rain. From Kakotopia we rode to the sea for three hours over a beautiful plain of the richest and best cultivated land I have seen in Cyprus, owing to there being a greater number of villages than usual collected together. It was laid out in continued fields of maize, corn, and vines. At half-past six, we arrived by moonlight at a Greek convent, on the banks of the sea, dedicated to St. Sergias and Vaccha. It was very large but consisted of a quadrangle of miserable, low mud buildings. The small church appeared Byzantine; on one side of it lay a large stone, with a Venetian inscription in Greek. It contained twenty or twenty-five monks, who could give us only accommodations much inferior to what we should find in an English stable; and this being one of their banyan-days, it was with the greatest difficulty we could induce them to kill a fowl for us. However, we made the best of our situation, and contrived to sup and sleep tolerably. The villages we saw on our road to-day were, Ierolakos, Marmari, *Tha*inia, Argatzi, Menikon, *Zoth*ia, Kakotopia, Nitzeta, Prassion, Morphon, Kazivera, Elea, Petra, and Sirleenkhori.

Thursday, October 19th. (Thermometer 92.)—At a quarter past six we mounted and set off. For one hour and a half we continued on the same plain along the sea-coast. It was every where rich and cultivated, abounding in corn, melons, some few vines, olives, mulberries, and figs, which were growing close down to the sea. To our right we had the bay, and to our left the large Turkish village, of Levka (white). In the bay were anchored three large boats, which came here for the facility of smuggling corn. We crossed a broad, though dry, bed of a mountain-stream, filled with the finest oleanders and cistus, from which the spot derives the name of the Ξήρον Πόταμον (dry river). At eight o'clock we ascended the mountains, which shewed us by far the most beautiful scenery I have seen in Cyprus. They were very high, sometimes of earth and sometimes of stone (which latter had a red volcanick appearance,) covered above with pines, oaks, caroba trees, all of the largest dimensions (except the oaks, which were dwarf), and brushwood, and with the richest verdure. In the deep valley below ran a considerable mountain-stream, which was crowded with, and frequently hidden by, immense plane-trees, oleanders, cistus, and brushwood, among which latter were great quantities of blackberry bushes: our road sometimes lay along the top of these mountains on roads overhanging tremendous precipices, whose abrupt fall was softened by the trees growing out of their sides, and sometimes along the banks of the stream below, whose murmuring was an agreeable accompaniment to the beauty of the prospect. Many burnt trees were lying along the mountains and across the valleys, of which the peasants make great quantities of charcoal, and this forms a considerable branch of commerce between Cyprus and Alexandria. At a quarter past ten, we stopped under a large plane-tree by the side of the stream, where we dined, and repaired our last night's bad rest by a two-hours' sleep. At half-past twelve we set forward again, not fearing the sun, as our road was completely shaded and frequently darkened by the copiousness of the foliage around it. At two o'clock we came to a part of the mountains which was cultivated, where we found superlatives wanting to express our admiration. The whole valley and the rise of the mountains (covered with rich reddish mould) were every where crowded with vines, mulberries, olives, figs, planes, oaks, brushwood and fern. This continued for the rest of to-day's journey, and a considerable quantity of wine is made here. The villages in the neighbourhood (except Levka, all we saw to-day) were Morgon, Xaki*th*ira, and Ampeli (grapes). These, though small (yet all built of stone), formed a pretty addition to the scenery, whether perched on the top of the mountains, or half hid by foliage at the bottom of the valley. The inhabitants were all black with the juice of grapes, which they were washing in the stream below. At half-past four, we saw the bay of Levka behind us: for the last hour we road along the tops of high mountains (on roads that overhung tremendous precipices), whose pine-clothed rock formed a magnificent contrast with the luxuriant cultivation of the valley below. At five we stopped at the convent (dedicated to the Virgin) of Kikkos, the largest in Cyprus. It is built, though irregularly, after the European fashion, and being on the top of a height, commands a superb view that extends on a clear day to the coast of Caramania. It is built of stone, but we found carpenters at work in it, all the interior having been burnt two years ago, when a considerable number of manuscripts which it contained were all lost. It is manned by above two hundred priests and caloyers; but as it possesses a great number of farms throughout the island (particularly an extensive one near Nicosia), these are distributed among them, and there were now not above sixty at Kikkos. Here we were very hospitably received, and supped and slept well. There were a number of cottages round the convent, which I took for a village, but was told they were a farm belonging to the convent. We saw in the mountains to-day a great many large spreading trees, with red bark and a broad leaf, called by the natives ἀντρούκλια; but as I know nothing of botany, and there is no one in Cyprus sufficiently versed in it to tell me their botanical name, I cannot explain what trees they are; I conclude, however, that there is nothing in them rare or remarkable, for they are too numerous here not to have been observed by former travellers; and Hasselquist, whose forte was botany, expressly states (Voyage à Cypre, page 246), that the island produces no rare plant.

Friday, October 20th. (Thermometer 84.)—At seven we left Kikkos, and for five hours passed over and between very high mountains, adorned with the same natural productions as those of yesterday, the rocks still bearing a strong appearance of being volcanick, but with less cultivation. Among these mountains we saw three villages, Melikhori (the village of Apples), Treiselees (three Olives), and Ievrekon. One of these consisted of three houses, and another of five. At half-past twelve, we descended into a beautiful part of the valley, through which ran a crystal stream, shaded by all the trees named before, whose verdure was a delightful contrast to the grey rock hanging over it.

Here we found a small farm belonging to Kikkos, inhabited by six or seven priests, provided with a good corn-mill turned by the mountain stream, and with a large garden, plentifully stocked with olives, figs, pomegranates, mulberries, and vines, from which the caloyers made silk, oil, and wine. Here we made a tolerable dinner, and rested two hours, which we should not have done, had not our guide deceived us as to its distance from Paphos, in the hope (as we paid him by the day) that he should prevent us arriving there to-night. We left this delightful spot at half-past two, guided by one of the priests, (for our guide did not know the road), and proceeded along the banks of the stream in the valley. The farm is very considerable, and is joined by another no less so, belonging to another convent. At four we reached the village of Sinti situated in the valley, here abounding in olive trees, of which much oil is made in the village. Here we changed our guide, finding luckily a Greek just setting off for Paphos, and proceeded immediately. The mountains here and hence forward were lower and more naked than those we had passed, but the bed of the mountain-stream, though nearly dry, was from sixty to eighty feet broad, and every where filled with foliage; half an hour after sun-set we passed the village of Nata, when the evening became dark, and the road difficult and stony. Near this village, on the east, we passed a small ruined Venetian church. We now ascended low mountains, over which we clambered for nearly an hour through terrible roads. On the other side of these mountains we came to a low plain watered by a considerable, though half dry, mountain stream, which we crossed from time to time. On the beginning of it we passed the small village of St. Barbara, whose inhabitants were every one of them swept off by the plague two years ago. On this plain, of which the road was stony and difficult, we continued two hours. The moon, on whose aid we had calculated, was completely hidden by thick clouds which poured on us a little rain, and we were mortally tired; the more so, as for the last three hours our Greek companion constantly assured us we had only half an hour to go, fearing that if we knew the real distance, we should push on, and leave him behind.

At length, to our great delight, we reached, at ten o'clock, the village of Ieros Kypos (the sacred garden.) We went immediately to the house, or rather cottage, of Signor Andrea, an old Zantiote, who has for many years been English consular agent for Baffo, and who asked me after Sir Sidney Smith with great earnestness. He gave us a supper of delicious fish, and a room in which were made up for us two tolerable beds, on which we slept like tired people.

Saturday, *October* 21st. (Thermometer 86.)—Ieros Kypos is supposed to have been the site of the gardens of Venus, whence it derives its name. There are no remains of antiquity in it, and it is now only a miserable village, containing about thirty stone houses. As it is built on an elevated hill, which is one entire rock, it is not probable that the sacred gardens were *on*, but near, its site on the plain below. At nine we mounted donkeys, and went to Baffo, which is at one hour's distance, and this hour we rode over a rich plain, in some parts well tilled and laid out in fields of corn, but in general barren and uncultivated. The town, now on or near the site of New Paphos, is divided into three quarters. The metropolis, where live the Turks, which contains about 150 houses,—the Greek quarter, which is called Ktema, containing about fifty houses,—and the Marina, retaining the ancient name of Baffo, and containing about eighty families, Greeks and Turks. The metropolis and Ktema form a continued town, and are built on a low hill of rock about half a mile from the sea. These houses are all built of rough unformed stone.

We went first to the Greek convent of Ktema, and afterwards called on the Cogià Bashee of the Aga, who lived in the same quarter, with whom we took pipes and coffee. This man is paid one piastre a year by every peasant in his master's jurisdiction; this would give him about 1,500 piastres a year, but by fraud and tyranny, he increases it to 10,000 piastres a year; he was a complete Levantine—fat, lazy, ignorant, and proud. Near his house, in the Greek quarter, were some large square caves, cut in the rock, which apparently were tombs, as they lead to caverns now choked up, and there are several small squares cut in them (like the ground of a basso-relievo) three or four feet square. From the manner in which they are cut, it appears that the materials of ancient buildings were hewn out of them. We walked with the Cogià Bashee to the Aga, who had a wretched, half-ruined house in the Turkish quarter. I shewed him my firman, which, as he could not read, he handed to his secretary, who went right through it. The Turks have built a mean insignificant castle on the beach at the Marina; and he, supposing it was this, I came to see, hummed and hawed, said I should have done well to bring an order from the governor at Nicosia, and (by the suggestion of his secretary) added that my firman only said I was to *pass through* Cyprus, and not to inspect it. To this I answered, that of course my object in passing was to see: that I would not give a para to see the castle, which was as wretched a building in the way of fortification, as I ever remembered to have set my eyes on. That my only object in visiting the Aga was to pay him a compliment, as I was only come to see the antiquities which he could not prevent me from doing, or if he did try to do so, I should then know how to act: he replied, that he had no intention of preventing me, and we left him.

The metropolis is composed of half-ruined houses of stone, and in a stony valley below the hill on which it is built, are a few gardens, which, being in the middle of the town, have a very pretty effect: as we passed through the Turkish burying-ground, Signor Andrea (these people think all stones an object of curiosity to Franks) made me observe two stones now covering the tombs of Turks. One contained a Gothick inscription, and, on the other, were engraved three *fleur-de-lys*, which seems to carry it back at least to the date of the French kings of Cyprus, possibly to the time of the Arabs. We returned to the convent of the Bishop of Baffo (for whom Mr. Vondiziano had given me a letter, but he was at a village two hours distant) where we made a bad dinner off onions and cheese,—after which we mounted our donkeys and rode to the ruins of New Paphos. We first visited those most to the west, which are about a quarter of a mile south of the rock, on which stands Ktema, and the metropolis (this rock runs east and west,) and are close to the sea, on the low plain. These ruins are called by the general name of Palaio Castro, and their appearance is most extraordinary. They occupy a spot of ground (about a quarter of a mile long, and very nearly as much broad) which is covered—except in a few spots where the communication is broken—by a mass of solid rock, more or less high, but seldom more than forty feet, and hewn into numerous caves, which appear to have been catacombs, but are now so choked up, that it is impossible to see whether they all communicate with each other. These caves are more or less large, and within them are others cut of a shape evidently meant for tombs, about ten feet long, three broad, and four high. We entered most of these caves, and found them of various sizes, some about twenty feet square, but in general they were smaller, *i.e.,* those above ground, for there are some subterraneous ones which Signor Andrea, who probably was a better fisherman than anti-quary, did not advise us of.

Sometimes the rock was so low, and the ceiling consequently so thin, that the ex-cavated part, to prevent its falling in, was supported by Dorick fluted columns, ten feet high, hewn out of the rock, which the Turks have broken off and carried away to adorn their mosques, leaving, however, frequently enough of the capital and shaft to see what was there. There are many small excavations, one or two feet deep, and three or four feet square, like the ground of a basso relievo, which were probably devoted to the reception of images: over the entrance to many of the caves are carved architraves, slightly adorned in various ways . . .

Many stairs are cut on and towards the top of the rocks. The rock is of a very soft grey sandstone, and the ruinous state in which it now is, must have been produced by some earthquake or tremendous convulsion of nature, as immense masses of it are sev-ered, and lying at some distance from the main body. On the top of the rock, nothing is visible. The excavated caves are on every side of it. There are above fifty of the larger ones, and above 100 of them in all. As their floor is generally of earth, much I have no doubt might be discovered by exploring and digging them, but the watchful jealousy of the Turks being carried in Paphos to a most rigid excess, their passages are blocked up by dirt and dust, and they serve as stables to the donkeys of the neighbourhood; we dis-lodged at least a hundred of these animals, nor did we observe any other cattle among the ruins. On leaving these ruins, we rode about half a mile along the plain, which was badly cultivated, and stopped at some other ruins (situated exactly south-east by east of Palaion Castron) named, I could learn no reason why, Afrikee. The spot at which we stopped was a low rock, about 200 paces long, and 150 broad. Round the sides of this rock were hewn out numbers of caverns, mostly larger than those of Palaion Castron; (some of these were from forty to fifty feet square,) but differing from them, in that there were no tombs cut within them except in one chamber, which was about thirty-five feet long, and thirty broad. Of these caves I counted about thirty, all cut in the sides of the rock below. On its top, there is little to be seen, except three ruined arched chambers, and these I should suppose to be Venetian. These chambers are about sixty feet long, fifteen broad, and fif-teen high. The breadth of the chamber is the span of the arch which roofs it, and the three chambers and arches join each other. They are built of stones of unequal size, but none of them more than four feet long, and eight inches high. On the hill are to be seen some marks of foundations of buildings, but not sufficiently clear to enable one to trace out chambers. The hill commands an extensive view of the plain of Paphos (which is very rich land, and in some parts tolerably cultivated) and of the low brown mountains that bound it. As the sun set, while I was examining the remains at Afrikee, I could only take a hasty walk round Baffo (the Marina) which, having been under the Venetians a consid-erable town, is full of ruined houses and churches. During this walk, Signor A. showed me a small hill, on which were some granite columns, and under which he told me were subterraneous chambers. This spot he told me was called by the inhabitants τὸ Τάφος τῆς Ἀφροδίτισσης (tomb of Venus): as it was quite dark, when we came to it, we de-ferred our departure (which had been fixed for day-light to-morrow) another day. At seven we returned over the plain, which, for the hour we rode back was covered with thistles, to Ieros Kypos.

Sunday, October 22nd. (Thermometer 92.)—At eight we rode on donkeys to the Marina, over the same plain, (cultivated, but covered with thistles), as we returned by last night. Baffo, formerly a Venetian town of some magnitude, is now like Famagosto, choked up by its own ruins. Palaces and churches are every where seen crumbling to the ground, and about eighty families inhabit the patched remains of as many palaces, of whom two thirds are Turks. Every house has its garden, which gives a richness to the scene, and contrasts finely with the ruins around. The bay is large, but the port very unsafe, as the Mole remains only in part to the east and west, and not at all to the south, which is thus left quite open: to this port, bad as it is, vessels frequently resort for the advantage of smuggling corn; there were two small Idriote vessels anchored in it while we were there: the port is commanded by an insignificant castle built on its banks by the Turks: on the east side, opposite to the castle, is a small ruined Greek church. We walked immediately to the hill where is the ruin which the inhabitants call the tomb of Venus, which is about 100 paces north of the port. Over its surface, (which is of very considerable extent) and in its immediate environs, are scattered a great number of grey granite columns, of which all I saw were broken; they were two feet in diameter. As we were bathing in the port, we found two of these under the water, and as it is difficult to know whether these scattered remains are in their original situation, or have been displaced by the hands of man or nature, it becomes nearly impossible to judge what was the extent of the building they supported, or to decide whether that building was the temple of Venus. I think, however, that the fact of the Marina *alone* being still called Baffo by the inhabitants, and the name given by them to the ruins on this hill, are great evidence in favour of its identity. Signor Andrea told me that he had counted above 150 of these columns, but the hill and its environs being cultivated, most of them are now buried under ground. The subterraneous passage is immediately under the hill. The entrance to it is a square of about four feet: the passage below was so choked with stones and dirt, that though I worked hard to remove them, I found it impossible to penetrate above eight feet; of these eight feet the descent was rapid, and the roof formed like the under part of a staircase; possibly if the ground above were cleared away, a staircase might be found from above to the chambers below. This is all that remains of the splendour of Paphos. Signor Andrea told me, that twenty years ago, a Turk who had murdered another, and was hotly pursued, took refuge in these subterraneous chambers, to which despair made him find the passage, not then entirely choked up; after wandering three days under ground in utter darkness, he came out at Afrikee, about a quarter of a mile distant from the hill of the temple: his report was that he had passed through chambers full of stones, with some skulls and other bones. Having money he escaped, by distributing it, the punishment of his crime; and he is the only man, as I was told by several, ever known to have entered. The whole neighbourhood of Baffo and the metropolis, and Ieros Kypos is full of large masses of rock, hewn into caves, like those I have described, probably all communicating subterraneously with each other. The villages in the vicinity of Paphos, in sight of Ieros Kypos, are Peyia, Marathounta, Anavarkos, Eba, Konia, Armo, Mesoe, and Phlyraka. The Fons amorosa is one day's journey to the north of Baffo, in a village called St. Nicolas, too distant for the scope of our excursion. At two, we returned to Ieros Kypos. This village is built on a rocky hill; in the valley below it, to the south, are gardens watered by a stream gushing from the rock, and this stream is said to have been the baths of Venus. About half a mile east of Ieros Kypos, towards the termination of the gardens in the valley, is a spot in the gardens called Sazousa, on which, said Signor Andrea, were killed many children by the (ancient Greeks). What he meant by this I could not discover, except it was some memorial of the cruelties practiced in the ancient temples standing formerly here, one instance of which may have been handed down by tradition. At half-past four we took leave of our host, and quitted Ieros Kypos. All our ride this afternoon lay along a fine plain, on the banks of the sea, mostly uncultivated, but containing a few fields of corn, cotton, and tobacco. (Considerable quantities of this latter are prepared in Baffo, and by many thought superior to that of Latikea). To the left of our road, which lay east, was a line of low earth mountains covered with brown verdure. Our last hour was surrounded by gardens and trees, and we passed a large mountain-stream, over which lay a handsome Venetian bridge, yet entire. (We passed three or four of these bridges in the valleys near Kikkos, but all in ruins). The villages which we passed in four hours of this afternoon's ride, were Colona, Akhelia, Timee, and Man*th*ria. At seven we stopped at the village of Coukklia, which is built on the site of Old Paphos, and found good accommodations in a large ruined house, of which the master, an intelligent Greek, received us very hospitably. He told us, that Coukklia, with six other villages, was a farm of the Sultan, of which he was the manager, and which yielded twenty purses a year. Coukklia was formerly a considerable town under the Venetians, but is now nothing but a mass of ruined churches and houses, of which latter about thirty are inhabited, half by Turks and half by Greeks. The inhabitants however of this, and indeed of almost all the villages we have seen since leaving Nicosia, are happier than those of Larnaca and of the capital, in having good stone-houses over their heads, whereas those of the three chief towns of the island are only of mud, and require yearly reparation to resist the periodical rains.

Monday, *October* 23rd. (Thermometer 92.)—In the morning early I strolled about the ruins of Coukklia, among which I did not discover the remains of any considerable houses. There are three or four churches, which from Venetian became Greek, and are now quite in ruins. One only remains sufficiently entire to be still used: in the wall of this is a coarse black stone, about two feet long and one and a half high, bearing a Greek inscription, which, from the rude formation of the letters, appears of remote antiquity, and of which the note contains all I could make out *[Plate 7 c.]*; by this it appears to have been taken from a temple of Venus. In the ruins of another church was a large stone of grey granite, with another Greek inscription of Roman date, which I have also copied in a note below. *[Plate 7 d.]*

At eight we left Coukklia: for four hours our road lay over low mountains mostly naked, but at intervals scantily clothed with brushwood, pines, planes, and caroba trees. The fruit of this latter is very sweet; and when Cyprus was Venetian, it formed a branch of commerce, which still continues in miniature; for the Venetians make an agreeable paste sweetmeat of the caroba, and those of Cyprus are the most esteemed. At two hours from Coukklia, we passed the small village of Alektora, near the sea which we had all day close on our right. At twelve, we stopped at the village of Misour, which is on the top of a high mountain. The land round it was well cultivated and very productive of olive and mulberry trees. Here (and indeed in several villages we have passed) we found many peasants ill, mostly of fever and inflammation of the eyes, (very common in Cyprus,) who, when they find themselves unwell, lie down listlessly on their beds, and wait patiently till nature works their cure or their death; for their neighbourhood seldom affords them medical assistance, and that of the priest with book and crosses, in which they place most reliance, is not to be had gratis.

At two we left Misour, and rode for five hours over the mountains which bore every where the same appearance of nakedness and rockiness, our road being varied between smooth sheets and rough-pointed paths of whitish stone. Two hours and a half east of Misour, we saw lying near our road two broken columns of granite, whose isolated situation (for there was no other remnant near them) makes it impossible to guess of what they formed part. The descent of the mountain was so terribly precipitate and rocky, that we were forced to walk down, and even then, it being quite dark, feared for our beasts, which, as well as ourselves, often stumbled. At half-past seven we stopped at Episcopi, a large Turkish village, at the eastern foot of the mountains. Dark as it was, we could perceive that the village was very pretty. A mountain-stream, very copious, runs through it, and it is surrounded by rich gardens. I saw in it the ruins of a large Roman aqueduct. The Turks here not being willing, they said, to admit Giaours into their houses, and proposing to lodge us in a dark dirty crowded coffee-house, we would not stop there, but left them after half an hour. We rode towards Limesol over a fine smooth plain, and at nine stopped at a farm belonging to some inhabitants of Limesol, consisting of half a dozen houses: here we were again unfortunate, for the first we entered was occupied by a Turk, whose wife, he being absent, positively refused us admittance, and railed like a Stentor at our guide, who in vain pleaded ignorance, for daring to conduct us there. At length we found at the door of another house, a Greek who gave us lodging, a supper, and beds which were so well peopled, that we could not close our eyes all night.

Tuesday, October 24th. (Thermometer 86.)—At half-past six we mounted and rode for two hours along the plain of Limesole, which, though very level and rich, was mostly uncultivated, and covered with brambles and brushwood, except, as usual, in the neighbourhood of villages, of which we saw two in these two hours, Colos, and Zakatzi. At Colos are some ruins of the age, it is said, of the French kings of Cyprus, and there is one large square tower built, it is reported, by our *Coeur de Lion.* At half-past eight we entered Limesole. It is a miserable town, consisting of 150 mud houses, of which 100 are Greeks, and 50 Turks: yet of the fifty ship-loads of wine which Cyprus exports annually, twenty are on an average dispatched from Limesole: a mountain stream runs through it, over which is a broken Venetian bridge. We stopped an hour at the house of the English agent, and at half-past nine set off again. We continued till eleven, along the plain of Limesole, which is cultivated in the immediate vicinity of the town, but beyond it is quite barren. All the cultivation on it is of corn, and indeed since we left Sinti we have seen no vines except a small plantation at Misour. At eleven we entered a line of low mountains, along which we continued till half-past three. These were generally naked, but at intervals clothed with carobas, brushwood and brambles. We rode always by the side of the sea, and at half-past eleven had to our right a precipitate cliff, of which the sides contained a few ruins, but so nearly washed away that it was impossible to distinguish what they were. The villages we passed on these mountains were Monaphrouli, Pentakhoma, (five Mounds), and Maroni. At the termination of the mountains we stopt to snatch a bread and cheese dinner, near a small pool of bad water. Thence we rode along an uncultivated plain covered with brambles and brushwood, with the sea close on our right, and low brown mountains to our left, till eight o'clock, when we were glad to stop at the village of Mazoto, where, in the cottage of a Greek peasant, we got a good supper of fowls (which, as usual with us, were killed, picked, cooked and eaten in twenty minutes), and slept not a wink all night for the same reason as last night. My companion during our excursion has carried his gun with him in the hopes of finding game, but he has not once had an opportunity of firing it. In the proper season red-legged partridges and Francolinas are very common in Cyprus.

Wednesday, October 25th. (Thermometer 84.)—We set off at dawn, fagged and feverish from want of sleep. The whole of our road lay along a fine level plain, little cultivated except in the neighbourhood of the villages, and even there overgrown with thistles. Half an hour to the west of the Scala of Larnaca is an extensive salt-pit, near which is a considerable aqueduct built but seventy years ago by a Turkish governor of Cyprus. At nine o'clock I reached the Scala, or Marina, left my horse with his master, and returned to the house of Signor Vondiziano, where I passed the rest of the day with the exception of a visit or two in the afternoon. The villages round Larnaca, within three hours, are Anaphoti*tha*, Kyphino (a Turkish village), Anglisi*the*s (this name appears to have some connection with our nation), these two last are small villages close together, Alethrikon, Chivisila, Klavia, Kyttion (Citti), Tertzephanon, Arpera, *Th*romolazia (Ditch-road), Meneoo, Tekeh, Kalon Khorion, and Ara*th*ippon . . .

Monday, October 30th. (Thermometer 80.)—In the afternoon I went with Monsieur and Madame La Pierre (the wife was born in Constantinople, and I knew her there; the husband is dragoman to the French Consulate here) to the village of Ara*th*ippon, an hour north-east of Larnaca on the plain; this being the Greek fête of Saint Luke, to whom the church there is dedicated. All the peasants in the neighbourhood go there on this occasion in gala, but we arrived too late, most of them having gone in the morning. The village contains only a few mud cottages, and the church is small and mean. We returned therefore immediately.

Tuesday, October 31st. (Thermometer 80.)—In the evening while I was sitting in the house of Monsieur L. P.; an old Greek woman came in frantick with terror, and on her knees begged for protection, swearing her neighbour's wife wanted to murder her. It appears that this old woman, having some money, at sixty years old had persuaded a young peasant of thirty-five to marry her. He naturally soon grew tired of her, and fell in love with his neighbour's wife, who returned his love. After this, he and his dulcinea amused themselves by thrashing his old wife whenever she fell in their way. The husband is now fled to Nicosia to avoid his wife, whom he detests, and she is preparing to follow him, and entreat the archbishop there to force him to live with her. Meantime, her rival met her this evening, and regaled her with her accustomed salutation. I forget who is the traveller (I believe it is Sonnini) that calls Turkey and Greece the land of chastity and conjugal decorum! . . .

Thursday, November 2nd. (Thermometer 79.)—I walked down to the Marina in the morning to look after an opportunity for Rhodes. I found there was only one ship going, a Turkish one, which is now loading corn in Famagosto, whence it will not return for some days. I therefore accepted an invitation I had from Monsieur L. P. to accompany him and his wife on an excursion to Nicosia for a few days. At half-past two I set off with them, attended by two of their servants. We rode over the same road as I passed before, and at six stopped at Athiainon, where we passed the night with tolerable comfort in a cottage, to whose tenants my companions had sent notice of our coming. In the evening we went to pay a visit to a Russian female pilgrim, who by chance was passing the night in the same village: of her appearance, the little that was human was more masculine than feminine, particularly as to dress and voice. She spoke scarcely intelligibly in French, and could not utter three words of English, which at first she pretended to know. We made out that after having lost 300,000 roubles by the burning of Moscow, in whose neighbourhood lay her estates, she resolved on making the pilgrimage of Jerusalem which she had just completed, having stopt there ten days, and being now on her return.

Friday, November 3d. (Thermometer 77.)—We set off from Athiainon at four in the morning, and, till the sun rose, were intolerably chilled by damp and cold. At eight we entered Nicosia, where, as I had nothing new to see, and the female part of the party was very tired, we stopt in-doors the rest of the day, except a visit we paid in the evening to the bishop, with whom we supped. We are lodged in the house of an Italian who has been a soldier in the French army, and fought in the battles of Jena, Austerlitz, and Eylau. He now exercises in Nicosia his trade of a cabinet-maker, in which he is an excellent workman, and has to his great regret married a woman of Cyprus,—I must not say a cyprian.

Saturday, November 4th. (Thermometer 80.)—In the morning we strolled about and paid visits to two or three Greeks. One of these was an old fellow who was very vain of his knowledge of Hellenick, and of some miserable rhymes in Romaick which he composed twenty years ago on the marriage of a relation, and which, having had them printed at Venice, he has framed and hung up in his room. In the afternoon I strolled a little about the bazaars, which are most wretched, and passed the evening and supped *chez nous* . . .

Monday, November 6th. (Thermometer 82.)—At half-past four we left Nicosia to sleep at a convent two hours off. These two hours we rode over a fine plain, plentifully watered, wooded with numerous olive trees, and sown with corn and cotton. We passed two villages, Strovilos, and St. *Th*emetissa, and at a quarter past six stopped at the convent of the Archangel Michael, a farm of Kikkos, in which, while that monastery is undergoing repair, is deposited that precious treasure the Παναγία τοῦ Κίκκου, *i.e.,* the picture of the Virgin painted by Saint Luke, of which there were said to be three in the world, one here, one, I believe, at Venice, and the third I forget where. Here they gave us tolerable good beds, in one of which I deposited myself immediately, having felt symptoms of fever all day, which grew so strong towards evening that I could hardly sit on my horse.

Tuesday, November 7th. (Thermometer 76.)—In the morning we attended mass in the church, which, though small, is richly ornamented: In the centre of the wall, fronting the principal entrance, is fixed the picture, which the priests have wisely covered with gold, silver, and precious stones (inlaid to represent the Virgin and Infant) and round it are hung pearls, sequins, &c., the offerings of the devout, only a small hole being left in the middle for the people to kiss. The peasants have a great idea of the efficacy of this picture in devotion, and I remarked some of them prostrating and crossing themselves before it seventeen or twenty times. At nine we set off and rode along the plain of Nicosia, scattered with low hills (sometimes of marl) and bounded by low mountains, consisting of a rich soil very little cultivated at a small distance from the city, and, where it was so, abounding in olive trees, and thinly sown with corn and cotton. We passed the village of Cheri and at noon reached that of Neson where we stopt to dine. This latter was a very pretty village, full of fruitful gardens and fields of cotton, watered by a copious mountain-stream running through it, and surrounded by brown mountains, which formed a fine contrast with its vegetation. We left it with regret at four o'clock, and for one hour rode through the same pretty scenery as that which surrounded it. We then passed the village of *Th*ali, whence we rode . . . over a stony road, and hilly uncultivated country (as I have described it in my ride to *Th*ali last February) till the last hour when we passed the plain of Larnaca, and passed (at half-past seven) the village of Ari*th*ippon. Through all the afternoon we had frequent and vivid flashes of lightning, and for the last half hour, light rain.

We stopped at Larnaca at half-past eight, and had scarcely sheltered ourselves within doors, when there arose a furious gale of wind with violent and incessant rain, both which continued the whole of the night. To-day is the Greek fête of Saint Demetrius, on or near which day, say they, there always blows infallibly a heavy gale of wind, and so settled is their belief in this, that no Greek vessel will put to sea in this season till the time of the expected storm be over. I felt no other mark of fever to-day than weakness and an utter want of appetite.

Wednesday, November 8th. (Thermometer 77.)—In the morning I went down to the Marina to inquire for the Turkish captain, whom I found not yet returned from Famagosto. While here, the fever seized me suddenly with aguish shiverings, and so weakened me, that, finding myself unable to reach Larnaca, I crept into bed at Mr. H.'s, where I staid till Thursday the 16th. The fever lay very heavy on me for four days, and the other four I was so weak from the remedies applied to me and my almost total abstinence, that I could not leave my bed till the eighth day. The Turkish captain then called to say, he should positively sail that evening; and though still so weak as to be unable to walk without a stick, I had such dread of the air of Cyprus, that I resolved to accompany him. I walked Mr. H.'s horse to Larnaca, took leave of my friends, packed up, and at a quarter-past ten pushed off in a shore boat to follow the ship, which had sailed an hour before, and was some way off with a light north-east breeze. By firing frequently we succeeded in bringing her to, and I got on board at midnight. She was a large three-masted polacca, of about 150 tons, with a captain and crew from the Black Sea, the latter all Greek. I lay down directly on a wretched bed, in a hole about six feet long and three broad, for the captain not expecting me, had given his cabin, which he had promised me, to other passengers.

The vessel went smoothly and slowly all night, with a light north-east wind.

Cyprus, though nominally under the authority of a Bey appointed by the captain Pasha, is in fact governed by the Greek archbishop, and his subordinate clergy. The effects of this are seen every where throughout the island, for a Greek, as he seldom possesses power, becomes immediately intoxicated by it when given him, and from a contemptible sycophant is changed instantaneously to a rapacious tyrant. Accordingly the peasants of Cyprus, both Mahometans and Greeks, (not a single Jew is allowed to live in the island) are so insufferably plundered that their labour is barely capable of supporting their existence, and they yearly desert in great numbers to the coasts of Caramania and Syria. The least kharatch they pay is of thirty piastres, and the greatest sixty-five, *i.e.,* each whole family. Their utmost gains are from 400 to 500 piastres a year, and of this they pay annually to the government and to the Greek convents 250, but for the sum paid to the convents (by far the greater part) they are forced to give sixty-five paras to the piastre, though the regular change in the island is only forty. They live accordingly in the greatest wretchedness. Their houses (in the central parts of the island, near the sea-shore, they are more generally of stone) are of mud, and consist of two small rooms, with mud floors, and ceilings of platted rushwork, plastered outside with mud, with one half of the floor raised above the other, and generally with no other furniture than a ricketty wooden bedstead. Their food is of coarse wheatbread and herbs, with, at rare intervals, an occasional home-fed chicken, and the wine of the country, which, fortunately for them, is bought very cheap; the sharp-tasted (red) at from six to eight paras the oke. The mud floors contract such immoderate quantities of vermin, that it would be utterly impossible for the inhabitants to sleep, if their skins had not by long practice become as tough as that of a horse. Their misery is sometimes increased by a sort of locust, which, at intervals, over-spreads the island, and destroys entirely every species of vegetation. As their taxes are not diminished when this calamity occurs, in these disastrous years they are forced to sell their small stock of furniture, and frequently every disposable thing they possess, to satisfy the rapacity of their unfeeling tyrants.

The wine of Cyprus being brought (*i.e.,* the red) from the villages in skins tarred inside, has so strong a taste of tar, that I could not drink it. The common white wine is very good and not very sweet. It does not fetch the price of Commanderia till after being kept two or three years. It is called Commanderia, because the district in which it is made (lying between Limesole, Baffo, and Sta. Croce) formed part of the *Commandery* of the Knights Templars.

When a peasant marries, he takes his wife with nothing else than a box containing the few clothes she may have, and he is thought uncommonly fortunate if his father-in-law be able to give him, with her, a mule or a donkey. The consequences of this misery are such as might be expected. The peasant is sunk in a state of apathy and sullenness which a philanthropist cannot contemplate without horror. Being constantly forced to serve others gratis, his pride is to refuse the slightest favour when not forced. With his wretched wooden plough, dragged by two half-starved oxen, he hardly scratches the ground, and his harvest might frequently be doubled by a willing labourer. In many of the mountains of the island are mines of iron, of which the usual signs are visible on their surface. The peasants know this, but will not speak of it, lest their avaricious masters should make them work gratis at extracting the ore. The Venetians made sugar and vitriol in Cyprus. At Paphos are considerable quantities of the μίανθος, or uninflammable mineral. All these advantages are rendered useless by the rapacity of the government, which, as usual, is hurtful to its own interests.

The peasants of Cyprus have a curious superstition, which seems to have descended to them from the time of the ancient Egyptians, *viz.*; they never eat flesh of oxen, cows, or calves, nor ever drink cows milk. They nourish them, however, to sell to the ships at the Scala.

Independent of the fevers produced by its uncultivated land becoming marshy, Cyprus is unfortunate in its situation. It suffers from the cold of Caramania, from the hot sirocs of Syria, and from the plague of Egypt, which never fails to infect it when prevalent there.

The transit commerce of Cyprus is considerable, owing to the numerous vessels that come from other ports of the Levant, and from Malta. But this is only within a few years; Signor Vondiziano tells me that the average of the consular duties in Larnaca for the last four years, has been 30,000 piastres, of which he takes two sevenths, according to the rules of the Levant company, to which he sends the rest.

Having somewhere read (I believe in the Quarterly Review of Dr. Clarke's Greece) that the dress of the Greek women in Cyprus differs from all the others, and approaches more to the ancient model, I observed this point with particular attention, and am able to state with confidence that in all my rambles about the island, I have seen only two kinds of dresses that differed from the usual fashion of the Greeks, and of these but very few. One of these was a short yellow vest tight round the upper part of the body, with a red petticoat that came over it at the waist, round which it was tightened by a drawing tape; a handkerchief was carelessly tied round the head. This was worn by a villager, whom I saw at Santa Croce, and by another near Paphos. The other (worn by a pretty young girl of Nicosia) was all of white cotton, a loose vest, with pantaloons fastened by a drawing tape round the waist, and descending to the feet below the knot with which it was tied at the ancle *à la Turque*. The general dress (like that of all Greek women) consisted of a white cap (sometimes with a red border or embroidered, according to the circumstances of the wearer) round which the hair flowed loose before on each temple, and terminated behind in one, two, six, or even eight tails, generally lengthened by skeins of silk; strings of sequins, rubiehs, or paras, hung round the head and neck; a gown tightened at the waist, and bound by a simple handkerchief, or by a leathern girdle fastened by silver clasps which generally bore the shape of a circle or of a sloped heart, and an outer robe more or less richly embroidered, flowing to the feet; for this latter a red cloth is mostly preferred, they being here freely permitted to wear that colour as well as yellow shoes, contrary to the custom in Constantinople. They frequently throw a handkerchief loosely about the head to shade them from the sun, and none of them, even Turkish women, hide their face with scrupulous jealousy.

Poverty seldom consults fashion in dress, but if I observed one habit more common among the Greek peasants (men) than the other, it was one of coarse cotton, all white, consisting of a short vest tight round the body, with loose trowsers down to the feet, fastened round the waist by a drawing tape, or, if the wearer could afford it, by a girdle which was generally red. The turban was mostly of coarse white cotton, they being freely allowed to wear this colour on the head.

The Turks of Cyprus are in fact the tamest in the Levant. Many professed Mussulmans are in secret Greeks, and observe all the numerous fasts of that church. All drink wine freely, and many of them eat pork without scruple in secret; a thing unheard of in Turkey. They frequently marry the Greek women of the island, as their religion permits a Turkish man to marry an infidel woman, though to guard against an abandonment of Mahometanism, it forbids a Turkish woman to marry an infidel.

The Greek of Cyprus is abominably corrupt, being intermixed with Venetian, Turkish, and Arabick . . .

A Frank in Cyprus has the greatest difficulty to find servants, in consequence of which their insolence to their masters is insufferable. This is not owing to any want of serviceable subjects, but to the infamous conduct of the Greek priests, who, with their usual bigotry and pride, tell the peasants that it is a shame to serve, and no sin to rob, the Frank dogs. When a peasant robs a Frank, the priests do not enforce restitution, which they always do if the plunder be taken from a Greek.

In short, these Greek priests, every where the vilest miscreants in human nature, are worse than usual in Cyprus from the power they possess. They strip the poor ignorant superstitious peasant of his last para, and when he is on his death bed, make him leave his all to their convent, promising that masses shall be said for his soul. Madame Dupont (the mother of my companion) tells me that she once paid a visit to a Greek widow of a peasant who was dying, and asked her if she had made her will to dispose of what she had in the world. "I have only that," replied the woman, pointing to a handsome Venetian look-ing-glass, hanging up in the room, "and that I have left to my father confessor to pray for my soul."—"But your two children," replied Madame D. "Oh!" said the superstitious dupe, *"he says, Heaven will take care of them!"*

I found the climate of Cyprus delicious during my two visits. But in summer the heat is intolerable, and the winter generally is one continued torrent of rain. The rainy seasons are March and April (it is the rain of these months which, by filling the marshes, causes the fever) and November, December, and January. Up to my departure, the rain had hardly begun; we had only two days of it, in Nicosia, and the inhabitants attribute this unusual continuation of dry weather (which oppresses every one with colds or fevers) to the early cold which is wafted here from the snow on the mountains of Caramania. In winter a sort of tornado is not unfrequent, and the inhabitants have not yet forgotten one of these which occurred in a night of February, in the severe winter of 1812-13, during which hail-stones fell as big as walnuts that beat in the mud roofs of many of the houses. I did not see in Cyprus a single cypress tree, from which some assert that the island de-rived its name, while others deduce it from the Henné plant (in Botany, Lawsonia iner-mis) whence the Easterns prepare the yellow dye for the hair, and which, in Hellenick, was called Κύπρος. It grows very abundantly in the island.

I could not hear of any serpents in Cyprus. It seems to be now free from the an-noyance of those animals by which it was anciently so infested as to have acquired the epithet of ὀφιώδεα Κύπρον.

* * * * *

All the day of the 21st, we had light winds from the north easterly, and made from three to four knots an hour. At noon we descried the high mountains of Caramania, of which the projection forms the west-end Bay of Satalia, and at sun-set I bade adieu for ever to Cyprus, which we had seen but dimly all day.

Parsons 1821

The Reverend Levi Parsons was sent as a missionary to Smyrna in November 1819. He traveled the eastern Mediterranean in the troubled times of the Greek uprising against the Turks. He visited Cyprus twice in 1821 in the months of January and May. He died in 1822 barely two years after beginning his ministry. This account is from *Memoir of Rev. Levi Parsons, Late Missionary to Palestine,* compiled and prepared by Parsons' son-in-law, Rev. Daniel O. Morton and published in Poultney, Vermont: Smith & Shute, 1824. Morton quotes from Parsons' letters to his parents and to the American Board of Commissioners for Foreign Ministries. We include here Morton's introductory remarks along with the excerpt from Parsons.

[A long letter to his parents, January 1, 1821 concludes:]

[p. 354]

"P.S. *January* 25, 1821. *At harbour near to Paphos, (Cyprus.)*—In the morning I expect to commence a tour through the island to distribute tracts and bibles. I leave this letter in the vessel, to be forwarded to Smyrna."

[p. 355]

The following extracts, from a letter to the corresponding secretary of the A. B. C. F. M. dated Cyprus Feb. 7, 1821, contain an account of his missionary labours on that island, and mention several interesting facts respecting that once favoured and delightful place. "At the harbour of Baffa (anciently Paphos) I left the vessel, and proceeded by land forty miles to Limesol, for the purpose of distributing testaments and tracts. The first place which I visited was Paphos. The priests immediately conducted me to the church, where *they say* St. Paul preached the gospel; from thence to the hall, where he was condemned; and to the pillar, where he was bound and received 'forty stripes save one.' It was truly affecting to see so many churches destroyed; some used for stables, others for baths, others completely in ruins. Of three hundred and sixty-five churches, once the glory of Paphos, only four or five now remain. Twenty-five or thirty miserable huts are all that remain of the once most distinguished city of Cyprus.

From this place I went to the house of a Greek bishop in a village two or three miles from the shore. There I was received with the utmost cordiality; and all his proceedings were marked with great seriousness and dignity. He highly approved of the tracts which I brought with me, and engaged to distribute them among his people. Under his government are two hundred churches, but only fifty are now open for religious services. On the way to Limesol, spent one night in a village called Pissouri. The priest of the village purchased a testament, and received tracts" for distribution. "I sent to the bishop of Larnica two hundred tracts; one hundred for his own use, and one hundred for the archbishop of Nicosia. The next day the bishop in company with the principal men of the village came to the house of the consul to express their approbation of the truths contained in the tracts, and their gratitude. It was my intention to go by land from Limesol to Nicosia, but the rain prevented. The tracts which I send to that city will be distributed, as in other places, among the priests and schools." Mr. Parsons sent two Greek testaments to two poor churches, and fifty tracts to the monastery of "the holy cross." The English consuls at Limesol and at Larnica entertained him with great kindness.

Several pilgrims took passage from Cyprus, so that the whole number on board was seventy-five. It was with emotions not easily described that Mr. Parsons beheld the shores of Palestine, particularly the summits of mount Lebanon.

* * * * *

[p. 386]

May 12.—Early in the morning, arrived at the port of the ancient Paphos, Cyprus, two miles from the house of the Greek bishop. In consequence of contrary winds, and especially in consequence of sickness among the pilgrims, we were permitted to refresh ourselves on shore for the day. The bishop, hearing of our arrival, sent bread, cheese and wine for our refreshment.

May 13.—Slept the last night under a hovel upon a bed of bean pods. The weather is delightful, and the fields of grain are ripe for the harvest. Every object around us, the fragrance of flowers, the choice variety of fruits, the singing of the birds, the salubrity of the air, is calculated to excite our praise and gratitude.

May 15,—Had some profitable conversation with the Greek priest who accompanied us. I requested him to prove from the scriptures the articles of his creed; such as the duty of offering prayers to the virgin Mary, praying for the dead, &c. He declined, and appealed to the fathers. He added, "The bible is not capable of affording instruction without the aid of the holy fathers." But in what a deplorable situation, I replied, does this place the greater part of Christians! They must search a thousand folio volumes to learn their duty. Where is there one out of ten thousand, that would not die in ignorance of the will of God?

May 17.—With regard to confessions, the Greek priest said, "If a man commit a great offence, he must go to the bishop, tell his fault, and then supply the church with candles and oil, and give of his substance to feed the poor." Not a word said about repentence towards God, and faith in the Lord Jesus Christ.

May 19.—Off Castello Rosso.

Goodell 1823

William Goodell was one of the early Christian missionaries sent to the Levant by the American Board of the Commissioners of Foreign Ministries. After a stay in Beirut he became the first missionary in Constantinople and was considered a pioneer in the Protestant Reformation in Turkey. Sailing east he visited Cyprus in November 1823. Unfortunately he failed to comment on his week in Cyprus and only records the early Christian history there. He left, however, a journal and numerous letters, which his son-in-law, E. D. G. Prime, compiled, excerpted, and commented on in *Forty Years in the Turkish Empire or, Memoirs of Rev. William Goodell, D.D.*, published in New York: Robert Carter and Brothers, 1876.

[p. 75]

October 22, 1823. We have engaged passage on 'La Divina Providenza,' a Maltese brig, bound to Cyprus and Beyrout . . .

[p. 77]

Friday, November 7. Instead of being in port, as we had hoped, we are still 'sailing under Cyprus, because the winds are contrary.' An admirer of the Greek classics might easily fancy that his eyes now behold the very mountains which the poets have rendered immortal by making them the birthplace of Venus, and the abode of the Graces. In the Scriptures of the Old Testament this island was called 'Chittim.' In the Acts of the Apostles much mention is made of it under its present name. It was to Cyprus some of those came 'who were scattered abroad upon the persecution that arose about Stephen, preaching the word to none but unto the Jews only.' It was here Barnabas was born, who, 'having land, sold it, and brought the money, and laid it at the apostles' feet.' It was here 'one Mnason' lived, 'an old disciple with whom,' said Paul (when on his way to Jerusalem for the last time), 'we should lodge.' It was to Cyprus Paul and Barnabas sailed, after they had 'been sent forth by the Holy Ghost' to preach to the Gentiles. It was at Paphos, in this island, 'the deputy of the country desired to hear the word of God, and Elymas the sorcerer sought to turn him away from the faith,' for which he was smitten with blindness. And it was here Barnabas sailed, after he and Paul had contended, and 'departed asunder the one from the other.' The Lord in mercy grant 'that there may be no divisions among ourselves, but that we may be perfectly joined together in the same mind and in the same judgment'!

Friday, November 14. Left Cyprus at seven o'clock this evening.

Carne 1826

John Carne, Esq., of Queens College, Cambridge, published *Letters from the East*, London: Henry Colburn, 1826, recording his extensive journey throughout Turkey, Egypt, Syria, Palestine, Cyprus and parts of Greece. Portions appeared in the *New Monthly Magazine.* He also authored *Letters Written During a Tour Through Switzerland and Italy, in the year, 1825.*

Carne's visit to Archbishop Cyprian in Nicosia is of special interest as it apparently occurred shortly before Cyprian's execution by the Turks. Many Greek nobles had already been executed and there was a threat of Cyprian's imminent death. Carne claims to have had as a guide in Nicosia the "Sclavonian" swordsman who had executed so many Greeks and asked for money from Cyprian for dispatching them without pain. Although the execution of many of the Greek clergy and Cyprian occurred shortly after Carne's visit, he describes Cyprian as being beheaded, which is in contradiction to other accounts that speak of the archbishop as being hanged, while all the others were beheaded.

LETTER XXII

Having resolved to take a passage to Cyprus, we set sail on a fine afternoon from Beirout in a small boat, crowded with passengers, reckoning only on a passage of twenty-four hours. Four nights and five days passed over us in this wretched boat, which had no cabin but a dark hole sufficient for one person to drag himself into, and the space without was crammed with bales of merchandize. The weather was very hot, our water fell short, and the distress of the poor passengers, among whom were many women and children, was dreadful.

We were becalmed at last off a desolate part of the island, and two or three of the crew were sent on shore for some water, and in a few hours returned with a plentiful supply. The joy of the people on board was excessive, and they drank the water tumultuously, as if they were never to drink again; those who were unable to rise lifting up their heads with rapture, while the stream was poured into their lips by others.

On the fifth day we entered the port of Larnica, and proceeded to the house of the consul for England, M. Vondiziani, a Greek, to whom we had letters of introduction. This friendly and amiable man made his house quite a home to us: he was a widower, had five sweet children, and was perfectly domestic in his habits; he allotted us apartments commanding extensive views of the country, where we were served with breakfast in the English style, and his table was covered with a variety of dishes at mid-day and at eight in the evening.

The country around Larnica is perfectly naked and rugged, and the climate sultry and unwholesome. The consuls for the different European nations reside here, and their houses are fitted up in a good style. With the exception of some patches of verdure in what are called the gardens of some of the houses, the territory around is destitute of shade, and the ground parched with heat. In the apartments of the consul's house, the sun was excluded; but for several hours in the day the heat in the streets was insupportable.

The island was at this time in a state of deceitful tranquillity; the massacres of the Greeks were for a while partially suspended, only to be renewed with greater fury. At the consul's table each day appeared an unfortunate Greek family, who resided in his house, and received from him the utmost kindness. It consisted of a widow in the prime of life, her eldest son, a fine young man, and two or three children. The father, who was a rich Greek boyar, had been murdered, and all his effects confiscated. This poor lady was most anxious for every detail of the war, and to know if the English would assist her oppressed country.

The governor of the island was a brutal and savage character; and the Greek monks trembled at his threats to destroy and ransack their monasteries. The fathers were most unfortunately situated in this war: timid from their habits, they saw only certain destruction in store; or else girded on a sword and joined the ranks, in which they cut but a sorry figure. Several priests had been slain a short time before our arrival; and one evening, while sitting quietly in the consul's parlour, an unhappy Greek was shot at the door, while passing along, by a Turkish soldier.

The island having been placed under the pacha of Egypt's protection, he sent a body of soldiers to defend it; who not long after mutinied for want of pay. They resolved, about two thousand in number, to march to Larnica, seize on some vessels, and embark for Egypt. The intelligence reached us at Larnica on the evening of their approach: the greatest consternation instantly prevailed; the Austrian consul shipped off his most valuable effects, and went on board with his family. As the troops would arrive in the night, a general scene of pillage and tumult was likely to take place. The consul was most alarmed for his children, two or three of whom were pretty girls; and having mustered all the arms and domestics in the upper apartment, whose windows fronted the street, we took post there before dark, assured that the Turks would not stand more than one volley from a defensive position like this; and Mons. V.'s little garrison, mustering more than a dozen people well armed, made no contemptible appearance.

Report said the mutineers were only a few miles from the town: the women were dreadfully alarmed; but hour after hour passed away quietly, and we found in the morning that they had altered their course, and gone to Famagousta. A few stragglers only arrived, one of whom was shot in a quarrel by his comrade the same evening. At the latter town they committed several excesses, but were quieted at last by the interference of their commander, and promises of pay.

In the course of the revolution, several of the Greeks, to save their lives, had become Mahometans; among these was a rich merchant: this man we frequently met, and he invited us to visit him. He was a smooth, good-looking, and corpulent Greek, and confessed it was to save his head only that he had apostatised. It was now the fast of Ramadan, and he bitterly exclaimed against the Koran, and its absurd laws, which compelled him to fast from one sunset to the next, and this agreed dreadfully with his habit of body. "Sixty-three times to-day, said he, have I been obliged to prostrate myself towards Mecca, and touch the ground with my forehead;"—which could have been no easy matter, from his extreme corpulence. He cursed the prophet and his paradise too. "I must put myself to torment," said the Greek, "for what I care nothing about: and what are all his bowers and pleasures to me, while I am famishing?" Besides, the faithful had their eyes sharply upon him, and he was obliged to model his subtle face into a solemn and reverential expression, and keep from other indulgences, which mortified him more than the loss of the good cheer, for, from his own account, he was a thorough profligate.

Another Greek family were placed in a rather more tragical situation at Larnica. A certain time was allotted them to decide whether to embrace Islamism or die; the husband leaned to the former alternative, and strove to persuade all his family; but the wife was firmly resolved to adhere to the faith of her fathers, and, like many other Greek women in this warfare, showed a heroism, of which the men are too often destitute: the time allotted was not yet expired.

Cyprus, from its vicinity to the Egyptian power, the cutting off of nearly all the rich and distinguished Greeks, and the want of spirit in the remainder, was more unfortunately situated than the rest of the Greek islands; and yielded without resistance to the cruelties of its oppressors. The military force at this time dispersed over so large a space was weak; and had a body of resolute Greeks effected a landing in any part, the island would probably have been free, at least for a time.

It was sad to see this large and beautiful island so desolate and ravaged; chateaus and their rich gardens laid waste and deserted, and their surviving possessors dependant on others for shelter and support; women, bred up in luxury, deprived of their husbands and parents; and the sons of nobles imploring refuge from strangers. Large domains of land could be bought for a trifle; and a chateau, with a garden, together with a small village on the domain, and an extensive tract of land, were offered for a few hundred pounds.

We left Larnica on a fine evening, on a tour into the interior of the island. The Consul caused his secretary and one of his servants to accompany us; so that, with the Janizary and his servant, we formed a party of nine. The Turk was a fellow of humour and good nature, and, unlike these guards in general, accommodated himself entirely to our movements.

In about two hours, after travelling over a parched plain, we came to a fine fountain, with some trees, and stopped for a short time; and towards evening arrived at a hamlet of Greek peasants, and took up our lodging in a neat cottage. The fare the good people provided, with some additions from Larnica, furnished an excellent supper. The horses being ready to start soon after day-break, we took a simple yet luxurious breakfast in the court, and which, from its being so speedily provided, we often adopted afterwards: the new milk from the cow being placed over the fire, and a quantity of coffee thrown into it, made a repast in a few minutes, with a crust of bread, fit for an epicure.

The day was exceedingly beautiful; every day indeed was alike, and the atmosphere was so pure, that the outline of each mountain in the horizon, however distant, was traced with perfect distinctness. The way led over a plain, more verdant, however, than the one traversed the day before; and in a few hours we came to a deserted chateau, that had belonged to a wealthy Greek gentleman. It afforded a melancholy and affecting scene. The chambers were all empty, and the furniture destroyed or plundered. Through the small and rich garden ran a beautiful stream: we sat on its banks beneath the shade of the trees, and partook of some refreshment brought by a peasant, whom we found in the house, and who belonged probably to a village not far distant. The windows of the house looked over a spacious plain in front, and a range of fine mountains on the right. The owner had been murdered by the Turks; and his widow and children, some of whom were very young, were driven out to misery and dependence.

Leaving this spot, we travelled over the plain beneath a sultry sun, and saw with joy the rich and deep groves of Cytherea at a distance, which soon afforded a welcome shade. We proceeded to the house of a Greek priest, and ascending a long flight of steps, entered the garden, into which the dwelling opened. It was a sweet and retired place, full of orange and lemon trees; the fruit of the latter hung in quantities, and of an enormous size. The father seemed well pleased with our visit, and killed, not a fatted calf or kid, but a goat, which being made into soup, and two or three sorts of dishes, was served up in the corridor. This good man had a wife and family, and seemed to live in much comfort.

The village of Cytherea consists of detached cottages, each having its garden and rivulet; for so great is the abundance of streams around this spot, that they appear to flow close to every dwelling. The groves are chiefly of mulberry, orange, and lemon trees, and a quantity of silk is produced here. Next to the gardens, the chief attraction around this spot is the picturesque and irregular chain of mountains that rises above and around it, the waving and rocky outline of which is beautiful. Not far from the father's was the handsome dwelling of a Greek boyar, the coolness of whose garden and rushing stream almost invited us to become purchasers, and settle in this place, where the climate is healthy, and free from the scorching heats of the coast. The possessor of this mansion had been beheaded a short time before, and it was left desolate: the Turks would have sold it for a trifle, and an Englishman might have enjoyed it in perfect safety.

In the evening we visited the greater part of the scattered village: one seldom sees a more inviting and attractive spot; and we ascended, about sunset, one of the mountains to the west. The light was nearly faded when we had gained the top; yet we had a fine view of the sea, the coast beneath, and the high shores of Caramania on the opposite side, but it soon became indistinct, and we had to find our way back nearly in darkness. The descent over the rocks was very annoying, and we regained the priest's home with no little pleasure, and being parched with heat, had the table placed in the garden beneath the orange and lemon trees, and plucking the fresh fruit, drank insatiably of excellent lemonade. To lie down to sleep beneath the deep foliage was a luxury; and the perfume was wafted by the cool night-breeze around us.

We took leave of our host next morning, who, if subsequent accounts are correct, possessed not his sweet garden and cottage much longer, but was soon after numbered with his murdered countrymen. Ascending the mountains, the path soon became wild and rocky; and in a few hours we beheld the monastery of Chrysostom on the declivity above, and wound up a steep ascent to it. It is overhung on three sides by lofty mountains, and looks down in front on an extensive plain, in the midst of which is the city of Nicosia. The convent is very ancient, and contains about a dozen Greek monks; whose larder did not appear to be very well provided, as we soon found to our cost. They had abundance of room and solitude, and could inhabit only a part of their edifice. The church is paved with marble, and the walls adorned with the usual daubings of Greek saints, male and female, who must be all of one family, from their marvelous likeness to each other.

Whatever might have been the former reputation of the convent, it is little resorted to now, and its finances are probably very low. It was founded by a rich Cypriot lady, some centuries ago; and beneath the portico of the church is her tomb, over which a lamp was kept always burning. Two slaves, or domestics, to whom their mistress was strongly attached, are laid in the same tomb, according to her wish in her last moments. It is a wild and tranquil spot to be buried in, where the mountain-winds breathe fresh over her grave.

In the garden of the monastery are cypress-trees of immense size and beauty, exceeding all we ever beheld; and a fountain breaks away, and descends over the rocks into the plain beneath. These monks lead a cheerless life, being under a vow of poverty and chastity, besides other severe rules; for which they have, probably, to thank their lady foundress.—On the brink of a steep mountain, that rises to a great height over the convent, are the colossal ruins of a castle, whose position must have been almost invulnerable. It was built as a place of defence against the oppressions of the Knights Templars, at the time they possessed the island. A long, steep, and most toilsome path leads up to it; but the prospect from the summit, as well as the remains themselves, amply repay the trouble. A number of small and ruinous chambers, and massive walls, spread over the face of these craggy rocks, have a singular effect; and the view extends over the greater part of the island, the immense plain that intersects it, and its mountain border, with the coast below, and the sea and shores of Asia beyond.

On returning to the convent, the good fathers, who never eat flesh themselves, soon after introduced different parts of a goat for our dinner; but he must have been some venerable attendant on the convent, or else bound under the same laws of self-denial, for it was impossible to partake of a single morsel, and we bade the monk make us rid of it. However, he produced some excellent honey, for which Cyprus is famous, as well as for its wines.

In the evening we rode down the mountain and over the plain, entering the gates of Nicosia before sunset. Having sent a letter of introduction to the Greek archbishop of the island, he immediately provided an excellent house and garden for our residence, and after dark honoured us with a visit. Cyprian, so cruelly murdered not long after our departure, was a fine and dignified looking man. He came to accompany us to supper at his palace; for which we soon after set out, lighted by a number of torches. The archbishop walked at the head, and his priests followed in order, according to their dignity. His table was sumptuously spread, and the cookery exquisite; the Cyprus wine of the oldest quality. Every morning he sent us breakfast in the English style, which was served by his domestics; at mid-day we dined at the palace; and every evening he came to converse for an hour, and then conducted us to his home, in procession, as before, to sup and spend the evening. His kindness and attentions were excessive, at the very time that he was labouring under constant alarm and agitation of mind.

What situation could be more affecting and distressing? Chosen to his high office by the Porte, as well as by his people, he formerly possessed great temporal influence in the island, even beyond that of the governor, till the breaking out of the revolution caused it to be taken from him. For some time, he had been compelled to look on the massacres of his countrymen and the plunder of their property, and stifle every expression of feeling. The oppressed and menaced Greeks often sought him for refuge; but, watched vigilantly by the Turkish authorities, he dared not afford protection to any, save by his private charities, for which he had numberless objects. But now affairs were assuming a darker and more threatening aspect, as it regarded his own safety: he had been frequently insulted by the Turkish soldiers; the governor had spoken in abusive terms of him. "My death is not far distant," said Cyprian to us; "I know they only wait for an opportunity to dispatch me!"—and this was very evident.

One evening as we sat at supper, he was called out by one of his attendants respecting a message from the governor. We accompanied him to another apartment, where the soldier waited, who spoke in the most insulting terms: the calmness of the archbishop forsook him, and he replied with great warmth, refusing to obey the message. The soldier departed, and we returned to the table, but its harmony was completely destroyed. The ecclesiastics looked pale and terrified, and Cyprian sought by every effort to encourage them: he was deeply agitated and affected; but his fine features were lighted up with a noble energy, as he dwelt on the cruelties of their oppressors, and protested his determination no longer to submit to such aggravated insults, at the same time that he warned his hearers to prepare for the worst.

No one interrupted him, for it seemed like the farewell address of this excellent pastor to his trembling people; who felt, no doubt, that when the high and noble spirit that had guarded and consoled them, took its flight, they would fall a helpless prey into the hands of their enemies. The lamp-light, falling on the group of listening ecclesiastics, and on the remarkably fine countenance of their leader, whose long white beard descended nearly to his girdle, rendered this a scene not easily to be forgotten. It grew late, and we waited with anxiety the return of the soldier, who would probably bring a fiercer message from that wretch the governor; but, to the satisfaction of all, he returned no more.

Highly eminent for his learning and piety, as well as for his unshaken fortitude, Cyprian was the last rallying point of the wretched Greeks; and his frequent remonstrances and reproaches had rendered him very obnoxious to the Turkish authorities. He often shed tears when he spoke to us of the slaughter of his countrymen. We asked him why, in the midst of such dangers, he did not seek his own safety, and leave the island; but he declared he would remain to afford his people all the protection in his power to the last, and would perish with them.

The garden attached to the residence afforded a very pleasing walk amidst the burning heat of the day; having plenty of shade, and fountains. The climate of Nicosia, from its situation in a wide and flat plain, is oppressively hot, and it was scarcely possible to walk in the streets in the middle of the day. The construction of the houses and

streets being more Venetian than Turkish, the city does not enjoy the shade and coolness of most other Oriental towns. It is surrounded by a very strong wall, in which are
three handsome gates.

We went one day, by the governor's permission, to visit the large and splendid
mosque of the city, and were attended by a fierce and brutal Sclavonian soldier, who had
been the executioner of the unfortunate Greek nobles, in the great square, a short time before. This mosque was formerly the Christian church of St. Sophia; it was built by the
Venetians in the Gothic style, and consists of three aisles, formed by lofty pillars of marble. Around are the tombs of princes, of knights templars, and Venetian nobles. Every
vestige of the Christian worship was destroyed when the Turks stormed the city in the
fifteenth century; but it has been impossible to give it the air of a mosque. The imaun's
pulpit is erected where once, probably, stood the altar, and the walls are covered with inscriptions from the Koran, in large letters of gold: the pavement is of marble. At the time
we visited it, the imaun was seated a few steps above the floor, on which sat a circle of
Turkish gentlemen, each with the Koran in his hand, to whom he was expounding with
much earnestness, and they listened very attentively.

This noble edifice conveys an impressive idea of earthly vicissitudes. The ancient
kings of Cyprus were crowned within its walls, where also their ashes were laid: the warriors of the Temple have their tombs here, and many a haughty Venetian senator; but now
the Turk tramples on their ashes, and invokes the Prophet over the graves of those who
shed their blood in defiance of his name.

It is difficult to form an idea of the population of the town at present,—so many of
the Greeks have fled or been sacrificed, or keep concealed in their houses.

We went to the palace to have an audience of the governor: he was absent in the
country, but his chief officer, a young and handsome man, received us with great politeness. Some of the apartments of the palace were very elegantly furnished, with a double
row of windows on three sides of the walls, for the admission of air. Refreshments were
served, and the Turk assured us of perfect safety in travelling to any part of the island,
and requested, that, if we wanted any thing, we would make it known to him. The palace
stands in the great square, in the midst of which is a beautiful fountain: it was here that
the cruel execution took place, of the Greek nobles and merchants. The governor sent to
inform them, that he had just received dispatches from Constantinople, which not only
assured them of protection and safety, but granted them some additional privileges; and
he invited them, from different parts, to attend at his palace on a certain day, to hear these
documents read. Too credulously trusting to the governor's professions, almost all the
principal Greeks in the island assembled, and were admitted into the chamber of audience, from which they were almost instantly conducted by a passage, one after the other,
into the square without, where the sight of a strong guard, and the executioner with his
naked sabre in his hand, revealed at once the base treachery practised on them. The latter,
who was a Sclavonian soldier, boasted to us of his dexterity in the execution, for he had
struck off every one of their heads with a single blow of the sabre. The father of the family who found refuge at the consul's at Larnica, was among the number. The unhappy
men bore their fate with singular resignation, and submitted their necks to the blow without a murmur or complaint. Their houses and effects, lands and villages, were instantly

seized and confiscated, and their families rendered desolate! It is not easy to estimate the misery occasioned by this sudden and cold-blooded cruelty.

The archbishop described this scene, which was quite recent; and the anguish of his feelings was bitterly augmented on the following day, when the Sclavonian soldier waited on him and demanded a reward. Cyprian asked for what? The other answered, because he had put the archbishop's countrymen to death with so little pain, having beheaded each at a single blow, and that he deserved a recompense. But this wretch had been richly paid before; as he affirmed on our way to the mosque, that he had received a certain sum of the governor for every head.

While at Nicosia, we passed some part of every day in visiting the Greek families, with the consul's secretary, and were always received with the most attentive politeness. They, in general, lived retired, and many of their residences were handsome, opening into a pleasant garden, and surrounded with a corridor; the interior was furnished in the Turkish style. The women of the family were always present, their long tresses unconfined, of a dark colour, as well as their eyes; their complexion was seldom fair. One of these ladies, the wife of a merchant who was ill, was a remarkably intelligent and clever woman: she sometimes sat with us in the corridor, and conversed with deep feeling on the distresses of her people. Her husband, to save his life, and his family from ruin, had assumed the turban, and then every para of his property became as secure as in a fortress.

Coffee, sherbets, and wines of the finest quality, were introduced on these occasions. One species of the latter, forty years old, was exquisite.

The often boasted beauty of the women of Cyprus has long ceased to exist: they are now a plain race; the Grecian cast of features in some measure survives, but the form of symmetry, slender and elegant, is looked for in vain. It is, perhaps, doubtful how far the women of ancient Greece were a generally handsome race; the statues which survive might be the *beau ideal* of the sculptor, or rather an assemblage of the beauties of various women, than the possession of any single one. Whenever this exquisite beauty really existed, it became the theme of the poet, and the subject of the painter, who lavished all their powers in the description, which would hardly have been the case if beauty was the common or frequent gift. Immured as they were in the seclusions of their own walls, their lives and minds in general insipid and uncultivated, their society must have been, in some degree, regarded with a similar esteem and respect by the intellectual Greeks as the Ottoman ladies are by the Turkish lords of the present day. —Another circumstance, unfavourable to the growth or preservation of beauty in the Greeks, was, that they confined their connexions chiefly to their own country, and did not generally intermarry with other nations. It is evident, that the personal advantages the Turks possess over other nations, are exclusively owing to their taking wives from all countries; Arab, Grecian, and Persian blood all flow in the veins of an Ottoman, and conspire to make him the handsomest of human beings.

One afternoon, a messenger came to invite us to an audience of the governor, who was returned. He was sitting on a cushion, in a small and cool apartment, and was a most ferocious and savage looking fellow. He had none of the gentlemanly and dignified manners which generally characterize Turks of rank. We were scarcely seated, before he broke out in furious terms against the Greeks, on whom he lavished the foulest epithets. He abused the excellent Cyprian; and bitterly menaced a Greek monastery on the sea-shore, a few leagues from the city: it would make an excellent post, he said, for his soldiers, and those dogs should not possess it long. This convent, in a noble situation, was inhabited by a few poor monks, and during our stay in the city some soldiers entered it, and grossly insulted and beat one or two of the fathers, and plundered whatever they could lay their hands on. Not long after our departure, it was attacked and taken possession of by the troops, and all the fathers were murdered. The behaviour of the governor during our interview with him was more like that of a wild beast than a man; he evidently looked forward with delight to the heaping fresh cruelties on the wretched Greeks.

On leaving him, we visited the General of the Egyptian troops, sent by Mahmoud Ali to secure the island. He was seated in a small and beautiful kiosque, in the middle of the garden; the roof, in the form of a cupola, was light and gilded, and the windows, which looked into the garden, were surrounded by a number of fine trees. This commander was an elderly man, with a dissolute, yet inanimate countenance; he was attended by several of his officers: he conversed freely, and asked if England was not as hot as Cyprus; the air at this time was quite oppressive. The pipes brought by the attendants were very richly ornamented, and the napkins of purple silk, flowered with silver. The chibouques we smoked at the palace every day were splendidly enamelled, and valued at thirty guineas each; those of the general were little less valuable. We quitted this chief with pleasure, and returned to the archbishop's, who gratified us, after dinner, with an exhibition of sword-playing. Two men, armed with sword and target, and who were habited like mountaineers, and of a wild aspect, displayed considerable skill in attacking and warding off each other's blows for some time: the shield was of the size and form used by the Highlanders in former times.

The church of the Greek convent at Nicosia is adorned with costly ornaments, particularly a small image of the Virgin, almost covered with precious stones. Demetrie, who was a bigoted Greek when he joined us, had lost so much of his intolerance by associating with Michel, that he warned those around him, to our no small amusement, not to put faith in idols, such as this splendid Virgin. An old Greek, who stood by, raised his hands and eyes in utter astonishment at such blasphemous discourse.

We took leave, at last, of the excellent Cyprian, whose fate, as it was easy to perceive, was near at hand. He gave us his blessing, and requested us to remember, and carry to our country, the details of his sad and melancholy situation. Indeed, he appeared weary of his life: many of his ecclesiastics having been executed almost before his eyes, others imprisoned, or plundered of all they possessed, and the remainder subjected, with himself, to constant insults and persecutions.

Leondias, son of the late Vicar, was seized, and suffered cruel tortures during several days, to compel him to reveal the place where the nephew of the Archbishop was concealed.—This young man, Theseus by name, had bribed the executioners sent to arrest him; and, having paid large sums to some of his chief enemies, succeeded in saving himself by flight from Nicosia, into some of the remote parts of the island. Leondias, who was an old man, either not knowing or refusing to tell the place of his concealment, expired at last, after enduring extreme tortures. The prelate was filled with anguish at the unhappy event.

It was not long afterwards that the perfidious governor invited Cyprian to summon his chief ecclesiastics, saying that he wished to impart to them some intelligence which particularly concerned their safety and welfare, and requesting an immediate interview. All the clergy who were summoned to attend, were filled with suspicion of some treacherous design; but all hope of escape, or of avoiding this assembly, was vain, as the island was filled with the troops of the pacha of Egypt. But these unfortunate ecclesiastics hoped, that by offering all that remained of their property, they might satisfy the rapacity, and appease the fury, of the governor.

The next day, the prelate and his devoted flock were assembled in the Turkish palace, in the great square of Nicosia; when the governor, having placed guards at the gates and in all the passages, ordered the massacre to begin. Cyprian, in this trying moment, behaved with uncommon courage and dignity: he demanded of the governor, what crime these ill-fated men were guilty of, that they should suffer so dreadful a fate; recounted the spoliations and insults they had already endured, declared their entire innocence, and that, if nothing but blood would satisfy the governor's cruelty, he was ready to shed his own rather than they should perish.

The Turk returned a short and brutal reply; and the bishop's self-devotion only accelerated his own destruction. Many insulting questions were put to him; but he declared he had always served the sultan with perfect integrity, who, he now found, had deserted him, and given him up to the malice of his enemies. He requested a few moments to spend in prayer. By this time, his beloved people lay murdered around him, and he knelt down amidst their dead bodies, and commended his spirit into the hands of God. His head was then struck off, and he died without a murmur, evincing the same serenity and exalted piety, which through life had endeared him to all his people.

Filled with horror at the death of their revered prelate, many of the wretched Greeks of both sexes took refuge in the churches; but these retreats were soon violated by the infuriated Turks, and the pavement streamed with blood. The altar itself did not protect those who clung to it from violation; and the dreadful scenes of Scio, although to a smaller extent, were acted over again on those fatal days at Nicosia!

LETTER XXIII

Leaving Nicosia in the morning of a beautiful day, we travelled through a country that had little interesting in its appearance, till, in the afternoon, we came to the small plain and village of Dale, the ancient Idalium, and gladly sought shelter from the heat in one of the cottages. Michel brought a small sheep for our evening's repast, which did not prove too much to satisfy so large a company, increased by two or three of the inhabitants. In the mean time, the good cottagers set before us some delicious honey, and a preparation of cream.

As soon as the heat was in some measure abated, we sallied out to explore the neighbourhood, which is very beautiful, shaded by a variety of small groves, and abounding in fragrant shrubs. A fine stream, on the banks of which the village is built, runs through the plain. The soil is excessively rich, though only partially cultivated. A large and confused heap of ruins, the remains of the ancient city, are on the plain, at about a mile from the village; but not a column or fragment possessing any beauty, is left to tell of its former magnificence. A lofty eminence, on the right, is covered with remains of a similar kind, but more massive in their appearance: a circular wall, in spite of its decayed state, may be distinctly traced. The view over the plain from the summit of this hill is uncommonly fine; a more delightful and superb site for a city can scarcely be imagined. We watched the sun going slowly down on its groves and stream with great delight, and then bent our way to our rude habitation.

Near the foot of this hill, in a most lonely spot, and in a wretched cottage, lived a family of lepers. These unfortunate people were avoided by all the other inhabitants, who dreaded to come near their dwelling. The disease was hereditary; for every one of this numerous family was afflicted with it. Some of them stood at the door, and looked the pictures of sadness and solitude. They would be starved, did not some of the people who lived in the plain bring food occasionally, and place it at a short distance from the cottage. So great is the horror entertained of this disease, that the Mosaic law is fulfilled to the letter, of thrusting them out from all society, without the hope of ever returning to it.

Returning to our cottage, by the river side, we found the sheep ready to be served up, cooked in half a dozen different ways, and accompanied by some very good Cyprus wine. The table was spread in the court, and the air was now delightfully cool. The twilight at this season of the year (June) was longer than it is often thought to be in eastern climates, affording us excellent light for nearly three quarters of an hour. Some of our party danced in high glee to a guitar, played by one of the natives, till the lateness of the hour induced us to retire to our rude couch.

Early the next morning, after a hasty breakfast, we took our departure from the pleasant environs of Idalium, and bent our way towards Larnica. Some parts of the country were romantic, particularly a long and winding defile, on each side of which the rocks rose precipitately; and a monastery perched on the top of a small and conical hill, that was perfectly bare, was on the right. In the afternoon, we came to Larnica, and the hospitable home of the Consul.

It was now time to think of proceeding to Greece, as Cyprus became every day more and more a prey to tumults and massacres. But we waited some days in vain for a passage to the Morea: it was a dangerous destination, and no vessel was likely to undertake it.

The new superior of the Catholic convent at Jerusalem arrived here on his way: he was a good-natured, cheerful monk, and preached on the Sunday an eloquent sermon, in Italian, in the convent chapel. He seemed to like his destination uncommonly well. So fond are these ecclesiastics of power, that many of them would go again to the rocks and caves of the Thebais, to have dominion over their brethren.

Our resources for amusement at Larnica were very few; the occasional visits to the families extended only to sitting for an hour on the divan, or beneath the trees in the garden, and the refreshment of a cup of coffee, or a glass of Cyprus wine. The Consul, though a Greek, and perfectly secure beneath the protection of the English Government, would most gladly have left the island with his children, to place them out of danger during the present unhappy state of affairs. His eldest daughter, a fine young woman, was married to a merchant of good property in the town, with whom she appeared to live very happily: we passed a very pleasant evening at their house. The Consul had a covered caleche, of curious appearance, in which we sometimes drove during the sultry hours of the day, and passed some hours in a sort of coffee-house, chiefly to enjoy the cool breezes from the sea, beside which it stood.

Demetrie, Mr. G.'s servant, drove his bargains here to vast advantage; he was a merchant whenever opportunity offered; and he never omitted to embrace it. When at Jerusalem, he carried to the holy sepulchre a large heap of necklaces of beads, and crosses, and laid them on the sacred marble, that they might be rendered precious, and have the incense sprinkled on them. These he was sure to sell among his countrymen at home at a very high price. Milk of the Virgin, relics of all kinds, were treasured up with the same irreverent purpose. But he was rigid in all his observances, and contended stoutly for the excellence of the Greek faith, though he confessed himself to be a desperate sinner, and even doubted sometimes if the saints would be able to do any thing for him.—He contrived, while at Larnica, to buy a large quantity of wine at a very low price, of a young Greek, whose father had been beheaded some time before. The merchant declined parting with his wine so cheaply; but Demetrie completely frightened him into it, by declaring he was servant to some Lords Inglese, who would not be trifled with in this manner, and who had power to have his head taken off, as his father's had been, and with as little ceremony.

An Ionian vessel, bound to Trieste, afforded me an excellent opportunity of visiting the Morea, as the captain engaged, for a handsome douceur, to deviate from his course, and put me on shore at Navarino. Mr. G. resolved to visit Constantinople; and a large Austrian ship, that lay in the harbour of Famagousta, being about to sail for that city in a few days, he engaged a passage; but the Ionian brig was ready to depart first, and we parted with deep regret, having passed through various and trying scenes with the greatest delight, and with a harmony that scarcely ever experienced a moment's interruption.

Frankland 1827

Captain Charles Colville Frankland of the British Royal Navy kept a personal journal for his family and friends of his "three years' rambles upon the continents of Europe and Asia." He was prevailed upon to publish it, and a first edition was printed followed closely by a second edition, from which the following excerpt was taken, published in two volumes by Henry Colburn and Richard Bentley in London in 1830 with the extended title *Travels to and from Constantinople in 1827 and 1828 or Personal Narrative of a Journey from Vienna, through Hungary, Transylvania, Wallachia, Bulgaria, and Roumelia, to Constantinople; and from that City to the Capital of Austria, by the Dardenelles, Tenedos, the Plains of Troy, Smyrna, Napoli di Romania, Athens, Cyprus, Syria, Alexandria, etc.* Frankland made a brief stop at Cyprus in December 1827, but did not disembark. He made a longer visit in August 1828, reproduced here from Volume I.

[p. 315]

AUGUST 9.—In the morning, we made Cape Blanco, in the Island of Cyprus. All the day running with a fine breeze along-shore, towards Larneca. We passed Cape Gatto and Cape Salines, and made the point Chitti about sunset. At about nine, sounded off Cape Chitti in five fathoms. We anchored in the roads of Larneca, about 11 P.M. in eight fathoms. [N.B. Give Cape Chitti a wide berth.]

AUGUST 10.—In the morning, the British Consul came on board . . . I went on shore in the evening with Dalling. The Marina of Larneca is a wretched place, consisting of a long row of mud-built houses with flat roofs: it has a bazaar and a castle. The palm-

trees which are thinly scattered about the back of the town, give it a very Egyptian appearance, and I am told make it very much resemble Alexandria. The Consul sent his carriage for us, to convey us to his residence at Larneca, about three quarters of a mile from
the Marina. It was an open kind of caléche drawn by one horse, just such a one as Gil
Blas and his friend Scipion went down in to Andalusia, to take possession of his Quinta
at Leria.

On our way out saw a few *Cyprians*. God only knows how this island ever attained its celebrity for beauty; for, to judge of it from the specimen we saw, one would
have said it was the last place which Venus would have chosen in which to fix her favourite residence. I am told, however, that in the neighbourhood of Paphos (whose temple
still exists), *il y a le plus beau sang possible*. The male part of the population is handsome
and robust; and perhaps the laughing and wanton Goddess had an eye to this circumstance. The Consular residence is spacious and cool. The old gentleman received us with
much politeness and urbanity, offering us beds, &c. &c. He has several daughters; but I in
vain looked for a Haidee among them. Indeed, as far as I have hitherto seen in the Levant,
it strikes me that female beauty is a rare plant, and that all the poetical accounts which we
have been in the habit of reading upon this subject, are gross exaggerations. Pipes and
coffee employed the evening, and at about nightfall we returned to our bark.

AUGUST 11.—All the morning at the Marina with Dalling.—At noon we drove
out *à la Gil Blas* to Larneca.—We dined with the Consul, and saw several of the European Consuls.—Tutti, Illustrissimi Signori.—I observed at dinner that the fair *Con-
sulesses* had tinged their finger-nails with henna, *à la Turque*. It is curious to observe how
much the Greeks, in their humiliation and slavery, imitate their masters in their fashions
and absurdities. I should have remarked, that our Consul is by birth an Ionian, and that he
had married a Greek Cypriote; his daughters, therefore, are Greek in costume, language,
and ideas.

I observed that in most of the houses at Larneca, the ceiling of the large rooms is
supported by a Gothic or rather Saracenic arch. The beams likewise rest upon such
wooden projecting supports or buttresses as we see in old churches in England, under the
wood work of the roof. Many of the houses have a kind of façade, extending half the
height of the house, of stone, and of the same order of Saracenic architecture. I think that
some antiquarians trace the origin of this style of building in England back to the days of
the Crusaders, who are said to have found it existing in Cyprus and Palestine, and to have
imported it into Europe on their return. I observed likewise several columns with such
capitals and pedestals as we see in cathedrals and churches of the Gothic style.

There are by all accounts about two thousand troops of Mehmet Ali Pasha in Cyprus, Albanians: the whole population consists of about twenty-five thousand souls, of
which five-sixths are Greeks. The island remains in a state of uncultivation, owing to the
rapacity and tyranny of the Government, and is depeopling very fast. The population,
both Turk and Greek, are represented as extremely indisposed towards the yoke of the
Sultan, and as ripe for revolt upon the appearance of any thing like an auxiliary force.

The neighbourhood of Ali Pasha is, however, a formidable obstacle to the eman-
cipation of Cyprus; and I fear that, unless that tyrant should be blockaded in his port of
Alexandria, there is but little chance of the Cypriotes shaking the Ottoman yoke from off
their shoulders. Dalling and Elliot are purchasing Cyprus wines. The old and superior

wines are rare and dear, but the ordinary sorts cheap and abundant. The Commanderia, as it is called, is one of the best sorts. The Muscat is a perfect liqueur, but is about a dollar and a half the okka. The bread of Cyprus is excellent . . .

AUGUST 13.—I was awakened by a salute from the fort, in honour of the arrival of the Governor of Cyprus, (Mootselim,) upon a visit to Mr. Elliot. The weather very hot. In the evening I walked with Dalling in a cotton plantation near the beach. We enjoyed the cool sea-breeze and the splendour of an Oriental sunset upon the picturesque mountains of Cyprus exceedingly.

AUGUST 14.—A grand field-day on board; exercising the ship's company in firing the great guns at a mark. Some very good shots. I received a contusion on both my knees in firing a carronade, the gun recoiling farther than I had calculated upon. I stayed all the evening on board, my knees being too stiff and uncomfortable to admit of walking. Mr. Elliot came off, having had an interview with the Mootselim . . .

AUGUST 16.—His Majesty's ship Raleigh fired a royal salute upon the occasion of the rehoisting the Consular flag, which had been struck, owing to some misunderstanding between the British Consul and the Governor of Cyprus (Mootselim); and indeed this misunderstanding was the cause of Mr. Elliot's being sent hither by Mr. Stratford Canning, with instructions to bring the Governor to his senses (backed as his representations would be by the thirty-two-pounders of the Raleigh). The Turkish fort saluted likewise with twenty-one guns, the last of which, according to their custom, was shotted, throwing the ball a little ahead of the ship.

At noon Captain Dalling and myself, both in uniform, went on shore to dine with and felicitate the Consul. After dinner, we all went to call upon the Mootselim, in the house of the Cogia Bashi.

Our procession from the Consular residence to the Cogia Bashi's house was rather ludicrous, but appeared to produce a very grand effect upon the minds of the good inhabitants of Larnaca, who all came out at their doors to stare at us. I could hardly retain my gravity on witnessing the awkward attempts made by an old Turk of the Consulate, in his long scarlet robes, and grey beard, to stand up behind the ricketty carriage of the Consul (*à la chasseur*) with a large truncheon in his hand, as an emblem of his office and dignity.

We found his Excellency seated upon his divan, and surrounded by his Albanian guards. We were ushered into his presence with considerable pomp, and invited by him to seat ourselves on his divan. He told us that we were welcome, and that he was delighted to make our acquaintance, and so forth.

As usual, we were regaled with pipes and coffee; after which, we were each presented with conserves in little filagree cups of silver, (closed at the top by a hinged cover); then followed excellent sherbet with embroidered napkins; and next, we were sprinkled with rose-water, and perfumed with incense contained in filagree silver censers. His Excellency was very desirous that Captain Dalling should go over to a port in Caramania, and take under his charge a vessel, on board of which his Excellency's charem was to be embarked. This unusual and extraordinary request was naturally declined. On taking our leave of the Mootselim, he requested Captain Dalling's acceptance of two casks of Commanderia wine and four bullocks.

In the evening, we paid some visits of ceremony to the various Consuls and their spouses, and reembarked about eight o'clock. To-day and indeed the day before yesterday, two vessels arrived, having been plundered by a piratical schooner on the north-east side of Cyprus. We read a proces-verbal, taken before the French Consul, of the treatment received by one of the passengers: it was indeed most atrocious. We hope to fall in with the pirate on our return from Baruti. We hear from Alexandria that the Egyptian fleet of eighty-nine sail, had sailed for the Morea; two ships of the line, nine frigates, twenty corvettes and brigs, and forty-eight transports with four thousand troops on board.

Average height of thermometer, 82° in the shade, on board. Much ophthalmia and fever at Cyprus.

Exports, silk, cotton, wine.

AUGUST 17.—We weighed at about 2 P.M. for Baruti.

Wilson 1829

In *Travels in Egypt and the Holy Land,* published by Longman, Hurst, Rees, Orme and Brown, in London in 1823, William Rae Wilson, Esq., described setting out from London on 26 October 1818 and visiting Cyprus during April 1819. Wilson added copious footnotes from Bacon, the Bible, Denon on Upper Egypt, Morier's *Journey through Persia*, and Clarke's *Travels.*

On leaving Bayreuth, I sailed to Cyprus, in company with a medical gentleman, who fully confirmed the fact of the Druses worshipping the calf, having lately been witness to it. This place is distinguished by visits received from an apostle "who went through the isle," preaching the word of God, and joined by Barnabas, a native. I disembarked at Larnica, and proceeded to the convent. Among other places I visited Nicotia, the capital, and on returning from it to Larnica, was surprised at finding myself almost enveloped in a cloud, or thick body of locusts, covering the ground, and skipping like grasshoppers, with hissing noise, and a sight so altogether novel, that it occasioned some degree of apprehension. Any person who has read Scripture with the slightest degree of attention, cannot fail to reflect with horror on these "grievous swarm of flies," sent forth by the incensed majesty of heaven on a guilty world. The vengeance, indeed, of an almighty power in such visitations can only be figured by those who have witnessed their sweeping ravages; and in some countries the inhabitants actually lay in provisions against famine created by the devastation of locusts. It has been presumed they have a government similar to that of bees, and when the king rises he is followed by the whole band, but I apprehend this is contradicted by him who was possessed of wisdom. It is further mentioned that Arabs salt and eat locusts, although I had no opportunity of remarking this fact in any intercourse I had with this tribe, although, on the other hand, there is decisive evidence they were permitted as a species of food under the Jewish dispensation, and also partaken by John, precursor of Christ, in the wilderness. In allusion to the infelicities of old age, the grasshopper, which I presume to be meant for locust, is also referred to.

On return to the convent, having informed the monks of this phenomenon, they treated it lightly, and assured me that at particular seasons locusts came in such formidable numbers, as to actually darken or obscure the sun itself, and the work of destruction was incalculable. Their grand objects of attack, in particular, were the vine and fig-trees, which are stripped so completely bare of leaves as to convert the trees almost in one moment, into an image of winter, and a husbandman, who at the rising of the sun beholds his fields fair and luxurious, finds these before it goes down, absolutely bare, like a desert. In this island they arise from an immense track of waste land, affording shelter, with the powerful heat: in short, desolation attends their progress in every direction, and a more destructive scourge, I believe, a country never was visited with, and when antiently set loose as a judgment upon this earth. These devouring insects were of an enormous size. How much ought it not to be a subject of gratitude, that the island of Albion has been exempted from such visitations, which have also extended to other places of the earth.

I embarked at Larnica, and skirted along the western side of this island, having often distinct views of Paphos, a small town at the bottom of a mountain, where the goddess of idolatry had been demolished by the presence of St. Paul, and his eloquent persuasion had attracted the notice of one person in authority there, who was attempted to be drawn aside from the faith by artifices of another, which not only called forth the marked indignation of this apostle, but was followed up by demonstrative proof of that power with which he was armed from heaven, in depriving such an officious character of the organs of vision; an event that struck terror in the mind of that chief person, and founded a firm belief of the truth of the doctrine which had been proclaimed by this chosen vessel of Christ.

Disraeli 1831

Benjamin Disraeli, later Lord Beaconsfield, and prime minister of Great Britain visited Cyprus for one day in 1831 during a trip to the Mediterranean in 1830 and 1831. He wrote one sentence about the island he was so instrumental in bringing under the aegis of Britain at the Congress of Berlin. A talented literary writer as well as politician, his novel of 1847, *Tancred, or The New Crusade* prognosticated occupation of Cyprus when one Levantine, speaking of the death of an English prince, says to another, "If he was killed accidentally, there will be negotiations, but the business will be compromised; the English want Cyprus, and they will take it as compensation."

This selection is taken from his Letter XIII. written at Alexandria, March 20,1831 to his sister Sarah Disraeli. It is reproduced in *Home Letters written by the late Earl of Beaconsfield in 1830 and 1831*, London: John Murray, 1885 (Kraus Reprint Co., New York, 1970).

After some days we landed at Cyprus, where we passed a day on land famous in all ages, but more delightful to me as the residence of Fortunatus [*footnote:* in the fairy tale of *The Wishing Cap*] than as the rosy realm of Venus or the romantic kingdom of the Crusaders. Here we got a pilot to take us to Jaffa.

Gordon 1832

Thomas Gordon's two volume *History of the Greek Revolution* was published in Edinburgh by William Blackwood and in London by T. Cadell in 1832. Gordon (1788-1841) was educated at Eton and Oxford and served in the British service until 1810 after which he held commands among the insurgents in the Greek Revolution. In his lengthy study of the 1821 revolution of the Greeks against their Turkish rulers Gordon describes its impact on Cyprus "towards the end of May," in Volume I.

[p. 192]

That celebrated island (140 miles in length and sixty-three in breadth) is intersected by a range of mountains, called Olympus by the ancients, terminating towards the east in a long promontory. The soil is fruitful, and although but a small part of the land was under cultivation, the merchants of Larnaka nevertheless exported annually, during the late wars, many cargoes of excellent wheat to Spain and Portugal. Its population (thought in 1814 not to exceed 70,000) was daily diminishing; half were Greeks under their Metropolitan, and the remainder Turks, with the exception of a few Franks at Larnaca. A Mutesellim, appointed by the Capitan Pasha, ruled the isle, and next in authority to him were the Archbishop and Dragoman, (the latter a Greek nominated by the Porte,) charged with the affairs of the Rayahs, and responsible for their contributions. As those functionaries played into each other's hands, no division of the Empire was more heavily taxed; and the peasants, reduced to total indigence, embraced opportunities of expatriating themselves. The most fertile and agreeable region is near the old Paphos, where flourish fine forests of oak, beech, and pine, with groves of olive and mulberry trees. Cyprus is renowned for the quantity of its fruit, wine, oil, and silk; it abounds in oxen, sheep, fowls, and game; and the natives boast, that the produce of every soil and climate will not only flourish there, but attain to the highest perfection. Its trade is carried on at Larnaka, a town of 5000 souls, built on the site of Citium, at the bottom of a deep bay, making an excellent roadstead. Nicosia, the capital, is an inland and more populous city: Famagosta, on the east coast, once a strong place, is now dismantled and ruinous. The military force consisted of 300 guards of the Mutesellim, and 4000 Janissaries, badly armed, and without discipline or courage. The character of the people is mild; and it is said that few instances of cruelty occurred, and that the Mussulmans lived on a very amicable footing with their Rayahs. Separated from European Greece by a wide expanse of sea, the Cypriotes beheld with a sort of indifference the commencement of the revolution, vainly flattering themselves that it would not disturb their tranquility. But towards the end of May, certain Turks, gratifying private malice under political pretexts, assassinated some individuals, and the principal Greek merchants then fled. This transient gloom might perhaps have passed away, had not the Porte resolved to secure its dominion of the island, by introducing a body of forces from the neighbouring provinces; a resolution that ruined Cyprus, but which was notwithstanding reasonable in itself. The insurgents in their vessels hovered round its shores: the native Mohammedans were unwarlike, and a plan to revolutionize it was already hatching by the Archbishop's nephews then in France. In obedience to firmans of the Sultan, the Pashas of Aleppo and St John d'Acre assembled 10,000 Syrian troops, the scum of that barbarous country, and shipped them off from Acre and Tripoli, whence their navigation was short and prosperous, the hostile cruisers having withdrawn, to co-operate in defending the Archipelago. Hardly had those vagabonds disembarked at Larnaka, (in June,) when they gave themselves up to every species of villainy; the remonstrances of the French consul having obliged the Mutesellim to provide for the safety of Europeans, he ordered the Syrians to march to Famagosta, but this measure only tended to spread their ravages more extensively. Seduced by their example, the militia of the Isle joined the strangers in their career of crime; the Metropolitan, five bishops, and thirty-six other ecclesiastics were executed. Nicosia was sacked, as well as Famagosta, and the whole of Cyprus converted into a theatre of rapine and bloodshed.

Kirkland 1832

Rev. John Thornton Kirkland was president of Harvard College from 1810 to 1828 when he retired due to ill health. To regain his health he and his wife Elizabeth traveled in Europe, Egypt, and the Holy Land for the next three years. Mrs. Kirkland in a series of letters recorded their travels, and a letter dated May 2, 1832 from Nazareth spoke briefly about Cyprus. It is published in Volume 19 of the Second Series of the *Massachusetts Historical Society Proceedings,* 1905, Boston: Published by the Society, 1906.

We left Jaffa the 14th for Cyprus and had our usual fortune of a long passage. Cyprus is a dreary looking island, though much famed for its wine and an amorous fountain held in great veneration by the Turks. After contending a long time with baffling winds we reached Rhodes, where we remained a day and a half.

Burton 1837

Rev. Nathanael Burton, a military chaplain, reported his extensive wanderings under the extensive title, *Narrative of a Voyage from Liverpool to Alexandria, Touching at the Island of Malta, and from thence to Beirout in Syria; with a Journey to Jerusalem, Voyage from Jaffa to Cyprus and Constantinople, and a Pedestrian Journey from Constantinople, through Turkey, Wallachia, Hungary, and Prussia, to the town of Hamburgh, in the Years 1836-37.* It was published in 1838 by John Yates of Dublin. Burton visited Cyprus in March 1837.

[p. 163]

On Wednesday, the 8th of March, we anchored in Scala di Lanarka bay, in the island of Cyprus: the weather had by this time cleared up, and the sea was calm; I was pleased at the sight of a number of European ships, thinking I might be able to make a short cut by Italy or France. We had scarcely anchored when the lazaretto-boat came alongside, with its little flag, to inquire if there were any victims on board; after a short parley with the captain, and the present of a few oranges, they departed. One of my reasons for making Cyprus my way was, that I understood there was no quarantine—the intelligence was too good to be true, for I found a pretty little lazaretto was completed by the sea-side.

A fire was now kindled on board, and I prepared myself a cup of coffee, as did also my friends the Jews. We remained that night in the vessel. On the morning of the 9th of March the boat was lowered, and I was conveyed to the lazaretto; the Jews, who were on their way to Russia, were allowed to remain in the vessel till, I suppose, some opportunity occurred. I now found I was doomed once more to this species of confinement. A respectable person has less chance of escape than another from this thraldom, as they consider him possessed of means; but I must confess, the lazaretto at Scala, in Cyprus, is really a desirable residence. The apartments are large, clean, and comfortable. The upper rooms, one of which I occupied, communicate with a handsome balcony, which runs round the whole building—the sea on one side, and a mountain like the Sugar-loaf [*footnote:* in the county of Wicklow] on the other. There were very few inmates, and I really felt comfortable. I had a whole apartment to myself, with a fine view of the town of Scala in front. The guardian, Signior Ricini, did all in his power to render my condition easy, and sent me up a bedstead. From the advantages in the way of quarantine, I would recommend travellers who purpose visiting Palestine to make Cyprus and Jaffa their way.

The town of Scala, which has the appearance of a neat watering-place, is now the chief port of commerce in the island. I am sure I could not have procured more comfortable lodgings in the town than those I now possessed. A person was appointed to attend me, as a compliment, because they said he understood English. He was a native of Alexandria, a truly Egyptian figure—a perfect antique—the high ears handed down to us in the statues of that early enlightened people—in short, the bust of Memnon stood before me. I used sometimes call him the Sphynx. I am persuaded his ancestors were veritable Egyptians in the days of the Pharaohs. The poor fellow seemed quite proud of having been selected to attend me; but such an attempt at English. He certainly must have heard the language spoken. The two or three words he attempted, he harped on, as a novice in music would the gamut—"What want, vauther? Me serve Inglis sips, Scanderia." He was, however, an obliging creature, and seemed proud of attending an Englishman.

Wine and *aqua vitae* are exceedingly cheap in Cyprus, and the best bread I had yet tasted in the Levant; these, with some of the cheese of the island, constituted my diet. The Cyprus cheese, though much used through the East, I by no means admire: it is white, and has a heartburn flavour. They make it up like small twopenny loaves; it gives the idea of being the manufacture of persons who were beginning to learn how to make cheese, and had botched their work.

The English vice-consul, Signior Antonio Honoliziano, an Ionian, sent his son-in-law and chancellor to visit me, and offer his services. I understood there was a vessel bound for Marseilles, and I begged of him to make an agreement with the captain to take me for ten dollars. The avaricious captain would not consent to take me for less than thirty, and, of course, I was to provide myself; the present state of my finances would not permit me to give so much.

Contrary to my expectations, I was only detained at the lazaretto from the 9th to the 11th of March, and then entered the town of Scala. I was now in the dominions of the Sultan of Turkey, and I perceived a greater lightness, and, if I may use the expression, taste and elegance in the appearance of every thing. The roofs of the houses were somewhat sloped, and had a more cheerful appearance than the towns of Syria. Most of them had courts before, and reminded me, with their balconies, of the ancient inns, which have now disappeared in London. Scala is a small place, but appears to have a brisk trade. Its principal exports and chief productions of the island are cotton, corn, wine, wool, colloquintida, wax, skins. Ah! were Cyprus in other hands, what a granary, what a treasury! Land is for little or nothing, yet fertile in the extreme. And what has the Grand Seignor done? He has sold Cyprus, for so much a year, to an ignorant wretch, who, some years ago, kept a shop in the little bazaar of Scala, and who, of course, prompted by his contracted mind, rack-rents it, to make the most he can. I found the kindest interest expressed for me on my appearance in the town. One Mr. Sticho, a Venetian, who saw me at the lazaretto, devoted a whole day, introducing me to every one whom he thought might be of use to me: amongst the rest, to the British consul, a fine old man, dressed in the European costume, and wearing a rosette in his hat. He speaks French well, and, though of the Greek Church, is a great admirer of the American missionaries, and, I believe, is a subscriber to their labours. He was particularly anxious as to his inquiries about Mr. O'Connell; his manners are very much those of a gentleman of the old school. They are not accustomed to English visiting them, and looked upon me as a kind of rarity: yet there is one native of England residing in Scala; and oh! how truly has she supported the character of a genuine British female! This lady is a Mrs. Hamiat: she is married to a Swiss gentleman, who had been an officer of flying artillery in the army of Ibraham Basha, but is now engaged in the cotton trade at Scala, and has got a cotton-press which, affording such facilities, and doing away the necessity of manual labour, has incensed many against him; and they have made a complaint to the bishop to prevent him, who I cannot conceive has any thing to do in the business. Mrs. Hamiat's maiden name was Stevens, and her father had been an eminent merchant at Aleppo. This young lady, when she heard I had arrived, wished much to see me, and expressed the interest of a relative, and asked me, with almost tearful eye, what induced me to visit that part of the world. "We are all wondering," says she, "what brought you here." The excellent creature, I believe, supposed me entirely destitute, and I could perceive in her a resolution to befriend me to the utmost. Though there is an extensive convent of the Latins in Cyprus, yet, by the exertions of Mr. Sticho and a worthy little Greek, dragoman to the American missionaries, I obtained an apartment in some buildings belonging to the Greek Church of St. Lazaro, or Lazarus. These buildings enclosed the church and church-yard; two or three caloyers, who serve the church, occupy a few of the rooms. The place has become a kind of khaun, where pilgrims, muleteers, farmers—in fact, all wayfaring persons stop; there were continual arrivals whilst I was there. The egoumen, or chief priest, had given me the key of my apartment, and I had just procured some wine, bread, and cheese, when a servant arrived from Mrs. Hamiat to conduct me to her house, where I found both her and Mr. Hamiat seated at a comfortable dinner, awaiting my arrival. In the kindest manner, they invited me to take an apartment in their house. Whilst I rejoiced at this expression of friendship, I was resolved not to try it to the utmost, lest it might end in disgust; and, therefore, continued in my homely ecclesiastical residence, whilst I occasionally dined with my kind friends, who wished me to go every day, and were interesting themselves, without my knowledge, in making every inquiry about what ships were sailing, and whither bound, and endeavouring to procure me a cheap and comfortable passage. I must attribute the extreme kindness of Mrs. Hamiat, and the manner in which it was expressed, to an inspiration from that gracious Lord, who, though the most unworthy and worthless of his creatures, has ever unremittingly watched over me. The church of St. Lazaro, or Lazarus, in the convent of which (as it is called) I was domiciliated, is an ancient structure, similar to some of the old parish churches in the country parts of England. It stands in the centre of a church-yard, round which was the range of buildings, one story high, with a shed in front, where travellers lodge, and here, also, the priests have their apartments. The door of my apartment was within five or six feet of the tomb-stones, on which those who dressed any thing placed their small stone kitchen with fire.

The British consul informed me that Lazarus, whom our Lord raised from the dead at Bethany, having been persecuted by the Jews as a living monument of Christ's power, fled to Cyprus, where he became instrumental in establishing the gospel; he lived fourteen years after, and at his death was buried in this church, where his tomb is still to be seen under the sanctuary; his remains were afterwards removed by the mother of Constantine the Great to Constantinople; I considered it a coincidence worthy of my regard, that I had ever been interested in the case of Lazarus, and used to take a pleasure, whilst at Jerusalem, of frequently visiting Bethany, though in its present condition far from being attractive, and now, without seeking it, I find a shelter, I may say, under his roof.

The apartment I occupied was a large chamber, stone-floored, having two wide, wooden fixture-beds, similar to soldiers' guard-beds, on which to lay bedding, which the person procures himself; there was an article in the room, which for a long time I had supposed was a bier for the dead; it had a domed canopy; I certainly considered this piece of furniture, together with the church-yard as rather sombre company, and I remember that when a boy I should have wasted to death under such circumstances; I was, however, afterwards informed that it was a canopy for carrying in procession the effigy of a dead Christ, during the paschal solemnities, I now, therefore, considered it an houourable ornament to my apartment.

Being the Greek lent, there was service twice a day in the church of St. Lazaro; the nasal, monotonous voice of the caloyer awoke me every morning; I occasionally attended the service; at one time I observed the deacon, who always assists the priest, entering the sanctuary with a round basket on his head containing a large loaf, which after consecration was cut into small pieces and distributed to the congregation; this I conceive to be the true mode transferred from the early church, and the deacon acting in his genuine capacity "of serving tables;" the morning service was the Greek mass, the even-song consisted of psalms, lessons, and prayers, chanted alternately; the constantly repeated prayer, and the response of the people, were *Kyrie eleison! Eleison me O Theos!* after which the officiating priest issued from the sanctuary with the censer, incensing every individual as he passed along; in the Greek church the women are separate from the men.

The Greek is the vernacular language of Cyprus, and differs little from the ancient, but it is difficult for an English Greek scholar to understand their manner of pronouncing it, and one is not a little surprised to see the characters we used so to venerate in college, as the prerogative of the learned, scrawled with charcoal on the walls, and used on the most common occasions.

The English vice-consul and his son-in-law, Mr. Poullachi, invited me to reside at their house, and signed my passport, remitting the usual fee; in short, though a perfect stranger in Cyprus, I was treated with a kindness and consideration I could not have expected.

The present capital of the island is Nikosia, which contains about twelve thousand inhabitants; the famous church of St. Sophia, like its namesake at Constantinople, is a mosque. The ancient capital, Famagusta, which still exhibits the traces of former magnificence in several noble ecclesiastical structures, is now almost deserted.

During the time of the crusades, this island was of importance to the European princes who were engaged in them; they established commanderies here, *i.e.* districts which were under their command; to this day they are so termed, and still retain some of the beneficent effects of European residence and culture, being the most productive parts, and yielding a fine white wine, which is called commandery wine, and brings a higher price than other wine of Cyprus.

The small town of Scala is built of broad, flat, burnt bricks, mixed with straw, which soon decay; the principal street is Bazaar, which is narrow, and consists of sheds supported on rough, wooden pillars, behind which is a kind of warehouse, and in some cases a dwelling; the mosque here has more the appearance of a Christian church; instead of the blunt, tasteless minarets of Syria, this of Scala resembles more a slender steeple, pointed, and covered as to its top with polished lead.

The market was not at this season well supplied; the only meat I saw was lamb, which is good and cheap; I ate peas at Mr. Hamiat's, which, though early in the month of March, were already old. But here, as in every other part of the Turkish dominions, vegetables are rather scarce, and not cultivated to the extent that the richness of the soil would warrant; I, however, saw a greater quantity of potatoes than I expected; they are brought in, in baskets, but do not appear to have the strength or body of ours; they have none in Jerusalem or Jaffa; in the same description of baskets, they bring to market a large kind of field snails, with handsome shells, which seem a favourite food with many of the inhabitants; the family occupying the apartment next to me in the convent, boiled them with their shells in a large pot for their dinner repeatedly. There is a comfortable little auberge in Scala, kept by a native of Turin; it resembles a neat, country tavern in England; here, at a very trifling expence, a person can dine off seven or eight plates, (as the Europeans in the Levant term it,) of different meats, with wine, bread, fruit, coffee, and a pipe of tobacco. Not having had a regular dinner, I may say, since leaving Alexandria, I was glad to avail myself occasionally of the advantages this place afforded; my bill amounted to five piastres, a sum equivalent to little more than a shilling of our money.

During my stay at Scala I attended a funeral in the church of St. Lazaro; the corpse was wrapped in a shroud without a coffin, and carried into the church on a bier, like a cradle hand-barrow; the priest and deacon offered up prayers and incense; the congregation approached, and severally kissed the breast of the body, where the cross had been laid, after which it was conveyed into the church-yard, where the prayers and incense were continued; the deacon cast the earth three times on the body, (as in the church of England,) and then poured a glass of oil on its breast; here the ceremony ended, and the monumental clay was heaped upon the defunct.

My anxiety to leave the island became now very great. I feared much the diminution of my small funds, and was desirous to get on European ground, where a stout pair of legs, with perseverance, would at length carry me to my much-longed-for home.

* * * * *

[p. 176]

The next morning I waited on Mr. Marino, an Italian gentleman, and American consul, who I understood could give me some account of the vessels at Limasol. He told me there were no vessels there bound for Constantinople, but that there was one in the very harbour of Scala, where we then were, which was to sail for Constantinople in four or five days: "And here, Signior," said he, introducing me to a young man of interesting appearance, who was seated near him—"here is the captain."

They had some conversation together, and Mr. Marino informed me that the captain would take me. I was anxious to know the terms, but was told that it was time enough to speak of them. This I considered a manifest answer to prayer, and, as it were, a divine intimation that, having been cared for so far, I should not be forsaken during the rest of my journey.

The captain was not more than one-and-twenty years of age, the son of a rich Venetian merchant. We afterwards met at the auberge, when I became anxious to settle with him. So great was his kindness, that he would have taken me for four dollars (finding my own provisions); I, however, gave him five, which make a sovereign. The ship's cargo consisted of karobs, the fruit of the locust-tree. The ultimate destination was Odessa, a port of Russia on the Black Sea. These carobs are principally used for cattle, but many of the human species relish them highly. They consist of a large black, clammy pod, which, when chewed, is of a very luscious, liquorice flavour. Though a tree, it is leguminous, or of the pea kind. Many have supposed it to be the locust which constituted the food of St. John the Baptist in the wilderness, but, I believe, without foundation. The karobs of Cyprus are esteemed the best—I fancied they tasted very much like dates.

* * * * *

[p. 179]

The name of the ship in which I was about to sail for Constantinople was the Il Persiano, and that of the captain, Signior Vianello. There were two passengers besides myself—one, a Mr. Passera, a gentleman of some property from Turin, devoted to the study of chemistry, and who had lived in Syria two years; the other, a Mr. Micheli, an Italian also, who had married in Cyprus, and was going to Constantinople to obtain an employment. Though Mr. Passera had never visited England, yet he spoke the language in a manner that agreeably surprised me. This I did not expect to find in Cyprus. We met at the little auberge, and contracted a friendship for each other: he took every opportunity of paying me attention. The superiority of his mind and the urbanity of his manners exalt the people of Italy in my regard.

The captain's father, a wealthy Venetian, was owner of six ships. I felt truly thankful for being placed amongst liberal and enlightened persons; nothing could exceed the youthful captain's interest on my behalf.

I had just ordered at the auberge a quarter of cold roast lamb, ten loaves of bread, and a canister of coffee, for my sea-store, to which I would have added a small stock of wine and arech, when Mrs. Hamiat's servant arrived with a basket, containing half a dozen of good Cyprus wine, part of a Dutch cheese, and a Bologna sausage. I was quite overcome by this fresh demonstration of kindness from that excellent lady, and immediately accompanied Mr. Passera, to visit and take my leave of her, and express my sincere thanks for all her kind attentions to me.

Before leaving Cyprus, I should not omit to mention the labours of the American missionaries, who have an establishment here, and are really the ministers of much good to Scala. They have printed a variety of works in Greek, as well as Arabic; and I was happy to see amongst them some extracts from the fathers of the Greek Church, as such would prove acceptable to the members of that communion—these, together with a well-finished atlas, with Greek names, are bought up with avidity by the people, to whom they are sold at a very low price. The missionaries are supported entirely from America. Mr.

Thomson, of Scala, with his little Greek dragoman, are continually employed in every good work.

Cass 1837

General Lewis Cass was the American ambassador to France who traveled in the Mediterranean and wrote about his travels for American magazines. The excerpts here are taken from his article "The Island of Cyprus," Part 1 (in two parts), in *The Southern Literary Messenger*, Vol. VII., No. 2., February, 1841.

[p. 81]

Cyprus, the kingdom of Venus, where are Paphos, Cytherea and Olympus; or truly, where the sacred mountain rises now as it did in the earliest ages of the heathen mythology, but where the favorite seats of the voluptuous goddess are as abandoned as her worship, as desolate as her shrines! What powerful words are these, also, to stir up the imagination! What associations do they awaken between the past and the present! What interesting reflections and anticipations did they excite, as a favoring breeze drove us onward, and on the 29th of September, 1837, brought us in sight of a range of mountains . . .

* * * * *

[p. 91]

As we cast anchor we were visited from the shore; but there being no quarantine regulations, we were at liberty to land without delay; and, availing ourselves of this power, we left the ship immediately, and repaired to the house of the American Consul. We found this gentleman, Mr. Mattei, and his amiable family, prepared to render us all the services in their power. He is himself an Italian, and his wife is an Arab, from some part of Mount Lebanon; and they have one son, an intelligent, promising young man, and two daughters. The young ladies preserved in their costume, a mixture of Frank and Oriental fashions, which was something picturesque, and in unison with the style of their beauty. While we remained at Larnica, we often visited this family, and they were always kind and hospitable. But we still made the frigate our home, as we could find no where else in the East, the comforts which an American ship of war carries with her. Even, however, in this distant and secluded spot, two of our countrymen had established themselves—Messrs. Pease and Thompson,—induced by a noble zeal to spread the truths of the gospel, and to be useful in the education of the Cyprian youth.

We found that these worthy missionaries and their families had won for themselves general esteem, and were indefatigable in the execution of their self-imposed task. We have since learned, with great regret, that Mr. Pease has fallen a victim to the insalubrity of the climate, the martyr of his own generous self-devotedness.

It is generally agreed that Larnica occupies the site of the Necropolis of Citium. Ruins of that extinct city yet exist, pointing out its position and extent; and the stones of its ruined edifices yet furnish building materials for the construction of Salamis and Larnica. The Abbé Marite, who wrote a very good work in Italian upon Cyprus, describes Larnica as the most agreeable place in the island; and we might be unjust if we withheld the reason, which does more honor to his frankness than to his taste: "for I know," says he, "nothing more interesting than a commercial place." However this may be, its port is the most accessible to the interior of the country; and it is, in fact, the great mart of Cyprus. We examined everything in the city and its environs, worthy of observation. It contains nearly a thousand families as well Greek as Turk. There are some wealthy merchants and proprietors, but a large portion of the inhabitants are not merely poor—they are miserable. The house of the consul was built of stone, and may serve as a type of the residences of the rich Cypriots. It had two stories, and was entered by a *porte cochére,* whence a flight of stairs led to the second story, the habitation of the family. Upon these stairs, we always found posted the kavass of the consul. This is an important functionary in the East, who well deserves a passing notice. Originally from contempt, but now perhaps from fear, the governments of the Mahometan countries refused to take cognizance of disputes between Christian residents, subjects of other powers. These differences are left to their proper consuls to arrange, and thence has grown up a peculiar jurisdiction in those regions. The consuls are powerful personages, exempt from the Turkish local authorities, and enjoying important privileges: among these, the dearest to the natives of the country who are selected for foreign consuls, is their freedom from taxation. These consular offices are therefore sought with great avidity; and happy is the oppressed Greek or Armenian, who can put on the livery of a Christian nation, and hoist its protecting flag upon his mansion. As, however, an *infidel dog,* even when enjoying the highest immunities, cannot interfere with the *true believer,* it was necessary, in order to conciliate this fundamental maxim of Mahometan law, with the duties and privileges of the consul, to provide them with an agent charged with their protection, and with the execution of their orders. During the existence of the Janissaries, a member of that powerful corps was always selected for this purpose; for whatever else may have been the faults of their organization, or of their conduct, they had won for themselves a reputation of great fidelity towards the persons in whose employment they were placed. The Consular Janissary was called a *kavass,* and the name and function still continues, though the turbulent body has been abolished from which these functionaries were chosen. Our friend the Cyprian *kavass,* was a fine specimen of the Ottoman race. Well proportioned in stature, with a black piercing eye, a proud look, and a flowing beard, he stood there the representative, as it were, of the haughty warriors who professed to maintain by the sword, what by the sword they had acquired. His costume was in admirable keeping with his physical properties: his head was covered with an immense turban. He wore a close tunic of silk, girded by a belt which contained his richly ornamented *handjar* and pistols, and loose flowing pantaloons. Over these was his large red robe, and in his hand he held a long baton, ornamented with a silver hook. Woe to the unhappy Greek who should pass him without due reverence.

Ascending the stone staircase thus guarded, the visitor passes through a large ante-chamber, whence he is introduced into the *salon* of reception, which is an extensive apartment, well lighted, and looking out upon the sea, with a high ceiling, having the floor covered with matting. It is plain, and with little furniture, the principal article being a silk divan, which extends around the room. There are neither chairs, tables, looking-glass, nor pictures. The oppressive heat of the climate seems the enemy to be feared; and a cool temperature the *summum bonum* to be sought. An extensive courtyard was in the rear of the house, and a garden ornamented with flowers, shrubs and trees, whose shade and foliage were in agreeable contrast with the parched country which surrounded the town.

We wandered through the streets, gazing upon all that was worthy of a look, and upon much that was not. These streets are narrow, crooked and dirty, and exhibit a most stoical indifference to all regulations of police. The common houses are built of dried brick, mixed with straw, which in the rainy season, admit the water in abundance. Their external color is red, but the interior is painted with a white pigment, found in the neighboring hills; and some of them are commodious. They are covered with earth, mixed with clay, and floored with stones.

One of our first visits was to the mosque. It was formerly a Latin church. It is a Gothic edifice, whose front is ornamented with six marble columns, divided into three naves, by four pillars which support the roof. We found the Mahometan ecclesiastics of Cyprus more liberal than in any other part of the Turkish Empire. Whether this relaxation of fanaticism was toleration or indifference, we know not; but the fact is certain. Wherever else we had sought entrance into a mosque, we had found difficulties, which sometimes the local functionaries removed, and sometimes we declined to encounter, freely acknowledging the danger of contending against prejudices which time had not softened. With every disposition to promote our wishes, and with all the influence which high rank and extensive power, civil and military, gave him, the Governor General of Syria, Sheriff Pasha, freely told us at Damascus, that it would be dangerous for us to enter the great mosque of that city, a peculiar object of veneration; and so far was this caution carried, that our guide in this ancient place, built before the days of Abraham, Seid Ali, who was attached to the British Consulate, and whose natural shrewdness had been augmented by foreign travel, as much as his *true faith* had been diminished, allowed us only to cast a stealthy glance into this holy edifice, as we passed the doors, which were opened for the entrance of all true believers.

But in Larnica no one was excluded from the mosque. Our sailors entered it at pleasure, and we roamed through it as freely as we should have done through a Catholic church; and in the midst of the performance of the most holy ceremonies of the Mahometan religion. It was a curious and interesting spectacle, and we returned again and again to observe it. On the ruins of the former steeple, a minaret has been erected, and it is from this tower that the muezzin calls the faithful to prayers. The Mahometans interdict the use of bells, both in their mosques and in the Christian places of worship; and in the Latin and Greek churches, we found the time of worship announced by the striking of a long board, which gives out a most lugubrious sound. But the Turkish hours of prayer are proclaimed by a peculiar officer, who is called a muezzin, who ascends the minaret, which rises from each mosque, and from the top, calls out towards the south, then towards the east, and the north, ending with the west. The summons is a fixed formula, every where alike, and is an invocation of the name of God, and of Mahomet, his prophet. It is expressed in a kind of howl, uttered with the full force of the lungs, while the fingers are held to the ears. While lying in the beautiful basin of Constantinople, with Europe on one side, and Asia on the other, we many a time watched the muezzins of the neighboring mosques, as they wound their way slowly up the minarets, and have there seen and heard them address themselves in succession, to the four cardinal points of the heavens, announcing that the hour of prayer was come. And at night there was something affecting in these loud warnings, issuing from a thousand towers of a populous and sleeping capital, and coming mournfully to us over the waters, announcing the existence of God, and the duties of man. These cries are uttered five times in the twenty-four hours,—at dawn, at noon, at three o'clock, at sunset, and at midnight. At each annunciation, every true believer should repeat the stated prayer, and on Friday, the Mahometan Sabbath, a sixth prayer is enjoined, which should take place an hour before sunset. At noon is the principal ceremony in the mosques; and we observed at Larnica that the attendance at that hour was numerous. Infidelity has no doubt made great havoc in the ranks of Islamism; and we were given to understand in the East, that most of the high functionaries, and of the enlightened men, were the veriest skeptics in their religious faith. It cannot but be that the progress of information will reveal the nakedness of Moslem pretensions, and the absurdities of the dogmas of Mahomet. Still, however, fanaticism usurps the place of rational belief; and high or low, whether sincere or hypocritical, must practice the outward observances enjoined by the Arabian prophet.

* * * * *

[p. 94]

We found the interior of the mosque of Larnica destitute of all ornaments. There was a kind of elevated tribune, or pulpit, near one corner, which was occupied by the imaum, or attending priest. There were neither divisions nor seats: all was perfectly plain. The congregation kneeled each upon a mat, carpet, or corner of his garment, and seemed to recite his prayer with much fervor. Their genuflexions and motions were not the least curious part of the ceremony. They first kneeled down, and struck their foreheads against the floor; they then arose upon their knees, bowing repeatedly; and then upon their feet, raising their hands towards the heavens; and then crossing them upon their hearts. Sometimes they were motionless, apparently engaged in earnest devotion; and these alternations of posture continued during all the ceremony. It is difficult for a spectator, who has not often been present upon these occasions, to convey an adequate conception of the ceremonial. It was obvious, however, that the whole was regulated by an established ritual, for all the congregation followed the same form, and went through their motions in perfect unison. While this ceremony was going on upon the floor of the mosque, the imaum in the tribune was not idle. He addressed the auditory in an uninterrupted monotonous tone; and the only definite explanation we could gather from our interpreter of the meaning of his discourse, may be summed up in these words, *"God is great, there is but one God, and Mahomet is his prophet."* His sermon, if it may be so called, continued about twenty minutes; and though we were not fortunate enough to comprehend the tenor of his remarks, yet other travellers, with better means of information, have said that the Mahometan priests, in their addresses, and in their expositions of the Koran, dwell with some force upon great moral duties, and inculcate the necessity of a holy life, as well as of a pure faith.

We sought the remains of the ancient city of Citium, whose site Larnica has usurped. But nothing satisfactory could be seen. The foundation of the walls, and of a few edifices, may yet be traced; and there are ruins, which mark the former existence of extensive aqueducts—those structures which seem to have been so indispensable to the cities of antiquity. The ditch, too, may be followed, but the monuments of Citium have given way before the cupidity of Salamis and of Larnica; and the quarry was too convenient, not to furnish building materials for these modern cities. This is the constant course of things in the East; and Turkish lime-kilns and miserable habitations have absorbed some of the most beautiful works of art, which had survived the revolutions of twenty centuries.

We desired to survey the condition of the Cyprian women, and to form a correct estimate of their station in society, and of their qualities, physical and moral. But our time was too short, and our opportunities too unfavorable for anything more than a passing glance. We shall tell however what we saw.

It must be recollected that this island is divided between the Greeks and the Turks: and there is a no more marked difference in the whole social state of the Mahometans and Christians than is found in the customs which regulate the condition of the women. Any general portrait would be fallacious. The common features are too few to appear upon the same canvass. To be faithful, there must be two sketches—one for each religion. We do not aspire to present either. We shall content ourselves with a trace or two, which may serve as a *"relief"* to the works of other artists. We have often met the Mahometan women in the streets, but their uncouth costumes on such occasions deprived them of all interest. Covered with a long dark hood or mantle, their features, and even their forms, were wholly concealed: but the holes in their *masks* enabled them to survey that world to which they were impenetrable. Sometimes a bright look would pierce through these windows, revealing the fire of intellect and emotion, which might be hid, but not smothered. Under these circumstances the nearest kinsman cannot recognize his relation, and a husband may be jostled by his own wife without suspecting who is near him. No doubt the pictures of Eastern life, so richly traced in the Arabian tales, contain many a faithful portrait of female infidelity. But the painting is overcharged; and we believe there is neither that eternal jealousy and caution on the part of the husbands, nor that disregard of their duties on the part of their wives, which we have been taught to suppose exist in all Mahometan countries.

* * * * *

Desirous to visit the interior of Cyprus, we formed a numerous party for that purpose, and, guided by the son of the Consul, and attended by his Drogueman, and accompanied by our countryman, Mr. Pease, we mounted our mules, and passing out of Larnica, we found ourselves in the midst of a most desolate region. There is no doubt of the ancient prosperity of this island, but still it is difficult to reconcile its present appearance with the accounts of its exuberant fertility which have come down to us. The soil appears sterile; there are almost no streams, and everywhere a deficiency of water: shade is nearly unknown, and not the slightest trace remains of the natural woods, for which the country was formerly celebrated. The eye wanders over a dreary region, with here and there a miserable village, and in its neighborhood a field of wheat or barley, wretchedly cultivated. Scarcely a moving thing is seen through all this dreary space, but once in a while, a solitary traveller upon an ass, or a flock of goats, seeking a scanty subsistence, and guarded by a goatherd and his dog.

The computed distance from Larnica to Nicosia is eight hours, equal perhaps to twenty-four miles, but we accomplished the journey in six hours. The first village we passed was Lividia, some distance to the right of the road. A century ago it was a prosperous place, surrounded by meadows and cultivated fields; but these are now converted into marshes, and a malaria has been generated, that has ruined and depopulated the town.

Four hours from Larnica, brought us to Attien. We passed many hills in the distance, furrowed with hollows, and did not find a single object to redeem the dreariness of the country . . .

We found Attien the most comfortable looking Cyprian town we had seen. It is said to contain one hundred and twenty houses, and six hundred inhabitants. These houses are built of stone and clay, or of stone and brick, and though without any pretension to beauty, yet they are neat and pleasant. The Greek cross is upon each door, and there are ruins of ancient edifices, which mark the former importance of the city, whose site is now occupied by this village.

Another hour brought us to Piroi, a small town inhabited by Turks, which possesses the advantage of a rivulet, to which it owes its importance. Here are some mulberry trees, and fields planted with cotton . . .

We followed our guides, and entered the city by the gate of Famagosta, whose sculptured crosses and lions indicate its Venetian architecture; and passing through the principal street, repaired to the Greek convent, the residence of the Archbishop. The Latin and Greek religious establishments in the Levant receive the Christian travellers, and in all the interior cities they are the only places where these strangers can find hospitality. They are not often very neat, and sometimes not very well provided, but what they can do, they seem to do with good will; and a pilgrim must be more than usually fastidious, who does not welcome even their roughest fare and hardest couch, after a long day's ride under a burning sun. Custom has established the right of the traveller to remunerate his hosts, by an adequate present to one of the serving brothers; and this convenient arrangement, though it does not diminish his thanks for the kindness of which he finds himself the object, yet removes an obligation, which otherwise he would be unwilling to encounter. Our guide led us through a narrow gate, constructed evidently for security, into the court-yard of the convent, where dismounting, he preceded us into the building, with the air of an old acquaintance, who is sure of a good reception. And in this he was not mistaken; for the venerable Archbishop and all his clergy seemed to vie with each other in kindness to their trans-Atlantic guests. We were ushered into a large apartment, furnished with that never-failing appendage in the East, a divan, and were soon offered coffee, pipes and sherbet.

We found this Episcopal mansion an old building, and somewhat dilapidated. It contains many rooms, with naked walls, long dark corridors, which connect them, and a little chapel; and surrounds a small paved court-yard, and is furnished with a neat garden, ornamented with fruit trees and flowering shrubs.

The Archbishop soon entered, and we were introduced to him. He was a venerable looking man, clad in a long black serge robe, covered with a kind of bonnet, and wearing a cross upon his heart. He is the most considerable Greek personage in the island, and, as we shall see by-and-by, is a sort of intermediary between the Turkish authorities and the native Greeks. In his ecclesiastical polity, he has three suffragan bishops under him: one at Paphos, one at Larnica, and one at Cerines; and an appeal, though we do not know how regulated, lies from his decisions to the Patriarch at Constantinople. He was frank in his conversation; but his reading, whatever it may have been in the polemical books of his own church, had evidently been otherwise very restricted, and many questions, which he and his clergy put to us, indicated great ignorance of the condition of other countries and the state of modern literature. The resistance of his countrymen to Turkish oppression had terminated by the establishment of the new Greek kingdom, and Cyprus had not been re-deemed by making part of it. But it was evident that the hearts of the Cyprian Greeks were in the cause, and the Archbishop alluded with great feeling to several afflicting events, which, during the progress of the struggle, had spread fear and distress among his flock. We have already recounted the striking catastrophe by which his predecessor, two bishops, and many of the heads of the principal Greek families, were entrapped and put to death, in the court of the Governor, by virtue of a firman from Constantinople.

Here, as elsewhere among the Greeks, as well continental as insular, we found that the sympathies manifested for them in the United States in the perilous struggle through which they had passed, and the substantial aid which had been sent to them, were well known and justly appreciated; and much of the cordial reception we every where met with, was due to these circumstances.

Supper was soon announced, and we accompanied the Archbishop to the refec-tory, where a most tempting refreshment awaited us. We took our seats with that digni-tary, and with some of his clergy, and there were several serving brothers in clerical hab-its, who filled the offices of servants. Before we sat down, a short prayer was recited by the Archbishop. The Greeks have adopted the Turkish process of cooking, and their dishes also consist partly of mutton and partly of fowl, where the original material is so disguised that it is difficult to recognize it; but its taste is really exquisite, drawing com-mendation from the nicest epicure. There is, too, an abundance of the choicest vegetables and fruits.

Sherbet was served, and the celebrated Cyprian wine, called *Commandeira,* which they said was thirty years old. This island has been renowned for its wines since the earli-est ages, and Solomon the wise King of Israel—no bad judge by-the-by—praises the vine of Cyprus, with a warmth which shows that the taste of its juice was yet upon his lips. The Greeks, with their usual inflation of style, call it a *panacea,* endowed with the prop-erty of rejuvenation. The Archbishop was temperate in his habits, and did not drink wine, contenting himself with sherbet. Some of his guests, however, took a double share with-out difficulty; and left no doubt of their hearty acquiescence in the praises of this favorite cordial, for such truly is the old *Commandeira.* The Prelate gave two toasts in compli-ment to his visitors, one to the President of the United States, and the other to the Ameri-can Democracy. And well they struck upon our ears, in this old hall of the convent of Nicosia! After supper we were conducted to our sleeping apartments, where we found comfortable beds and clean sheets.

In the morning we gave notice of our arrival to the Governor, or *Mutzelin,* and asked at what hour he would receive us. He sent a prompt and polite answer, which was brought by two of his subordinate officers, splendidly equipped, and armed with pistols, daggers, and batons. Placing themselves at our head, they led us in grand procession—a rare spectacle no doubt to the Nicosians—to the palace of the Governor. We found this an old mansion, built by the Venetians, presenting nothing in its architecture or distribution worth description, but constructed, like all the larger edifices, around a court-yard. As we crossed this paved enclosure, our Greek attendants intimated to us, in a whisper, that it was the place of the execrable tragedy where their countrymen had perished. We could not mistake the expression of their piercing eyes. It said, as plainly as eyes could say, that a day of vengeance was ardently desired. The stables form part of the palace, and open upon this court-yard; and some beautiful horses are always kept tied here by the leg, and adorned with splendid caparisons. This is a piece of magnificence in which the Eastern grandees are fond of indulging.

We then entered the first large apartment, or vestibule, where we found a numerous crowd, composed of the suite and servants of the Governor, and of persons brought there by business. Passing through this room without stopping, and then through several others, we were at length ushered into the presence of the important functionary, upon whose nod depends the life or death of the unfortunate subjects who now occupy the kingdom of Venus.

The first aspect of the apartment was rather imposing: not from its furniture, for this was only the eternal divan, where rich Turks and Greeks spend so many of their hours, sleeping and waking; but from the display of arms, with which its walls were hung. Such a profusion of pistols, and guns, and swords, and daggers, we had not seen in the East. The passion of the Turks for these rich instruments of destruction is well known. They are scattered through their houses with a barbarous magnificence. But the *armourial* (not *armorial*) bump of the Cyprian ruler must have been prodigiously developed. He must have devoted years of care, and expended large treasures upon the acquisition of his collection. And truly it was a spectacle well worth inspection, and it was arranged with excellent effect.

Turning our eyes from this exhibition to the representative of royalty, we found him comfortably reclining upon his divan, smoking his pipe. He barely saluted us by an almost imperceptible nod of the head, as we entered the room. He might have been fifty years of age, and his figure and countenance were prepossessing. With the pride of his countrymen he nourished a black flowing beard. This is an appendage, which, though we do not admire, yet we can tolerate among a people who still retain many of the barbarous traits which they brought with them from the plains of Central Asia to the banks of the Bosphorus. It is associated with our idea of a Mussulman, and is perhaps necessary to give full effect to his person and bearing. But the efforts of modern fashion to bring back the hair upon Christian chins, is to us one of the most disgusting and strangest freaks, by which the waywardness of change has distinguished itself. It is Gibbon, we believe, who somewhere says there is little probability that a civilized people, who have once renounced the custom of wearing beards, will ever resume it. But the acuteness of this shrewd observer failed him in this remark. He did not count enough upon foppery and folly. He was a better historian than prophet. From the progress already made in the revival of hairy envelopes for the countenance, and the consequent destruction of much of its expression, he would be a bold writer, who would now renew the prediction of the historian of the Lower Empire. For ourselves, we confess that we never see the lip disfigured by these protuberances, fit only to defile the drink which is brought to the mouth, without a mixed feeling of dislike and contempt. And whether upon the Boulevards of Paris, or the Broadway of New York, if we meet a young fop with more hair upon his face than brains in his head, turning up his nose, and twisting his *whiskers,* or *mustaches,* or *imperials,* or *favoris*—or whatever other title the emptiness of fashion may have given them,—our mind is instantly carried back to the dirty, miserable streets of Jerusalem, where this operation may be seen in all the vigor of its native climate. There we have many times passed the beggars, as wretched as hunger, nakedness and hopelessness can make them, extended under a powerful Syrian sun, and curling and twisting their mustaches, with all the pride of an American or European dandy! So much for taste. But we must return from this digression to the governmental palace of Cyprus.

Every Moslem functionary, civil or military, whom we have seen, through the whole extent of the Turkish empire, had worn a red Fez cap and a blue frock coat. Damascus presented the only exception to this remark, but its well known fanaticism had preserved for it this immunity. But this man, with a taste we could not but admire, and with a courage which commanded our respect, had on the turban which his ancestors had worn since the days of Ishmael, a full red robe, and slippers, or babooshes. How he dared to risk the bowstring, by thus neglecting his Imperial master's orders in this point, considered so important at Constantinople, we know not. But his was no common danger, for Mahmoud was equally obdurate and inflexible.

We had now passed through a large part of the Turkish empire, and had been introduced to many of the highest functionaries,—to the Capitan Pacha, to Mehemet Ali, to Ibrahim Pacha, and a host of governors, and of other officers, civil, military, and ecclesiastical; and we had everywhere been received with marked attention. Mehemet Ali descended from his divan, as we entered his large salon, and advanced half way down the apartment to meet us, from consideration, not to us, but to our country, and gave us the post of honor at his side. The time had evidently passed by since the Moslem authorities imitating their master, the Padischah, cast their eyes upon the Christian stranger, and said, "What does the slave want?" But the Cyprian Governor belonged to the old school of Turkish etiquette, and, no doubt, anticipated the pleasure of mortifying the *"Infidel dogs."* But we had had too much experience of the Mahometan character to be disconcerted by any affectation of superiority, and we well knew how to treat it; and besides, as one of our countrywomen is said to have remarked to the Pope, with some *smartness* indeed, but also with some truth, we were from a land where every person is his own sovereign, and we felt little disposition, in the corner of a remote island, to tolerate the childish vanity of this slave of the Grand Vizier, himself the slave of the Sultan. As we entered the room, we had taken off our hats, which was our usual custom on similar occasions, as a mark of proper respect; but observing the part which our new friend intended to play in this little comedy, we instantly took our resolution, and replacing our hats upon our heads, we marched to the divan; and without further ceremony, seated ourselves by his side. Our American party followed the example, and very comfortably ensconced themselves in the cushions. But it was too much of an effort for the Greeks. They remained standing, and at a respectful distance, except the *"Friend of the People,"* for such was his title—one of the Greek primates, who are always in attendance upon the Governor, and who had come to the monastery to escort us to the palace. He fell upon his knees before this redoubtable functionary, and preserving that humble attitude during the whole interview, he repeated in Greek to Mr. Pease, the remarks of the Governor, and our countryman interpreted them into English. The *Great Man*, observing the turn which affairs had taken, accommodated himself to this change of circumstances, with more good sense and good humor than we could have expected, and relaxing his gravity, entered into conversation.

He affected a good deal of state in his domestic establishment. He had many servants, and they were richly dressed. Presently entered the never-failing relief for Turkish taciturnity, tobacco and coffee; and the master was no less curious in his pipes than in his arms. He had a splendid collection of amber mouth-pieces, and many of the bowls and stems were inlaid with precious stones. During our visit, the pipes were repeatedly changed, which is the very *quintessence* of Turkish hospitality. The coffee was served in small China cups, and these were placed in golden saucers. Then came the incense-bearers, with odoriferous gums, lighted in silver censers, which gave out a strong perfume, almost too strong for our olfactory nerves, which were not disciplined to so severe a trial. After this followed the sprinkling, we might almost say the aspersion, with rose-water, which was carried around, and thrown upon us with an unpleasant profusion. Handkerchiefs, richly embroidered, were then presented to each guest; but it evidently was not their first tour of service; and their employment did not excite that feeling of useless expense, sometimes almost painful, which is felt, when these costly articles receive for the first time, the impression of the fingers, after a meal *á la Turque*.

Our host felt much interest in the condition and prospects of Mehemet Ali, and was evidently a partizan of the Egyptian Pacha. He asked us many questions respecting the Viceroy and his son Ibrahim, and the state of affairs in those portions of the East where we had travelled. He became quite sociable before the visit was finished, and when we took leave, his gravity had softened into an appearance of confidence. At our request, he gave orders for our admission into the principal mosque, and sent one of his officers to accompany us there.

This edifice was formerly the metropolitan church of the island, dedicated to St. Sophia, and in it the kings of Cyprus were crowned and buried. Some half-effaced inscriptions in the marble floor still indicate the last dwelling places of royalty. The edifice is in the style of the middle ages, and little change was necessary to convert it into a Mahometan place of worship. On the exterior its towers have given place to two minarets, and in the interior the sanctuary and all the monuments have been removed. The followers of Mahomet are allowed no decoration in their mosques, and there was nothing to break the nakedness of the architecture but a niche in one of the walls, where a copy of the Koran was deposited, and the tribune or little pulpit, for the imaum or officiating priest. There is something, however, impressive in one of these old structures, thus despoiled of all its ornaments, and delivered to a false worship. Their very nakedness approaches sublimity.

We strolled through the town to examine its features, and then visited the bazaars. The streets are tolerably regular, and some of them are wide for an Eastern city. To our surprise, we found them quite clean, a rare virtue in these regions. But they were sadly desolate, and the whole place presented unequivocal symptoms of rapid decay. Some of the Venetian edifices, and yet more of their ruins, remained, and attest the ancient magnificence of their capital. But most of the houses are miserable huts, contrasting strangely with these evidences of its former splendor. We found the principal bazaar well supplied with provisions, and with the articles in general consumption among the Turks. We then visited the ramparts, and made the tour of a considerable part of the fortification. Their elevation gave us a favorable opportunity to complete our *reconnaissance* of the city, and of its environs. A near inspection confirmed the notion we had at first formed of the original extent and importance of these works. Their circuit is about three miles, and they were surrounded by a broad moat, now dry, or converted into a marsh. We found many brass pieces upon the walls, bearing the winged lion of St. Mark, showing their Venetian origin. Historians say, that at the capture of this place two hundred and fifty cannon were taken by the Turks, many of which have rested upon the fortifications ever since that period. But the government of Constantinople is not much given to reparation, and the defences of Nicosia exhibit the same aspect they did on the day when the Mahometan army marched over them into the fallen city, except the gradual dilapidation which time has occasioned.

We looked over the town, and upon the surrounding country; and our position, lending more effect to the view, presented us a more cheerful prospect than we had at first anticipated. Nicosia contains many gardens, which appear to be well cultivated, and are planted with orange trees. The palm tree, too, flourishes here, and its tall slim trunk, rising over the buildings, is a beautiful picturesque object, far more pleasant than the funereal cypress which it displaces, and which is so common at Constantinople, and in most other Turkish cities. The roofs of many buildings are covered with earth, in which fruit trees and flowering plants take root, and overshadow these edifices. This extent of foliage is broken here and there by the elegant kiosks, which belong to the rich inhabitants, and whose curious architecture is in happy unison with the general panorama. But the picture is lifeless. Turkish despotism presses upon Nicosia, and this unhappy city is marching to that solitude, which too often follows the trace of Moslem conquest.

The great plain in which the capital is situated was before us; but we have already sufficiently described its melancholy and sterile aspect. The spurs of Olympus approach the walls, and at a short distance the whole ridge rises in all its lofty and rugged magnificence. In some of its clefts snow is always found, and a Greek village is exempted from other tribute, upon the condition that it supplies the Governor with that refreshing article: but, with the true fiscal refinement of Turkish rapacity, the treasury loses nothing by this arrangement, the rest of the Island making up the quota, and the Governor thus receiving both his taxes and his snow.

Upon a plateau, near the very summit of the range, they pointed out to us the remains of a chateau, erected by one of the last queens of Cyprus for a summer residence. It occupied indeed a most aeriel position, and commanded, it was said, a magnificent prospect. Near us, at the foot of the mountain, was the village of Cytherea, occupying an agreeable position, and containing about two hundred houses. They are all cottages, situated at a little distance from one another, and are surrounded with mulberry, citron, orange, and olive trees, which have quite a forest-like appearance. There are many springs, that issue from the neighboring hills, and which spread fertility over the fields, which are well cultivated. This place is a favorite resort of the Cypriots, and is perhaps the most agreeable residence in the island. From all antiquity it has been renowned for its beautiful landscape. Especially dedicated to Venus, its very name recalls, even in our days, images of voluptuous pleasures. In his adventures of Telemachus, where the young hero is exposed to all the temptations incident to this licentious island, Fenelon depicts, in glowing colors, the natural beauties of Cytherea. But however agreeable are its shade and water, it requires a strong effort of the imagination to discover, in the aspect of this poor Greek village, the features of the ancient residence of the Cyprian goddess, so *luxuriously* described by the poets of antiquity.

In the evening we took leave of our monastic friends, and commenced our return to Larnica. We passed through a different part of the country, but its general configuration and appearance were very similar to those we had observed in the former part of our excursion. We thought, however, that the fields were somewhat better cultivated, and the villages more numerous and less wretched. Aradippe particularly, at the distance of three hours travel from Nicosia, made a favorable impression, from the comparatively comfortable condition of its inhabitants. It contains about fifty houses, and possesses the singular privilege of being the only place upon the island where hogs are suffered to be bred. We know not the cause of this exemption. Aradippe has also a church, dedicated to St. Luke; and upon his festival a fair is held, to which large crowds resort.

At nightfall we reached the village of Dale, and were conducted to the house of the miller, a substantial man, where we *stayed*, till morning. His habitation was a cottage of sun-dried brick, comfortless enough, according to our notions—for it possessed little in the interior but walls and floors. By robbing the hen-roost after our arrival, and searching the garden, they spread us a tolerable supper of fowls and vegetables: and we carried to the table a good appetite, the best remedy of the traveller against any of the *little inconveniences* to which the kitchen department may expose him. Our attendants at the table were two Greek priests, called from the clerical mansion to officiate in this humble employment, so different, in our estimation, from their proper functions. It was a trait of life which revealed the true condition of the Greek priesthood. This class of society is in the lowest state of poverty, laboring in the fields for their support. It is impossible, under the circumstances, that they can possess the necessary information for the instruction of their flocks, or that moral influence, which is its result, and which now enters as an element into the institutions of all enlightened Christian countries. These two priests had the aspect of extreme poverty, and, as far as we could judge, they were as ignorant as they were poor. It was a sad spectacle; but they did not feel it so, and the few *paras* they gained they no doubt considered an ample compensation.

Our sleeping apartments were indeed none of the best, for our host could give us nothing but the floor, with the exception of two planks, raised upon stools, which were couches *par excellence,* and where the elders of our party sought repose. As to beds and blankets, these were supplied by our own cloaks. But we had too often passed the night in the middle of the forest, with less peaceful *appliances to boot*, than this quiet cottage furnished, to be kept awake by the poverty of its resources.

In the morning we arose, and issued forth with much interest, to examine the environs, for we knew we were upon classic ground. The village of Dale has indeed preserved the name, as its position has preserved the site, of the ancient Idalium, which was one of the four cities consecrated to Venus, as she herself declares in the tenth book of the Æneid:

> "Est Amathus, est celsa mihi Paphos atque Cythera
> Idaliaque domus."

We ascended the hill where this favorite city formerly existed. It commands an extensive prospect, and when the country was cultivated and prosperous, the view must have been beautiful. But time has swept away, even to the foundation, every edifice. Not one stone rests upon another within the circuit of the walls. These, indeed, can be traced, and pieces of pottery, those indestructible evidences of the existence and ruin of the early Greek towns, may be picked up; but the most complete desolation rests upon the place. It is difficult to describe the emotion which the traveller experiences, when standing upon the site of one of these old cities, which had run its race before the records of authentic history,—constructed and destroyed before there were any written monuments to carry down the story of its fate. Even in the time of Pliny, Idalium *had been*—the beautiful and touching expression of the Romans to indicate past existence combined with present destruction. After enumerating many other cities of Cyprus, that author adds, "fuere et ibi Cyneria, Malium, Idalium."—*Plin., Lib.* v. c. 31.

The vicinity of Dale was rendered pleasant by some springs of water, always the cause of fertility in the East; and there were trees in the gardens of the village, which lend it an agreeable aspect. It may be too, that its odoriferous plants give out the same fragrance which they did in the palmy days of the island, but none such saluted our nerves. If Virgil, in his beautiful picture, where he paints a rural scene, and Innocence dwelling with Beauty, drew the local details from this region, and not from his own imagination, the change in the circumjacent country has not been less than in the lost city:

> "At Venus Ascani placidam per membra quietem
> Inigat, et fotum gremi dea tollit in altos
> Idalire lucos, ubi mollis amaracus illum
> Floribus, et dulci adspiranes complectitui umbra."

Early in the day we reached Larnica. Our ship had previously touched at Limasol, and after leaving Larnica, we run down the island to the west, keeping the coast full in view, and sufficiently near to be able to form a general conception of the physiognomy of the country. The result of our observations, and of the information we procured, we shall briefly state.

There are two Limasols, the old and the new. The former, which occupied the site of the ancient city of Amathuntum, was destroyed by Richard Coeur de Lion, and is now a heap of ruins. The new, which was erected in its vicinity by one of the Lusignans, in the twelfth century, is now following rapidly the fate of its two predecessors. It is a miserable place, with a tolerable port, however, and serves as an entrepot, whence the wine, the principal production of this part of the island, is sent to Larnica, and from thence exported to the Levant, and to Europe.

Continuing down the coast, we passed the Cape of the Cats, the western point of the island, and the sites of many towns whose names are recorded in history, and whose ruins attest their former existence, but of whose annals little is known, and which are now desolate. Paphos, however, now Baffa, was too renowned not to claim the tribute of a passing notice. The aspect of the mountains in its rear was lofty and rugged, and the country appeared poor, with a whitish sterile looking soil. Its port has become almost inaccessible, being obstructed by a bar, and the anchorage is bad even for the vessels which can enter it. It possesses a castle of the middle ages, but we know not its means of defence, nor are they likely to be known, by any trial it is destined to endure. It has a bishop too, but he is as poor as his flock; and that is poverty enough, even for the sternest advocate of Episcopal abjuration of wealth. But here, too, the Moslem tax-gatherer finds something to tempt his rapacity, and Paphos has, or not long since had, its digdaban, its cadi, its aga, and its other officers, with barbarous epithets in the Turkish civil hierarchy, who gathered something for themselves, and something for their masters.

It was in this part of the island, where were found various mineral productions; among these a kind of crystallized quartz, highly esteemed in the Levant, and called "Baffa diamonds;" and the asbestos stone of a superior quality, known as the "cotton stone," the fibres of which are white, fine and flexible. It derives its name, *Ameanthus,* from the place in whose vicinity it is found. It is often mentioned by the ancients, and Pliny describes the process of its manufacture into cloth, but so erroneously that no confidence can be placed in his information. He says, it was so common, that the Cypriots used it for sails for their vessels. It was certainly much esteemed, and wherever the bodies of the dead were burned, this material was sought for the purpose of enclosing them, and this preserving their ashes more pure.

As to the mines of gold, of copper, of iron, and of tin, which are described by Ptolemy, by Strabo, by Pliny, and by many other authors, as existing in Cyprus, and by their products contributing to a part of its wealth, they have been not only abandoned long since, but their sites are unknown. We might almost doubt their existence, were not the evidence of antiquity so strong upon the subject.

For the sake of geographical accuracy, it may be well to state, that four sites have claimed the name of Paphos, two in ancient, and two in modern times, but all occupying the same region, succeeding each other, as some of the calamities to which the island has always been subject, have struck their predecessors in succession. Alas for the mutability of the things of this world! It would puzzle the Paphia goddess to trace the foundation of her own temple; to tell where were the hundred altars, which smoked with the blood of animals sacrificed to her worship, and which sent up the perfume of the richest odors of Arabia.

Before bidding adieu to this branch of our task, we are tempted to introduce to our readers one of the most distinguished families of Cyprus, whose honors are not indeed recorded in the Herald's College, but which are commemorated in the Cyprian annals. They trace their descent from the earliest times, even from the period of the Roman domination. It is well known that Cyprus has always been, more or less, infested with venomous snakes, whose bite is fatal. Among these, the most dreaded is the asp, and popular credulity has given faith to the pretensions of *charlatans,* who affect to cure the patient by various tricks and incantations. But this *Esculapian* family possessed a hereditary virtue, and did not depend for its renown upon any superstitious practices. Their name was Ophiogenes, and their power over the serpent tribe was so great, that these would caress and lick them like little dogs, without doing any injury. The cure was operated by the simple touch of a member of the family, and was infallible. Exagon, who was ambassador from Cyprus to Rome, and who claimed this descent, gave an irrefragible proof of confidence in his power. He placed himself naked in the present of the consuls, in a large barrel, filled with serpents. To the great astonishment of the Romans, the reptiles did him no injury, but caressed him, and exhibited marks of pleasure in his company. An old historian thus writes: "I do not know if any of this family remain, or if some other has inherited its virtue, but I do know that in 1701, there was a man at Famagosta, who, by pronouncing some words quite low, cured the bite of asps, serpents very venomous, and very common in that island."

As late as 1831, not only was public confidence not weakened in this curative power, but the incidents of the process are gravely given by Messrs. Michaud, of the French Academy, and Poujoulat, two French authors, who have jointly written a book of travels in the East. After recounting that a man who was bitten by an asp, sent an express to the favored mortal who had the power to heal, and that the latter "brought a glass of water, in which he threw some dust, and presented it, pronouncing some unknown words, and saying *return to the sick person,* you will find him cured,'" they add, that in effect, "the sick man on the return of the express, was found standing, and felt no more pain." Then follow some remarks upon human incredulity, and upon "that ignorance which does not believe any thing," through which it is easy to perceive that the learned authors were disposed to give faith to the exhibitions of this hereditary curative power, in the island of Cyprus.

Now, though we firmly think with Hamlet, that

"There are more things in heaven and earth, Horatio,
Than are dream'd of in your philosophy,"

and have long since abandoned the proud principle of believing nothing we do not understand, yet upon this occasion our travelling predecessors in the regions of the East make rather large demands upon our stock of credulity, and we have witnessed too many clever tricks among our own Indians, not to invoke the testimony of our reason, when reading the narratives of similar efforts among the mountebanks of Cyprus. But we will not forestall the judgment of our readers upon this important subject, and shall content ourselves with repeating after the *Minstrel,*

"I cannot tell how the truth may be,
I say the tale as 'twas said to me."

We have already passed the bounds of our own judgment, and probably of the reader's patience, in the unreasonable length to which this article is extended. And yet we have not touched upon the government, population, revenues, productions, nor commerce of Cyprus, nor upon many other subjects connected with the present condition of the inhabitants, and illustrative of the operation of Mahometan institutions over a subjugated country. In another number we shall give the result of our observations upon these topics.

Wilde 1838

In September 1837 Sir William Robert Wilde was engaged as a "medical attendant to a gentleman about to make a voyage for the benefit of his health . . . Mr. R. Meiklam . . . in his own yacht of 130 tons, with all the comfort such a mode of transit could command . . ." They arrived on Cyprus 7 March 1838 and departed 9 March 1838. This selection is taken from Wilde's book, *Narrative of a Voyage to Madeira, Teneriffe, and along the Shores of the Mediterranean, including a visit to Algiers, Egypt, Palestine, Tyre, Rhodes, Telmessus, Cyprus and Greece, with Observations on the Present State and Prospects of Egypt and Palestine, and on the Climate, Natural History, and Antiquities of the Countries Visited*, 2nd Edition, Enlarged and Revised, published in Dublin: William Curry and Company, 1852.

We left Kastelorizo on the 6th; and being favoured with a fair wind, we made the eastern point of the island of Cyprus next day, and continued coasting along its undulating shores, under stun-sails, till the evening. The weather had improved, and now all was sunshine. Some parts of the scenery here are very beautiful; the ground is pleasingly diversified with hill and dale; and in other places the headlands present a white, chalky appearance, not unlike Dover Cliffs; from between which we obtained occasional glimpses of the distant Mount Olympus. We "brought up" in an open roadstead off the town of Limasol, which is situated upon a low bank of sand, with a surfy beach before it. It has little calculated to interest the visitor, except the minarets of its mosques, that rise into lofty spires covered with tin, and which have a pleasing effect when burnished by the beams of the setting sun. A large plain stretches to the east of the town, and behind it is a range of barren hills, which are by no means picturesque. A quarantine of three days was imposed upon us here, on account of our having touched at Macri; and this rendered our situation very uncomfortable, as there was a heavy swell in the sea, caused by the gale that we encountered off Kalamaki, which had not yet quite subsided. The principal trade of this place is wine, of the fame of which we had heard much; and to procure some of it was one of our reasons for visiting the island. The accounts generally given of this wine are either very much exaggerated, or those who have given these coloured statements must have acquired a vitiated taste that few Englishmen would desire to possess. Mix honey, vinegar, and tar with brandy and water, to the taste of a Cyprian, and you have this much esteemed beverage of the Levant; and if you wish to prepare it for Greece, add a certain quantity of resin; or for Spain or Portugal, put in the same quantity of anise-seed. Strength and sweetness are the qualities looked for; and the tarish flavour which it possessed, I found to arise from its being kept in large unglazed earthen jars, which, to prevent filtration, are coated on the outside with tar. There are two kinds of this wine, red and white. It is carried from the country into the port in skins, as at Madeira; but of its mode of preparation the merchants engaged in the trade are totally ignorant, and they generally dispose of it as soon as possible.

We found Limasol to be but a poor place. Its streets are, however, broader than those of most oriental towns. An old castle at the entrance mounts a couple of long brass Venetian guns of the date of 1543. The population is mixed, and consists of Greeks and Mohammadans, who have all (particularly the women) a wan and sickly look, that at once discovers the influence of malaria. There is no place upon, or in the vicinity of, the coast of Asia Minor where fever is so prevalent as this. It continues the entire three months of summer, and we were told that those who may have suffered from it previously are still liable to its repeated attacks. With some it remains, though in a more modified form, during the whole year, so that the place can never be said to be entirely free from its influence; and when I visited the consul, both his wife and child were just recovering from a fit of ague. On my recommending to some of the inhabitants to seek a higher elevation during the time in which the fever is most prevalent, they smiled, shook their heads, and said that they were perfectly aware of the propriety of following my advice, but that they had been accustomed to it from their youth, and, as it seldom caused death, they were unwilling to lose the chance trade, of which they might be deprived by a summer's residence in the mountains. None, even of the better classes, remove from the place, preferring to suffer this intermittent from year to year, to a removal to a more healthful situation during its continuance. The men seemed a slothful race, and the women, as far as we could observe, bore no resemblance to their great progenitrix.

On the 9th we left Cyprus, and sailed for Syria.

Summer 1839

George Summer (1817–1863), an American who travelled in Europe from 1838 to 1852, wrote frequently for American periodicals and newspapers. In August 1839 he visited Cyprus briefly and although he does not record it, he met Lorenzo Pease an American missionary in Larnaca. Pease's wife recorded Summer's visit days before Pease died from fever on August 28. Summer's letter of August 31, 1839 to his sister Mary from Damascus includes his stop in Cyprus. It appears among his letters in the *Massachusetts Historical Society Proceedings*, Volume 46, published by the Society, Boston, 1913.

From Rhodes I went to *Cyprus,* the island so famous of old as the birthplace of *Venus,* the *Paphian* queen. Paphos still stands, a miserable Greek village with a few houses built of mud, while near by are the fallen columns of the temple that once stood there for the goddess. All around the island, which is about 500 miles in circumference are ruins of ancient temples and cities. *Laonica,* where I stopped for one day, is near [the site] of the ancient *Citium,* which was the birthplace of *Zeno* the stoic. You see Mary, how completely I have been for some time past mixed up with those who flourished in antiquity. I shall become an *antique* myself almost, if I poke about in this way much longer, stumbling over old ruins, measuring columns, and climbing into tombs, etc.

From Cyprus I went down upon the coast of Syria, and passed along by Tyre and Sidon to Jaffa, thence returned again and landed at *Beirout,* which is near the spot of the rencounter between St. George and the Dragon. He being my patron saint, I of course went to see the spot of his mighty deeds.

Neale 1842

Frederick Arthur Neale was attached to the British Consular Service in Syria and took the advantage to travel through the surrounding areas. He recorded his journeys in two volumes, *Eight Years in Syria, Palestine, and Asia Minor from 1842 to 1850*, London: Colburn and Co., 1851.

The time of his trip to Cyprus during those nine years is not documented. He apparently visited only Larnaca and Nicosia briefly and recounts little but a romantic human interest story from each city.

Larnaca, the principal sea-port of Cyprus, has an extremely pretty appearance from the sea. But the white ranges of houses built along the beach are principally shops and warehouses: the residents live inland, about half a mile from the beach.

Mr. Niven Kerr, who was our Consul when I visited Cyprus, was extremely hospitable and kind to me during my stay, though I lived with Mr. Cerrutti, the Sardinian Consul, than whom it would be difficult to meet a more excellent or better-informed man.

Larnaca is celebrated for its wines, the Camandaria, dry and sweet, and red wine. For my own part, I think all of them execrable. Here we were once again among carriages, which are hardly known in Syria or Palestine. Every respectable person in Larnaca has his phaeton or gig, though, to say the truth, they are, at best, most wretched turn-outs. The churches are permitted to have bells, a privilege unknown in other Turkish towns. From a tall spire of the Catholic church, which for security is built in the precincts of the Sardinian consulate, the bell every Sunday morning tolls the hour for public worship.

The people are exceedingly fond of gaiety, and I often had my night's rest interrupted by fond youths serenading their mistresses. Balls and evening parties are of continual occurrence, and the Polka was introduced just previously to my arrival, by the officers of one of the Queen's ships.

The climate is anything but healthy; and Larnaca, like a great number of Eastern towns, is surrounded by marsh miasmas. The trade is inconsiderable. Plenty of vessels frequent the port, but they merely come for the purpose of buying provisions, which are both cheap and good. French and Italian vessels, which are homeward bound, lay in a stock of wine and biscuit here for the use of the crews, and the biscuits of Larnaca are, in my opinion, equal to those made in any part of Europe.

Every traveler who has ever visited Cyprus has heard of Signor Baldo Matteo, the Ebenezer Scrooge of the East. While I was at Larnaca, a sad adventure, furnishing ample materials for a melodrama, nearly terminated old Baldo's life, and all his speculations. His only daughter, and heiress, lost her heart to a needy Austrian, who had come to Cyprus expressly to make his fortune by marriage. Hearing of the wealth of old Baldo, and of his daughter, he fixed upon him at once; but Baldo was not to be easily caught, and totally repulsed every advance. The Austrian grew desperate, and, as a final resource, became fanatically religious, attending the Catholic chapel morning, noon, and night. Nothing could exceed his devotion to a certain old priest troubled with the cramp, on whose leg he sat, whenever it was attacked, till the pain passed off. When, after this, he whispered to him the sin that preyed most heavily upon his mind, which was a wish to possess riches, that he might bestow them on Mother Church, and hinted at a passion for Miss Baldo, he received immediate absolution, and was next day dining at old Baldo's table, in company with the Padre Presidenti, and seated next to the object in whom all his hopes were concentrated. Miss B. was luckily placed on his right, and heard with unspeakable rapture all his protestations of love and devotion. Had she been on his left, these would all have been lost, as she had been perfectly deaf on that side from her birth.

To be brief, the Austrian proposed, and was accepted, and all that he had now to obtain was old Baldo's consent. Baldo, however, as a man of the world, saw clearly through his designs, and knew him to be a knave, though he had too much reverence for the priestly clique, who had introduced the Austrian, to give a decided negative. All he asked was time—a year—to consider so important a measure. This was accorded, and Baldo devoutly prayed that the true character of his daughter's suitor might before that time be unmasked. His prayer was granted, but in a way the least expected, and certainly the least agreeable to himself.

The lover of the Signorina Baldo, finding his exchequer rather low, and being sorrowfully conscious of his inability to increase his wealth, so as to enable him to keep up necessary appearances, came to the desperate resolution of grasping, without further delay, his intended wife's fortune, by sending poor old Baldo out of the world. Accordingly, armed with a loaded double-barrelled pistol, which he concealed about his person, he proceeded to Matteo's house at an hour when he knew he would find him alone, the daughter and servants being in the habit of attending high mass on Sunday mornings; and he knocked at the door, which, after a little hesitation, was opened to him. Old Baldo, though believed to be an honourable man, and fair and just in his transactions with others, was a confirmed miser. He had accumulated great sums in hard cash, which, unseen by human eye, he had buried in his garden, and hidden in various parts of his house. The house was going to ruin, and wanted whitewashing and repairing in many parts. The garden was a perfect wilderness of weeds and thistles; but these he set fire to regularly once a year, and by this means, to a certain extent, kept them under. As for gardeners armed with a spade, which might dig up and bring to light all kinds of secret hoards, if there was one trade Baldo detested, it was this. He kept the key of his walled-in garden, and on Sundays, when all his family were absent, he strolled about in it till their return.

He was thus occupied when he admitted his would-be son-in-law; and the first thing this promising youth did, was to draw forth his pistol and take deliberate aim, discharging it at the breast of the feeble old man, who, tottering backwards a few paces, fell to the earth apparently a corpse. For such the murderer took him; and depositing the pistol close by his side, to make it appear he had died by his own hand, he rushed into the street, closing the door after him.

Running with the haste of a man charged with some important news, he came suddenly on a gentleman attached to the Austrian Consulate, whom he breathlessly informed that passing near Baldo's house, he had heard the report of a pistol, followed by a sound like that of some heavy body falling to the earth, that he had in vain knocked at the door for admission, and that he had no doubt in his own mind that some sad catastrophe had occurred.

In a few seconds a perfect mob was collected at Baldo's door, which they broke open, and rushing in, beheld old Baldo stretched upon the ground, his clothes literally saturated with blood, and a pistol lying close by his side. The assassin, who never dreamt that the old man was still alive, witnessed this spectacle with fiendish triumph, though loudly lamenting the loss of him, whom he called his best friend on earth. But it happened that the ball, though it struck against a part where a wound would have been mortal, had come in contact with the sharp edge of a bone, which turned it in another direction, and it was now safely lodged between the skin and the spine. Baldo, who had fainted from fright and loss of blood, now, to the amazement of all, recovered his senses, and hearing the voice of his late assailant, slowly raised himself up, and denounced him on the spot. Having done this, he fell back, and again became unconscious. The wretch was immediately seized and handcuffed, and safely borne away to the Austrian Consulate, where he was placed in confinement.

Doctors were now assembled from all parts of Cyprus, and all examined the wound, and declared it fatal, expressing the greatest surprise that the patient should have lingered so long. The blood being staunched, and Baldo suffering from no real injury, but labouring under a sense of approaching dissolution, begged that a confessor might be sent for. To this confessor, he acknowledged, amongst other offenses, the commission of one sin which weighed heavier than all the rest upon his guilty conscience. It appeared that his niece, who was then married to a French merchant at Larnaca, had been left at a very early age an orphan, and had become his ward. She had, however, been well provided for by her parents, and a large sum of money had been deposited in his hands, which, after covering the expenses of her education and board, &c., would still leave a considerable surplus as a marriage portion. Now old Baldo, never forgetting his thrift, had more than twice turned this capital over before the date of the niece's marriage, but he had retained the proceeds as his own, handing over the principal to the bridegroom on the nuptial day. But on the approach of death, as it seemed, he felt considerable qualms of conscience, and confessed his unworthy stewardship, and indicated the spots where these savings were concealed. The husband of the niece quickly dug them up, and came into possession. Scarcely was this done, when Baldo recovered, and would almost have forgiven the attempt upon his life, had it not involved such serious results.

The Austrian was by the Turkish authorities handed over to his own Consulate, and was eventually removed to Trieste, but I believe, for lack of sufficient testimony, escaped punishment. This affair, as it may be imagined, created a great sensation in Cyprus, which was once the scene of the memorable tragedy which terminated the life of Desdemona.

From Larnaca I proceeded to Nicosia, the capital of all Cyprus. It is a fine healthy town, approached through a subterranean gate. The fortress is still in excellent condition, and is always well garrisoned. The houses are the handsomest I have ever seen in the East, and are all detached, each house having a fine garden round it.

At the house of Signor Chelibi Yanko, the principal Greek in the Island of Cyprus, I have tasted some Camandaria that had been forty-five years in barrel. This was something like wine; a fine oily old wine, unequalled in flavour by any I have tasted in the East.

It was in Nicosia, about the year 1840, that Dame Fortune once more played off one of her eccentric frolics on the person of a poor Greek priest, who had little to depend upon in this world, save such meagre offerings as the more charitable of his parishioners bestowed upon him. As the story goes, he was a devout and holy man, but beyond being able to go through the regular routine of his priestly office, possessed but scant learning, and was equally ignorant of the world's ways and manners. At the commencement of a fast, fearing he should, from his defective memory, forget its exact duration, he carefully filled his pockets with so many dried peas as there were fast days, and each day extracting one from his pockets, as the peas diminished, he was warned of the proximity of a feast, and prepared accordingly. On one occasion, his wife happening to find a few peas in her husband's pockets, and imagining the devout man was fond of this Eastern luxury, very affectionately replenished his pockets from her own store of cadamies, or roasted peas. Great was the consternation of his congregation, when on the eve of the feast day, instead of proclaiming its advent from the pulpit, as is usual, he informed them that eight or ten days yet remained for the approaching festival. A discussion on this point immediately ensued, when the priest, in confirmation of what he asserted, produced from his pocket the remaining peas, making known at the same time his method of calculating. Upon this,

his wife stepped forward, and acknowledged what she had done, and great merriment ensued, in which the priest joined.

To this poor man, fortune now brought one of those rare windfalls which are more frequently heard of than experienced. One summer's evening he was seated in the courtyard of his humble house, watching with satisfaction and delight the gambols of his little children, who were amusing themselves with throwing stones at a hole in the wall. At length he remarked, that whenever a stone chanced to go near the crevice, he heard a ringing sound, and to convince himself that he was not deceived, he stepped nearer, and hit it repeatedly with a stone, each time hearing the sound distinctly. It now occured to him that there was some concealed treasure within, and the thought made him tremble with expectation. He went to bed early, but not to sleep, having formed the determination that he would that night make a rigorous search. When all was still, he rose from his sleepless couch, and going out stealthily and noiselessly, commenced, by aid of a small pickaxe, breaking into the wall, removing stone by stone. He had hardly worked an hour, when out fell a bag of doubloons, followed by a second and a third. This was indeed a treasure, sufficient to satisfy a more covetous man; but he felt there would be no safety with it in Cyprus. That very night, he carefully stowed his riches in two saddle-bags, and before daybreak, awoke his wife and acquainted her with their good fortune, when horses were hired at a neighbouring khan, and priest, wife, and children turned their backs upon Nicosia, and arriving early at Larnaca, embarked that very day on board a vessel sailing for Italy. The priest became the head of one of the wealthiest mercantile firms now established at Leghorn, and is, I believe, still living.

The population of Nicosia is computed at nine thousand souls, *i.e.* seven thousand Greeks, and two thousand Turks. In Cyprus there are three times as many Greeks as Turks, and taking one with another, they are about the greatest set of scamps that were ever accumulated in one country.

I left Nicosia, and returned to Larnaca, and from Larnaca sailed in a British schooner for England.

Kinglake 1834

Alexander W. Kinglake, educated at Eton and Cambridge, made a historic journey in 1834 and 1835 through the Levant during the "Great Plague of Egypt." His brief stop in Cyprus plays only a small role in the travels and it is not known exactly when he was in Cyprus, or anywhere else, during those two years as he wrote and rewrote his manuscript over a nine-year period carefully eliminating detailed references. His book *Eothen* ("from the early dawn" or "from the East") *Or Traces of Travel Brought Home from the East* was valued for some years for capturing the essence of the Ottoman lands he traversed rather than for minute details.

The first edition was published in 1844 by Ollivier partially supported by Kinglake followed by other editions in 1864, 1889 and one in 1906 by Henry Frowde, London. Oxford University Press has published editions as recent as 1982 and 1991.

In the introduction and notes of the 1906 edition D. G. Hogarth points out that Kinglake failed to correct an "error in classical lore, his belief that he had seen ruins of the great temple of the Paphian Aphrodite at Baffo (Nea Paphos). That shrine lies in reality ten miles away at Kuklia (Palaia Paphos), and Kinglake must have passed almost in sight of its ruins on his way from Limassol."

Kinglake saw only the districts of Limassol and Paphos which he thought beautiful, but Hogarth felt that he missed the extremes of the picturesqueness of the castles high on the Kyrenia range and the barrenness of the gypsum country inland from Larnaca.

There was a Greek at Limesol, who hoisted his flag as an English Vice-Consul, and he insisted upon my accepting his hospitality. With some difficulty, and chiefly by assuring him that I could not delay my departure beyond an early hour in the afternoon, I induced him to allow my dining with his family, instead of banqueting all alone with the representative of my sovereign, in consular state and dignity. The lady of the house, it seemed, had never sat at table with an European; she was very shy about the matter, and tried hard to get out of the scrape, but the husband, I fancy, reminded her that she was theoretically an Englishwoman, by virtue of the flag that waved over her roof, and that she was bound to show her nationality by sitting at meat with me. Finding herself inexorably condemned to bear with the dreaded gaze of European eyes, she tried to save her innocent children from the hard fate awaiting herself, but I obtained that all of them (and I think there were four or five) should sit at the table. You will meet with abundance of stately receptions, and of generous hospitality too, in the East, but rarely, very rarely in those regions (or even, so far as I know, in any part of southern Europe), does one gain an opportunity of seeing the familiar and in-door life of the people.

This family party of the good Consul's (or rather of mine, for I originated the idea, though he furnished the materials) went off very well: the mamma was shy at first, but she veiled her awkwardness by affecting to scold the children. These had all immortal names—names, too, which they owed to tradition, and certainly not to any classical enthusiasm of their parents: every instant I was delighted by some such phrases as these:— 'Themistocles, my love, don't fight.'—'Alcibiades, can't you sit still?'—'Socrates, put down the cup.'—'Oh, fie! Aspasia, don't oh! don't be naughty!' It is true that the names were pronounced, Socrahtie, Aspahsie--that is, according to accent, and not according to quantity, but I suppose it is scarcely now to be doubted that they were so sounded in ancient times.

To me, it seems that of all the lands I know (you will see in a minute how I connect this piece of prose with the Isle of Cyprus), there is none in which mere wealth— mere unaided wealth—is held half so cheaply, none in which a poor devil of a millionaire without birth or ability occupies so humble a place as in England. My Greek host was chatting with me (I think upon the roof of the house, for that is the lounging place in Eastern climes), when suddenly he assumed a serious air, and intimated a wish to talk over the British Constitution,—a subject with which, as he assured me, he was thoroughly acquainted. He presently, however, remarked that there was one anomalous circumstance attendant upon the practical working of our political system which he had never been able to hear explained in a manner satisfactory to himself. From the fact of his having found a difficulty in his subject, I began to think that my host might really know rather more of it than his announcement of a thorough knowledge had led me to expect; I felt interested at being about to hear from the lips of an intelligent Greek, quite remote from the influence of European opinions, what might seem to him the most astonishing and incomprehensible of all those results which have followed from the action of our political institutions. The anomaly—the only anomaly which had been detected by the Vice-

Consular wisdom—consisted in the fact that Rothschild (the late money-monger) had never been the Prime Minister of England! I gravely tried to throw some light upon the mysterious causes that had kept the worthy Israelite out of the Cabinet, but I think I could see that my explanation was not satisfactory. Go and argue with the flies of summer that there is a power divine yet greater than the sun in the heavens, but never dare hope to convince the people of the South that there is any other God than Gold.

My intended journey was to the sight of the Paphian temple. I take no antiquarian interest in ruins, and care little about them unless they are either striking in themselves, or else serve to mark some spot very dear to my fancy. I knew that the ruins of Paphos were scarcely, if at all, discernible, but there was a will, and a longing, more imperious than mere curiosity, that drove me thither.

For this, just then, was my Pagan soul's desire—that (not forfeiting my inheritance for the life to come) it had yet been given me to live through this world—to live a favoured mortal under the old Olympian dispensation—to speak out my resolves to the listening Jove, and hear him answer with approving thunder—to be blessed with divine counsels from the lips of Pallas Athēnie—to believe—ay, only to believe—to believe for one rapturous moment that in the gloomy depths of the grove by the mountain's side, there were some leafy pathway that crisped beneath the glowing sandal of Aphrodētie—Aphrodētie, not coldly disdainful of even a mortal's love! And this vain, heathenish longing of mine was father to the thought of visiting the scene of the ancient worship.

The isle is beautiful: from the edge of the rich, flowery fields on which I trod, to the midway sides of the snowy Olympus, the ground could only here and there show an abrupt crag or a high straggling ridge that upshouldered itself from out of the wilderness of myrtles, and of a thousand bright-leaved shrubs that twined their arms together in lovesome tangles. The air that came to my lips was warm and fragrant as the ambrosial breath of the goddess, infecting me—not (of course) with a faith in the old religion of the isle, but with a sense and apprehension of its mystic power—a power that was still to be obeyed—obeyed by *me*; for why otherwise did I toil on with sorry horses to 'where, for HER, the hundred altars glowed with Arabian incense, and breathed with the fragrance of garlands ever fresh?'

I passed a sadly disenchanting night in the cabin of a Greek priest—not a priest of the goddess, but of the Greek Church; there was but one humble room, or rather shed, for man, and priest, and beast. The next morning I reached Baffa (Paphos), a village not far distant from the site of the temple. There was a Greek husbandman there who (not for emoluments, but for the sake of the protection and dignity which it afforded) had got leave from the man at Limesol to hoist his flag as a sort of Deputy provisionary-sub-vice-pro-acting-consul of the British Sovereign. The poor fellow instantly changed his Greek head-gear for the cap of consular dignity, and insisted upon accompanying me to the ruins. I would not have stood this, if I could have felt the faintest gleam of my yesterday's pagan piety, but I had ceased to dream, and had nothing to dread from any new disenchanters.

The ruins (the fragments of one or two prostrate pillars) lie upon a promontory bare and unmystified by the gloom of surrounding groves. My Greek friend in his consular cap stood by, respectfully waiting to see what turn my madness would take now that I had come at last into the presence of the old stones. If you have no taste for research, and can't affect to look for inscriptions, there is some awkwardness in coming to the end of a merely sentimental pilgrimage, when the feeling which impelled you has gone: in such a strait you have nothing to do but to laugh the thing off as well as you can—and, by the by, it is not a bad plan to turn the conversation (or rather allow the natives to turn it) towards the subject of hidden treasures: this is a topic on which they will always speak with eagerness, and if they can fancy that you, too, take an interest in such matters, they will not only begin to think you perfectly sane, but will even perhaps give you credit for some more than human powers of forcing dark Earth to show you its hoards of gold.

When we returned to Baffa, the Vice-Consul seized a club, with the quietly determined air of a brave man, resolved to do some deed of note; he went into the yard adjoining his cottage where there were some thin, thoughtful, canting cocks, and serious, low-church-looking hens, respectfully listening, and chickens of tender years so well brought up as scarcely to betray in their conduct the careless levity of youth. The Vice-Consul stood for a moment quite calm—collecting his strength; then suddenly he rushed into the midst of the congregation, and began to deal death and destruction on all sides; he spared neither sex nor age; the dead and dying were immediately removed from the field of slaughter, and in less than an hour, I think, they were brought to the table, deeply buried in mounds of snowy rice.

My host was in all respects a fine, generous fellow. I could not bear the idea of impoverishing him by my visit, and my faithful Mysseri not only assured me that I might safely offer money to the Vice-Consul, but recommended that I should give no more to him than to 'the others', meaning any other peasant. I felt, however, that there was something about the man, besides the flag and cap, which made me shrink from offering coin, and, as I mounted my horse on departing, I gave him the only thing fit for a present that I happened to have with me, a rather handsome clasp-dagger, brought from Vienna. The poor fellow was ineffably grateful, and I had some difficulty in tearing myself from out of the reach of his thanks. At last I gave him what I supposed to be the last farewell, and rode on; but I had not gained more than about a hundred yards, when my host came bounding and shouting after me, with a goats' milk cheese in his hand, and this (it was rather a burthensome gift) he fondly implored me to accept. In old times the shepherd of Theocritus, or (to speak less dishonestly) the shepherd of the 'Poetae Graeci', sung his best song; I in this latter age presented my best dagger, and both of us received the same rustic reward.

It had been known that I should return to Limesol, and when I arrived there, I found that a noble old Greek had been hospitably plotting to have me for his guest. I willingly accepted his offer. The day of my arrival happened to be my host's birthday, and during all the morning there was a constant influx of visitors who came to offer their congratulations. A few of these were men, but most of them were young graceful girls. Almost all of them went through the ceremony with the utmost precision and formality: each in succession spoke her blessing in the tone of a person repeating a set formula,— then deferentially accepted the invitation to sit,—partook of the proffered sweetmeats and the cold, glittering water,—remained for a few minutes either in silence or engaged in very thin conversation—then arose, delivered a second benediction, followed by an elaborate farewell and departed.

The bewitching power attributed at this day to the women of Cyprus is curious in connection with the worship of the sweet goddess who called their isle her own. The Cypriot is not, I think, nearly so beautiful in face as the Ionian Queens of Izmir, but she is tall, and slightly formed; there is a high-souled meaning and expression—a seeming consciousness of gentle empire that speaks in the wavy lines of the shoulder, and winds itself like Cytherea's own cestus around the slender waist; then the richly abounding hair (not enviously gathered together under the head-dress) descends the neck, and passes the waist in sumptuous braids. Of all other women with Grecian blood in their veins, the costume is graciously beautiful, but these, the maidens of Limesol—their robes are more gently, more sweetly imagined, and fall like Julia's Cashmere in soft, luxurious folds. The common voice of the Levant allows that in face the women of Cyprus are less beautiful than their majestic sisters of Smyrna, and yet, says the Greek, he may trust himself to one and all the cities of the Ægean, and may still weigh anchor with a heart entire, but that so surely as he ventures upon the enchanted Isle of Cyprus, so surely will he know the rapture or the bitterness of Love. The charm, they say, owes its power to that which the people call the astonishing 'politics' (πολιτική) of the women, meaning, I fancy, their tact, and their witching ways; the word, however, plainly fails to express one-half of that which the speakers would say. I have smiled to hear the Greek with all his plenteousness of fancy, and all the wealth of his generous language, yet vainly struggling to describe the ineffable spell which the Parisians dispose of in their own smart way, by a summary 'Je ne sçai quoi'.

I went to Larnecca, the chief city of the isle, and over the water at last to Beyrout.

Barclay 1859

The first American consulate in Cyprus was established in 1835 with the elevation of Marino de Mattey to consul from the title of consular agent that he held from 1832. Upon the death in 1859 of de Mattey, who was a native of Cyprus, John Judson Barclay was appointed as the first American to serve in the consulate in Larnaca. Three other Americans were subsequently appointed to the post, but never arrived due to ill health or reassignment, so Barclay served until he was replaced by Luigi Palma di Cesnola in 1865.

The following is his dispatch to Lewis Cass, Secretary of State, on May 20, 1859, from *Despatches from United States Consuls in Cyprus, 1835-1878,* Vol. 1 (Washington, D.C., National Archives, Microcopy T-463).

U.S. Consulate - Cyprus
Larnica, May 20th 1859

Hon. Lewis Cass
    Secretary of State,

        Sir,

        I have the honor to submit the following Commercial and Statistical Report for the Island of Cyprus.

The Island of Cyprus, the Ancient Cupros (*Kupros*) has since the year 1572 been under the Dominion of the Sublime Porte having been taken in that year by the Moslems from the Venetians. At the time Cyprus became a Turkish Province it had a population of two million souls, which number has been reduced by oppression of their Rules, Resolutions and immigration to about one hundred and eighty thousand which is the gross amount of the present population, not sufficient to afford (illegible) labor for the cultivation of one third of the rich soil of an Island 164 miles long, by 63 broad. At present large tracts of the most fertile ground are uncultivated, and an Island, which under the Rule of the Venetians, exported to Europe large supplies of cotton, wheat, barley, silk and wool, and the minerals, of which copper particularly yielded rich revenues to that enterprizing nation, does not at present yield one twentieth part of its former productions, and its mines of copper, lead, silver, coal and iron, are now almost entirely neglected, although the expense of working them would be small and the returns large.

The exportation of cotton alone during the Venetian Dynasty amounted to 30,000 bales annually while at present the amount exported, does not exceed 5,000 bales.

An experiment is being made by an English colony under the auspices of the Manchester Cotton Supply Association to restore, as regards the growth of cotton the palmy days of the Venetians to the long neglected Island, by opening again so large a field for the cultivation of that plant, and if during the occupation of the Island by the Venetians with their primitive implements for the cultivation of the soil, the exportation of cotton amounted to 30,000 bales annually, what would now be the yield under the improved systems of agriculture, with our modern inventions in machinery &c &c.

The principal part of the cotton now grown in the Island is shipped for France and Austria.

To the antiquarian, the ruins of the ancient Salamis, Kolossi, St. George and Acamas, open a most interesting field for investigation and research where marble statues, and gold, silver, and copper antique coins are constantly found, not only in these places, but everywhere in the Island. To the mineralogist, the ancient mines of silver, copper, lead &c, mentioned in Virgil, present a field for speculation rarely met with.

The government of the Island is under a Civil and Military Pacha. The former resides at Nicosea the capital of the Island—a well fortified town, and contains a population of 15,000 inhabitants. About twenty one miles from this city is Larnaca the principal seaport where the military Pacha resides, and which is also the residence of a *Mudir* (or Agent of the Governor) and of the numerous Consular representatives of which there are some fifteen—the Consulates of France, Austria and Russia being handsomely appointed.

At present, the laws of the Empire are, as far as I can learn, impartially and justly administered, and crime of any magnitude is of rare occurrence, robbery being seldom heard of and murder but rarely committed. The inhabitants are a peacible & hospitable race, and friendly to strangers, particularly Americans—who here, as everywhere in the East have left the best of names. They are about 3/4 Christian and 1/4 Turks, the former being principally of the Greek Church, the Catholics not numbering over 1500 & a small number of Protestants.

The income derived by the Turkish Government annually, from this Island, exceeds £120,000. The principal port of shipping being Larnica, where there were last year 749 vessels discharged and freighted, and from which during the same period nearly £140,000 value of the produce of the island was shipped for Europe.

The import and export returns for the last two years for the Port of Larnica are given in the next pages.

* * * * *

The principal articles of importation here are sugar, coffee, leather, silk & woolen & cotton manufactures—lead, iron & copper—which are imported from France, England, Austria & Turkey.

The principal exports are raw cotton, wool, linseed & sesame, wheat, barley, madder-roots--native manufactures in silk and cotton--locusts & wine. The latter is shipped in large quantities to Egypt and Syria.

* * * * *

An enterprizing Swiss Protestant Gentleman has lately located in this place a steam flour mill with all the requisite machinery of the best description for the manufacture of fine & coarse flour, with every prospect of success there being a large demand for fine flour both here, and at the several Syrian Ports.

There is still a traffic carried on here in slaves, tho' from all the information I have gathered there have not been any lately imported. There are at present three or four thousand in the Island & I am informed they are in general well treated by their masters who are principally Greeks or Turks. The price of a male is about $75 and of a female $40.

The climate of this place is not healthy—feavers prevailing during the greater part of the year.

The preceeding Report has been made from reliable data, collected since my residence here and is respectfully submitted for the present in lieu of a more extended minute the which I shall prepare after a longer residence.

> I have the honor to be
> Yr. Obt. Servant
> J. Judson Barclay

Warner 1865–1876?

Charles Dudley Warner (1829-1900) was an American essayist and editor who collaborated with Mark Twain in writing *The Gilded Age*. He describes his visit to Cyprus in his book *In The Levant,* published in Boston and New York by Houghton, Mifflin and Company, 1893. He writes so glowing a description of the accomplishments of "General" Cesnola, that a dash of the critical and skeptical eye of his co-author Twain would be welcome. Warner visited Cyprus while Cesnola was American consul from 1865 to 1876.

In the early morning we were off Cyprus, in the open harbor of Larnaka,—a row of white houses on the low shore. The town is not peculiar and not specially attractive, but the Marina lies prettily on the blue sea, and the palms, the cypresses, the minarets and church-towers, form an agreeable picture behind it, backed by the lovely outline of mountains, conspicuous among them Santa Croce. The highest, Olympus, cannot be seen from this point.

A night had sufficed to transport us into another world, a world in which all outlines are softened and colored, a world in which history appears like romance. We might have imagined that we had sailed into some tropical harbor, except that the island before us was bare of foliage; there was the calm of perfect repose in the sky, on the sea, and the land; Cyprus made no harsh contrast with the azure water in which it seemed to be anchored for the morning, as our ship was. You could believe that the calm of summer and of early morning always rested on the island, and that it slept exhausted in the memory of its glorious past.

Taking a cup of coffee, we rowed ashore. It was the festival of St. George, and the flags of various nations were hung out along the *riva*, or displayed from the staffs of the consular residences. It is one of the chief fête days of the year, and the foreign representatives, who have not too much excitement, celebrated it by formal visits to the Greek consul. Larnaca does not keep a hotel, and we wandered about for some time before we could discover its sole *locanda*, where we purposed to breakfast. This establishment would please an artist, but it had few attractions for a person wishing to break his fast, and our unusual demand threw it into confusion. The *locanda* was nothing but a kitchen in a tumble-down building, smoke dried, with an earth floor and a rickety table or two. After long delay, the cheerful Greek proprietor and his lively wife—whose good-humored willingness both to furnish us next to nothing, but the best they had, from their scanty larder, and to cipher up a long reckoning for the same, excited our interest—produced some fried veal, sour bread, harsh wine, and tart oranges; and we breakfasted more sumptuously, I have no doubt, than any natives of the island that morning. The scant and hard fare of nearly all the common people in the East would be unendurable to any American; but I think that the hardy peasantry of the Levant would speedily fall into dyspeptic degeneracy upon the introduction of American rural cooking.

After we had killed our appetites at the *locanda*, we presented our letters to the American consul, General di Cesnola, in whose spacious residence we experienced a delightful mingling of Oriental and Western hospitality. The kawâss of the General was sent to show us the town. This kawâss was a gorgeous official, a kind of glorified being, in silk and gold-lace, who marched before us, huge in bulk, waving his truncheon of office, and gave us the appearance, in spite of our humility, of a triumphal procession. Larnaka has not many sights, although it was the residence of the Lusignan dynasty,—Richard Coeur de Lion having, toward the close of the twelfth century, made a gift of the island to Guy de Lusignan. It has, however, some mosques and Greek churches. The church of St. Lazarus, which contains the now vacant tomb of the Lazarus who was raised from the dead at Bethany and afterwards became bishop of Citium, is an interesting old Byzantine edifice, and has attached to it an English burial-ground, with tombs of the seventeenth century. The Greek priest who showed us the church does not lose sight of the gain of godliness in this life, while pursuing in this remote station his heavenly journey. He sold my friend some exquisite old crucifixes, carved in wood, mounted in antique silver, which he took from the altar, and he let the church part with some of its quaint old pictures, commemorating the impossible exploits of St. Demetrius and St. George. But he was very careful that none of the Greeks who were lounging about the church should be witnesses of the transfer. He said that these ignorant people had a prejudice about these sacred objects, and might make trouble.

The excavations made at Larnaka have demonstrated that this was the site of ancient Citium, the birthplace of Zeno, the Stoic, and the Chittim so often alluded to by the Hebrew prophets; it was a Phoenician colony, and when Ezekiel foretold the unrecoverable fall of Tyre, among the luxuries of wealth he enumerated were the "benches of ivory brought out of the isles of Chittim." Paul does not mention it, but he must have passed through it when he made his journey over the island from Salamis to Paphos, where he had his famous encounter with the sorcerer Bar-jesus. A few miles out of town on the road to Citti is a Turkish mosque, which shares the high veneration of Moslems with those of Mecca and Jerusalem. In it is interred the wet-nurse of Mohammed.

We walked on out of the town to the most considerable church in the place, newly built by the Roman Catholics. There is attached to it a Franciscan convent, a neat establishment with a garden; and the hospitable monks, when they knew we were Americans, insisted upon entertaining us; the contributions for their church had largely come from America, they said, and they seemed to regard us as among the number of their benefactors. This Christian charity expressed itself also in some bunches of roses, which the brothers plucked for our ladies. One cannot but suspect and respect that timid sentiment the monk retains for the sex whose faces he flies from, which he expresses in the care of flowers; the blushing rose seems to be the pure and only link between the monk and womankind; he may cultivate it without sin, and offer it to the chance visitor without scandal.

The day was lovely, but the sun had intense power, and in default of donkeys we took a private carriage into the country to visit the church of St. George, at which the fête day of that saint was celebrated by a fair, and a concourse of peasants. Our carriage was a four-wheeled cart, a sort of hay-wagon, drawn by two steers, and driven by a Greek boy in an embroidered jacket. The Franciscans lent us chairs for the cart; the resplendent kawâss marched ahead; Abd-el-Atti hung his legs over the tail of the cart in an attitude of dejection; and we moved on, but so slowly that my English friend, Mr. Edward Rae, was able to sketch us, and the Cyprians could enjoy the spectacle.

The country lay bare and blinking under the sun; save here and there a palm or a bunch of cypresses, this part of the island has not a tree or a large shrub. The view of the town and the sea with its boats, as we went inland, was peculiar, not anything real, but a skeleton picture; the sky and sea were indigo blue. We found a crowd of peasants at the church of St. George, which has a dirty interior, like all the Greek churches. The Greeks, as well as the other Orientals, knew how to mingle devotion with the profits of trade, and while there were rows of booths outside, and traffic went on briskly, the church was thronged with men and women who bought tapers for offerings, and kissed with fervor the holy relics which were exposed. The articles for sale at the booths and stands were chiefly eatables and the coarsest sort of merchandise. The only specialty of native manufacture was rude but pleasant-sounding little bells, which are sometimes strung upon the necks of donkeys. But so fond are these simple people of musical noise, that these bells are attached to the handles of sickles also. The barley was already dead-ripe in the fields, and many of the peasants at the fair brought their sickles with them. They were, both men and women, a goodhumored, primitive sort of people, certainly not a handsome race, but picturesque in appearance; both sexes affect high colors, and the bright petticoats of the women matched the gay jackets of their husbands and lovers.

We do not know what was the ancient standard of beauty in Cyprus; it may have been no higher than it is now, and perhaps the swains at this fête of St. George would turn from any other type of female charms as uninviting. The Cyprian or Paphian Venus could not have been a beauty according to our notions. The images of her which General di Cesnola found in her temple all have a long and sharp nose. These images are Phoenician, and were made six hundred to a thousand years before the Christian era, at the time that wonderful people occupied this fertile island. It is an interesting fact, and an extraordinary instance of the persistence of nature in perpetuating a type, that all the women of Cyprus to-day—who are, with scarcely any exception, ugly—have exactly the nose of the ancient Paphian Venus, that is to say, the nose of the Phoenician women whose husbands and lovers sailed the Mediterranean as long ago as the siege of Troy.

It was off the southern coast of this island, near Paphos, that Venus Aphrodite, born of the foam, is fabled to have risen from the sea. The anniversary of her birth is still perpetuated by an annual fête on the 11th of August,—a rite having its foundation in nature, that has proved to be stronger than religious instruction or prejudice. Originally, these fêtes were the scenes of a too literal worship of Venus, and even now the Cyprian maiden thinks that her chance of matrimony is increased by her attendance at this annual fair. Upon that day all the young people go upon the sea in small boats, and, until recently, it used to be the custom to dip a virgin into the water in remembrance of the mystic birth of Venus. That ceremony is still partially maintained; instead of sousing the maiden in the sea, her companions spatter the representative of the goddess with salt water,—immersion has given way here also to sprinkling.

The lively curiosity of the world has been of late years turned to Cyprus as the theatre of some of the most important and extensive archaeological discoveries of this century; discoveries unique, and illustrative of the manners and religion of a race, once the most civilized in the Levant, of which only the slightest monuments had hitherto been discovered; discoveries which supply the lost link between Egyptian and Grecian art. These splendid results, which by a stroke of good fortune confer some credit upon the American nation, are wholly due to the scholarship, patient industry, address, and enthusiasm of one man. To those who are familiar with the magnificent Cesnola Collection, which is the chief attraction of the Metropolitan Museum of New York, I need make no apology for devoting a few paragraphs to the antiquities of Cyprus and their explorer.

* * * * *

From time to time during the present century efforts have been made by individuals and by learned societies to explore the antiquities of Cyprus; but although many interesting discoveries were made, yet the field was comparatively virgin when General di Cesnola was appointed American consul in 1866. Here and there a *stele*, or some fragments of pottery, or the remains of a temple, had been unearthed by chance or by superficial search, but the few objects discovered served only to pique curiosity. For one reason or another, the efforts made to establish the site of ancient cities had been abandoned, the expeditions sent out by France had been comparatively barren of results, and it seemed as if the traces of the occupation of the Phoenicians, the Egyptians, the Assyrians, the Persians, and the Romans were irrecoverably concealed.

General L. P. di Cesnola, the explorer of Cyprus, is of a noble Piedmontese family; he received a military and classical education at Turin; identified with the party of Italian unity, his sympathies were naturally excited by the contest in America; he offered his sword to our government, and served with distinction in the war for the Union. At its close he was appointed consul at Cyprus, a position of no pecuniary attraction, but I presume that the new consul had in view the explorations which have given his name such honorable celebrity in both hemispheres.

The difficulties of his undertaking were many. He had to encounter at every step the jealousy of the Turkish government, and the fanaticism and superstition of the occupants of the soil. Archaeological researches are not easy in the East under the most favorable circumstances, and in places where the traces of ancient habitations are visible above ground, and ancient sites are known; but in Cyprus no ruins exist in sight to aid the explorer, and, with the exception of one or two localities, no names of ancient places are known to the present generation. But the consul was convinced that the great powers which had from age to age held Cyprus must have left some traces of their occupation, and that intelligent search would discover the ruins of the prosperous cities described by Strabo and mentioned by the geographer Ptolemy. Without other guides than the descriptions of these and other ancient writers, the consul began his search in 1867, and up to 1875 he had ascertained the exact sites of *eleven ancient cities* mentioned by Strabo and Ptolemy, most of which had ceased to exist before the Christian era, and none of which has left vestiges above the soil.

In the time of David and of Solomon, the Phoenicians formed the largest portion of the population of the island; their royal cities of Paphos, Amathus, Carpassa, Citium, and Ammochosto were in the most flourishing condition. Not a stone remained of them above ground; their sites were unknown in 1867.

When General di Cesnola had satisfied himself of the probable site of an ancient city or temple, it was difficult to obtain permission to dig, even with the authority of the Sultan's firman. He was obliged to wait for harvests to be gathered, in some cases, to take a lease of the ground; sometimes the religious fanaticism of the occupants could not be overcome, and his working parties were frequently beaten and driven away in his absence. But the consul exhibited tact, patience, energy, the qualities necessary, with knowledge, to a successful explorer. He evaded or cast down all obstacles.

In 1868 he discovered the necropoli of Ledra, Citium, and Idalium, and opened during three years in these localities over ten thousand tombs, bringing to light a mass of ancient objects of art which enable us to understand the customs, religion, and civilization of the earlier inhabitants. Idalium was famous of old as the place where Grecian pottery was first made, and fragments of it have been found from time to time on its site.

In 1869 and 1870 he surveyed Aphrodisium, in the northeastern part of the island, and ascertained, in the interior, the site of Golgos, a city known to have been in existence before the Trojan war. The disclosures at this place excited both the wonder and the incredulity of the civilized world, and it was not until the marvelous collection of the explorer was exhibited, partially in London, but fully in New York, that the vast importance of the labors of General di Cesnola began to be comprehended. In exploring the necropolis of Golgos, he came, a few feet below the soil, upon the remains of the temple of Venus, strewn with mutilated sculptures of the highest interest, supplying the missing link between Egyptian and Greek art, and indeed illustrating the artistic conditions of most of the Mediterranean nations during the period from at about 1200 to about 500 B.C. It would require too much space to tell how the British Museum missed and the Metropolitan of New York secured this first priceless "Cesnola Collection." Suffice it to say, that it was sold to a generous citizen of New York, Mr. John Taylor Johnson, for fifty thousand dollars,—a sum which would not compensate the explorer for his time and labor, and would little more than repay his pecuniary outlay, which reached the amount of over sixty thousand dollars in 1875. But it was enough that the treasure was secured by his adopted country; the loss of it to the Old World, which was publicly called an "European misfortune," was a piece of good fortune to the United States, which time will magnify.

From 1870 to 1872 the general's attention was directed to the southwestern portion of the island, and he laid open the necropoli of Marium, Paphos, Alamas, and Soli, and three ancient cities whose names are yet unknown. In 1873 he explored and traced the cities of Throni, Leucolla, and Arsinoë, and the necropoli of several towns still unknown. In 1874 and 1875 he brought to light the royal cities of Amathus and Curium, and located the little town of Kury.

It would not be possible here to enumerate all the objects of art or worship, and of domestic use, which these excavations have yielded. The statuary and the thousands of pieces of glass, some of them rivaling the most perfect Grecian shapes in form, and excelling the Venetian colors in the iridescence of age, perhaps attract most attention in the Metropolitan Museum. From the tombs were taken thousands of vases of earthenware, some in alabaster and bronze, statuettes in terra-cotta, arms, coins, scarabaei, cylinders, intaglios, cameos, gold ornaments, and mortuary *steles*. In the temples were brought to light inscriptions, bas-reliefs, architectural fragments, and statues of the different nations who have conquered and occupied the island. The inscriptions are in the Egyptian, Assyrian, Phoenician, Greek, and Cypriote languages; the last-mentioned being, in the opinion of the explorer, an ancient Greek dialect.

At Curium, nineteen feet below the surface of the ground, were found the remains of the Temple of Apollo Hylates; the sculptures contained in it belong to the Greek period from 700 to 100 B.C. At Amathus some royal tombs were opened, and two marble sarcophagi of large dimensions, one of them intact, were discovered, which are historically important, and positive additions to the remains of the best Greek art.

After Golgos, Paleo Paphos yielded the most interesting treasures. Here existed a temple to the Paphian Venus, whose birthplace was in sight of its portals, famous throughout the East; devotees and pilgrims constantly resorted to it, as they do now to the shrines of Mecca and Jerusalem. Not only the maritime adventurers and traders from Asia Minor and the Grecian mainland crowded to the temple of this pleasing and fortunate goddess, and quitted their vows or propitiated her favor by gifts, but the religious or the superstitious from Persia and Assyria and farthest Egypt deposited there their votive offerings. The collector of a museum of antiquity that should illustrate the manners and religion of the thousand years before the Christian era could ask nothing better than these deposits of many races during many centuries in one place.

The excavations at Paphos were attended with considerable danger; more than once the workmen were obliged to flee to save their lives from the fanatic Moslems. The town, although it has lost its physical form, and even its name (its site is now called Baffo), retains the character of superstition it had when St. Paul found it expedient to darken the vision of Elymas there, as if a city, like a man, possessed a soul that outlives the body. We spent the afternoon in examining the new collection of General di Cesnola, not so large as that in the Metropolitan Museum, but perhaps richer in some respects, particularly in iridescent glass.

In the summer of 1875, however, the labors of the indefatigable explorer were crowned with a discovery the riches of which cast into the shade the real or pretended treasures of the "House of Priam,"—a discovery not certainly of more value to art than those that preceded it, but well calculated to excite popular wonder. The finding of this subterranean hoard reads like an adventure of Aladdin.

In pursuing his researches at Curium, on the southwestern side of the island, General di Cesnola came upon the site of an ancient temple, and uncovered its broken mosaic pavement. Beneath this, and at the depth of twenty-five feet, he broke into a subterranean passage cut in the rock. This passage led to a door; no genie sat by it, but it was securely closed by a stone slab. When this was removed, a suite of four rooms was disclosed, but they were not immediately accessible; earth sifting through the roofs for ages had filled them, and it required the labor of a month to clean out the chambers. Imagine the feverish enthusiasm of the explorer as he slowly penetrated this treasure-house, where every stroke of the pick disclosed the gleam of buried treasure! In the first room were found only gold objects; in the second only silver and silver-gilt ornaments and utensils; in the third alabasters, terra-cottas, vases, and groups of figures; in the fourth bronzes, and nothing else. It is the opinion of the discoverer that these four rooms were the depositories where the crafty priests and priestesses of the old temple used to hide their treasures during times of war or sudden invasion. I cannot but think that the mysterious subterranean passages and chambers in the ancient temples of Egypt served a similar purpose. The treasure found scattered in these rooms did not appear to be the whole belonging to the temple, but only a part, left perhaps in the confusion of a hasty flight.

Among the articles found in the first room, dumped in a heap in the middle (as if they had been suddenly, in a panic, stripped from the altar in the temple and cast into a place of concealment), were a gold cup covered with Egyptian embossed work, and two bracelets of pure gold weighing over *three pounds*, inscribed with the name of "Etevander, King of Paphos." This king lived in 635 B.C., and in 620 B.C. paid tribute to the Assyrian monarch Assurbanipal (Sardanapalus), as is recorded on an Assyrian tablet now in the British Museum. There were also many gold necklaces, bracelets, ear-rings, finger-rings, brooches, seals, armlets, etc., in all four hundred and eighty gold articles.

In the silver-room, arranged on the benches at the sides, were vases, bottles, cups, bowls, bracelets, finger-rings, ear-rings, seals, etc. One of the most curious and valuable objects is a silver-gilt bowl, having upon it very fine embossed Egyptian work, and evidently of high antiquity.

In the third room of vases and terra-cottas were some most valuable and interesting specimens. The bronze-room yielded several high candelabra, lamp-holders, lamps, statuettes, bulls'-heads, bowls, vases, jugs, patera, fibula, rings, bracelets, mirrors, etc. Nearly all the objects in the four rooms seem to have been "votive offerings," and testify a pagan devotion to the gods not excelled by Christians generosity to the images and shrines of modern worship. The inscriptions betoken the votive character of these treasures; that upon the heavy gold armlets is in the genitive case, and would be literally translated "Etevandri Regis Paphi," the words "offering of" being understood to precede it.

I confess that the glitter of these treasures, and the glamour of these associations with the ingenious people of antiquity, transformed the naked island of Cyprus, as we lay off it in the golden sunset, into a region of all possibilities, and I longed to take my Strabo and my spade and wander off prospecting for its sacred places. It seemed to me, when we weighed anchor at seven o'clock, that we were sailing away from subterranean passages stuffed with the curious treasures of antiquity, from concealed chambers in which one, if he could only remove the stone slab of the door, would pick up the cunning work of the Phoenician jewelers, the barbarous ornaments of the Assyrians, the conceits in gold and silver of the most ancient of peoples, the Egyptians.

Poole 1869

Although R. (Reginald) Stuart Poole visited Cyprus in 1869, he did not record his trip until his article "Cyprus: its Present and Future" in pages 137-154 of the August 1878 issue of *The Contemporary Review*, London. The major part of his article summarizes consular reports from Riddell and Lang on the status of Cyprus agriculture, mining, forestry, commerce and ports. Poole attempts to weigh the desire of the area for British administration, the past depredations of Cyprus by the Turks, and the many questions about its potential.

Any Englishman who has visited the Eastern Mediterranean, and spoken to the natives in their own languages, has not seldom been perplexed by the question, "When are the English coming?" A Greek or a Syrian Christian has been put off with a sketch of the international difficulties to be encountered, a Muslim by some such simpler reply as "God is with the patient."

It is not hard to find the cause of this wish for English government. Profoundly dissatisfied with the rule of Constantinople and Cairo, the subjects desire a system which shall be at once strong, just, and tolerant. Where the two religions live side by side, without actual civil war, there is little craving for the creation of small principalities, administered in the interests of one part of the community, or the annexation to some little state already overstrained by the struggle of existence. No doubt Nemesis rightly decided that the Muslim should be expelled from the young kingdom of Greece, but the barbarity of the manner in which this was done, retribution being changed to revenge, has had its effect in limiting that interesting state. No doubt every Greek would wish to be a subject of the Hellenic kingdom, but many would desire that the difficulties should be smoothed over by that kind of administration which preceded the transfer of the Septinsular Republic to its proper ruler.

It is not difficult to understand why the native Christian, even when he is of the ambitious and intelligent Greek race, should be not unwilling that the difficult task of government should be given to safe hands; but at first sight it seems strange that the Muslim should desire this more strongly . . . Muslim pilgrims, Armenian and Parsee merchants, carry about them, consciously or unconsciously, the evidence of what English government is; and the desire for it in the Levant constantly increases.

It is not surprising, therefore, that the occupation of Cyprus should be welcome to the people, nor that their neighbours should rejoice at the effect which a well-governed province of an empire, protected on the condition that it shall reform its administration, must inevitably produce. Even the Constantinople Turk may see the moral of a contented country with a constantly increasing revenue.

* * * * *

[p. 145]

It is obvious that much of what is needed, if done at all, will be the work of private enterprise. Therefore it is necessary to ascertain how far Cyprus is adapted to Westerns as a residence. There are very different opinions as to its healthiness. The unfavourable one is probably founded on the malarious climate of Larnaka, due to the immediate neighbourhood of the salt-marshes. Places on the coast, well above the sea level and in dry neighbourhoods, such as Pyla, to the east of Larnaka, and villages in the interior above the plain, are healthy. I would advise English settlers to establish themselves within a few hours' ride of Larnaka until the administration has been thoroughly established. The immediate neighbourhood of a Turkish village might at first be undesirable. It is important to add that it is doubtful whether English children can be safely reared in the island; certainly Larnaka is ill-suited to them.

Our interest in the material well-being of Cyprus implies an interest in the population. What are its races and religions, and how proportioned, and are there any serious difficulties in the way of their living peaceably together? Ethnologically, the Cypriotes are of the old stock of the island, not Hellenic, perhaps, but rather proto-Hellenic,—I would, if I dared use so dangerous a term, say Pelasgic. No one who looks at them with archaeological eyes, not through the tinted glasses of the most picturesque of modern travellers, but sees before him frequently the type of the old sculptures—the round head, the large black eyes set a little obliquely in the plane of the face, the marked projecting nose, large and slightly hooked, the full lips, and the curling black hair, with the strong, thick-set, short frame—characteristics marking a vigorous race, in which the Aryan most nearly approaches the Shemite. It may be that there is a touch of the Phoenician. In character the Cypriote is patient, frugal, hard-working, law-abiding—Greek Christian and Muslim natives alike. The Greek has the domestic virtues which are the glory of the Hellenic race, without the cunning which is its shame. Like all the Levantine populations, he is timid of disease, and hence the barbarous treatment of the lepers, touchingly described by General di Cesnola (Cyprus, 244 seqq.).

The population of Cyprus, like that of the other provinces of the Turkish Empire, is not known with exactness; I believe it is about, certainly not more than, 120,000, two-thirds of whom are Greek Christians, the remaining third Mohammadans. Here I am forced to digress in order to remove the current error which speaks of the whole Mohammadan population of Turkey as Turks. This population should be divided into the true Turk, who may be considered as comprising various Tatar stocks, at the head of which stands the 'Osmánlee; and the descendants of converts, who may be called neo-Muslims. It is very important to the true understanding of the present Eastern Question that we should discriminate the two groups. The Turk, like all Turanians (I use the term in the ethnographical sense), is not intolerant, though like the Chinese he does not scruple to raise the weapon of fanaticism for political purposes. This has brought him into fierce conflict with the Greek Church, the most patriotic Church in the world, which at every moment of national effort has put itself at the head of the people, to retire the moment that freedom has been won—a profound historical truth I owe to M. Gennadius the Hellenic Minister. It is moreover hard for a Muslim to be tolerant. There have been noble examples, as of the Arab Prince of Spain who observed Sunday, no doubt for the sake of his Christian slaves. An administration in the hands of half-breeds and renegades, a press led by a renegade, the editor of the Constantinople *Jawáïb*, and religious doctors under foreign influence, and many of them foreigners, added to the love of dominion, have neutralized the tolerant element in the Turk. The learned men of Turkey have still to discover what their Indian brethren are elaborating, that Islám must move with the times, and that the Kurán and the Traditions contain the materials for the necessary changes. The 'Osmánlee again is of three classes—(1) the official Turk, usually a half-breed, the son of a Circassian mother to whose influence he owes his first and strongest training, who when he arrives at years of discretion takes to himself as many Circassian favourites as he can afford, and usually lives upon the plunder of the poor; (2) the tradesman, a refined and honourable gentleman, usually the husband of one wife of his own race, who is rarely divorced; (3) the peasant, honest, patient, frugal, without much initiative or desire to work for his own profit, and not without the tradesman's domestic virtues. The Turkish woman, the wife of the middle and lower classes, is active, thrifty, and faithful, but ungifted with physical beauty. She is the bravest of civilized women, loads her husband's gun in a siege, and, if he is in bad health, grooms the most unruly horse for him. [*Footnote:* This is no flourish. I am thinking of an honest Turkish woman who groomed the most savage horse I ever saw to keep her aged husband in service. She managed Bucephalus admirably, never losing her presence of mind or her face-veil.] I would except from the general condemnation of the mushroom aristocracy the honest old Derebeys, and such greater magnates as Kará 'Osmán Oglu, who governed Smyrna and put down the brigands fifty years ago. These landed gentry, the hope of the Turkish Empire, have been destroyed or reduced to beggary by the bureaucrat of Constantinople, who hates nothing so much as his opposite, an honest 'Osmánlee in power.

The descendants of converts, whom I have called neo-Muslims, are to be found in every part of the Empire. Their characteristics depend on the qualities of each race and the reasons for which they are Muslims. It is essential to understand these factors, for the history and present state of Turkey loudly proclaim their importance. It was to the Janissaries, forced converts, that the Turks owed their conquests, and with their destruction the decline of the Empire was fixed. At the present day the seats of the fiercest strife are not where a Turkish and a Christian population are side by side, but where a ruling stock of neo-Muslims, like the Bosnian Beys and the Bulgarian Pomaks, are in danger of losing their prerogative or being actually destroyed in a religious war. Crete, inhabited by a population of Greek Christians and Greek Muslims, is already in a state of ferment, and there is a risk of the recurrence of the last general war. These are instances of Slav, Tatar-Slav, and Greek Muslim, races in each of which fighting qualities have been fostered by Islám. Among these neo-Muslims there are, however, many secret Christians or politic neo-Muslims, whose children are baptized as well as admitted Muslims, and consequently have two names, one Christian the other Mohammadan. This whole section is either anxious or not unwilling to return to its former faith, and the European Governments would do well to look carefully to the interests and safety of the timid brethren, nor less to protect the section who are rather politic than sincere, but whose return to the Church would make them more manageable citizens.

I can now return to the constituent parts of the population of Cyprus. The Mohammadans, about one-third of the whole or roughly 40,000, are either Turkish or neo-

Muslim. The Turks are mainly confined to the towns (such as Nicosia, Famagosta, and Paphos, also Leuca), and are probably for the most part 'Osmánlees. They are more fanatical than the other Muslims, and thus the general condition of the Empire is reversed and the work of government incomparably easier. The neo-Muslims are of Greek origin, speaking Greek, and similar in character to the native Christians: many of them are Christians in secret. It speaks well for the Cypriotes that the indigenous Mohammadanism has not developed fanaticism.

The Greek Christians are in manners as in language similar to their cousins the Hellenes. Their dialect is marked by many peculiarities which would make ordinary Romaïc often of little use in the villages. I would advise any one intending a lengthened stay in the island to supplement a good colloquial knowledge of Romaïc by a careful study of Professor Mullach's "Grammatik der Griechischen Vulgarsprache" in relation to Cypriote. In creed the Greeks of Cyprus are of the Orthodox Church, which is wealthy and has several convents. They have their own schools, though education is far below the level of the Hellenic kingdom and Ionia. It is to be hoped that the great revenues of the archiepiscopate of Nicosia, which I have heard put at a sum I am afraid to state, for I cannot believe it to be correct, will be partly used for educational purposes. Freedom will no doubt stimulate the Cypriote Christians to rival the other Greek communities in this direction. The Greeks, the Syrians, and the Armenians have the future of the Levant in their hands if they seize the present opportunity.

The Christian population, enjoying in common with all Greeks family life in its purest and most unselfish form, is sure to increase under a good government. [*Footnote:* The old Greek at whose house I lodged at Dali in 1869 had a son of forty. "It is time," he had said, "the child should marry." Accordingly he gave him house and land, and with his old wife lived in a corner.] The Muslims are undoubtedly diminishing. General di Cesnola (Cyprus, p. 193) assigns the same cause for this which the author of the most remarkable and valuable of late works on modern Turkey (The People of Turkey, ii. 18 seq.) states of the Turks generally, the deliberate destruction of unborn offspring, and, if polygamy be added, no one need wonder. General di Cesnola and the authoress referred to appear to speak of the 'Osmánlees; this is important in reference to the character and prospects of the Muslim Cypriotes. A people which does not wish for children and which maintains a social system tending to the extinction of any but a barbarous race must be content to die slowly away, leaving its lands to their lawful heirs.

It may be asked in what manner English government will affect the different sections of the population. Beyond the great relief they will feel from being freed from the abominable over-taxation, there are circumstances which will render our rule especially welcome. At the head of these stand civil and religious liberty. Civil liberty will not be at once understood, and the freeing of the negro slaves held by the Muslims will be unwelcome, although where they have been fairly used they will remain as freedmen with all the advantages and none of the drawbacks of what is certainly the best form of modern slavery. In the matter of religious liberty the gain will be enormous. The Greeks will not be afraid to avow the wealth of their Church, and openly to use that wealth as already suggested for all the good purposes to which it can be applied. The Muslims will find their religious foundations, never yet secure from alienation under the 'Osmánlee rule, absolutely guaranteed by the English Convention. It is to their honour that nothing could tend so much as this, not even the removal of the intolerable burdens of taxation, to reconcile them to the change of rule.

A word may be added to travellers. They should not visit Cyprus unless they are prepared for rough travelling. In 1869 I passed a delightful fortnight there without post, newspapers, gas, roads, carriages, milk, butter, or drinking water; but this was in the great drought. Now that the "milordos" has come, the rate of living will soon rise, and the necessaries of life rapidly appear. Without a yacht the best mode of reaching the island is from Beyroot to Larnaka. It may be doubted whether any but a powerful steam-yacht should risk the open roadsteads of Cyprus, particularly on the storm-beaten north coast. There is no inn deserving the name at Larnaka or any other town, but the Consuls and the officers of the Ottoman Bank will give information as to quarters. The best plan is to engage servants at their recommendation and leave Larnaka as soon as may be. The Marina, the port and European quarter, is malarious, and on no account should windows be left open at night in sleeping rooms, nor is it wise to be out after sunset in the immediate neighbourhood. Mules may be hired here. A good cook and a small canteen, to be carried by one mule, are indispensable. For the summer, tents may be taken; in the winter, quarters may be obtained for a small sum at the Greek villages, where the inhabitants readily give up their best rooms for hire. If possible those chosen for sleeping rooms should be above the ground-floor, and the servants should be sent in first to clean them out and spread the travelling mattresses. In the case of the towns hospitality will be readily given by Greek merchants. In return some acceptable present,—a Greek Bible of an edition authorized by the Church, a tract of St. Chrysostom, or a Homer,—would be very welcome to an old-fashioned Cypriote. In all cases the servants of the host should receive presents, on a scale ascertained at Larnaka before starting, which in no case should be exceeded. In associating with Turks a few rules of etiquette should be carefully observed if the traveller wishes to be respected. These are easily learnt. In all cases familiarity should be discouraged by gravity of manner. Those who wish to understand the people would do wisely to pass a few weeks before starting in learning Romaïc.

Larnaka is a good central point for excursions to Salamis, Dali, Nicosia, Paphos, and Curium, as well as for the ascent of Mounts Olympus and Stavro. Other places are nearer to several of these points, but would be far less suitable as a basis of the traveller's operations. What he has most to observe will be stated almost immediately. The lover of scenery may be disappointed unless he can see beauty in almost bare mountains and wide-stretching plain. The naturalist will, whether geologist, zoologist, or botanist, find much to repay him, and it is to be hoped that the national love of destruction will not scare away or exterminate the rarer animals.

The mineral wealth of Cyprus may be uncertain, but there can be no doubt of its archaeological riches. Some sites may indeed have been well-nigh exhausted by that fortunate explorer General di Cesnola, but others are almost untouched. There is little to be seen above ground of the remains of antiquity: the traveller will be disappointed if he expects to be rewarded by such sights as those of Egypt, Italy, or Greece. Cyprus, like Assyria, is a land of buried cities. Nor will ordinary taste, even of a very cultivated kind, be rewarded by exploration. The work is interesting alone to the serious student of the remote annals of the Mediterranean. To him the antiquities of the island are a precious connecting-link between Egypt, Assyria, and early Greece, and the less attractive they are to the artistic eye the more valuable are they to his comparative vision.

It is not long since I endeavoured to show the place and value of Cypriote antiquities. Here I will only repeat that they probably range from the Trojan age, perhaps B.C. 1200, to the close of the Greek dominion, in a series of monumental records unrivalled for continuous succession anywhere in the world save in Egypt, that they are in origin and characteristics Phoenician, bearing the impress of the art of the nations which in turn ruled the Eastern Mediterranean, Greek art alone being but faintly represented. The character of Oriental taste was too firmly fixed for Hellenic art, late in arrival and never wholly welcome to the national instincts, to plant itself securely here. Had Cyprus enjoyed the good fortune of Rhodes, the next stepping-stone westwards of Phoenician commerce and the last eastwards of true Hellenic culture, we might anticipate dazzling results from excavations in the island. Not alone the national taste forbids this hope: the soft limestone of the island lends itself with a fatal facility to the production of inferior art, and thus Cypriote statues are little superior to the lower class of terra-cottas in force of execution and attention to detail.

Any one who wishes to know the general characteristics of the art monuments of Cyprus has only to examine the good typical series of statues and statuettes from the famous city of Idalium in the British Museum. They are arranged at the entrance of the great Egyptian gallery on the ground floor. They comprise everything of importance found by Mr. Lang in an ancient temple which had been destroyed on the overthrow of paganism. Among the archaic vases and terra-cottas in the upper gallery will be found good typical examples of Cypriote work. Those who would gain a fuller knowledge of the subject should consult General di Cesnola's "Cyprus," where in the excellent plates they will see not alone many more specimens of the statues of each period of Cypriote art, but also many fine examples of metal work, in which his excavations were unusually productive.

The most interesting remains have been found in the ancient royal cities, capitals of the small kingdoms into which the island was divided for at least four centuries before it became part of the kingdom of the first Ptolemy. The Annals of Sargon, repeated in the Larnaka stele, mention the submission of the seven kings of Cyprus . . . Esarhaddon enumerates the ten kings of Cyprus as subjects . . . The capitals vary at different times, and the number of the kingdoms also. The minority of the kings were Phoenicians, the rest Cypriotes, the royal race of Salamis boasting of a Greek origin. When the kings were confederate, the ruler of Salamis seems to have taken the lead, and the famous Euagoras, in the middle of the fourth century, was virtually king of the whole island, waging for ten years a successful war with Persia, which left him independent. Paphos was the chief seat of the worship of the national goddess Aphrodite, whose cultus was originally Phoenician. Citium, from its position, was a great port of the island, only rivalled by Salamis. These three cities were the chief places under the rule of the Ptolemies, and we find the governor uniting the functions of high priest, admiral, and general, for Paphos, Salamis, and Citium, though we do not yet know which of the two ports was the chief naval station.

Paphos has not yet yielded any very important results to the explorer, in spite of the efforts of General di Cesnola. The great temple, as rebuilt by Vespasian, in the archaic form, after it had been destroyed by an earthquake,—well portrayed, with its fish-pond, sacred doves, and strange conical stones, on the Roman coinage of Cyprus,—is now only represented by shapeless ruins, owing perhaps to the effect of successive earthquakes, as General di Cesnola remarks. His explorations here were unproductive.

At Citium the harbour and the walls of the ancient city may still be traced southward of the modern town of Larnaca. Besides a remarkable tomb of Phoenician style, there is little above ground. Excavations have however been rewarded with some objects of interest. The Assyrian stele, bearing the figure and annals of Sargon, was found here, and is now in the Berlin Museum (Cesnola, p. 47). A low hill on the edge of the salt-marsh which represents the old harbour has yielded an abundance of small terra-cottas of Greek style. Being of the Macedonian period, they are far inferior to the figures of Tanagra, but on the whole they will be more interesting to the generality than anything else in the range of the antiquities. With them Cypriote figures are found, either older, or, as is more probable, preserving the traditions of hieratic art: among these General di Cesnola notices the cow-headed goddess (pp. 51, 52).

Salamis has been even less productive than Citium. Probably in both cases the remains have been used for building purposes by the mediaeval rulers of the island and the Turks.

Idalium, Golgos, Curium, and Amathus have been the scenes of the happiest explorations. It may be doubted whether more than one of these sites has not been worked out. Yet here, as elsewhere, many small antiquities, as well as inscriptions, are still to be looked for . . .

Nothing undoubtedly Egyptian has yet been discovered in Cyprus. as far as I know, except a little mummy-figure of the time of the Twenty-sixth dynasty (B.C. 664-525), found in Carpás, which either General di Cesnola or Mr. Lang showed me at Larnaka. But it is not at all impossible that some record of Egyptian conquest, like the stele of Sargon, may yet be discovered. Egyptian objects, anterior in date to the Assyrian age would be of the greatest interest.

More Assyrian remains may confidently be looked for, in the shape of tablets, documentary clay cylinders, and ornaments.

All remains in the Cypriote character should be carefully preserved. It is by no means impossible that they may reach up to a very early age, far beyond the oldest Greek records. A word is due to this character and its interpretation, the latest fruit of the brilliant labours of the schools of Champollion and Rawlinson . . .

Coins will be the commonest of interesting antiquities brought to the traveller. The most important are those bearing Cypriote inscriptions, probably ranging from the sixth century to the middle of the fourth. The Phoenician coinages of the kings of Citium and Idalium, dating in the fifth and fourth centuries B.C., deserve the next place. Both these illustrate the religion and history of the island. A few fine Greek coins of Paphos and Salamis have come to light, but they were evidently scantily issued. Under the Ptolemies the mints of Cyprus struck abundant money, and as the greater part of the silver coins are dated, the class is of unusual historical interest. The Roman coins of Paphos with the representation of the great temple of Aphrodite are not uncommon. Of subsequent currencies the most interesting is that of the Lusignan kings of Cyprus, a complete representative series of which is very hard to obtain.

The mediaeval remains, particularly those of the Lusignan dynasty at Nicosia, and of the Genoese at Famagosta, merit careful study, and the architecture of the convents should also be examined.

I cannot end this imperfect essay without expressing a wish that the act which the satisfaction of the English nation and the joy of the people of Cyprus has ratified may be increasingly welcome to both,—to us welcome as the fulfilment of a promise to which our honour is bound, to them welcome as a pledge of better times, which shall see the East renewed,

"And bring all Cyprus comfort."

Cesnola 1871

Luigi Palma de Cesnola, the second American to serve as consul to Cyprus, was one of the most colorful visitors to Cyprus. An Italian army officer, he emigrated to the United States, where he cultivated important families in New York as a translator and language teacher. With their help he raised a company to fight for the Union in the Civil War and rose to the rank of colonel. He gave himself the rank of general after the war, but the army never confirmed it. Hoping to return to northern Italy as a consul, he accepted appointment to Cyprus and served from August 8, 1865 to August 17, 1876 when the consulate was closed while he was on leave.

Known for his rapacious excavation and collection of Cypriot antiquities during his consulship, he failed to sell significant portions of his collection to the Louvre, the British Museum, the Berlin Museum, or the Hermitage. He negotiated successfully with a group of important citizens in New York including his earlier friends which resulted in the founding of the Metropolitan Museum of Art based on his collection of well over 30,000 pieces. After his consulship he returned to New York to become the first director of the Museum.

The full account of his excavating activities is contained in his *Cyprus; Its Ancient Cities, Tombs and Temples;* New York: Harper and Brothers, 1878 and reissued in 1991 in Nicosia. The collection in the Metropolitan Museum is detailed in his multi-volume publication *A Descriptive Atlas of the Cesnola Collection of Cypriote Antiquities in the Metropolitan Museum of Art;* Boston: James R. Osgood and Company, 1885. Cesnola also authored *The Antiquities of Cyprus Discovered Principally on the Sites of Ancient Golgoi and Idalion,* with photographs by Stephen Thomson, published in London, 1873, by W. A. Mansell & Co.

The selection included here, an early account of his work at Golgoi, was reported in Italian to the Royal Academy of Sciences at Turin, which published it in the Annals of the Academy, 1871. Cesnola translated it into English and included it in a consular report to Assistant Secretary of State Hunter on July 5, 1871; the text, written in Cesnola's clear hand, is contained in *Despatches from the United States Consuls in Cyprus, 1835-1878* Vol. 1. (Washington, D.C., National Archives, Microcopy T-463). Cesnola's footnotes have been omitted; except for obvious slips, his spelling and punctuation have been retained.

U.S. Consulate at Cyprus
Larnaca, July 5, 1871

Hon. W. Hunter
          Asst. Secretary of State
                    Washington, D.C.
Sir   I have the honor herewith to enclose a translation from Italian of a Report I was requested to make to the Royal Academy of Sciences at Turin (of which I am an honorary member) upon my archaeological researches in this island which have resulted in the very important discovery of a large Phoenician Necropolis and of the fa-

mous Temple of Venus at Golgos one of the most ancient cities of Cyprus. This last discovery has been for many years past the constant object of fruitless researches made by order of and at the expense of the Imperial Government of France.

I have translated this report into English because I believe that if the Department thinks fit to have it published it may be found of some interest especially to our American archaeologists and classical scholars.

I have the honor to be
Most Respectfully
Your Obdt Servant
L. P. de Cesnola
U.S. Consul

Enclosures
1. Report on archaeological discoveries.

Archaeological Researches

Discovery of a Phoenician Necropolis, and the Temple of Venus at Golgi, in the island of Cyprus.

Report of Gen. de Cesnola read before the Royal Academy of Sciences at Turin, by one of its Members (Prof. A. Fabretti,) and published in the annals of the Academy, 1871.

The ancient history of Cyprus, up to the epoch of the Crusades, is so wrapped in obscurity, that it is impossible to be able to assert any fact whatsoever, with the assurance of not being mistaken.

The practical archaeologist, and by this I mean the intelligent and learned excavator, will be able to throw on this darkness, a clear light, if his future diggings, are superintended by himself in person, and he keeps a journal or diary of whatever he finds and also of whatever matter of interest falls under his observation.

There is not, in my opinion, another locality which presents like the island of Cyprus, an agglomeration, so to say, of all the ancient arts belonging to so many different Nations, which for long centuries have ceased to exist: for the reason, that this island although it had a particular language of its own has always from the remotest period, been dependent from other powerful Nations; such as Egypt, Assyria, Persia, Greece, Rome, etc; though governed by its native kings.

In fact 707 years before the Christian era, Cyprus was ruled by seven Cypriot kings, who sent ambassadors with their tributes consisting of gold and silver vases, etc to Sargon King of Assyria (the father of Sennacherib) who from Nineveh, or more probably from Khorsabad, had transferred and held his court in Babylon, which he had just conquered.

These Cypriot Ambassadors, when they returned to Cyprus, brought to their kings as a proof of their submission, a bas relief on black basalt, upon which there was sculptured the effigy of King Sargon, and a long inscription in cuneiform characters. This stone was discovered here in Larnaca (the ancient Citium) in the year 1846 and is now in the Royal Museum at Berlin.

From the ancient authors, very little information can be gathered, in regard to the true history of the past of this island; some being in open contradiction with each other. We find in Pausanias that when Agapenor from Troy, brought his colony of warriors to Paphos, (afterwards one of the most famous cities of Cyprus) in order to build the Great Temple dedicated to Venus, the Cypriots were already worshipping this divinity, in a Temple at Golgi; and that the city itself was also dedicated to Venus. Another author (Lycophron) assures us instead, that it was at Paphos where the first Temple dedicated to Venus was erected in this island; but such assertion is not founded on any other authority, than his own, and he asks if by chance Golgi and Paphos, might not have been the same city. Pliny in his 5th book, makes a very clear distinction between these two cities, which in fact did exist at a distance of 97 miles from each other, as was recently proved beyond all doubt.

Strabo and Ptolemy, who wrote of the existence in ancient times of two cities called Paphos, do not make any mention of Golgi.

The Byzantine Stephanos, and the latin Poets who spoke of Golgi, mentioned one Paphos only. The above named Stephanos states, that Paphos was in ancient times known under the name of Erythree and that Golgi, was a Cyprian city so called, after the name of its founder, who had come from Lycion (now Basilicata) to inhabit the island of Cyprus prior to the Troyan war.

Catullus speaking of the worship of Venus says "Quae Sanctum Idalium uriosque apertos. Colis quaeque Amathunta quaeque Golgos," and the same author in another place thus expresses himself, "Quaeque Regis Golgos, quaeque Idalium frondosum," and in fact these two cities Idalium and Golgi or Golgos, by my recent discoveries, have been proved beyond question, to have existed at short distance from each other.

Theocritus in his 15th Idilium thus speaks of Venus "Goddess who loves as much Idalium as Golgos," and affirms that she was also called Venus of Golgos.

During my residence in this island, I have visited attentively all the localities, which tradition more than anything else, pointed out to me the sites, whereupon existed once the famous historical cities of Salamis, Carpassium, Golgos, Idalium, Citium, Curium, Marium, Amathunta, Soli, Kithrea, Tamasus, and the two Paphos; and thereupon I undertook excavations more or less extensive, which sufficiently convinced me, that such cities must have effectively existed in those neighborhoods.

Archaeological excavations in this island, present many more difficulties than elsewhere; and this for three essential reasons:

The first, because there does not exist any ancient history of this island, worth such a name, which points out to the archaeologist the exact site, whereon were built the ancient cities; and he is compelled to be guided by what the inhabitants of the neighborhood tell him, and not unfrequently he is misled, through their ignorance as has happened to me more than once.

The second reason is, because no ruins or traces of any kind, can be seen on the surface of the ground; and it becomes necessary at a great expense, to search for them sometimes at several yards beneath; because the ancient buildings, were made of earth or bricks dried at the Sun which in progress of time, having decayed, fell upon their stone foundations, and covered them entirely. Some years afterwards these sundried bricks, were by the yearly rains reduced to their primitive condition of loose earth, and formed upon said foundations a compact kind of covering, which after so many centuries took a natural form; and the Cypriot with his plough which is still the facsimile of the ancient Roman Aratrum opens with it only the few inches of ground necessary for his farming purposes.

By their traditions however, when the natives require stones for building, they generally know what spot to select for that object; and thus have become reliable aids to the scientific inquirer.

The third reason, is the not small difficulty presented by the fact, that the ancient names of these localities, have nearly all been changed; and if one excepts Dali, Amathos, Kithrea, which have more or less preserved up to the present day their ancient etymology, the other cities would be quite impossible from their actual name, to recognise. In fact Citium, (the Chittim of the Scriptures) is called Larnaca; Golgi or Golgos, has changed its name into that of a village built with its ruins called Athieno (perhaps a corruption of Athens); Curium and its beautiful bay have received the name of Episkopi; Soli is called now Karavastasi; Paphos where Agapenor built the famous temple, and known under the Roman denomination as old Paphos, is called Kouklia; the other Paphos which was just rebuilt by the Romans, when St. Paul came there to preach the Gospel is denominated Ktima and so on.

In 1866 I went first to visit the few ruins brought to light by the French Archaeologists where once existed the oldest city of Cyprus which is Golgi. This is only two hours and a half distant from Larnaca. In its immediate neighborhood, there is the village of Athieno which as I said before, was chiefly built with its ancient stone.

It is at this place that the distinguished French Archaeologist Count de Vognè, Mas Latrie, Du Toit, De Gauley, and others of less note, undertook excavations, some on their private account, others in behalf of the French Government; always with the object of discovering the Temple of Venus, but without success.

In 1864 the French Government, I am told, sent here a person who must have spent large sums of money, from the extensive ground explored by him in search of the Temple. But this gentleman allowed himself to be guided too much in his researches, like his predecessors, by the fact that the ancients in general, built their places of worship upon heights like the Greeks on their acropolis; and as Athieno is surrounded by hills he had excavations made upon all those, which form a semicircle around Athieno in the northeastern direction, but as I said before without success.

It is true nevertheless, that these gentlemen if they were unable to find the Temple, they have established beyond doubt, that the site called by the natives Yorgos was the ancient Golgos, Golgi, or Golghiou as it is denominated by different ancient authors.

Remaining but a few days at Golgi in 1866, I caused excavations to be made in several places, but also without any satisfactory result.

Thence I went to visit the village of Dali, which from what I saw, I became convinced, is built if not on the identical spot, at least very near where the far famed Phoenician city of Idalium once existed. I stopped for a few days in that poor village, and invited by a peasant to visit an old tomb which he had discovered, while searching for stones to repair his house I soon convinced myself, that I was walking upon the Necropolis of

Idalium; and in fact, in the course of three years diggings, I opened with my men over eight thousand tombs!

Encouraged by that important discovery, I decided in the winter of 1870 upon re-visiting Athieno, for the purpose of making diligent researches, for the necropolis of Golgi, which could not fail to be either in the valley, or at the feet of the neighboring hills and verily I had the good fortune, not only to find it, but without expecting, or hoping it, I discovered the Temple itself, the object of so much labor, and as many fruitless re-searches during half a century; not upon the summit, or on the slope but precisely at the foot of a hill, upon which the French Archaeologists, had made very deep and extensive excavations, but in a wrong direction.

The area occupied by the Temple, was well delineated by its stone foundations, which I discovered at a depth of 3 and a half yards, and was 60 English feet in length, and 29 in width; and yet in such a small enclosure, I found the remains of upwards of one thousand statues of every dimensions!

They were dug out with precaution, but nearly all of them were found more or less mutilated; this would go to prove, that the Temple was either destroyed by hordes of for-eign invaders before the Christian era, or by the Christian fanaticism in its earlier period. It is more probable that the latter hypothesis is the correct one; because towards the center of the Temple, I found on the stone pavement coals, and a considerable strata of ashes of several inches in thickness.

About one third of these statues were of lifesize; two colossal; several gigantic or semicolossal; and the remainder of every size; from three feet and a half in height, to a few inches only. The form of the Temple was quadrangular; to what order of archi-tecture it belongs, was not easy to decide. The bases of columns however, which I found at the doors of the Temple belonged to the two oldest known; that is the Doric, and Ionic. The Columns could not be found; probably because they were merely of wood, a thing which Pausanias assures us to have been greatly in use in ancient times, especially in Asia Minor.

This Temple had two doors; one opening on the Southeastern wall, and the other on that facing Northwest. If it had opposite to these doors two others I was unable to as-certain it, for the reason that the diggings of Count de Voguè (now French Ambassador at Constantinople) directed by him several years ago, extended diagonally down the hill, and destroyed without knowing it, the Southwestern corner of the Temple.

A strange, and not usual thing in ancient Temples, is that the two doors were not in the center but towards the extremity of the walls.

Attiguous to the two longitudinal walls of the Temple, still placed in several lines, I found a great quantity of pedestals of every dimension, some with bas reliefs upon; oth-ers with Cyprian inscriptions but the largest number of them without anything.

In the center of the Temple, at distances which I forgot to measure, but which very probably were equal with each other, there were three files of double pedestals, upon which it appears, statues were placed back to back; this would explain satisfactory to me at least, the reason why, almost all these statues therein found, had only the front part sculptured.

Amongst the rubbish in the Temple, were found two stone chairs, one of which much mutilated and several small vases which I believe contained the necessary oil to feed a great number of lamps.

A large stone vase (similar to that found at Amathunta by the French Count which is now at the Louvre) was discovered all in pieces; near the Southeastern entrance which doubtless must have been used for their religious ablutions. A smaller one was found entire at the other entrance of the Temple.

Scattered here and there in the pavement of the Temple, I discoverd a great quantity of votive offerings in stone; such as nurses or mothers with babes, eyes, ears, fingers, very much like those one sees at the present day in the Greek, and Catholic sanctuaries; but what characterises principally the Temple of Golgos, is the abundance of votive Phalluses or Priapes found therein.

The height of the Temple, if I have to measure it, or rather calculate it from one of the two colossal heads I found therein, must have been at least from 30 to 40 feet; because the head alone measures over three and a half feet in length; so that, considering it as the seventh portion of the body, that statue when whole, must have been about 25 feet high; the rain or sun, have not left any visible traces upon the stone, to lead me to suppose, that the Temple was without roof; as in the remotest times they used to be.

I greatly doubt if the Temple had windows; because of the great quantity of stone lamps, which were found scattered all over the pavement. Two of them had the form of a little Temple with two columns painted in red of the Ionic order; a lamp was cut in the stone, which bears yet the black traces of smoke.

The Temple was dedicated to Venus, but even if the ancient authors had not mentioned it, some of the votive offerings, and the bird sacred to that goddess, in the hands of many of the statues found therein, would have proved it.

It is true among the statues some were found representing Hercules, and Apollo; but it is known, that although the ancients used to dedicate a Temple to a particular divinity, they used nevertheless to place in it also other gods.

The Temple of Golgi, shows signs of having existed for many centuries; because therein were found statues which are of the epoch of the 2nd Assyrian Monarchy, and others of the Greco-Roman period, thus showing a difference of nearly one thousand years between one statue, and the other; but this is not impossible as we have here in Larnaca the Greek church of St. Lazarus, which is nearly 1,100 years old. Among the votive statuettes in stone & terracotta, some of which represent the Egyptian Deities of Thoth and Apis, there were several representing Mylitta or the Assyrian Venus; the Astoreth or Phoenician Venus, and others representing the Egyptian and Greek Venus.

Something of the Assyrian art is found in several statues; especially in the semi colossal one, holding a patera in its right hand; the Egyptian art is seen in many of them: the Phoenician art is also well represented, but the Greco-Roman only by few. It is strange, that none were found denoting the Persian period of domination in this island which was for more than a century.

A thing worthy of study is, that all these statues, with the exception of the few Greco-Romans, have certain artistic affinity between them, which makes me believe, that they do not represent any of the above named nations art, but are purely Cyprian art; which however has not yet been proved. Still it would not be extraordinary that a people, who had a language to themselves, which they spoke and wrote also, as the 34 inscriptions in that language in my possession found in the Temple testify, should have also had a style of art peculiar to themselves.

And when some European or American Paleologist will be able to read one day, this interesting language, I am convinced, that he will find out that I was right in my conjectures.

What is a positive fact is; that all these statues found in the Temple, are without exception of the calcarean stone, which so much abounds everywhere in Cyprus, and which would therefor indicate that they were without doubt sculptured in this island.

The Cyprian sculptors may have perhaps at different epochs imitated somewhat the art of their conquerors; but they have always preserved something of their national character in them. The Cyprian features of today for instance, being frequently very strongly marked in the heads, even to the formation of the skull.

Among other stone votive offerings not named above, found in the Temple were lions, cats, cows with their little one sucking, doves, sheep, masks of bearded men, of women, and bulls, most of which have holes to hang them to the walls of the Temple.

In all my diggings in this island, and especially in the discovery of this Temple I have never found any indication of those obscenities, which several ancient authors and especially Herodotus assure us, the Cypriots were so addicted to, in their worship of Venus.

No Cyprian writers contemporary to the worship of this goddess exist, that I am aware. Those who wrote when it no longer existed, based their assertions probably upon traditions which they obtained already exagerated; and they have perhaps amplified them still further so as to render their writings more palatable to the depraved taste of the readers of those times.

The Priapos found in the Temple, prove nothing; except perhaps that they might have been offered to the Goddess, in acknowledgment of some cure, as the other votive offerings were.

Among so many statues, I did not find a single one, which was indecent; on the contrary its seems to me to see in their physiognomies, a certain majestic air, very little in accordance with the obscenities related by Herodotus.

It is positive that the subterranean Cyprus, may be said to be virgin yet of excavations, if we except Dali and Golgos.

At Paphos I merely surveyed the ground, and fixed the exact spot, upon which was erected the famous Temple of Venus, and I purchased it; but for want of funds, was unable as yet to explore it.

I believe if serious diggings are made at Kouklia, there will be found objects not only of great importance to science, but also of great artistic value, because it is well known, that the paleo Paphos which gave the material to Alfieri for his tragedy of Myrra, was destroyed by an earthquake. The inhabitants of that epoch, no doubt dug there soon afterwards, to find the treasures of the Temple, and other precious objects, but if their artistic taste was then, such as it is today in the natives of this island, I am quite sure, that they have not carried away one single statue; were it from Praxiteles, or by the great Phidias himself.

Therefor everything leads me to believe, that among the deeply buried ruins of that famous Temple, to which all ancient Greece used to go in pilgrimages, as we do now to Jerusalem, may be found some work of great value, and by these matchless sculptors.

I have annexed to this Report, some topographical sketches, and a series of photographs, to make it more intelligible.

At your request I prepared this report; but I must beg, that it be received with forbearance by your scientific body; as I had no library to consult in this semibarbarous place, and I may be wrong in some of my assertions.

The object of this paper is merely, to acquaint the Royal Academy with the discoveries I have made in this island; especially of that of the Temple of Golgos, its topographical position, the description of the objects found therein, and for what use they were probably made.

If these informations such as they are, may prove of some service to science, and interest to the honorable Body, over which your Excellency presides, I shall be most simply rewarded.

Larnaca, January 1871   L. P. de Cesnola

To His Excellency Count Lelopis de Salerano
    Minister of State, Senator of the Kingdom, etc, etc,
    President of the Royal Academy of Sciences at Turin.

Riddell 1873

The following "Report by Acting-Consul Riddell upon the Commerce of Cyprus for the Year 1873" is excerpted from Fred. H. Fisher, *Cyprus—Our New Colony and What We Know about It*, George Routledge and Sons, London, 1878. Riddell appends to his report tables of imports and exports, which are not reproduced here.

In my report for the year 1872, I mentioned that, owing to the want of sufficient rain, the harvests of 1873 were likely to turn out a failure. This has proved to be the case to an extent even exceeding the worst apprehensions, and unfortunately applies to nearly all the products of the island; so that not only have large quantities of grain been imported at high prices, with an accompanying strain upon the financial resources of the island, but, also, there having been little produce for exportation, trade has suffered severely throughout the year. The prices of grain continued until the end of June at about the same as stated in my report of 1872; say £1 14*s.* for wheat, and 16*s.* 6*d.* for barley, per imperial quarter. By the end of August it would become apparent that a considerable importation of grain from abroad would be required to carry through the winter; but although imports then commenced, and prices also began to advance, it was not until the last two months of the year that any serious rise in prices took place. By the end of the year, and notwithstanding considerable importations of grain from Turkey, prices here had risen to £2 16*s.* for wheat, and £1 17*s.* for barley.

Owing to prices having continuously advanced in Syria, Caramania, and Anatolia, from whence supplies for Cyprus could be brought, imports not only cost more money to the importer, but supplies began also to fall off in quantity; so that by the end of March of the present year stocks in Cyprus were well nigh exhausted, notwithstanding that prices had risen to about £3 15s. for wheat and £2 7s. for barley, with an insufficient supply for the wants of the island till next harvest. Great numbers of the quasi-starving peasants were obliged to subsist on the edible roots of such indigenous plants as they could dig up in the fields, using also locust beans to a large extent in lieu of cereals. The tithes of the year collected by the Government amounted to only a small amount, which had all to be given out to the peasant farmers for seed, without which they had not the means of re-planting their fields for the harvests of 1874.

Altogether, 1873 has proved in every respect one of the most disastrous years remembered in Cyprus, and owing to the great scarcity and high price of food, the borders of famine have been touched and the hardships and suffering are great. Fortunately the rains commenced in November, and continued, with unusual abundance, till so late even as the end of March 1874. This fortunate occurrence served to revive and sustain the hope of the entire population, and abundant harvests are looked forward to in 1874. The winter was unusually wet and cold. The rich and extensive grain-producing district of Massaouri has been abundantly watered by the descent of the torrents, and the grain fields were sown under more favourable and auspicious circumstances than have been experienced these many years past.

As regards cotton, the result of the crop of 1872 turned out very deficient in quantity and inferior in quality. The influences which caused such an unfortunate result were alluded to in my report of 1872, but the yield of the whole crop fell much below the estimates then formed. In the accompanying Table of Exports the quantity of raw cotton sported in 1873 is shown as 827,704 lbs., but of this quantity, down to the end of the year, only 32,980 lbs. belong to the crop of 1873. The gathering of cotton in Cyprus rarely begins earlier than the month of October, and there is none ready for export before November. Only a very insignificant quantity was exported to Great Britain in 1873, owing in part to the want of regular opportunities of shipment, and also that, down to about the middle of the year, the prices obtained for raw cotton in the markets of Marseilles and Trieste were relatively much higher than those current at the same period in Liverpool; hence the bulk of the shipments in 1873 went to foreign ports, as shown in the Table of Exports. From this it will be seen that of a total export amounting to 827,704 lbs., only 19,430 lbs. went direct to Great Britain. Prices here, based upon quotations of value in the Mediterranean ports, became greatly inflated, and there is too much reason to believe that very great losses have been sustained by exporters. The crop of 1874, owing to the larger area of cotton land which the torrents have permitted to be well watered, will, it is expected, be both large and good, unless subjected, as in 1873, to unusual and deleterious influences.

The production and export of sheep-wool in 1873 having been of all kinds 478,860 lbs., rather exceeds the average yield. This quantity, however, comprises 43,040 lbs. of old wool, i.e., wool which has been used for various domestic purposes, and which the poverty of the owners has obliged them to sell in order to procure subsistence. Deducting this from the whole quantity exported leaves 435,820 lbs. as the yield of 1873.

The pasturage having been early dried up by the drought, the flocks were reduced to a very poor condition, and the rapid growth of new grass which succeeded the first rains produced great mortality, so that through the reduction of the flocks the quantity of wool to be raised in 1874 will be probably below the average in quantity, but the quality may turn out superior in cleanness and fibre. The quantity of madder roots produced in 1873 has scarcely fallen off, notwithstanding its reduction in value in the markets of Europe. The falling off in the quantity sent to Great Britain is remarkable, being only 230 cwts., against 4,980 cwts. in 1872. Of the entire quantity (about 4,700 cwts.) exported, 4,250 cwts. went to France; it would appear therefore that prices have been more remunerative there than in England. Growers in Cyprus are turning their madder-root lands to other purposes, as they affirm that present prices render other crops more paying. I am unable to report any important public works completed or undertaken in the island. The extension of the telegraph wires from Nicosia to Larnaca has been commenced. The mercantile classes of Larnaca, in their anxiety to obtain the boon, have contributed £100 towards the cost of construction.

The material prosperity of this island depending, as it does, mainly upon its products, of which grain forms the most important, it appears a matter of regret in every point of view that the Imperial Government should not have exempted Cyprus from the additional impost of 2 ½ per cent. upon all tithes due to the State, to take effect from the 13th of March of 1874, thus adding one-fourth to this already heavy tax, and raising the rate from 10 to 12 ½ per cent. Such a measure applied throughout the empire, and embracing all kinds of products, may be deemed at any time a most questionable policy in the best interests of the State; and applied to Cyprus immediately after a series of bad and insufficient harvests, which culminated last year, as I have said, in the nearest approach to actual famine, and with the peasant farmers reduced to actual poverty, it can be only viewed as a most impolitic if not really unjust impost. Nor must I omit to mention the greatly increased rate in the current value of moneys which has taken place in Cyprus during the year 1873, mainly owing to the large importation of copper money. The Imperial Ottoman Bank Agency here maintains a fixed rate of currency, their £ sterling being 114 piastres; and but for the check which this establishment exercises upon the currency, it is impossible to guess to what extreme rates the coins in circulation might attain. At the beginning of the year, gold coins circulated in commerce at an agio discount of only 1 per cent. to 2 per cent. on the bank rates, whilst the Beshlik (or base) currency was at par. At the close of the year the difference had risen to nearly 20 per cent., the £ sterling circulating at 130 to 134 piastres. I need not dwell on the sufficiently obvious depreciation thereby in the value of landed and other real property when transactions are conducted in piastres. For a time (but only for a time) the change operates in favour of exporters, who effect the purchase of produce in piastres with the £ sterling at 130 piastres in lieu of 114 piastres; but it is manifestly against the importer, who must also sell in piastres, and be paid at the same rate, whilst he has to remit the cost of his goods in sterling value: in other words, the rate of exchange, which at the beginning of the year was about 114 piastres per £ sterling, is now at 130 piastres, without anything nearly approximative in the currency price of the imported articles. Apply this to debts and obligations due in piastres, and entered into long previously, but which must now be liquidated at current rates, and the ruinous consequences to the creditor become easily apparent.

LARNACA, *April* 25, 1874.

Alexander Palma di Cesnola 1873, 1876

Alexander Palma di Cesnola was the brother of Luigi Palma di Cesnola, the American consul to Cyprus from 1865 to 1876, who carried out extensive archaeological excavations in Cyprus and shipped thousands of antiquities to New York to form the basis of the collection of the Metropolitan Museum of Art. Alexander served as consular agent for his brother for the "Province of Paphos" in 1873 and as vice consul during Luigi's extended absence in 1876.

This selection is the Preface to the first edition of Alexander Cesnola's book *Salaminia, the History, Treasures, & Antiquities of Salamis in the Island of Cyprus*. It is taken from the second edition published in 1884 by Whiting & Co., Lim., London. The remainder of the book is devoted to the details of his Cyprus expeditions in 1873 and 1876 and his finds, which became the Lawrence-Cesnola Collection in England.

Ere the reader takes up the following pages, I beg leave to say a few words about the book, and the explorations it describes.

I make no profession of archaeological knowledge, nor does my book even now pretend to be more than a simple narrative and description of explorations in the Island of Cyprus. These pages have been prepared in order to place before students and the public the principal relics which I discovered; but it is not expected that they can exhaust the interest and associations of those remains. My own position is that of an enthusiastic digger-up of antiquities. I went to Cyprus in the year 1873, and remained there until the end of 1874. After an absence of about eighteen months, which were spent in London, I returned to Cyprus.

During this interval my days were freely spent in the British Museum, the vast Oriental treasures of which are arranged in a scientific manner, prodigiously to the advantage of those who, like myself, diligently study them. It was while thus occupied that I had the honour of making the acquaintance of Dr. Samuel Birch, the all-accomplished and learned keeper of the Oriental antiquities in the museum. This acquaintance ripened, on my part at least, into a very devoted friendship, and I am at this time indebted to Dr. Birch for the abundant aid he has given me, in writing the introduction to the following chapters. My previous engagement in Cyprus having been broken, not through my own wish, nor with my consent, but by others, I accepted the generous offer of Mr. Edwin H. Lawrence, F.S.A. to supply a sum of money to enable me to commence digging on my own account, a condition being that if I succeeded in forming a collection of antiquities of sufficient importance, it should be offered to England before any other country. On arriving in Cyprus at the end of July 1876, I engaged the same house and servants in Larnaka I had before, and also a country house at Ormidia, the latter being near to Kitium, Idalium, Salamis, and other localities which are rich in ancient monuments. In the month of August I was ready to resume researches, and had collected, partly in Larnaka and partly in Dali, twenty skilled workmen, putting at their head an excellent aged digger, who soon proved himself an affectionate and faithful assistant. My intention was to secure a collection of vases and glass, so as to have one or two specimens of every shape and kind used by the ancient Cypriotes. The vases being mostly funereal were not difficult to discover. My men and I knew where to search; all that was required was patience and time.

As to the glass, the case was not so simple; some of the natives, and even my own men, were disheartened. Very little glass had been found, they declared, within the last two years; but I am happy to say that in the end I obtained a large number of specimens, and a vast variety of glass relics, as well as terra cotta vases, the number now in the Lawrence-Cesnola collection, which is hereinafter described, being about four thousand of each material. Many specimens, among this multitude of ancient art-relics, are remarkable for their shape and character. With objects in glass, coins are always found, therefore I have been able to obtain a most valuable and exceedingly interesting collection of more than one thousand six hundred examples, which include specimens, in gold, silver, and bronze, of every dynasty which has occupied the island in ancient times; the reader will, amongst other descriptions in my book, find an account of the more important of these relics. As coins are found with objects in glass, so lamps are found with terra cotta vases, and I thus collected more than two thousand lamps, of which two hundred bear makers' names stamped upon them in Greek or Roman characters. All excavators have a fancy for one particular kind of relic, and I was not exempt, my ambition being to find inscriptions in the Phoenician and Cypriote languages; therefore my men had strict orders to bring to me everything which bore an indication of an inscription, and I also was always on the look out for such things. The result of these efforts the reader will find in many interesting examples as described in this book, for the translations and explanations of which I am greatly indebted to friends, but most especially to the learned and Rev. Professor A. H. Sayce, of Queen's College, Oxford. The first objects I found with inscriptions were two vases in terra cotta, bearing Phoenician lettering, such as was used for cinerary urns. Inside one of these vases I found burnt matter, probably the remains of a child: the only differences between the two vases were in respect to the places where they were found, and the inscriptions they bear. One came from ancient Kitium, and has a Phoenician inscription, the other came from Idalium, and is enriched with Cypriote letters. Another vase, which I found in the village of Athieno, has Cypriote letters, and was probably used as a family cooking pot.

From the end of June until October 1876, I was obliged to suspend work on account of the heat of the weather. I occupied this interval in an excursion to Salamis, and with the aid of some natives of two villages, I dug near to the ruins of the ancient city; but I was deceived, and after much outlay and trouble left the place without finding anything of great importance. Although I lost money in this research I did not regret it, as I met there two very intelligent natives, who were large proprietors of land in the ruins of Salamis, and well informed about digging. Having furnished them with money, and incited their diligence with many promises of future payments, I left them, to seek tombs at Salamis. I think, and my men had the same opinion, that neither I nor those who worked before me among those ruins, had failed to find the proper place for successful explorations. I may explain here why I sought the site of the tombs in Salamis before commencing any other diggings. The manner I adopted was that of my predecessors.

Be it noticed, that there are two methods of exploring the antique world—digging in the ruins of the cities, and digging in the tombs of their inhabitants. Tombs are found generally near ruins. Digging in ruins is always uncertain, and can only be carried out at great expense, which sometimes may be continued for months without producing anything of importance; but if the excavator should find but one fine object, it will pay more than all the expenses incurred. When digging in ruins I always sunk shafts at the spots which bore indications of temples, palaces, or other large buildings. These shafts were sunk a few feet apart, and were made more or less deep, the depth of each being dependent on the men finding rock or virgin earth. When either of these substances was reached, I knew there was no hope for researches in these directions; therefore, abandoning the pits, I tried other parts and dug again. When the shafts disclosed a foundation or pavement, I continued working in the direction indicated, feeling sure that something would surely be found there. I have many times hoped to find a famous temple and other remains, and was often ready to draw plans, and began to take measures for the elucidation of these *chateaux d'Espagne*, but all of these visions ended in nothing except foundations of common buildings. It is only an excavator who can enter into my feelings. At the moment of expectation, the excitement of a digger can only be compared to that of a gambler. I must, however, say that if a digger has many disappointments, he has great pleasures and much satisfaction in the progress of his work, and this satisfaction I experienced in mine, especially at Salamis. Searching for tombs was conducted nearly in the same manner as among the ruins, the only change in the manner of seeking being due to the different constructions of the tombs, and this depended upon the people who had buried their dead in them, for of course the antiquities were in accord with the people to whom they had belonged. In digging in the tombs I always recovered antiquities to the full value of the expenses incurred, because the objects found are generally gold.

My system of work was generally to divide the diggers into small parties of three or four each to work in the tombs, and one party in the ruins, I myself remaining with the latter, ready to run to the spot when my men opened a fresh tomb. In this manner also, it I found it necessary to have more men in the ruins, I could easily call for those who were working in the tombs. To the workmen I generally paid the fixed wages of one shilling a day, paying them every Saturday also for the objects they had found, at a rate fixed beforehand by my foreman and the workmen. The gold was paid for by weight, adding sometimes a little more when there was art in the work. Under this system I continued digging for about three years. I will take this opportunity of stating that all this time of my diggings, I was never cheated, nor had I any trouble with these poor workmen (as many excavators in other countries have had), but, on the contrary, I received from them most faithful work; and, on their part, they had confidence in me. If I had occasion for complaints, it was not against Cypriote people; and it must be remembered that, although I always employed men of both religions, orthodox and Mahommedan, I could not say which of the two was more faithful. I had great confidence in men of both classes, and have sometimes left in their hands large sums of money, and never experienced misgivings about its safety; and I do not think there is any other island or country where the people are more honest or trustworthy than the folks of Cyprus are. When I parted from them it was with great regret.

In October and November of 1876, I was digging at Timbo, Ormidia, and other villages, and I collected in those places a very large number of vases and fine specimens of glass. It was at this time that I sent two parties of five men each, the one to Kurium, and the other to Soli; but they came back with very few spoils of the spade and pick.

This was the last time I sent out independent parties of diggers, for I found it better to discontinue this system, and to keep all the men with me. I returned home to Larnaka for the winter, and began to pack the relics which had then been unearthed for conveyance to Mr. Lawrence in England. My first cargo consisted of six large cases dispatched in an Austrian Lloyd's steamer. For the success attending this shipment, I am indebted to Messrs. Osmiani Brothers. At Alexandria the cases were passed to another company, *en route* to Messrs. Moss and Co., Liverpool, who, in their turn, delivered them safely in London.

My life in Larnaka was very solitary, and I received very few friends. My time was taken up in sorting the antiquities, and arranging and studying them. I was, and am, greatly obliged for many explanations given by my dear friend, Mr. Demetrius Pierides, a great antiquary and numismatist, who is thoroughly acquainted with Cypriote monuments, which he has studied indefatigably for about half a century. He is an honourable gentleman, whose presence adorns the island of Cyprus. The reader will see that the kindness of Mr. Pierides towards me was not limited to the time that I spent in Cyprus, but that it continues now; for in reading this book it will be observed how kindly he has aided me in many things. I thankfully remember, too, the kindness of H. E. the Bishop of Larnaka, of the Archimandrite himself, and of the Venerable Dr. Valsamacchi, and the goodness of others, who were the only friends I received during this winter. In March 1877, I visited Paphos, and while on the way thither spent many hours in the ruins of ancient Marium, visiting the spot where the learned German, Dr. Sigismondi, met his death while examining a tomb. These ruins were one hour's distance from Limassol, and halfway between Larnaka and Paphos. I received kind hospitality from M. Teodoro Peristiani, a learned lawyer from the University of Paris. This gentleman was in every instance most obliging towards me. During my stay in Limassol I visited two collections of Cypriote antiquities, one belonging to a native, and the other to Dr. Gastan, but I could not succeed in buying either of them. The first of these collections comprised many objects that I liked, especially three pieces of a patera, with Phoenician inscriptions; but I could not obtain it, on account of the great price set upon it by the owner, and because I thought the inscription was not of one patera, but of three different specimens put together as one; and in spite of some savants in Paris, who said it was but one inscription, I retain my opinion.

I stayed at the Lusignan Castle, in Colosso, and received very kind attentions from M. Lobianco, proprietor of a large estate in Limassol. At Paphos I remained ten days, and dug in several places, where I found some fine gold objects and vases of a particular form, which are found only in this locality. I obtained at a village near Paphos-Nova a beautiful Cypriote inscription of three lines, and I there bought four other inscribed stones. Paphos is an excellent locality for digging in the ruins; but it is an extremely expensive place, and difficult to explore, because the ruins have been buried and reburied by earthquakes, so that it requires many men and very deep shafts to reach them.

In April 1877 I returned to my country house, and extended my diggings to Riso-Carpazzo. I remained in this line of mountains until July 1877, and collected there many very rare relics in gold, glass, vases, and inscriptions. It was at this time I found a square well, partly of brick and stone, which was full of fractured statuettes of a new form, and mixed with earth. I put together of these about two hundred statuettes; the reader will find illustrations of some of these in this book. This well was about two miles distant from Salamis. The statuettes probably belonged to a temple of the latter town, and were placed in this well in the early part of our era. The statuettes were found thus: first those of very ordinary and rough work; in the centre were those of much better art; and in the lowest stratum they exhibited most beautiful art. No news came to me from Salamis, but I knew that the man who was excavating there for me was keeping his promise, and working hard in our joint interest. On my return from Carpazzo I saw him, and bought from him some very good ancient Greek glass, such as is called Phoenician in Cyprus. He said to me, "No tomb yet; but I hope very soon to have news to bring you." In August I went again to Limassol; but only passed the ruins of Kurium, and began digging with ten men in the same spot in which one of my predecessors found a treasure, which is now in the New York Museum. I recovered many relics, principally in gold or silver,— fibulae, rings, ear-rings, and a beautiful necklace. After a fortnight's work, I was advised by a friendly Turkish officer and others in the village, that people in the coffee-houses were beginning to speak adversely to my operations, while one of the proprietors thought it would be better to inform the Kaimakan or Chief of the Province of Limassol, with a view to stopping my work. On hearing this, I decided to leave the place for a time, and went back to Larnaca. I left only one man to continue the work at Kurium.

After a month this man returned with many very good objects in silver and bronze, and twenty or more fine ear-rings. I must say that in this circumstance, as during all my digging in the island, I was most obliged to the Turkish authorities. If I have succeeded in gleaning the Laurence-Cesnola collection from Cyprus, it is due to the kindness of the Turkish officers, from the simple zaptieh or policeman, to the Governors-General; and I know that this kindness continued, although some jealous persons and others did their utmost to deprive me of this indulgence and regard. This, however, was not the same when, at a later time, they tried to injure me with the new Government. This jealousy was not limited to the authorities of the island; but resulted in a communication to the Minister of Foreign Affairs in Italy. In thinking of how much other diggers and archaeologists have had to suffer in foreign countries, principally in the East, before me, for instance, Botta, Layard, Schliemann, and others, I cannot but feel that my lot was not so hard as theirs, and so I continued my work without paying much attention to what was said and done against me. I always worked with the countenance and indulgence of the authorities and public officers. I had, indeed, made application in Constantinople for a firman, but never received a positive answer; so I continued digging without it. It is on this account that the reader will not find in the Lawrence-Cesnola collection many large monuments of the statuary class, such as my predecessors had been able to obtain. It was not because I did not find any, or made no researches for them; but I was unable to treat them like small articles which are easily removed. If I had tried to remove large works, it would not have been to my advantage; but, most probably, advantageous to others, and possibly they would have stopped my work. It is certain that if I had succeeded in obtaining a firman, England might have obtained some fine statues and monuments, and had no cause to regret what it has lost. Mr. Edwin Lawrence would, in that case, have had all his wishes fulfilled. In November 1877, my workman came from Salamis to Larnaka, and brought three statuettes in terra-cotta, one with a Greek inscription on it, which he had found in a tomb there. He brought, also, several pieces in marble and stone bas-reliefs, from a spot at which he hoped explorations might prove very successful. I ordered all my men directly to Salamis, and followed immediately, took a house in a village near the ruins, and remained there until the British occupation of the island. My collection at that time was not a third of what it afterwards became, in consequence of this discovery in Salamis.

On bringing to England the mass of the relics I had recovered from the soil of Cyprus, an exhibition of the whole was arranged, where it still continues, in Holland Park, in the mansion of Mr. Lawrence; but very few general visitors have seen it, on account of its display at a private residence.

Fortunately, no necessity of selling this collection exists, as many other collections have been sold at public auction, and for the sake of realizing their money value; and, certainly, no one would desire to disperse this one, until every means had been used of securing these works of antiquity to the public use in the fittest manner, and I should be glad, if it were possible, that they could be exhibited in a public museum.

The student will find every piece described in this book, with the name of the place where found; and this has been done so as not to fatigue the reader with a long preface. During all my diggings I have never sold a single antiquity. I have, on the other hand, presented many things, principally to English and American visitors, who honoured me with visits while they were passing through the island; but I always refused to sell anything.

I embarked on the Lloyd steamer from Cyprus in February 1879; and returned to London the 22nd of May 1879, after having stayed in Italy some time, in order to re-establish my health. Six months after, the collection was arranged in cabinets in two large rooms, in the house of Mr. E. H. Lawrence, 84, Holland Park, where they still remain. Many Englishmen and foreigners of learning have visited the collection. I invited Dr. S. Birch and Professor C. T. Newton, C.B., of the British Museum; and Mr. Wallis and Mr. Thompson, of the South Kensington Museum, to see the antiquities; which they did. In 1881, with Mr. Lawrence's consent, I offered to exhibit the collection in the South Kensington Museum, and for the benefit of art students. After four months I received an answer from the authorities, who placed at my disposal six small cases in a room near the Water-Colour Department. I took the advice of many friends; and every one agreed it was impossible to make a favourable exhibition in so small a place. I therefore declined the offer, hoping for a better occasion at a later time. At the end of the same year I offered to lend the greater part of the collection to the British Museum for temporary exhibition; but the offer was not then brought to a successful conclusion. With these offers I feel I have completed my duty to students and amateurs in antiquities. The Lawrence-Cesnola collection is too large for a private museum. It is my ardent wish that some day it may be in a public one.

Before ending this preface I heartily thank many learned friends, besides those I have previously mentioned, who have helped me with counsel and aid in this work, and I especially thank Professor E. Renan, Mr. F. G. Stephens, and Mr. Walter de Gray Birch, F.S.A.

After this explanation, I leave my book in the hands of the reader, begging him to show all leniency and benevolence towards my many shortcomings.

Farley 1877

J. (James) Lewis Farley set out to write about his experiences during a winter residence in Egypt, spring in Syria and summer on the Bosphorus. He had resided many years in Turkey and had specifically visited Cyprus and spent two years on the coast of Syria, so when the announcement of the British protectorate was announced, he felt compelled to expand his writings to cover Cyprus and the problems it posed. He had published *The Resources of Turkey, Turks and Christians*, and other works. The following is excerpted from *Egypt, Cyprus and Asiatic Turkey* published by Trübner & Co., London, 1878.

[p. 149]

On arriving early in the morning at Larnaca, the ancient Citium, now the chief port of Cyprus, sufficient time is allowed to go on shore, and inspect everything worth seeing. The streets are clean, and the interior of the houses—mostly only one storey high above the ground floor—is very comfortable; the apartments being generally paved with white marble, and the houses themselves surrounded by pretty gardens, in which the Cypriotes take great pleasure. Larnaca is the residence of the European Consuls, and carries on a considerable trade; but it is strange its roadstead should be preferred to the old part of Famagûsta, which offers the advantages of a safe and commodious harbour. If the marshes in the vicinity of the latter were drained, the harbour cleared, and the old works to seaward reconstructed, Cyprus would possess one of the finest harbours in the Levant. Before the Turkish occupation, Cyprus contained upwards of 1,000,000 inhabitants ; but it is now estimated there are not more than 180,000, distributed amongst 605 towns and villages, of which 118 are exclusively inhabited by Mussulmans, 248 by Christians, and 239 by Moslems and Christians. As a consequence of the diminished population of Cyprus, an immense breadth of land is lying waste and uncultivated; but if the population were sufficiently increased, and the soil were properly tilled, it would be difficult to estimate the future agricultural produce of the country . . .

There is probably no place where living has been hitherto so easy as at Cyprus; even the beggars—who are mostly blind, maimed, or worn out by age, and have generally a small house of their own—are able to live quietly at home, without begging more than one or two days a week. The island, too, has generally had the reputation of being one of the healthiest in the Mediterranean, although recent experience would rather indicate the contrary.

I am nevertheless inclined to believe that it is not so much the climate as imprudence which has caused the amount of sickness lately prevailing at Cyprus. No one accustomed to the East would think of travelling during the great heat of the day, and the culpability of marching troops under an August and September sun can hardly be excused. Lower Egypt, from my own experience, is very healthy, with proper precautions, but if the same imprudence were committed there, dysentery would inevitably ensue; in Syria, intermittent fever would be the consequence, and so it has been in Cyprus. The troops should have commenced their march an hour before sunrise, rested during the great heat of the day, avoiding all stimulants, and resumed their march two hours before sunset. Had this been done, I am convinced that much of the sickness prevailing among our troops in Cyprus would have been avoided. Another mistake that has been made was in sending the men immediately to hospital; and, as practice is better than theory, I shall give a case in point. Travelling once in Syria, I committed the imprudence of remaining for several hours under the mid-day sun, and, on arriving at Beyrout, I felt exceedingly ill with all the premonitory symptoms of intermittent fever. Instead, however, of going to the doctor, I went to the Turkish bath, and two hours' sweating killed the fever. Now, at Cyprus, our troops, in the first instance, ought not to have been marched during the heat of the mid-day sun, and, in the second, instead of being sent at once to hospital, they should have been sent to the bath. Occasional doses of quinine, judicious use of the Turkish bath, and protection from the mid-day sun, are the best preventatives of intermittent fever in the East.

[p. 159]

Ports.—Larnaca, the residence of the European consuls, is the chief sea-port of the island. Ships of war, steamers, and sailing vessels coming to Cyprus, usually cast anchor in the roadstead, which is formed by the two capes of Pilla and of Kitti, and affords a tolerable anchorage. Through Larnaca pass all the manufactured goods imported, as well as almost all the cereals, and considerable part of the wines, caroubs, and silks exported from the island. The population amounts to 15,000, of whom a third are Turks.

Limassol is the chief port for the wine and bean trades, and has acquired considerable importance within the past few years on account of the demand for wines and spirits. It would be difficult to calculate the possible produce of Cyprus if the island contained a million of agriculturists, for the entire place is one unworked mine of enormous wealth. The hills alone which surround Limassol might produce annually, to an almost unlimited extent, the currants so highly prized in Europe; and, although there is not a single vine in a circuit of more than four leagues from the town, Limassol, nevertheless, exports a million barrels of wine as the produce of the mountains of the province, of which hardly one-tenth is cultivated. The olive and caroub trees grow together on the chain of mountains encircling Limassol, without any cultivation being bestowed on them, while the hills are covered in some places with oaks planted in the time of the Venetians. Limassol contains between 5000 and 6000 inhabitants, of whom one-third are Turks.

Famagûsta, so famous under the Venetians, possesses an excellent spacious port, which, however, is now so choked up with mud that it can only hold about a dozen small craft. It is well sheltered from all winds, and, if deepened, which could be done at a small expense, would contain hundreds of large ships.

Roads.—The roads are rather better in Cyprus than in most other parts of the Ottoman Empire, but they still fall far short of the requirements of the island. From Nicosia, which is centrally situated, roads, varying in importance from bridle paths to bullock tracks, radiate to different parts of the island—one going through Larnaca, Limassol, and Famagûsta. A good road, however, from the capital to Larnaca is much needed, and before any important expansion of trade can take place, the whole of the roads will require to be substantially improved. At present, with only a small proportion of the arable area under cultivation, even the existing roads are quite inadequate. If the agricultural and mineral resources of Cyprus were but fairly developed, the island would yield a revenue which would justify a large expenditure on works of public improvement.

* * * * *

[p. 163]

Population.—In the time of the Venetians, the population of Cyprus was upwards of 1,000,000. In 1840, the entire population of the island was only 100,000; is it now, however, calculated at 180,000. The number of Turkish families is 7299, and of Christian families 19,215, making a total of 26,514 families.

Condition of the Inhabitants.—Those inactive masses who live from hand to mouth are not to be found in Cyprus; all who wish for employment can obtain it. The want of hands is so much felt that any one, having a distaste for the calling of fisherman or boatman, can find employment at once as cooper, porter, wine-gauger, broker for foreign captains, &c. The country enjoys perfect tranquillity; thefts are very rare, and robberies unknown. Many years have passed since an assassination occurred in the island; and altogether Cyprus enjoys the reputation of being the most peaceable island in the Mediterranean. Its present state is that of a country which once was celebrated, rich, and populous; which now is but the shadow of its former days, but for which a better destiny may be reserved.

* * * * *

[p. 261]

INDUSTRY.—Tanning is one of the chief industries. The tanneries at Nicosia turn out from 1500 to 2000 bales of leather per annum. The manufacture of silk stuffs is produced at Nicosia by women to the extent of about 10,000 pieces yearly for dresses, besides handkerchiefs and sashes. The printing of English grey cloths for divans and coverlets is also carried on; building and carpentering are entirely done by Greeks, who also make good tailors and shoemakers. The trades followed by Turks are those of barbers, butchers, calico-printers, shoemakers, and saddlers.

REVENUE.—The revenues for the financial year of 1877 are considerably under those of last year, in consequence of the unfavourable returns of the crops. The tithes were administered by Government officials, with a view to remedy certain abuses complained of by the peasants; but the experiment so far has not benefited either them or the Government. Of the dimes in grain 120,000 kilos. of barley were sent to Constantinople for the requirements of the army, and a matter of 30,000 kilos. of wheat were given to the poorer of the peasants for sowing.

PUBLIC WORKS and ADMINISTRATION.—Nothing has been done in the way of public works during the year, even the carriage-road between Larnaca and Nicosia, which was traced out a few years ago at a great outlay, has been greatly neglected. No other roads exist in the island save bridle paths, some of which are also used by bullock carts. There are no wharfs and jetties. The only facilities for shipping are a few wooden scalas, and these, as a rule, generally disappear in winter. The promised reforms have not yet been applied to this island. The peasants continue to be heavily taxed, and as their ability to pay has diminished, arbitrary measures are resorted to for their collection. The Government does not seem to have been very fortunate in the selection of its administrative and judicial officials for Cyprus, and as complaints have been made against some of them the vali of Rhodes sent a functionary, accompanied by an efficient staff, to make the necessary investigations.

CUSTOM HOUSE.—Complaints were lately made against the director of the Larnaca custom house because he insisted that all produce exported from this town should pass through the custom house instead of being shipped as formerly from the different scalas under the supervision of a custom house clerk, and after the required formalities of weighing, &c., had been gone through. As this was an impossibility, owing to the smallness of the building and the limited space in front of it, confusion and delay ensued, to the prejudice of the merchants and of the Government. This state of things having been brought to the notice of the superior authorities of Indirect Contributions at Constantinople, an inspector was sent over from Beyrout to make a full and complete report of the grievances complained of. No result has come of it as yet.

Lang 1860s–1878

R. Hamilton Lang was manager of the Imperial Ottoman Bank agency in Larnaca, Cyprus from the early 1860s to 1872 when he accepted a similar position in Egypt. In addition to his business activities, his antiquarian research, and his experimental farming, he served as British vice-consul for four short terms intermittently and was appointed Consul in 1871. His book, excerpted below, was begun in the late 1860s and completed as the British took over the administration of the island in 1878. It was published as *Cyprus: Its History, Its Present Resources, and Future Prospects* by MacMillan and Co., London, 1878.

CHAPTER X.
AGRICULTURE AND PRODUCE.

. . . The wines of Cyprus have long been celebrated. The best quality, known as "commanderia" wine, received its name from the Comandatore of the Knights Templar, and is highly appreciated in France and Italy. It was from Cyprus that the vine was introduced, with so much success, into Madeira, and during my residence in the island fresh vineshoots were applied for by the American consul at Madeira in consequence of the ravages of the vine-disease. The British public may therefore hope at no distant date to drink their Madeira from a British possession. The common wine of the country is very wholesome, but has a disagreeable taste from the tar with which the vessels in which it is fermented and the skins in which it is transported, are besmeared. Its cost is about a penny per quart-bottle, but in the opinion of competent judges it is a wine which, freed from its tarry taste, would be very valuable to the trade for mixing. Experiments were made by a Greek gentleman, Mr. Bargigli, in the manufacture of a wine fermented after the European system, and they were fairly successful. An American gentleman from Cincinnati also manufactured a white wine, which, considering the difficulties of an entirely provisional manufacture, was also a success. In both cases, however, it was evident that a small percentage of alcohol was required to make the wine good for shipment.

The culture of the vine in Cyprus has been very seriously affected by the excessive burdens imposed upon it by the Turkish Government. Like all other produce, an eighth part had to be paid to the Treasury, under the tax called "Dîmes;" but as the tax could not be taken in kind, seeing that the fresh grapes would not keep, it was converted into a money value, fixed yearly by the local "medjlis," or mixed tribunal. The basis of this value was the market price in the chief town of the district, instead of the value at the place of growth, and thus a tax which ought not to have exceeded twelve and a half per cent. in reality became one of over twenty per cent. Nor was this all. The grape converted into wine had to pay an excise duty, which represented a further tax of ten per cent., and an export duty upon shipment besides. The natural consequence of these excessive impositions was the diminution of a culture for which the island is particularly adapted. For many reasons it would be wise to free this production from all tax, except a moderate export duty. The result would be an extensive development in this branch of culture, which is profitable to the island and which may become very advantageous to the British consumer . . .

At present, with the exception of a small quantity of Commanderia wine to Trieste, all the exports go to Syria and Alexandria.

The linseed and sesame produced in Cyprus are of excellent quality, the former being equal in value to that of Bombay. The production is not large, and the export is chiefly to France.

McCulloch, in his *Commercial Dictionary*, upon "Cotton," quotes from Lewis Roberts's *Treasure of Traffic*, published 1641, as follows: "The Manchester weavers buy cotton wool in London that comes first from Cyprus and Smyrna, and at home work the same and perfect it into fustians, vermilions, dimities, and other stuffs." Cyprus was therefore a very early contributor to the wealth of Manchester. At the time of which Lewis Roberts wrote the London Corporation of the Levant Company had a factory in the island, and it was doubtless through it that Cyprus cotton got to London. In a little British graveyard attached to the church of St. Lazarus at Larnaca there are many gravestones erected to British merchants connected with the Levant Company Corporation, and several belong to the seventeenth century. The company did a flourishing business, and enjoyed exceptional privileges in Turkey. It was dissolved some forty years ago . . .

Cyprus is capable of producing most serviceable qualities of cotton wool. During the American war American seeds were introduced, and proved a great success. It was in connection with their introduction that I first interested myself in the agriculture of the island, not as a business, but as a pastime. I found that New Orleans was in several respects more sure of success than native seed, and my produce was classified in Liverpool at only five per cent. less than Middling Orleans produced in America. But the peasant cultivators found a difficulty in the production of cotton from American seed. The pod from the latter opens up at maturity so fully that unless the cotton contained in it is at once picked it falls to the ground and consequently deteriorates. Thus the picking requires to be done almost daily during the season. But the tax-gatherer, who had to receive his eighth portion, would not allow this, because he could not be in daily attendance. The pod from native seed (conveniently for the tax-gatherer) never opens fully, and may remain weeks in the field after maturity. This circumstance alone sufficed to prevent many native growers from adopting American seed, although they acknowledged its advantages. As nearly all the cotton grown in the island is exported, it would be much better to collect any tax imposed upon the produce at the time of shipment, and not when the crop is gathered. The increased cultivation of cotton is dependent upon increased means of irrigation, and this leads me to say that the question of water supply deserves the earnest attention of the new administration. I had in my possession a copy of the opinion of the most eminent authority in France as to the probability of finding in Cyprus water after the Artesian system. He indicated several localities where, judging by the geological chart of the island, . . . there is considerable certainty of success in boring Artesian wells. I brought the matter under the notice of the Turkish Governor, and was authorised to treat with competent parties in England for the execution of experimental borings. Very moderate terms were arranged with a firm of engineers in London; but, as often happens in Turkey, before the plans could be carried out, the governor was removed. The value of water for irrigation in such a country as Cyprus is incalculable, especially where it is found with the power to raise itself to the surface of the ground.

Twenty years ago the production of tobacco was very considerable, and the qualities grown at Omodos, near Limasol, were highly esteemed both in Syria and in Egypt. To-day the production does not represent a tenth part of the consumption in the island itself. The cause of this anomaly is a very common one—the fiscal arrangements of the Turkish Treasury. Every fresh effort at Constantinople to increase the revenues of the country led to the imposition of fresh taxes on tobacco. At last the tax reached the exorbitant figure of six piastres per oke upon the most inferior qualities. As this represented about fifty per cent. of the entire value of the produce, it is not to be wondered at that the culture of tobacco almost entirely ceased. But Great Britain has every interest in restoring this culture to its former importance, and she would act wisely in freeing it for a time from all burden except that of a moderate export duty. The value of such crops as tobacco to the peasant population is very great. They especially add to the comfort of the family, as the labour required is chiefly performed by the women and children, and does not interfere with the more important agricultural work.

The fruit of the caroub-tree, called in commerce locust-beans, is an important article of export. It is the pod referred to in the New Testament as the "husks which the swine did eat," and with which the prodigal son was content to appease his hunger. The chief export of the bean from Cyprus is to Russia, where it is esteemed and eaten as a fruit. The article has however been frequently and largely exported to England, it is used as food for cattle, and also in the manufacture of a kind of molass. The great obstacle to its free consumption in England has been the cost of freight, which represents about thirty per cent. of its price at the place of shipment. Now that British enterprise is especially directed to Cyprus, it is probable that means will be found to crush and manufacture it before shipment, so as to economise this heavy cost. The production is a very valuable one to the island, as it requires little labour and is largely remunerative. The present export is about 10,000 tons annually. Until about 1820 the fruit of the caroub-tree could only be sold to the Government, or rather to the Pasha who had leased the island from the Porte. The small price paid for the fruit by the Pashas, and the abuses perpetrated, discouraged the growth of the tree, and even led the peasants in many places to root it up. But in recent years, since the sale was left free, the tree is much disseminated. It is an evergreen, and consequently offers a most beneficent shade during the summer months. It grows spontaneously, but the fruit is not good unless the tree is grafted. The graft is a shoot from an already grafted tree. The best quality is produced near Limasol, and Cape Caroubiere, and at Lefkera, near Larnaca. Those produced on the northern coast and shipped from Kyrinia are inferior in quality and cheaper in price, because they are not suitable for the Russian market. From their cheapness they are in greatest request for the English market. Their usual price is £2 15s. per ton f.o.b., at Kyrinia. The natives manufacture from the bean a kind of sweet cake, which is highly esteemed and very nutritive.

The madder roots produced in Cyprus are inferior in quality to those of Smyrna and Naples, but greatly superior to those of Syria. It is from this root that the fast-coloured dye known as Turkey red is extracted. The article was largely traded in by the Levant Company, of which we have already spoken, and it was doubtless through its imports from Turkey into England that the cloths dyed by this root got the name of Turkey reds. Of all other cultures that of madder roots demands the greatest care, and the soil must have exceptional qualities. It only succeeds in highly fertilized sand, if I may use the expression. After being richly manured with goats' manure the land has to be carefully turned over with the spade to a depth of at least two feet, and every weed or stone removed. There must be considerable moisture, if not actually water, at a depth not greater than four feet. The crop may be sown from seed, but it is generally planted from shoots. The shoots first throw out a small leaf above ground which begins to dry up about the sixth month. There is no further growth above ground, but the plant shoots down roots into the ground. These continue to increase in thickness, and grow downwards in length until the moisture below affects them. When they get into too moist soil they become black, or, as the natives say, they rot. In inferior soils this rotting will begin after eighteen months, while in the superior soils the roots continue to improve during thirty-six months. Hence in the trade, Italian madders are distinguished as eighteen-month roots and thirty-six-month roots. The madders grown in the district of Famagusta in Cyprus can only remain eighteen months in the ground, while those in the district of Morphon may remain without injury fully thirty-six months. All the time the root is in the ground the surface must be kept thoroughly free from weeds. After the root is lifted, it is gradually dried. If packed before being perfectly dry it heats rapidly and deteriorates. The produce of an acre of good madder land is 2½ tons of dried roots, worth £40 to £50. In consequence of this yield, madder-root lands command a very high price, and I have known them bring £140 per acre. But the culture is chiefly profitable to the peasant-cultivator who has no wages to pay, but, assisted by his family, prepares and works a quarter of an acre. Since 1873 the value of madder roots has greatly decreased. Science has found the means of making fast-coloured mineral dyes which are procured much cheaper. It is therefore unlikely that the culture of madder roots in Cyprus will increase; many lands hitherto devoted to that culture will be more profitably employed as vegetable gardens.

Silk is not largely produced in Cyprus, but the quality of the cocoons from the district of Paphos is exceptionally good. Six pounds of these cocoons will produce one pound of silk, a proportion seldom equalled and not surpassed by the cocoons of any country. The silk is also very strong, and of a very brilliant hue. The exports of silk cocoons are small, and chiefly to France. Judging by the tithes paid the value of the whole produce of silk in the island does not exceed £35,000, of which £5,000 may be exported. None of the modern appliances for stifling the worms or spinning the silk exist in the island, and the Arabs who come over yearly from Beyrout for the purchase of cocoons bring with them small portable machines for stifling. The natives expose the cocoons to the heat of the sun, and thus destroy the silk-worm. As the soil and climate is very suitable to the mulberry-tree it is probable that its culture may become more extensive. When it is desired to hatch the silk-worm eggs the women of Cyprus wear the cloth upon which the eggs have been laid round their waists, and cause them to hatch by the heat of their body.

CAPITAL XI.
DROUGHT AND LOCUSTS.

. . . Another calamity from which Cyprus has suffered grievously in the past, and which is an important cause of its present low prosperity, is the scourge of locusts. Thanks to the intelligent efforts of Saïd Pasha, one of the few able governors who remained for too short a time, the destruction of locusts was accomplished a few years ago, and the new administration has only now to watch attentively to prevent their return. In one year 50,000 okes, or about sixty-two tons weight, of locust eggs were collected and destroyed, and at that time some interesting facts connected with that destructive insect came to my knowledge. It was ascertained that on an average every case of locust eggs contains the germs of forty locusts, so that each female locust deposits in mother earth, for future delivery, forty inveterate enemies of humanity. Every oke of locust egg cases represents fully one million of locusts, so that in one year the island was delivered from 50,000 millions of locusts. I leave to the curious the calculation of what the numbers would have been in the following years had not Saïd Pasha appeared upon the scene. I wrote the following account of them in 1870:—

"LARNACA, *April* 28, 1870.

"About twelve months ago I drew attention to the very praiseworthy efforts of Saïd Pasha for the destruction of locusts, which, from time immemorial, have been the scourge of this island. It is with especial pleasure that I again refer to the subject; for, wonderful to relate, the entire destruction of locusts is a *fait accompli.* It is perhaps a unique sample of the entire extirpation of locusts by steady, continuous effort, aided by what may be called scientific means. It appears especially wonderful to nine-tenths of the inhabitants of this island; for although some may have believed in the power to extirpate, few expected to see it practically exercised. Legion is the name of the fitful efforts which have been made to overcome this hitherto invincible enemy, but the peasants generally found that they simply fell 'out of the frying-pan into the fire.' The locusts ate their crops, and the would-be locust-killers swallowed their money. The zeal of some governors lagged after a year's toil; the inertness of others gave golden opportunities to the locusts to multiply; and in more than one case ministers at Constantinople unwittingly leagued with the locusts, and removed capable men just when they expected to reap the fruit of their labours. It has been reserved for Saïd Pasha not only to work, with the honest sweat of his brow, but to see the fruit of his work; and richly does he deserve the shower of blessings which, on his recent return from the last search after locusts, a grateful peasantry lavished upon him. Five thousand piastres were vainly offered for an oke. Three years ago we could not move without disturbing the locusts. No one is more ready than his Excellency to accord just praise to Mr. Richard Mattei for the untiring and patriotic assistance which he ably and heartily gave; and it must be with peculiar pleasure that both now receive the cordial thanks of many who only two years ago spoke of and considered them as blinded enthusiasts in a hopeless cause. One of these—a member of the consular body—who boldly declared that if in two years the locusts were destroyed he would allow the Pasha to cut off his head, admits to-day that he has justly lost his too rash wager.

The day of execution is not yet named; perhaps in his hour of triumph his Excellency may be magnanimous . . ."

* * * * *

From the days of a governor called Osman Pasha, some twenty-five years ago, the island had been continually bled for the destruction of locusts without any result. The labours of Osman Pasha were very meritorious, but he died before the task which he really had at heart was completed. His successors with few exceptions, made great professions of destroying the locusts, and for this purpose either levied a tax upon the peasants for the purchase and destruction of locust eggs, or ordained that each peasant should deliver a certain quantity. In the former case the money was punctually collected and declarations drawn up that it had been employed in the destruction of fabulous quantities of locust eggs. But in reality from 90 to 50 per cent. (according to the courage and ability of the officials) of the cash was misappropriated and accomplished nothing. In some cases an appearance of honesty was preserved, and one-fourth part of locust eggs and three-fourth parts of sand and earth were officially destroyed. When the peasants were ordered to deliver a certain quantity of locust eggs the operation was conducted differently. In that case a sum of money was taken by the peasant to the commission of his district which was charged with the honest execution of the Padishah's orders, and in virtue of that money a receipt was given attesting that the exacted quantity of locust eggs had been delivered and destroyed. This is no calumny but a positive fact, for I gave my farm employés the money necessary for the purchase of their discharge. I remember calculating how much the island had paid for the nominal destruction of locusts from the time of Osman Pasha, and the amount was fabulous. The merit of Saïd Pasha was that he personally superintended the weighing and destruction of the eggs at Nicosia and refused to allow earth to pass for eggs. At Larnaca, Limasol, and Kyrinia he put some Europeans upon the commission of reception, had the eggs stowed, and authorised their destruction only after a personal inspection by himself. All the operations were carried on in broad daylight and were open to the invited inspection of every one. Proof of the destruction was convincingly evident the year after when locust eggs could only be procured at a great cost, and in the third year the value of locust eggs became equal to that of silk.

Besides attacking locusts through the destruction of their eggs, an ingenious plan was adopted for their destruction when in march, before they are able to fly. The inventor of this plan was M. Richard Mattei, an Italian gentleman and large landed proprietor, who has rendered immense service to Cyprus by his labours. He had observed that in their march the locusts never turned back, whatever was the obstacle in their way. When they got into a town they would spend days in climbing over the walls of the houses if the direction of their march required it, rather than follow the streets and go round corners. This led him to conceive the following plan. Canvas-cloths of twenty-four inches in breadth were attached by ribbons to small stakes stuck into the ground and stretched across the march of the locusts on either side at an angle of about 135°. To the top of the canvass-cloth was sewn three inches of oil-cloth. The locusts, whose march was within the stretch of the oil-cloths, at once set to work to climb the obstacle presented to them; but when they got to the oil-cloth their feet slipped on the smooth surface and down they fell to the ground. A little further, and always a little further down the angle they tried to mount, but in vain. At a distance of about 100 feet apart were dug pits of five feet in length, three feet in depth, and two and a half feet in breadth.   Round the mouth of one of these pits a wooden framework covered with zinc four inches in breadth was fixed on the inside. The cloths came close to the ends of the pits, leaving no space for the locusts to pass between the cloth and the pits. After vainly trying to surmount the cloth barrier worked down to the pits the locusts jumped into them, but could not get out, for in climbing up the sides they came to the zinc, over the smooth surface of which they could not pass. Only those who have seen the march of locusts can easily form a conception of their numbers. The locusts of Cyprus are about one inch and a quarter long when they have attained to their marching stage. They march about an inch apart, and I have seen columns of them a mile and a quarter in breadth and half a mile in depth. When the sun is warm and the weather calm they will march about half a mile a day over uncultivated ground. If the cloths were set against such a column the pits would fill in about four hours, and so thoroughly would they be packed that I have seen peasants jump upon the mass and not sink more than a few inches. Fancy the myriads of locusts one and a quarter inches long and one quarter inch broad confined in a pit 5 x 3 x 2 feet. The Porte approved an outlay of 5,000*l.* for these systems, and, at the request of the governor, I got them prepared by Messrs. Wylie and Lochhead, of Glasgow. Without doubt the destruction by this invention was very great in the years when the locusts were abundant, but the most effective measure of destruction will always be by the eggs. When the locusts get their wings nothing more can be done against them.

The locusts in Cyprus are now indigenous, but they may possibly have been first imported from Caramania. They come out in early spring, and they have all died off by the end of July. The desolation which they cause can only be fully appreciated when seen, magnificent fields of grain being levelled by them in a few hours. They settle two or three on each stalk, and at once attack the most tender parts, following the blades into the stalk and thus breaking it over. Of vegetables not a vestige is left on the field. I have seen beds of onions which I passed in the morning in splendid condition, as thoroughly cleaned as if nothing had ever been planted. When hard up for better food they attack fruit-trees and appear to poison them, for parts of some of my orange and lemon-trees which they cleared of foliage, one year, showed the effects for two years after. All the open reservoirs stink with dead locusts. All the eggs smell of locusts and have a deep colour because the hens pursue and eat them all day. When the locusts are in march you cannot put down your foot without stirring them; and if you sit out in the open air you have continually to be on the watch lest they should shelter themselves under your clothes. Whatever they settle upon they mark with a purple stain. They strike against your face if you meet a column on the wing, and they darken the air, but are not then otherwise disagreeable. After they have got their wings they couple. They generally select an uncultivated hill-side for the deposit of their eggs, and large columns deposit in the same place. The female is provided with what has been called a sword-like appendage, by means of which she inserts the eggs into the ground. A glutinous matter which is discharged over them facilitates the future discovery of the eggs, for in early morning the shepherd can discern it glistening on the surface of the soil. This matter becomes perfectly hard round the eggs and forms a kind of case for their protection, which resembles in shape a diminutive silk cocoon. The eggs are placed one over the other like chambers of a honey-comb, and I have counted as many as eighty in a case. The coating round the eggs is so impervious that I have seen the cases exposed to a severe fire without the eggs inside being in the least injured. Boat loads were also thrown into the sea, and all the cases which got washed on the shore were perfectly unharmed, The only effective method of destruction is to bury them under the soil at a sufficient depth to prevent their hatching. A few inches below the surface suffices for this, so that in ploughing the ground where they are deposited all risk of their hatching is removed. The rapidity with which the locusts disappear after the females have deposited their eggs has led the peasants to fancy that the male locust devours the female when she is in the act of laying, and himself dies of indigestion after his repast. My observations in no way confirm this fancy, and I would suggest, as a more probable explanation, that the exhaustion of all green foods under the rays of the sun may deprive them of their natural aliment and lead to their consequent death from starvation. It was a singular coincidence that the severe drought of 1869 followed the destruction of the locusts; and many Turkish, as well as some Christian, peasants looked upon the drought as a punishment from God.

Exposed as the farmer in Cyprus has been to disappointment from drought on the one hand, and to the ruthless ravages of locusts on the other hand, the wonder is not that he is at the lowest ebb of prosperity, but that the island is not one vast desolate waste. If it is not, we owe it to the patience under suffering and the almost superstitious submission to a Divine will which are remarkable characteristics of the Cyprian character. During the summer of 1870 a large portion of the peasants lived chiefly upon roots of all kinds, which they dug up in the fields. It was sad to see the long lines of these poor people arriving daily at the market-places with their trinkets and copper household vessels for sale in order to carry back with them a little flour for their famishing families. And yet there was no bitterness in their heart, no cursing of their sad fate. The exclamation which you heard from the lips of every man during these weary months of hardship was no other than—"O Theos mas lipithee," May God have compassion on us! Never did 1 feel touched by, and never do I expect to join in, such a refrain of joy as when one morning, about two o'clock, the first blessed drops of rain fell which had been seen during twelve months, and when they increased to a torrential shower, men, women, and children, with torches in the dark of night, repaired to the mouth of the watershed to clear away every impediment which might delay the water in reaching their parched fields. It was a strange and touching sight. There was no drunken revelling, but the child-like gratitude which filled every heart found expression in the passionate "Doxa se O Theos!" The Lord be praised!

The horseleech which bleeds the peasant is the usurer from whom he is forced to borrow to pay his taxes and to subsist until his crop is matured. These advances he procures at an almost fabulous cost. Not only does he borrow at an interest of two and sometimes three per cent. per month, but the lender insists upon being paid in kind, with results invariably such as the following. If the peasant delivers ten kilos of grain, he may be thankful if he is credited for them as nine; and if the market value is ten piastres, the peasant will be exuberant in gratitude if he is accorded nine-and-a-half. With these deductions the cost of the advance exceeds forty per cent. per annum. But this is supposing the most honourable treatment. Unfortunately such treatment is the exception rather than the rule. The peasant keeps no account—he signs what he is told, and takes no receipt. A bad year comes, he is ashamed to go near his Shylock; and when the first good year comes, he finds a debt of a few hundred piastres swollen fourfold. In this is his chief misfortune, and the situation morally deteriorates him. Unable to struggle with, or to do without his Shylock, he resorts to all kinds of subterfuges, in the hope of diminishing his misfortunes. Hence the grain mixed with straw and earth which he delivers—the bale of cotton left for twenty-four hours in connection with a jar of water, and numberless similar artifices. It is to be hoped that means will now be found, in a wise and prudent manner, to put capital at the disposal of the agriculturist, and if this is possible the immediate result will be a great extension of his operations, and an amelioration of his whole condition.

CHAPTER XII.
MINERALS AND SALT.

So far I have only dwelt upon the agricultural interest of the island; but its mineral wealth in ancient times was also very considerable. Its mines of copper were extensively wrought as late as the time of the Romans, and we read of their having been leased from the Roman Senate by Herod the Great. No mining operations are now carried on, but it is quite possible that scientific investigations may lead to the discovery of important mineral wealth. The best known copper mines were those near the ancient Tamassus, now the village of Lithrodonto, about three hours ride from Larnaca.

The scientific researches of M. Albert Gaudry upon the mineral wealth of Cyprus are the most valuable material which we possess on this subject, and as I make no personal profession of either geological or mineralogical knowledge, I prefer to give a succinct account of the information communicated by that gentleman. In regard to copper he reminds us that Pliny says, "It was in Cyprus that the first discovery of copper was made; but the mines of the island lost their value in consequence of the discovery of better in other countries." Strabo says, "There are at Tamassus mines of copper of an extreme richness;" and Galen mentions Soli "as the site of copper works." M. Gaudry says that the principal mines were on the western slopes of Mount Troodos. At Lisso there are extensive heaps of scoriae, the refuse from the smeltings of the ancients. To the north of the same village of Lisso, malachite (carbonate of copper) appears to be abundant. At a place called Dginhoussa, situated to the N.N.W. of Lisso, the entrance to an ancient mining-gallery is still visible. Near Poly tou Krysocou (marked Arsinoe in many maps), three mounds of scoriae are met with along the shore. At Soli, or Solia, M. Gaudry presumes that accumulations of scoriae from the works established by the Greeks are to be found. Coming to the centre of the island, he says, that vast accumulations of scoriae are met with on going from Mospiloti to Lithkodonto (the ancient Tamassus). About a mile and a quarter from the village of Lefkara, mounds of scoriae are found on the borders of a torrent. Near the village of Corno there are also extensive mounds. But by the analysis of five specimens of scoriae from Cyprus, M. Gaudry obtained the conviction that little profit would result from their re-smelting. I think it not improbable that the Romans re-smelted the scoriae of the more ancient refiners.

"Iron," says M. Gaudry, "abounds in Cyprus: not only is it found in the conditions of sulphuret and hydrate of iron, but on Mount Santa Crocce I have seen specular iron ore, crystalline and scaly, of excellent quality. However, it does not appear that it was ever worked." M. Gaudry thinks it probable that zinc was worked in Cyprus, "because the ancients speak of pourprolyx and cadmium." " The best cadmium," writes Dioscorides, "is the cadmium of Cyprus which is called botryitis." Galen relates that passing by Solia he found a great deal of cadmium which came from the ancient furnaces. He sent some to friends in Asia and Italy, who pronounced it superior to all the cadmium known.

"The stone of Amianthus, also called Asbestos," says Dioscorides, "came from Cyprus. It is similar to alum slate. Veils for the theatre were made of it; thrown into the fire these veils inflamed and yet came out without being burned, indeed they were more bright than before they went in." Apollonius Dyscolus says, "Amianthus abounds in Cyprus. In descending from Gerandros to Soli it is met with to the left of Elme, at the foot of the rocks." Asbestos is called by the natives bambakopesro, that is, the cotton stone; and gets the name from the appearance of fibre like that of cotton which it contains. From information which is communicated to me by my friend Mr. Baird, there is at about two miles from Pelindria, seven hours from Limasol, a torrent and hill-side which gets the name of Amianthi, and he was told that *there* there was a large rock of Asbestos. This is confirmed by a statement of Sakellarios that asbestos is found at one hour's distance from Palindria.

The island possesses capital quarries of stone. The northern range of mountains gives good and durable stones, and in many places on the southern coast, such as between Cape Pyla and Cape Pedalion, and between Cape Gata and Paphos, any quantity of good stone is obtainable.

The production of salt is a Government monopoly. There are two extensive salt lakes in the island, one near Larnaca, and the other near Limasol. During the rainy season these lakes are filled with fresh water, which the heat of summer evaporates. The soil is strongly impregnated with chloride of sodium, which combines with the fresh water, and when the latter evaporates, a crust of pure salt is left upon the surface of the ground. M. Gaudry supposes that the proximity and action of the sea impregnates the soil with its saline ingredients, but I am inclined to doubt this. Certain it is that in places far removed from the sea, the same deposit of salt is observable. Thus near Nicosia, twenty miles from the sea shore, there is a lake which produces salt, although in small quantities, and I am assured that in the Salt Lake country of America the sea has no influence whatever in producing the salt deposits. In Cyprus the only precaution necessary is to prevent the influx of more fresh water into the lakes than experience has proved that the sun's rays can evaporate during summer. The increase in the value of this revenue to the Government has been very remarkable. Forty years ago the salt lake of Larnaca was leased for an annual payment of 400*l.*, to-day the same lake produces net to the Government over 25,000*l.* The revenue may still greatly be increased by economising the charges of shipment, and thus successfully competing with the salt lakes of Tunis, which furnish a large part of the supplies required on the coast of Syria. The price fixed by the Turkish Government is twenty paras per oke, or about 3*l.* per ton, and the yearly sales about 12,000 tons. No effort is made to refine the salt. It was hopeless to expect such efforts from the Turkish Government, but they deserve to be made by British enterprise, and are certain of success.

CHAPTER XIII.

TURKISH AND FUTURE ADMINISTRATION.

Under the Sublime Porte the island of Cyprus formed part of the Vilaet of the Archipelago. The chief residence of the Vali was at the Dardanelles. The Governor of Cyprus, called a Mutassurrif, resided in the island, at Leufcosia or Nicosia. He administered the affairs of the island with a Council, over which he presided. It was composed of the Mufti, or highest Mussulman religious authority, the Greek Archbishop, the Mubasebegi, or Financial Agent, the Evcaf-nazir, or administrator of Mussulman religious property, and three Mussulman and two Christian notables. The Council met as often as it was summoned by the Governor, and always once week. Its decisions were embodied in documents called "musbatas," which were signed by all the members present. These decisions relieved the Governor of much personal responsibility, and received the highest consideration at Constantinople. The Council occupied itself with all questions of public utility and general administration. From the large Musselman majority in the Council it will be evident that no initiative could be taken by the Christian members; indeed, as a matter of fact, all initiative came from the Governor. The Council was advantageous in giving the Governor, invariably a stranger to the island, the benefit of local advice, and in obliging him to act in harmony with the representatives of the country. To a good Governor it never proved a hindrance; to a bad one it was an impediment to be overcome, but it was no protection against the evils of an inactive administration. The island was divided into, I think, five districts and sixteen arrondissements. The chief functionary over a district was called a Caimakam, and that over an arrondissement was called a Mudir. The Caimakam, or Prefect, administered with a Council, and reported to the Governor. The Mudirs reported to the Caimakam. The Council of the Caimakam consisted of the Cadi, or judge, and four notables. Such was the system of administration which prevailed in Cyprus, and which is known in Turkey as the Vilaet system. It assigned to the representatives of the people an important position, but, partly from incapacity and partly from servility, the Christian population did not profit by the liberal advantages accorded to it. The result was that the Christian representatives were in reality, although not avowedly, the choice of the Governor and Caimakams; but this was a defect, not in the system, but in its execution.

It is evident that much of the system which we have just described might be profitably adopted by the British Government. Substituting British for the Turkish functionaries, who *ex officio* are members of the Councils, eliminating the ecclesiastical members, both Mohammedan and Christian, and giving to Mussulmans and Christians equal representation, there would be the elements of a very desirable Council, containing a highly civilised element, in whose hands would be all the initiative, and a less advanced section, possessing local knowledge and practical experience of the country. The evils of a too personal government would be avoided, and the people would be gradually trained to take an interest in the administration. It cannot be too often insisted upon that our task is not to Anglicise Cyprus, but simply to preserve order, to facilitate the development of the material resources, and to further the moral and intellectual interests of its people. We have to practise what we have so long preached to the Porte—to afford to the native races, by an enlightened and impartial administration, the means of moral elevation and material prosperity. In this view too much government would be nearly as detrimental as too little. Our administration must be only the enlightened conception which guides the native hand; and the Queen of England must not be the mere mistress of Cyprus, but the honoured object of the love and devotion of its native races. There is a vast gulf between the natives of Cyprus and the natives of India, which we must not ignore, and our rule will be an utter failure if we apply to it, without important modifications, our Indian notions of government. The prosperous days of Cyprus were those in which she enjoyed a large share of self-government, and it is to this elevated position that we must again raise her out of the depths of moral degradation and material bankruptcy into which an unenlightened foreign domination has plunged her.

The commercial law adopted by the Porte is based upon the Code Napoleon, and is an admirable condensation of it. There is a very good compendium of Criminal Law for the guidance of the courts, and these are published in both Turkish and Greek. Translations into English ought to be made at once, and the British public will be astonished to find that Turkey possesses such systems of law. It is not the want of proper laws which causes justice to fail in Turkey, it is their vicious application and the complete ignorance of their letter as well as their spirit on the part of those who have to administer them. Few of the judges have ever received an education suitable for the proper discharge of their duties, and as few have the inclination to study the new principles and ordinances of justice which have been decreed at Constantinople. Nor need this be wondered at. The cadis (judges) belong to a religious school imbued with all the bigotry of a Pharisaical sect, destitute of the legal training absolutely necessary, and living in a climate which particularly indisposes to assiduous application and prolonged attention.

I had the good fortune when in Cyprus to possess dragomans thoroughly conversant with Turkish law, and able upon any point to refer to the chapter and text of the code. To one of them especially the caimakam and judge used continually to refer for direction. Just as a Frenchman has by him his Code Napoleon for constant reference, these gentlemen had their Turkish and Greek compendiums always at hand for use. It is impossible for me to mention all the names of those whom I never hesitated to consult upon legal subjects, and who could justify their opinions irrefutably with chapter and verse; but the number was sufficient to prove that after a few years of a proper system of legal training Turkey need not want men able to administer justice and creditably to use her laws. And it will be wise on the part of the British administrators in Cyprus to make the fullest use of these laws; for the advantage to Turkey will be immense if we make her published laws the basis of our system of justice in Cyprus, and thus make apparent the good results of their intelligent application.

In the preceding remarks I do not refer to that part of the Mohammedan Law which is based upon the teachings of the Koran. The perpetuation of that part is as impossible as would be legislation in England based literally on the Old or New Testament. But just as the general principles underlying the injunctions of the Old and New Testament will seldom be found at variance with the spirit of our laws, the general principles of the Koran, when applied by enlightened and impartial minds, are far less inconsistent than most people suppose with the requirements of the nineteenth century. The great defect of the Mohammedan holy law is that there is room for too much elasticity in its interpretation, and that its interpretation is left to men of very varying dispositions.

The constitution of the chambers of commerce in Turkey is admirable. For a year I acted as a member of the Tribunal of Commerce at Larnaca, so that I was able to test the efficacy of its code and organisation. Both were perfect, but the thoroughly unbusiness-like quality of the president and other Turkish members deprived them of their value. There was no punctuality in the hours of meeting, and precious time was lost in unsystematic discussions. The only reform required was the election of a competent president and secretary; but as the former had necessarily to be a Turk, little improvement could be expected from change.

Questions of property and mortgage will probably present the greatest difficulty to the British administrators. By Mohammedan law the transfer of land is not valid unless the proprietor appears before the cadi and declares that he voluntarily transfers all his rights. Refusal to complete this formality has often sufficed to prevent a creditor obtaining his due, and it is commonly asserted, even by Europeans long resident in the country, that no mortgage upon land can be made effectual in Turkey. But even ancient Turkish law provides a very simple and sufficient way, little known and seldom applied, of securing a creditor against the bad faith of his debtor. To effect a solid mortgage, the debtor and creditor must appear before the cadi, state the amount and term of the debt, declare the property which is to be hypothecated, and exhibit the titles of possession. The cadi then names and constitutes a third party, the Vekeel, or agent of the debt. In the event of the engagement of the debtor not being fulfilled, and if there is occasion to realise the mortgage, it is the vekeel who sells the land and gives a valid title to the purchaser. The "takrir," or voluntary declaration of the third party, replaces that of the original possessor, and all opposition of the debtor upon that ground is ineffectual . . .

In a former chapter we explained the nature of the salt monopoly. It is simply an enterprise, worked by the Government for the exclusive benefit of the Treasury, and only in so far as it imposes a fixed price upon the quantity of salt consumed in the island is it a burden upon the population. Of the revenue obtained, 27,000*l.* is derived from salt exported to foreign parts, so that only about 13,000*l.* is paid by local consumers. The working of this revenue is very simple, and the new administration will not do wrong in continuing the system of accounts and control. Some years ago there were extensive abuses in the working of this administration, such as the charging to the Government of expenses never incurred, and the delivery of larger quantities of salt than was paid for to the Treasury. But these abuses have been, in great measure, put a stop to by a fairly perfect system of control. The revenue from salt may be expected to increase under the British rule. Greater facilities for shipment must be provided for export. The expensive and inconvenient transport by carts, from the salt mounds to the shore, must give place to a rapid and easy transport, either by tramway-waggon, or by wire tramway-bucket; and a good jetty should be constructed to facilitate the loading of small craft. With these facilities, and a slightly reduced tariff, the volume of export shipments may be considerably increased. As the chief object to be aimed at is the enlargement of the circle of consumption, it may be wise to supply the export trade for distant countries, such as England, at lower rates. The article is suitable for ballast, and will be cheaply carried. It is expedient that this source of revenue from export should be developed to its fullest extent, as it benefits the Treasury without being in any way a burden upon the island.

We have described the second item of revenue as a royalty upon the produce of all lands. This tax is called "dimes," a contraction for "decima," the tenth part. Its existence dates back from very ancient times, and it may justly be connected in the mind of the reader with the tithe or tenth part which Abraham paid to Melchizedek, King of Salem. In Turkey all lands are sold and purchased subject to this burden, and the natives regard it not so much as a tax, as the share of the Government in the cultivation of the land. It is upon this account that the tithe-tax, although apparently very heavy, is paid by the peasants with far less grumbling than any other tax, and the only disadvantage connected with it is the impediment which the measures necessary for its proper collection are apt to throw in the way of the freedom of the cultivator. This disadvantage is certainly very serious, and when speaking of the cultivation of cotton, I had occasion to give a very good example of the hurtful way in which it may operate. Many schemes have been proposed in Turkey for its abolition, but the difficulty is to find an equally profitable source of revenue which will vary according to the prosperous or adverse circumstances of the cultivator. One proposal met with considerable favour among Anglo-Turkish reformers at Constantinople—the imposition of a fixed tax upon each pair of bullocks. Taxing the possession of land presented the inconvenience of imposing a burden upon lands not under cultivation, a serious disadvantage in a country where proprietors of large estates often leave extensive tracts of land fallow for years; and it was argued, that by taxing the cultivator according to the number of his bullocks, this evil would be obviated. But a grave injustice would have been inflicted by the new system. The tax per pair of bullocks would be necessarily a fixed one, without regard to the value or quality of the animals; and in this the small peasant would have been sacrificed. A good pair of bullocks, such as most large proprietors possess, will easily cultivate forty acres of grain land, while the small bullocks, which the peasant rears and employs, cannot cultivate more than twenty to twenty-five acres. The burden of the tax would therefore fall with unjust severity upon the small cultivator. Fuad Pasha, without exception the most enlightened of Turkish statesmen, a man whose ability would have done honour to any country, was quite conscious of the disadvantages arising from the tax of tithes, and, as an experiment, in one of the provinces of the empire, he converted the tax into a fixed money value, based upon the average of five preceding years. But the experiment did not succeed, and he was obliged to revert to the old system at the urgent request of the inhabitants whom he had wished to benefit.

A somewhat similar experiment was made in Cyprus during my residence there. Upon the urgent representations of Halet Bey, then governor, the Porte did not lease the dimes, but agreed, during three years, to give their collection to each village for a yearly payment of the average amount of its tithes during five preceding years. In this way it was hoped that all arbitrary exactions, and all inconvenience to cultivators would be avoided, and that the farmers would benefit by the profits formerly gained by the tax-collectors. What occurred in the village of Pyla, with which I was connected, will exemplify the working and the defects of the experiment. All the three years were fairly good agricultural years. During the first the primates of the village administered the tax, and at its close declared that there was a loss of about 1,000 piastres between the value of the tithes collected and the amount fixed by the Treasury. The accounts, however, were very imperfectly kept. The loss had to be levied *pro rata* upon the cultivators, and gave rise to a great deal of angry talk—the result of which was that the villagers requested me to arrange for the future administration. This was comparatively easy for me, as more than a third of the tithe I had to pay. An accurate account was kept; every one was satisfied, and the village had a profit at the end of the second year of about 7,000 piastres, while the profits of the third year sufficed to pay the personal tax of the whole village. Unfortunately, the experience of the first year at Pyla was general throughout the island, and repeated during the remaining two years, so that at the end of the period there was a loud demand for a return to the old system. The mass of cultivators did not benefit by the profits, while all were responsible for the losses, and it was evident that if a bad year came round the consequences might be very disastrous. The danger to the Treasury and to the peasant-cultivators of the conversion of tithe into a fixed yearly sum was thus clearly demonstrated. In a good year the peasant does not set aside out of his profits for future contingencies. He invests all his profits in land or cattle if he is frugal, or he spends them thoughtlessly if he is not. In either case they are not available when a bad year comes round. The land becomes absolutely unsaleable, the cattle die off, and the credit of the farmer is so shaken, that he generally cannot borrow. In these circumstances, what comes of the claims of the Treasury? They are either not satisfied, which cripples the Treasury, or in being satisfied they cripple the peasant. Until he has become more provident, and places his savings where a bad year does not affect them, or until land is a sure source of credit at all times, it will be wiser for the Treasury to share the risk of the seasons with the cultivators, and to defend itself against the consequences of a bad year by encashing larger revenues in a good one. The Treasury will frequently find compensation for one bad crop in the goodness of another; but under the system of a fixed average tithe this advantage is lost. The tithe due by the unfortunate cultivator becomes a bad debt for which there is no compensation from his more fortunate neighbour. Some years ago it was the intention of the Sublime Porte, yielding to the outcry of Western critics, to substitute for the revenue of dime a tax of four per mille upon the estimated value of all lands, cultivated or uncultivated; and in Cyprus all the necessary estimations were made. To the peasant proprietor this system would generally be advantageous, because, as a rule, he possesses little uncultivated land; but even he regarded the change with disfavour, as he would become subject to the danger of capricious evaluation.

I have entered at some length into this question for two reasons: firstly because the revenue from tithes is the most important of all, and because I have reason to believe that the idea of imitating the Indian mode of treatment has found considerable favour in influential quarters. I do not deny the expediency of freeing agriculture from the inconveniences of the tithe-collector; all I insist upon is that any conversion into a fixed and invariable money value will be dangerous both to the Treasury and the island until land has come to be a sure and good source of credit, and that any substitute, such as a fixed rate upon valuations arbitrarily established, or a tax per pair of bullocks, is certain to prove in great measure unjust.

In the preceding remarks I have spoken of a real dime or tenth part, but it is right to say that the Turkish Government, in its extreme impecuniosity, exacted an eighth part during recent years. As the British Government happily is not in a similar condition, its first fiscal measure ought to be the reduction of "dime" to its true proportion of a tenth part, and this reduction will be most highly esteemed.

The dimes of Cyprus were leased to the highest bidder. When leased as one lot they invariably fell into the hands of a Turkish, Armenian, or Greek banker of Constantinople. But in recent years the Sublime Porte, before adjudging them at Constantinople, authorised the governor of the island to receive and transmit local offers, and these offers were generally made for the dimes divided into five portions —the dimes of the Messorie, of Larnaca, Limasol, Paphos, and Kyrinia. In this way a very advantageous competition was established. The smaller the lots into which the dimes were divided, the greater the number of competitors. The dimes were leased from the thirteenth of March of each year, but it was never found expedient to adjudicate them until after the "latter" rains of spring, when the prospects of the agricultural year could be fairly estimated. The Treasury had no expense whatever in the collection . . .

The revenue from "dimes" is certain to increase rapidly and considerably, and this will afford the Treasury an opportunity of favouring by reduction certain products which it may be for the interest of the country to encourage. Thus it will be very wise to abolish all dimes upon the product of trees. The loss from such a measure will not amount to £7,000 per annum, and the advantage will be immense in encouraging the plantation of trees—the surest remedy against drought. It will also greatly facilitate the collection of the revenue, for the tax upon the fruit of trees is paid in very small sums, and gives a disproportionate amount of trouble.

We now come to the taxes direct and indirect; but it may be well to draw attention to the fact that in the salt and dime revenues we have found more than half of all the revenues of the island.

Of indirect taxes that which is derived from customs is the most important. The customs tariff established by treaty represents eight per cent. upon all imports and one per cent. upon all exports. It is difficult to prove the justice of these proportions—the inconvenience is very great. Thus the collection of an export duty of one per cent. is scarcely worth the trouble—the gain is nearly all expended in collection, and great trouble is given to the merchant for very little benefit. There appears to be only one of two things to do, either to diminish the import duty and proportionately increase the export duty, or, better still, to abolish the export duty. The custom-house administration in Turkey is exceptionally good, and greatly better in the provinces than at Constantinople. The system of accounts gives an effective control, and the fact that all the *employés* of the custom house are punctually paid out of encashments before these are accounted for to the Treasury has had a great influence in raising the standard of integrity in that branch of the civil service. To his Excellency Kiani Pasha are due the reforms in the custom-house service; and while he was at its head the "comptabilité" of the department was quite equal to that of most European countries. The new administrators of Cyprus will find it an easy task to continue the work of reform which his Excellency so well began. All duties are paid in gold or silver moneys.

The monopoly of weighing and measuring produces about £2,300 per annum. This revenue is leased out by the Government annually in the same way as the dimes, but it is a revenue which ought to be devoted to municipal purposes.

Stamps and a fee upon the transfer of property produce about £3,300. This revenue may with advantage be considerably increased, and indeed the increase is justified, by the better commercial facilities and the superior administration of justice which are assured by British rule.

Since I left the island a Tobacco monopoly has been instituted, but I am ignorant of the amount of revenue which it yields to the Treasury. It cannot be great, and all such institutions are in direct antagonism to British notions, and only justifiable under extreme financial pressure. It might advantageously be replaced, if necessary, by an import duty on tobacco.

The chief direct tax is one called " Verghi," which is a personal tax levied upon all householders and bread-winners. The Treasury does not directly either apportion or collect this tax. Each village has to contribute a fixed amount, for the payment of which the villagers as a whole are responsible. They choose yearly from amongst their number a person who is recognised by the authorities as their representative, and gets the title of "Muchtar," the selected. This person is charged with the collection of the individual contributions, and pays them over to the provincial Treasury. The village pays him a sum varying from £5 to £10 per annum, according to its size. The Muchtar is generally chosen from among the notables. The quantum of the tax to be paid by each breadwinner is apportioned, according to his means, at a general meeting of the villagers. As may be imagined, absolute justice is not always meted out, but it would perhaps be difficult to invent a better system. Proportionately, the well-to-do pay less than the labouring man, for the simple reason that the former have most to do with the distribution of the tax. The sum usually paid by a working man who is not a proprietor of land is about twelve shillings per annum. His gross income may be estimated at twelve pounds, so that the tax represents an income tax, without deductions, of one shilling per pound. Few of the peasant farmers, however, pay more than two pounds ten shillings, and as their incomes frequently amount to one hundred pounds, their personal contribution only represents an income-tax of sixpence per pound. The large proprietors, not peasants, did not contribute their just share, and the Mohammedan proprietors especially got off easily. It will be necessary to obtain accurate statistics of the contributions of each class, and to adjust the burden more equitably. Many of the villages will be found to be considerably in arrear of their payments. Years of drought always left their mark in arrears of village contributions, and considerable sums must be due to the Porte from this cause. It is to be hoped, however, that the Porte will forego such claims, as it would be impossible to allow the Turkish authorities to prosecute them, and it would very disagreeable for British agents to exact them. In the majority of cases, the villagers would dispute the account furnished, and allege payments made to the provincial treasurers which were misappropriated.

A tax upon sheep and goats produced a revenue of £6,000 net. This tax was leased annually by the Government in the same manner as the tithes of land. If I remember right, the amount paid for each sheep or goat, of two years old and upwards, was four-and-a-half piastres annually, while the average value of each animal at that time was only thirty piastres, and the annual income from it did not exceed twenty piastres. As the proprietor of a flock of about 600 head, I found the tax exorbitantly heavy; but the peasant shepherds relieve themselves from great part of its burden by cheating the collector as to the number of their flocks. The rate fixed is the same all over the Turkish empire, which is very unjust, as the sheep of Roumelia are worth three times as much as those of Cyprus.

The last item of revenue which has to be mentioned is the indemnity paid by the Christian population for exemption from military service. Either this tax upon the Christian population must now be abolished, or it must be extended to the Mohammedan population; seeing that both will in future be exempted from military service. The sum produced by the tax is only £7,000, and it would seem most expedient to abolish it altogether.

From this brief and general survey of the taxation Cyprus under Turkish rule, my readers may be inclined to say that the inhabitants have no cause to complain of very severe taxation, which is true if we only take into account the taxes which reach the imperial Treasury. "Happy people," an inhabitant of one of the large towns in England may say, "whose morning appetite is not continually disturbed by disagreeable printed envelopes communicating demands for an endless number of rates and taxes of every imaginable kind and designation. My dog, my horse, my carriage, my servants, my water, my gas, my policeman, all are occasions for a claim of money, whereas the Cypriote has only his 'dime,' his sheep-tax, and his 'verghi' to distress him." But unfortunately in Cyprus, and all over Turkey, the amount of taxes which reach the Treasury does not represent all that the subject has to pay. Every year he is victimised for some new or exceptional object. One time it is an imposition for the establishment of an agricultural bank, which is to work miracles for the peasant. This brilliant idea was lauded to the skies at Constantinople, and gave occasion for innumerable little paragraphs (absolutely necessary from time to time for the delusion of European capitalists) about a new era being inaugurated in Turkey. And what was it? The Porte recognised that the great impediment to the development of agriculture was the high rate of interest which peasants had to pay for the advances of capital they required. Like other Turkish delusions, this agricultural bank was thus based upon a great truth. This impediment was to be removed by the magic wand of the legislator. As a part of the vilaet system (the establishment of which we may say, *en passant*, helped to float a loan in Europe) there was to be created in every province an agricultural bank, which was to supply the peasants with capital at eight per cent. per annum. What a grand thing for people who never paid less than twenty-four per cent., and who could not get money even at that rate! But where was the money to come from which was to be so cheaply invested? Out of the pockets of the peasants. It was enacted that each cultivator was to pay annually to the local administration of his district two bushels of barley and one bushel of wheat, which contribution was to be converted into money, and to form the capital of the "Provincial Agricultural Bank." When the capital had reached a sufficiently respectable amount, applications were to be received from needy cultivators, and they were to be gratified by a loan bearing eight per cent. interest. In other words, the Government said: "You agriculturists need money at eight per cent. I have none to give you; but give me each of you every year a part of the little you have, and with that I will make advances to those I think most needy at eight per cent. per annum." The conception was *bizarre*, a little of the nature of the poors' rates in England. But what happened? The rate was rigorously exacted. The grain was rapidly converted into money, but nearly a year passed before the organisation of the bank was sufficiently complete to admit of its beginning to make its advances to the peasants. The money was not allowed to enter into the accounts of the Treasury, for the Porte would not have it thought that it benefited by the deposits of the Agricultural Bank! The cash therefore was looked after by the provincial cashiers. At last the peasants were to make their applications for assistance. One village consulted me as to what it should do. I answered, "Ask all the money you contributed, and give it to the most needy amongst you." "We are all equally needy," was the reply. " Then divide it amongst you in the proportions in which you paid it." But that was easier asked than obtained. A certain number of applications only were accepted; for the bank must needs keep in reserve a part of its capital. Before the second year came it was found, however, that the reserve had disappeared. The cashier had been changed. The accounts of the Treasury were passed on to the new man in perfect order, but no one thought of the bank reserve. It was gone. The bubble was allowed to burst. The desired effect had been produced upon Europe. New schemes fully occupied public attention. The Government ceased to claim the decreed rate from the peasants, and after the third year no more was heard of the Agricultural Bank. All that is to be found of it and of the peasants' money to-day is represented by piles of printed matter, a constitution, laws, and an organisation, which were read, admired, and applauded by distinguished diplomatists and interested editors. Two parties always played an unenviable part in these comedies: the sanguine capitalist, who found that the whole thing had only been dust thrown into his eyes, and the Sultan's much-esteemed taxpayer, who had been mulcted as usual.

Another common source of bleeding was the construction of roads. In every message from the throne the faithful subjects were told that the construction of roads would receive the immediate attention of the Government. For the misfortune of the inhabitants of Cyprus every governor during the past fifteen years has found it his duty to construct a road from Nicosia to Larnaca without delay. An engineer was specially intrusted with the preparation of plans, and the Council at Nicosia set about to devise the ways and means for their execution. The peasants were each to contribute a certain number of days' work, or to pay a sum of money wherewith labour was to be procured. It was in 1865 that the work was said to be seriously begun, and the estimated cost was to be 4,000*l*. By 1867 twice that sum had been spent, in money and labour, and not a fourth of the road was made. The governor was changed, serious irregularities were discovered, money had been taken from the peasants and misappropriated; in short, the affair had been so mismanaged that the works were stopped for a winter or two, during which all that had been done was undone. Once again the work was begun and peasants dragged away from their occupations—new outlay and new burdens. The governor was again changed and the works again suspended. During the famine of 1870 a sum of £2,500 was granted by the Porte to afford help to the poor. It was wisely employed by Saïd Pasha in carrying on the works on the road to Nicosia, and all that yet exists of them is owing to the expenditure *then* made. Four times what was required to make the road was extracted from the island, and the road was never made.

I have already spoken of the yearly locust-bleeding and its results. Another favourite method was a forced loan. The necessities of the Treasury compelled it to appeal to the tax-payers. A receipt was duly promised which would be respected later! Besides this bleeding for imperial account there remain the continual exactions of the local collector. Every time the zaptiehs came to the village they had to be fed, nourished, and generally subventioned. When a heavy demand for money was made from Constantinople zaptiehs were dispatched to all the villages. The action of these scoundrels depended upon the necessities of the moment. If these were not very pressing they were contented to accept a bribe and return with some excuse which dispensed the village from a visit for a week or two. If the orders were positive to bring money, then the utmost brutality was exercised, and, "coute qui coute," the muchtar had to borrow what he could not collect, or be put under arrest. In short, it is no exaggeration to say that as much as all the personal tax was paid in abusive exactions. No attention was paid to the convenience of the tax-payer. His grain might not be reaped, or it might be still in the threshing-floor; it mattered nothing to functionaries from whom no excuse would be accepted. From all these evils the inhabitants of Cyprus are now delivered, and we may indulge the hope that many years may not pass before the rest of Turkey, through a better administration at Constantinople, may rejoice in a similar deliverance.

My brief survey of the taxation of Cyprus may also afford satisfaction to the British tax-payer. We have seen that the revenue derived from the island amounts to about £180,000, and that nearly a quarter of the whole is from a property belonging exclusively to the Government, and which is very slightly burthensome to the inhabitants. The tithes contribute more than one-third of the whole, and this source of revenue is certain to increase in proportion to the development of the agricultural resources. Customs contribute £23,000, and this income will also be largely augmented from the importations necessitated by a greatly increased population. British administration will certainly be more costly than that of the Turkish Government, but it will also be more effective. It will only, therefore, be mismanagement which will make Cyprus a burden to the imperial Treasury, and the remedy for this mismanagement will speedily be found when the accounts are published. The urgent necessity is that the accounts connected with the general administration of the island should not be mixed up with those which concern imperial interests. For works of general utility, such as irrigation, roads, and government offices, the local administration may well be debited with the interest upon the capital judiciously and economically expended, but the imperial Treasury alone must support the cost of barrack accommodation, a harbour for ironclads, and military depôts.

It has frequently been said that Cyprus is unsuitable for imperial purposes in consequence of its complete want of harbours in which the British fleet may find shelter. This defect, which must be acknowledged, is, however, I think, greatly exaggerated. In all the roadsteads on the southern coast ships have the very best holding-ground, and, with proper care, may ride out any storm without the least danger. The plans of the roadsteads given in this volume are reduced from the Admiralty map, and they show deep water near shore where there is good anchorage. It is otherwise on the northern coast, where the sea-room is more restricted; but the northern coast will never be of value for imperial purposes. The great disadvantage of the roadsteads upon the southern coast is the shallowness of the water for a considerable distance from the shore, and in consequence of which an ugly surf breaks in stormy weather. Anchored within the line of that surf, no vessel will hold in a storm, and native craft, which have not enough of chain to lie outside, come ashore yearly in considerable numbers. But during the nine years of my residence in Cyprus no casualty ever occurred to a European vessel at anchor, nor do I remember any such vessel being obliged to go out to sea for safety. January and February are generally the stormiest months, and it frequently then happens that ships in the roadsteads can hold no communication with the shore during several days. But there is no especial danger in ironclads or any seaworthy vessels with good anchors lying off Larnaca, Limasol, or Famagusta, in the worst of the winter months. At Famagusta the Venetians had a little harbour of sufficient size to hold a small fleet of ships of the tonnage of that day. The harbour is now much filled up, but with a moderate expense it could be cleared and repaired. The sea-wall is still sufficient to cause calm water within the harbour, and I remember a French steamer of the Frassinet Company entering the harbour and lying in it some days when undergoing repairs which could only be made in calm water. I do not pretend to be a competent authority, but I feel convinced that no difficulty will be experienced in greatly enlarging the Venetian harbour of Famagusta, and providing *there* good shelter for large vessels. Such a harbour would be an immense boon to the shipping which frequents that part of the Mediterranean, for there is no shelter for vessels along the whole coast of Syria. Any outlay, therefore, incurred in the construction of a harbour at Famagusta would confer great advantages upon very extensive shipping interests, and in a few years a revenue of some importance might be obtained from harbour dues. Famagusta also presents great advantages for a military depôt. In the time of the Venetians it must have had a population of fully 30,000 inhabitants, and the walls of most of the houses are still standing. The town is surrounded by a ditch, and inclosed within well-built walls of strong masonry, which are in good repair. For the accommodation of a garrison of 10,000 men little more would be needed than restoring the stones to their former places, covering the houses, and delivering the place from the stagnant pools which surround it, and the mounds of *débris* which encumber it. Famagusta might thus become the imperial military station, while Leufcosia or Nicosia in the centre of the island, would remain the seat of the local government.

CHAPTER XIV.

A TRIP THROUGH THE ISLAND

After these "dry-as-dust" details about taxes and administration in the preceding chapter my readers may feel pleased to change the subject. Equally glad were my sister and myself to vary our life in Cyprus with a yearly excursion of three weeks into the interior. Every year we went over new ground as much as possible and so came to know the island from end to end. I hope many of my readers may decide upon following our example, and I cannot desire for them more than as much happiness as we experienced. It was always about the middle of April when we started, just as settled weather might be fairly expected, and when the trees were still clad in foliage, the mountain-streams boisterous in their fulness, and the fields rich in waving corn, or carpeted in green. Our preparations were simple, for we made up our minds before starting to become, for the time being, children of nature, accepting the homely fare with which the land could furnish us. The only exception to our rule was that we provided ourselves with coffee, tea, claret, and brandy—the last only for medicinal purposes. Each had a travelling-bed, which folded into small compass, with its pliable mattress, pillows, sheets, and quilt; and the cavalcade, as it started, was as follows:—First a muleteer on his donkey, which all followed, and which was always the freshest at the end of the day's journey. Next on a mule came my cawass Hasen, from vanity, not necessity, bristling with pistols and dangling a sword; then myself on my own horse, and my sister on hers. The worthy old Arab groom, Mohammed, who followed on a mule, would allow no one ever to interpose between him and my sister's horse, which he watched with a kind of paternal solicitude. Next came Jacob, my servant, factotum, and paymaster; and behind him a muleteer on his donkey, followed by a pack-mule, with the beds and bedding. Thus we started about two o'clock in the afternoon, and made our first halt at the hospitable country seat of an Italian gentleman and large landed proprietor at Nisso, four hours distant from Larnaca. On the way we had passed through the ancient Idalium, and just as we entered it had looked up to a slight rising ground on the left, where was the site of the temple of Venus, which I uncovered, recalling all the pleasant reminiscences of intensely interesting days. All the valley lying to the left of the village of Dali was a vast cemetery, which the men of Dali turned over. The beautiful earrings of gold and the elegant vases which these tombs contained speak of a wealth and refinement in the past far greater than is to be found amongst the simple Daliotes who crowd around to see our cavalcade pass, and the contrast reminds us that the world has not always been progressing. But in the grateful shade of the wooded valleys through which we pass, the fine grain crops, and the well-tilled land prepared for cotton, we may easily comprehend the wealth of the past, and indulge in hopes for the future. After enjoying the hospitable welcome of Mrs. Matei, and having slept comfortably without unpacking our beds, we start next morning, as soon as it is day, for Nicosia, the capital of the island, three-and-a-half hours distant. About half-way we come upon a large bed of oyster-shells—jolly big oysters, such as are eaten in England, not the puny ones offered us in Constantinople—and in the moments of surprise we feel inclined to ask what oystermonger has been throwing out his shells here? Getting down, we pick up some of the finest specimens, thoroughly petrified, and look round to discover the sea which left these disconsolate oysters stranded high and dry. We are in the midst of a remarkable country of hill and valley, which seems to speak of volcanic action during which the sea retired and left dry land between the Bays of Morpha and of Salamis.

As the sun begins to feel warm we are passing on our left a little village in no way attractive, and two or three men and women approach us asking alms. Had we been on the other road to Nicosia by Athienou, similar poor creatures would have offered us a drink of water from an aqueduct which crosses the road. From the noses eaten away in some, and the fingers of others rapidly disappearing, we shudder before these sad victims of leprosy, and learn that the little village is inhabited solely by lepers, who procure themselves a livelihood by begging alms and cultivating a little soil around the village. It is a sad sight in all the different stages of the disease. Some are still comparatively fresh and fair, on others the gradual death has made considerable progress. Yet how insensible they seem to the dreadful reality. They clamour for food, and seem as thoughtless as other people.

We are glad when, a few minutes past this village, we find ourselves on the breast of a plateau, and see Nicosia before us, in what seems nearly the centre of a valley at the base of the rugged-peaked hills of the northern range of mountains. The view is very picturesque, and it is especially striking, because it comes upon us unexpectedly. The tall minarets over the once Catholic Cathedral of St. Sophia, the zinc roofs of the Greek churches glistening in the sunshine, and the rich foliage which surrounds all the houses, invest the first view of Nicosia with a peculiar charm. A quarter-of-an-hour's further ride brings us to the city gateway. The town is completely surrounded by a ditch and well-built fortifications. It is entered by three gateways, those of Famagusta, Kyrinia, and Morpha. The gate of Famagusta, through which we are now passing, looks as if it belonged to primaeval times. It is formed of massive rough-cut wood of about nine inches thick, and the primitive fastening is simply a large square-cut beam, fastened on a pivot to the one half of the door, and inserted, when closed, into an iron catch upon the other. When we enter the town all the beauty which we saw from the outside is dispelled. We pass along ill-paved, narrow streets, and the nasal organs rapidly attest that no attention is paid to the cleansing of the town, and the ruined houses here and the broken aqueducts there serve as a proof that we are in the neglected domains of the Crescent and the Star. We pass with difficulty through the bazaars, crowded with donkeys, mules, and camels bringing produce, and a noisy rabble squabbling over their sales and purchases. From this troublesome crowd, after resting and refreshing ourselves, we gladly repair to the church of St. Sophia. The iron chain under which we must stoop to enter reminds us disagreeably, as it is intended to do, that this once Christian cathedral is now sacred to Mohammed. The change has affected the noble Gothic architecture as disagreeably as our feelings. The minarets blemish the external view just as the dirty mats, faded carpets, and trumpery pulpits destroyed the interior. It requires some effort of the imagination to restore the building in thought to its once solemn and sacred aspect, when during three centuries the kings of Cyprus were crowned within its walls with royal pageant. We venture, with considerable misgiving, to disturb the rest of myriads of fleas, and uncover the marble slabs on the floor which mark the graves of some of the Lusignan kings. But we are glad to get up into the minarets, and look out upon the beauties of the nature which surrounds us. The peaks of the northern range of hills are very fantastic in their cutting. One is called Pentadacktylon, or the Five Fingers, from its resemblance to the half-closed fist, with the thumb distended. The next is Mount Buffavento, 3,200 feet above the level of the sea. On the summit of the next is the ruin of an old castle, and close to it the 100 chambers cut out of the rock. In Nicosia we find ourselves in the centre of a great plain, richly covered with grain, and stretching for sixty miles from sea to sea. The highest point of the southern range, 5,380 feet, is still hoary with snow, and is clothed with pines.

The next afternoon we start for Bellapais, or Dellapais, a convent of white-robed nuns, built in the time of the Lusignans. We cross the ridge of hills by a pass near the village of Dillerno, and, after winding through wooded alleys for nearly an hour, get the first view of the fine ruins. We enter at once, passing to the left into what was the refectory. Hardly can we tear ourselves from the exquisite view which meets our eye on looking out from the windows. I will not attempt to describe it. It is not like Naples, it is not like Constantinople, it is not like the Lebanon—it is a sweet sylvan scene which speaks of peace and plenty. I doubt not that ere many months pass the whole monastery will have been restored to its pristine completeness, and will shelter British functionaries instead of white-robed nuns. On leaving it we accepted the hospitality of a very quaint but worthy man, Haggi Sava, a notable of the village, blessed with the luxury of a one-storied house in the midst of a dense orchard of fruit-trees of every kind. On another occasion, in September, walking through these orchards, I was astonished to observe the ground thickly strewn with fallen bitter oranges, and wondered why this waste. On inquiry it was explained to me that it was not worth while gathering them, for the price which they could fetch in Nicosia barely covered the cost of carriage. My sister thought this would be a paradise of marmalade for Keiller of Dundee. The fruit-trees are *chiefly*, and in some cases *only*, valued for their flowers, from which are made deliciously fragrant waters. Caroub and olive-trees are in great abundance in this district, and our host gathers yearly from his own property 200 tons of locust-beans. Both these trees require to be grafted, else the fruit is not good, and the graft used is simply the insertion into the stem of a shoot, in the case of the olive, of what the natives call the male olive-tree; and in the case of the caroub, of an already-grafted caroub-tree. The trees grow spontaneously, and are grafted after they have attained a certain height. Our host, Haggi Sava, has grafted the worst of all his caroub-trees during his lifetime, and increases his wealth yearly by the same simple means. In the district at Paphos there are extensive tracts of wild olive-trees, which only wait for the hand of man to graft them.

I could with pleasure continue to carry the reader along with us in our pleasant tour from Bellapais to Kyrinia, thence by Lapithos to Morpha, thence by lovely Soli to the monastery of Chico, near the summit of Mount Troodos; thence to Paphos, old and new; thence, retracing our steps, to Limasol by the ruins of ancient Curium, and from Limasol to Larnaca. We accomplished the whole tour, without any great fatigue, in twenty-one days. But I gladly leave the pleasant task to the more able pen of some equally fortunate tourist, and I hope that ere long his name and number may be "legion."

I had some interesting conversation with the monks at the monastery of Chico, near the summit of Troodos. This monastery is the richest in the island. It shelters about sixty monks, who are not recluses counting their beads and devoted to contemplation. On the contrary, they are busily occupied with the property of the monastery—some superintending flour-mills, others administering farms: living without care, yet fully engrossed with temporal concerns. A large number of boys are attached to the monastery, from whom the ranks of the monks are recruited, and who have their time divided between a little schooling, much chanting, and all kinds of menial occupations in the fields and in the convent. Of anything like literary work or theological study the monks have none, and the consequence is that the clergy are inferior in intelligence to the upper classes of the laity. Of course there are some pleasant exceptions. During my residence in the island the Archbishop of Cyprus was a most enlightened man, and a devout and exemplary Christian. He was quite conscious of the necessity of giving the monks a more advanced education, and was doing the utmost which his limited means would allow to secure it by the support and personal encouragement which he gave to a superior seminary attached to the Archiepiscopal Palace at Nicosia.

The monastery of Chico possesses a much revered image of the Virgin, supposed to be the work of the Evangelist Luke, who, according to tradition, was an artist. Pilgrims from all parts of the East, and especially from Russia, come to worship before this image, and considerable presents are made to it with all sorts of expectations. Married couples go there with prayers like those of Hannah of old; and on one occasion I was assured that a young lady sent 2,000 piastres to the image in order that one of my colleagues might be inspired with loving sentiments towards her.

Finding myself at Chico on a Sunday I expressed to a deacon, with whom I had become friendly, my desire to assist at the morning service. About half-past four in the morning I went to church, and found a lad reading aloud from a book which he held in one hand, while in the other he had a wax candle. The book was the Psalter of David—a seventh part was thus read every morning. There was hardly any one in the church, and those who were there paid no attention to the reading. By the time it was completed it was daylight, and then a goodly number of people began to assemble. The priests were chanting and singing in the inner sanctuary with the doors closed, while the people were waiting without. At length my friend the deacon came out from the sanctuary, clothed in full canonicals and swinging in his hand a censer of incense. He turned and bowed reverently before the image of the cross, and then having walked down the church, diffusing the fumes of the incense around him upon the people, he re-entered the sanctuary. After a few minutes he returned, followed by the priest, and carrying a large finely-bound Bible. Turning again to the image of the cross, he held up the Bible before the priest, who kissed it, and both re-entered the sanctuary. At this point the monk Chrysanthus beckoned to me to enter by the side-door of the sanctuary, and obligingly put for me before a window to the right of the altar a large Bible, open at the lesson of the day. With this and the Book of liturgy I was able to follow the whole service. The three liturgies used by the Greek Church are those of St. Gregory, St. Chrysostom, and St. Basil. As the last-mentioned is the longest, it is always read on Sunday. The priest read all the prayers "mustikos," that is, to himself, kneeling before the altar; and while he was thus praying the people without were singing and chanting anthems. A little bell announced to the people when the priest had ceased praying, and the people responded "Kyrie eleison" (Lord have mercy), and crossed themselves. The deacon, facing the altar and standing before the people, then read the lesson of the day. This terminated, and the rest of the liturgy, the communion service, began. A silver cup full of wine and a platter of bread cut into small pieces were put upon the altar, before which the priest stood, with the deacon at his side. The former then read from 1 Cor. xi. 23. This ended, he asked a blessing, and after offering up a prayer he partook of the bread. The deacon then prayed, and had administered to him by the priest a piece of the sacramental bread. Similar ceremonies were gone through in partaking of the wine. The deacon then carried the cup and platter to a table at the left side of the altar, before which a few monks were assembled, who partook of the sacramental emblems. After this the monk Chrysanthus approached me, and politely asked me whether I desired to communicate. Fearing lest some of the monks, less liberal in their opinions, might be offended, I thought it wise to decline.

After service I visited the library of the monastery. It was carefully locked up, and very seldom if ever opened except at the request of strangers. It contains some fine editions of the old Fathers, and very possibly works and MSS. of far greater interest than the monks realise.

After dinner I had a long talk about sports and kindred subjects. It is on the Troodos that the "Moufflon," generally called a wild sheep, is found. This animal is only known to exist on Mount Troodos and in the Island of Sardinia. The natives call it "Agrina." The skin and hair is like that of a deer, but it has no tail, and the horns are like the horns of a sheep, curling handsomely back. It is excessively fleet, and until rifles came into use was very difficult to shoot. According to the natives it scents man at a great distance; and there is considered to be no chance of getting near enough for a shot if the wind is carrying his scent to the moufflon. Their numbers are decreasing considerably from the improvements in sportsmen's weapons. It is hopeless to attempt to tame them even when taken small. Some thirty years ago the venison of moufflon used to be part of every great dinner in Cyprus. Only on two occasions, however, was I able to have it in Larnaca, and then it was brought down stuffed with salt. The skins are much prized by the Turks as prayer-rugs. That of the male is the finest.

The conversation afterwards turned upon venomous reptiles, and of course upon the dreaded snake, which the natives call "kofi" (deaf). Sakellarios tells us that the Cypriotes pretend that this snake is half its time deaf, and the other half blind. From fear of it the peasants, both men and women, always wear long boots. Its bite is fatal. I had no actual knowledge of any deaths due to it during my residence in Cyprus, but I remember a man whose arm had been cut off by the shoulder to save him from the effects of a snakebite on the hand. The haste with which the amputation was effected saved him, and for all I know he is still living in Larnaca. The monks told me marvelous stories of what they described as a stone, which they said could be extracted from the head of the snake when asleep, and which was an antidote to its poison. According to them, this material, which when asleep was concentrated in its head, becomes dispersed over the body when awake. They told me of a man in the neighbourhood who had such a stone, and when I asked what I could purchase it for, they said I could not get it under 10*l*., because the proprietor got large fees from people who were bit. They told me also of people who got the name of snake-suckers, and who were applied to, often successfully, to suck the bite, and thus extract the poison. These men pretend to have drunk a fluid from the snake which enables them to suck the bites without harm. This fluid was said to be procured in the following way. Immediately upon a snake being killed it is hung up in the sun upon a tree with the head down. From the mouth a liquid matter begins to drop, and it is this fluid which the snake-suckers drink. It was said to shorten their life, and to give them a peculiar colour. I was so struck with many of these details, that I noted them carefully at the time, but alas! I lost my note-book between Chico and Limasol. A few years after I met an English doctor on board one of the Peninsular and Oriental steamers who had made Indian native traditions about reptiles his especial study, and when I told him the Cyprian belief about the snake-stone, he said he had met with the same in India.

A few particulars about the first British camping-ground in Cyprus since the days of Richard Coeur de Lion may be of interest. It has been called the "Pasha Cheflik," but the words ought to be transversed. Cheflik means a farm, and this farm gets the name of the farm of the pasha from the following circumstances. Some eighty years ago a wealthy pasha of Constantinople was banished to Cyprus. According to Mohammedans it is an act of the highest beneficence to give water to a town, and this pasha took pity upon the condition in which he found Larnaca. He dug pits about five miles to the west of it, and at a depth of from twenty to thirty feet found a good source. He led the water at his own cost by covered canal and aqueducts to Larnaca, and thus provided the water which our troops relished so much at their camping-ground. In the letter of a newspaper correspondent the aqueducts near the ground are called Roman, but this is a mistake. The worthy pasha was a practical man, and from fear lest his beneficent work should be neglected after his death, he established a farm in the neighbourhood of the watersource, the revenues of which he assigned in all time coming for the repair of the wells and the preservation in good condition of the watercourse of Larnaca. This farm is known as the Cheflik of the Pasha. By abuse its revenues have latterly been turned from their original destination, and now benefit an heir of the pasha in Constantinople. The act of dedication is, however, perfectly explicit, and was translated to me frequently by Mr. Elia Fatullah, who worked nobly with me, and after my departure, in connection with the water-supply of Larnaca. It was remarked in a correspondence from Larnaca that some mischievous people from time to time cut off the water-supply. The mischievous people invariably are the lessees of the farm, or others, with even less right, along the course of the canal, who turn the water into the fields during the night to water their cotton or vegetables.

Game is abundant in Cyprus, especially in the neighbourhood of Paphos. But the sport will not be fully enjoyed until a few shooting-lodges have been erected. I would suggest putting up a shooting-lodge at Laco Franca, some hours before reaching Old Paphos, on the road from Limasol. Near Paphos, and at Tricomo, beyond Famagusta, francolins are got, but their number is yearly diminishing from want of protection. The male francolin is a beautiful bird akin to the pheasant. I succeeded in getting home for Lord Lilford a male and female bird, both of which, if I remember right, lived for some time in his preserves. The chief difficulty in transporting them is in preventing them from injuring their heads. They are exceedingly timid, and upon the least alarm spring upwards. If they strike their heads against any hard surface, a few minutes suffice to make a wound from which death is certain. I found the best protection by drawing across the top of their cage a piece of cloth which had not sufficient play to allow the head of the bird to reach the roof.

The hares of Cyprus are especially good and abundant. The partridges are not red-legged, and are deficient in delicacy. Woodcocks come down into the plains when snow is on the mountains. Quails are abundant in many places. I remember Captain Wild and Lieutenant Fitzgerald, of H.M.S. *Raccoon*, bagging eleven brace in the garden of the Cheflik of the Pasha in a couple of hours.

Before concluding this chapter I may add a few words on the climate. The island is very commonly called unhealthy, but I object to the expression until I know what is meant. If it is meant that Englishmen cannot go out there without considerable risk during the summer months of catching fever and ague, I admit its correctness. But to what country, with the thermometer generally about 90° in the shade, can Englishmen, with their national love of heavy eating and alcoholic liquors, be sent without incurring a considerable risk of sickness of some kind? A large portion of those who go to Cyprus will enjoy as good health as they can hope for in any country. Further, I object to blaming the climate for evils which result from defective sanitary regulations, and especially from the over-crowding, without previous preparation, of towns without sewers, without street-cleansers, surrounded by stagnant pools and all that the laziness and indifference of man can accomplish to infect the air. I must judge of the healthiness or unhealthiness of the climate from its effects upon those who, from long usage, live in accordance with its requirements, and who inhabit places free from exceptional and removable disadvantages. Judged by this standard, the climate of Cyprus cannot be declared unhealthy. It is inhabited, as it has been from time immemorial, by a perfectly healthy and robust native population, free from all serious sickness, and living to a hale old age. The climate of which this can be said cannot be called unhealthy. Facts, however, often carry more conviction than reasoning, and it is a fact that I lived in Larnaca, and went about the island summer and winter during nine years, and never enjoyed better health anywhere. My sister spent four years there with a similar experience. The consular changes which I witnessed during my residence there were of three French consuls, three Italian consuls, three British vice-consuls, two American consuls, and the only casualties amongst them were the death of a French consul from cholera and of an Italian consul when absent from the island. All the others, although disgusted with an inactive life destitute of social resources, left the island in perfectly robust health, and never suffered from any serious sickness. Of the pernicious fevers recounted by Dr. Clarke, who spent ten days in the island, I can only say that I never heard of them during my residence, although they may have existed before my arrival.

The fever common to Cyprus is quotidian intermittent fever or ague. The premonitory symptoms generally are lassitude, a peculiar whiteness in the extremity of the finger-nails, and debility about the knees. Nearly all chills and derangements of the stomach produce this fever. Exposure with insufficient covering to the dews of evening or the low temperature of the early morning are a very common cause of chills; and unripe fruit, especially cucumbers and musk melon, are frequent causes in summer of a derangement of the stomach. The patient suffers first from a feeling of coldness, which produces a convulsive shaking, and then from excessive heat and feverishness, which passes off in a profuse sweating. During the cold fit everything should be done to produce heat, and during the hot fit to produce perspiration. Great care must be taken not to check the perspiration. After a profuse sweating the temperature of the body falls and the patient will soon feel perfect relief. It is then that he must actively attack the disease with quinine. Anyhow taken, either in coffee or in pills, twenty grains (that is the weight of twenty grains of wheat) should be divided into five portions, and four of the portions taken with an interval only of half-an-hour if the patient is strong. In nine cases out of ten this will thoroughly kill the fever. The fifth portion should be taken the next morning, or a few hours before the attack came on the previous day. Many people never succeed in killing the fever, because they take the doses after too long intervals, or from the use of bad quinine. If the attack has been the result of a derangement of the stomach, which the patient can easily discover, as soon as the fever is killed a purgative medicine should be taken; but care must be observed that the strength of the patient is not too much impaired.

There is nothing in the least dangerous in the attacks, although when under them the patient looks and feels very miserable.

Of itself exposure to the sun will not give fever, but exposure to the sun without proper protection for the head will produce sunstroke. This brings on a high state of feverishness, and generally delirium. The best remedy is ice at once applied to the head.

Watchfulness and proper precaution is the best preventive against intermittent fever and sunstroke. Excessive exertion is imprudent. All ices are to be avoided, they can only safely be indulged in when the body is perfectly cool, and even then they must be taken very slowly. My experience was that all cold drinks and too cool clothing are unsuitable to the climate of Cyprus. I had to avoid linen clothing from a tendency to catch a chill producing dysentery. This chill came upon me when I sat down in the cool day breeze, with the pores of the skin opened from perspiration. I found light flannel or tweed clothing the safest, with a silk "ceinture" round the waist. Wearing this "ceinture" I could dispense with a vest, which is a great relief. He will suffer least in the long run who bears patiently with the heat, and neither increases it unnecessarily nor tries to drive it out of him unnaturally. For the dysentery which chills brought upon me, I found a glass of good

Commanderia wine taken after coming from stool was better than brandy, and generally sufficient. Life under canvas and sleeping on the ground or without good cover from the dews are both to be avoided. Inactivity and a dull life predispose to fever. I never had a thorough attack, and when I felt the least premonitory symptom, a free perspiration after a good gallop and a pill of quinine sufficed to put me all right.

CHAPTER XV.
ARCHAEOLOGY.

. . . Some thirty years ago the interesting bas-relief which Sargon presented to the Cyprian princes in the eighth century B.C., was uncovered in a garden near Larnaca. I have heard that it was offered to the British Museum, but only £20 was offered for it. The Berlin Museum was more intelligent, and secured the monument for about £50. It is still the most valuable of all Cyprian statues, being in admirable preservation, and bearing upon itself its own history in a long cuneiform inscription. Some time afterwards, on a hill-top near the ancient Idalium, there was found what is known as the bronze tablet of Dali, a beautifully perfect inscription of thirty lines and some 1,300 letters in Cyprian characters. This precious relic, still unique of its kind, was acquired by Mr. Peritie of Beyrout for the Duc de Luynes.

*   *   *   *   *

In 1868, after a torrential rain, some peasants of Dali were passing along the base of a hillside to the north of their village on the summit of which is a well which gets the name of Laksha Nicoli. They found, evidently washed down from the hillside, a few pieces of ancient pottery in perfect preservation, and one of them representing a duck. The peasants at once thought that more might be found where these came from, and they set to work to turn over the ground on the hillside. To their surprise they got into tombs, and extracted pieces of pottery in great number, and some lances in bronze. News of the discovery soon spread, and as the villagers were in much distress, having lost most of their crops from the ravages of locusts, they repaired in great numbers to the pottery-diggings. The Sunday after, when walking with Mr. Pierides (who was my coadjutor in all connected with antiquities, and who was my instructor from his superior, nay, very exceptionably profound antiquarian and philological knowledge), I heard of these discoveries and without loss of time we arranged to send an intelligent *employé* to the seat of the find, with orders to acquire some objects and send them for inspection. This agent found Mr. Ceccaldi already on the spot. The objects were new and varied, and nearly all of them came to Mr. Ceccaldi or myself. This mine led to the discovery of many more, and the peasants of Dali came to spend all their time in searching for tombs and rifling them. The number of objects increased, and so did the purchasers. My friend Mr. Sandwith, the British vice-consul, began to acquire, and after him another friend came into the field, who, although he began last, was destined to carry on his explorations longer than any of us, and with the most brilliant results, I mean, the American Consul-General de Cesnola. The novelty began to pass away, and yet new arrivals came to us daily. Our houses became like earthenware shops. The pieces found might be counted by tens of thousands, and the tombs opened by thousands. The peasants of Dali attained a proficiency in tomb-finding quite extraordinary, and, unfortunately for the purchasers, became knowing in the value of the pieces. They were led chiefly by two men, the one, Hasen, a Turk of Dali, who became attached to the American Consulate, and the other old Hagge Georgi, the finder of the "Tablet of Dali." The former had an extraordinary aptitude for such work, and, guided by the intelligence and perseverance of General Cesnola, his discoveries were certainly the finest made in Cyprus. The latter was chiefly my man, and had wonderful luck.

One day in 1869, just as I was getting tired of the pottery and glass finds, Hagge Georgi sent me a pressing request, that I should come at once to Dali because he had made some wonderful discoveries. It would be a long story to tell all the difficulties I experienced in the new work put upon me, but it proved a pleasant change in my antiquarian amusements. A temple had been discovered at Idalium, with its ancient contents, nine feet underground, and I determined to uncover it in a systematic way. The recompense of my labour was far beyond my expectation. One piece of stone alone which came to my hand I would not have exchanged for all the treasures of the tombs of Cyprus. It had a bilingual inscription in Cyprian and Phoenician characters . . . Besides this precious bilingual stone, and several Phoenician, Cyprian, and Greek inscriptions, a large collection of statues and two treasures of silver coins belonging to the early periods of coining were found in the temple. The inscriptions, the coins, and the best preserved of the statues are now in the British Museum. Shortly after I had finished the excavations at Dali, my men found another temple at Pyla, which was also carefully uncovered, but with much inferior results. It was the turn of my friend General Cesnola to have announced to him, in 1870, the discovery by his men of large statues near Athienon, which could only belong to a temple. Ten days later another temple was struck about 800 yards distant, and the contents of both became afterwards known as "The Temple of Golgos," and are now in America. Both temples were rich in statues, which were very perfect in their preservation, and many are most interesting as specimens of archaic sculpture. The second temple contributed a number of Cyprian inscriptions.

In 1864 the family of Count de Maricourt (then French consul for Cyprus) was in the habit of making an evening promenade towards the Salt Lake, about a mile from Larnaca. One of the party turned up in the sand a diminutive statue in terra-cotta, and this find led to further investigations. Other pieces were discovered close by, and daily, during several months, the party of ladies and gentlemen might be seen repairing to the spot to turn up statuettes just as others go to pick wild-flowers. In a very short time the family had formed a considerable collection, including some exquisitely beautiful pieces. For some time the ground was respected by courtesy, and we satisfied ourselves with admiring the pieces when they were found. But this was not long the case. Many idle workmen went there to search, and for at least seven years they never searched in vain. The objects found were in terra-cotta, and generally of the later Greek and Roman epochs. In 1870 five young men were digging for statuettes in these same sand-hills, when one of them came upon a bronze vase. He raised it. It broke in his hands, when, to his amazement, he saw shining coins run out of it. His companions had not perceived what had taken place, and his first impulse was to cover it up till he was alone. He did so; but a short time after his anxious curiosity overcame him, and he turned the earth back to see if all was still there. This time one of his comrades caught sight of the shining metal, and concealment was no longer possible. The contents of the vase were divided amongst the five, each taking a handful at a time. They went home with their prize and kept it quiet for two days. But the wife of one of them, in her joy and fear, could not contain the secret. She went and told it to Mr. Pierides, who came and told it to me. In a few hours we obtained possession of about 600 gold staters of Philip and Alexander the Great, for an equal number of Napoleons. Still this was not all—some had been kept back—and it was not until after several months that we acquired the whole find with the exception of about 100 pieces. All were in good condition, some quite beautiful, just as they had come from the mint. I disposed of five hundred of the common impressions at Constantinople. I parted with fifteen beautiful pieces to the Duke of Sutherland, and the choicer types I carried to England to compare with those in the British Museum. By the kindness of Mr. Poole a thorough comparison was made, and it was found that ninety-nine types in my possession did not exist in the collection of the British nation. Thus five young men who were working in the hope of gaining a shilling or two a day stumbled upon a treasure which brought them about 800*l* . . .

Doubtless much is still to be found of archaeological interest in Cyprus, and happily all impediment to its discovery is now removed. Of all the consular body at Larnaca the British Consul was the only one who was unable to obtain from Constantinople a firman for excavating. I applied officially to the British Embassy, and privately to Mr. Pisani, but the answer was that as the Porte itself had the intention of forming a museum no firman could be obtained. Of course the British Embassy, sacredly respecting Turkish rights, was bound to accept such an excuse. The American Ambassador laughed at it, and year after year his consul's firman was renewed. Fortunately my position in the island sufficed to secure that I should not be molested, and when the governor told me one day, during excavations at Dali, that he ought to stop me because I had no firman, I answered him jokingly that he needed a firman to stop me, which he had not. The shipment out of the island was attended with considerable difficulty, but it was somehow managed. *Cela se fait, mais ne se dit pas.* One colossal statue from the temple at Pila, however, seemed destined to become Turkish property. It was about seven feet high and of a great weight. An Austrian frigate whose captain was an enthusiastic antiquarian was in the roadstead at the time. In conversation, I spoke of my statue and the change of proprietorship which was probably in store for it. He at once offered to remove it if I would sell it to him. A nominal price of a few pounds was arranged, and he engaged to remove it after sunset. About eight o'clock the frigate's pinnace came ashore at a jetty close to my house, and half-a-dozen sailors landed out of it a powerful stretcher. This was carried into the courtyard of my house. The gate was closed. The statue was laid upon the stretcher and a coarse sheet thrown over it. The sailors, without any ado, carried off their load and passed the custom-house guard, who remained impassive, probably wondering whether it was a dead or drunken man who was being carried off by his comrades.

CHAPTER XVIII.
MY FARM IN CYPRUS.

. . . The farm of Pyla, which I leased for ten years, is about six miles from Larnaca. It consists of about 1,000 acres of arable land, of which only sixty were what are called livadia lands, that is lands capable of producing summer crops without artificial irrigation. It possessed a perennial source of water, capable of watering seven to ten acres of cotton land. The farm had been thoroughly neglected by previous tenants, and when I received it only sixty-five acres of poorly ploughed land were ready for sowing. As my only object was an interesting pastime, though I had no intention of losing money over it, I began work with only four pairs of bullocks, purposing to increase the number gradually as my arrangements progressed. My first farm-steward was a Nubian, formerly a slave, who had worked the land long years before under his master. He was honest, and thoroughly understood the work of farming. Upon his death I engaged his son, who had all the good qualities of his father. Thus there was no exceptional capacity brought into play either in master or steward. All my ploughmen were natives, some Mohammedan and some Christian. My bullocks were the best that could be got in the island, capable of doing good work. Of the years during which I held the farm, two were years of exceptional disaster from drought, such as old men had not remembered. During four we were afflicted by locusts (an affliction which ought never more to be tolerated), and only two years out of the ten were really good years. Nature, therefore, was in no way propitious to me. Up to the fourth year all was outlay, clearing ground, thoroughly manuring the cotton land, and lightly dressing some of the best grain lands. By the fourth year, with four pairs of bullocks, I put under seed 72 acres of wheat, 117 acres of barley, 5 acres of beans, 27 acres of cotton land; and by native associates 30 acres of wheat, 26 acres of barley, 18 acres of cotton.

My outlay at that time amounted to 125,000 piastres, say 1,150*l.*

In the fourth year I increased my bullocks to five pairs, and in the fifth to six pairs. By the seventh year my sowings reached, by my own bullocks, 128 acres of wheat, 124 acres of barley, 6 acres of beans, 1 acre of oats, 27 acres of cotton land. By native associates: 73 acres of wheat, 78 acres of barley, 18 acres of cotton.

My arrangements with native associates were that I gave the land and seed, and we shared the produce equally.

The last year of my lease my sowings were, by my own bullocks: 262 acres of wheat, 202 acres of barley, 5 acres of beans, 27 acres of tares, 25 acres of cotton land. By native associates: 135 acres of wheat, 202 acres of barley.

My bookkeeping was perfect, and in it was the secret of my control as to results. The rent which I paid represented fully five per cent. interest on the value of the farm, and upon all the capital which I invested interest was debited to the farm at eight per cent. per annum. By the seventh year (the sixth had been a year of drought) I had covered all expenses and had 201*l.* of clear profit, and by the end of the tenth (after another disastrous year of drought) the clear profits amounted to 901*l.* My outlay at its highest point only reached 1,150*l.*, and that only for a few months. For that outlay I got eight per cent. per annum, and had at the end of the lease over 900*l.* of profit, after selling off everything and some things at a considerable depreciation. But during that period I had paid for a clerk and a steward 770*l*., by which amount the profits would have been swollen had I been, as I easily might have been, both clerk and steward. In any event the salaries paid these *employés* would have sufficed to administer operations of three times the extent. Supposing, then, the operations to have been of three times the extent (and I would not recommend anything less), the results, even with my bad luck in years and my personal inactivity, would have been eight per cent. return for capital and 4,240*l*. clear profit at the end of ten years.

Devoting oneself personally to the work, and having the advantage of cultivating rich soil, the return ought to be two-fold. It must be added that living at the farm is very inexpensive. A farmer feeds from his flock and his barn *without* cost.

* * * * *

I have the pleasure in saying that my experiences in Cyprus prove that the Cyprian peasant is a good debtor. Of some seventy villagers in Pyla, to whom I made constant advances at twelve per cent. interest per annum, all, with hardly an exception, repaid me capital and interest, notwithstanding the sufferings of two years of drought. They prospered to such an evident degree that whereas I found the village sunk in debt, and in the greatest misery, I left it prosperous and cultivating a much larger extent of land. In order that advances to the peasant may be safe, title-deeds must be sure, mortgage simple, and land easily realisable. The first two of these essentials it will doubtless be the care of the British Administration to attain as early as possible, and the third will follow as a necessary consequence of general prosperity. It will be essential to interest British capital, and offer it a basis so sound and sure as may inspire it with confidence, for the greater the confidence which can be inspired the cheaper will be the rate at which capital can be attracted. It is too soon to enter into detail on this question, and these pages are not the place to do so in, but I have no hesitation in saying that it will not be difficult to devise a simple and efficacious system to satisfy both the British capitalist and the Cyprian landed proprietor.

CONCLUSION.

In the preceding pages I have endeavoured to give a fair and impartial account of the past and present of Cyprus. The island has known many masters and paid homage to nearly all the great conquering dynasties of the past. Their object was ever either dominion or gain. But it is *now* united, under the beneficent sceptre of the Queen of England, to a rich and generous people, whose aim in its acquisition is neither empire nor profit, but the diffusion of the blessings of civilization and of the elements of an enlightened progress. With a population docile and peace-loving, and a Government which emanates from neither a military nor a dynastic despotism, but from the paternal solicitude of a nation whose watchword is *Freedom, Justice,* and *Tolerance,* it needs no prophet to foresee the future prosperity and enviable happiness of both the Mohammedan and Christian populations of Cyprus.

AMEN!

INDEX

C

PLATE 1

Mount Croce   Mount Olympus

Arpera

Chitty

Larnica

Salines   Livadio

Cape Pilo

Salines Bay

a. Salines Bay (Drummond p. 173)

ὅρα καλῶς τῷ μοναχῷ του ἀληθῶς τον βίον
πῶς πανῦθεν ἐσαυρῶ]αι ζαρκιτε καὶ τω κοσμω
ὁμεν ςαυρῷ. γαρ Φανερως την νεκρωσιν σημαινει
ἀιδε λαμπαδες ἀληθῶς των ἀρεΐων την λαμψιν
ἠκλεισις δε των ὀφθαλμων τομη ὁραν καθολυ
τα μά]αια καὶ ἀςα]α τουτυ τουπλανυ κοσμυ
του ςομα]ῷ. δε ἡσιγη τομη λαλειν ἀκαιρως
ὕβρεις κὴ λογια αισχρα αἰωνῷ. τῳ παρον]ῷ.
ὁι ἥλοι δε ὁι των πoδων τομη βαδισειν ὁλως
ὁδον την πανενρυχωρον καὶ μη τρυφᾶν ἀσωτως

ἀλλα ἀγαπη καὶ σιγη ἀ⁔νο]ητιτε βιυ
λαμπειν τω κοσμω νοητως ὑπὲρ ἀυγας ἥλιυ
διαπανΐος⁔ε πολεμειν ἀπα]αιωνι κοσμω
κὴ της ζαρκῷ. τοις παθεσι κακιςω διαβολω
ὁ γαρ δεσπότης του παν]ῷ. ζυν τοις ἀυτου ἀγΐελοις
προς την αυτα βοηθειαν πλησιον αυτυ ἐςι
κὴ ςεΦῷ. κὴ διαδημα ἐν ταις χερσι κα]εχει
εἰγε νικηση τῆς ζαρκῷ. τυ κοσμυ τε τα παθη
ἵνα την τυτυ κορυφην ἀξιως ςεφανωση
κὴ βασιλειας ὀυρανων ἀυτυ κα]αξιωση
α. ψ. μ. δ.   ιυλιω.

b. Inscription (Drummond p. 265)

PLATE 2

a. Tower at Colos (Drummond No. 1, after p. 270)

No. 1.

See Page 267.

Church of St. Mamas, at Morfou *from a. to b. 53 ft. pt.*

b. Church of St. Mamas at Morphou (Drummond No. 1, after p. 270)

PLATE 3

South East Front of Agios Largos or St Hilarion?

b. St. Hilarion (Drummond No. 3, after p. 270)

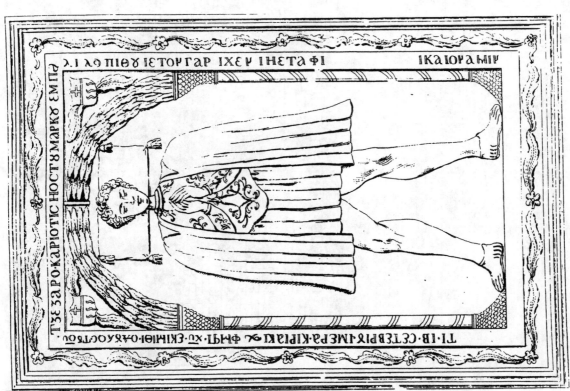

a. Stele (Drummond No. 2, after p. 270)

PLATE 4

Dela-Pays (Drummond No. 4, after p. 272)

PLATE 5

South View of Buffavento Castle or Queens Palace.

a. Buffavento (Drummond No. 5, after p. 270)

West View of Cantara Castle

b. Cantara (Drummond No. 6, after p. 276)

PLATE 6

....DOVAIRIN OLASPASSA AXXIX IORS DDILAB U AD D CLAXVIIID'
CL....

a. Inscription at Dela-Pays (Drummond p. 272)

b. Kanakarga (Drummond No. 7, after p. 276)

✠ ICI GIST DAME MARGVERITA
D' BOVDAPRA ESPOVZA OL RV.
D'MESSIRA ANGOINA D'GABO
LINLA OL LLAC GS PASSAAXXX
IORS D'ACVTA RLAD D'MCOGAXX
IIIIX' aST

c. Inscription (Drummond p. 279)

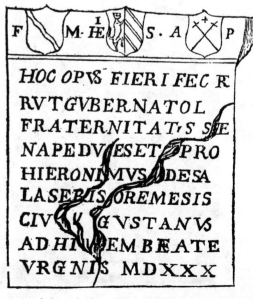

d. Inscription (Drummond p. 275)

PLATE 7

CONVENT OF STA THECLA.

a. Convent of Sta Thecla (Light p. 236)

ΩΕRSIDLℛΘℲDILℍΘ,SAℬℲƎℲƎℲℲSSℏↄ.

b. Inscription (Turner p. 538)

```
* ΑΦΡΟΔΙΤΗΙΙΙΑCΙΑΜ....................
ΑΙΟΝΟΥ..ΜΙΑΙΟΝΤΗ · ΗΤΙΝΑ · ΟΥΑΔΡΑΤΟΝ
ΤΟΝ ........................,...........
ΤΟΝΚΑΙΠΑΝΤΑΥ....ΙΑΝΟΝΤΑΙΟΥ..........
............ΤΗΡΗΤΙΝΑ..................
ΟΥΜΜΙ....ΙΟΥΠΑΝΤΑΥΧΟΙΥΙΟΝ...........
ΤΟΥ ............................,.....,....
ΧΗCΑΙ.......................ΑΙΙΦΑΠΟΝ
ΤΕΥΚΕΟΥΘΥΓΑΤΗΡΗΑΡΧΙ...........ΑΤΩΝ
ΑΤ..........ΡΟΝΔΗΜΗΤ..ΟC............ΩΝ
ΤΟΝΕΑΥΤΗ.....................,.........
............................................
```

c. Inscription (Turner p. 565)

```
* ΝΙΚΙΑΙΦΙΛΙΠΠΟΥΘΥΝΑ.......ΕΝΙΑΙ
ΚΑΙΣΑΡΟΣΘΕΣΩΣΕΒΑΣΤΟΥΓΥΝΑΙΚΙ
ΠΑΥΛΟΥΦΑΒΙΟΥΜΑΞΙΜΟΥΣΕΒΑΣΤΗΣ
ΠΑΦΟΥΗΒΟΥΛΗΚΑΙΟΔΗΜΟΣ
```

d. Inscription (Turner p. 566)

PLATE 8

Nicosia (Lang, facing p. 307)